# The Neuroscience of Psychotherapy

## Second Edition

# The Neuroscience of Psychotherapy

*Healing the Social Brain*

• Second Edition •

## Louis Cozolino

Foreword by Daniel J. Siegel

W. W Norton & Company

New York • London

Unless otherwise noted, figures were created by the author.

For information about permission to reproduce selections from this book, write to:
Permissions, W. W. Norton & Company, Inc.
500 Fifth Avenue, New York, NY 10110

For information about special discounts for bulk purchases, please contact
W. W. Norton Special Sales at specialsales@wwnorton.com or 800-233-4830

Manufacturing by Courier Westford
Book design by Martha Meyer, Paradigm Graphics
Production manager: Leeann Graham


Library of Congress Cataloging-in-Publication Data

Cozolino, Louis J.
 The neuroscience of psychotherapy : healing the social brain / Louis J. Cozolino. --
2nd ed.
    p. cm.
Includes bibliographical references and index.
ISBN 978-0-393-70642-0 (hardcover)
1. Psychotherapy. 2. Neurosciences. 3. Brain--Research. I. Title.
RC480.5.C645 2010
616.89'14--dc22
                          2009043708


ISBN: 978-0-393-70642-0

W. W. Norton & Company, Inc., 500 Fifth Avenue, New York, N.Y. 10110
                      www.wwnorton.com
W. W. Norton & Company Ltd., Castle House, 75/76 Wells Street, London W1T 3QT

                 1 2 3 4 5 6 7 8 9 0

This book is dedicated to my family:
my mother's courage, my father's determination, and
the memory of my grandparents. Together they somehow
instilled within me the belief that all things are possible.

# Contents

# Foreword

Louis Cozolino's contributions to the Norton Series on Interpersonal Neurobiology have been instrumental in moving this new interdisciplinary field forward. The first edition of *The Neuroscience of Psychotherapy* inaugurated the series, which now includes 16 titles. With this second edition, Lou has extended and deepened interpersonal neurobiology's basic view that integration is at the heart of well-being. I loved the first edition and have learned a tremendous amount from reading this exciting and extremely accessible updated edition. Readers new to interpersonal neurobiology (IN) will find this a wonderful place to start their journey, as Lou deftly brings the latest in cutting-edge science together with the healing art of psychotherapy. Those familiar with the field will find this a welcome addition to their IN library of texts written with the clinician in mind.

As the founding editor of the IN series, I have been proud to oversee the publication of these books that explore various dimensions of psychotherapy and science. Though each of the individual authors of and contributors may not articulate their work with the same vocabulary, their contributions have all added to the research and clinical synthesis that forms an educational foundation for IN as a multidisciplinary and synthetic way of knowing about what it means to be human. Ours is a complex species: We have inherited a nervous system whose evolution has left us with many mechanisms not suited to modern life. And we live within relationships that have shaped and continue to shape how our social brains are constructed within families, communities, and society. Cultural evolution continues to mold our synaptic architecture, influencing how we experience our inner, subjective lives and learn to communicate with one another.

This complexity could easily make us as clinicians move away from science to approach healing from an intuitive way of knowing alone. My hope in founding the field of IN has been that we would be able to see the forest for the trees, so to speak, and not get distracted by details, with all of their fascinating and nuanced complexities, but rather become enriched by all of this cutting-edge unfolding of new knowledge and ideas. But, this certainly is a challenge. In the busy lives of clinicians (and just plain everyday life), the tremendous amounts of data emerging from ever-expanding fields of science can be daunting. What we are trying to do with the IN series is to provide a forum for those working at the creative boundary between the chaos of overwhelming knowledge and the order of an intellectual framework. Lou Cozolino rides that edge like a master surfer, bringing together emerging findings from neuroscience with the beauty and power of healing relationships. It's a magnificent adventure, and you will need to take a deep breath and hold on as he takes you along with him through the various dimensions of science to see psychotherapy from new and helpful vantage points.

A framework that can be helpful in this important quest views clinical work as involving a triangle of well-being comprising the three points of Mind, Brain, and Relationships. This is a visual metaphor depicting the most foundational dimensions of our human lives, the essence of our subjective and our objective lives. This is a triangle revealing the flow of energy and information. Relationships are how we share energy and information with one another. The brain is here the extended nervous system distributed throughout the entire body, which is a mechanism through which energy and information flows. And the mind, in part, is how that flow is regulated—how we see and shape energy and information as it moves through our bodies and through our relationships.

Psychotherapy entails shaping these elements of our triangle toward well-being. From the IN perspective, health is achieved by promoting integration in our lives: Our minds come to monitor and modify our internal and interpersonal worlds toward the linkage of differentiated elements. The mind is a process that is both embodied and relational. In this view we can use our minds to cultivate integration, which promotes harmony; the lack of integration leads to chaos or rigidity. From the IN standpoint, we can see, for example, the various psychiatric symptoms and syndromes as revealing the chaos and rigidity that emerge from impairments to integration. Clinical assessment can detect when chaos and rigidity are present and identify the neural or interpersonal domains in which integration is lacking. Focusing on the need to enhance differentiation and promote linkage, an IN clinician is offered the framework with which to evaluate, so he or she can then create a treatment plan based on the centrality of integration in the cultivation of well-being. Beyond just eliminating symptoms, this view defines health and offers practical steps to promote the integration at the heart of living a harmonious, creative, and meaningful life.

Providing us with a rich and varied tapestry that weaves up-to-date science with his decades of fabulous work as a clinician and master educator in the field of mental health, Professor Cozolino is our guide in this eye-opening exploration of integration and the pathway toward health. Both our patients' and our own lives can greatly benefit from this fruitful journey of discovery. Welcome to the world of integration and interdisciplinary thinking!

Daniel J. Siegel, MD
Founding Editor, The Norton Series on Interpersonal Neurobiology

# Preface to the Second Edition

It has been extremely gratifying to witness the first edition of *The Neuroscience of Psychotherapy* play a role in introducing a new generation of therapists to the complex and fascinating world of the brain. Over the years, this book has created many opportunities for me to interact with students, teachers, and therapists who are curious about the biological basis of human behavior. Their enthusiastic feedback has strengthened my belief in the relevance of neuroscience to clinical practice and my dedication to the integration of mind and brain.

There are a number of reasons for this new edition. The first is that I've discovered the truth of the saying "writing is the process of rewriting what you have already rewritten," an urge that, for me, didn't diminish with the publication of the first edition. Second, the energy and enthusiasm generated by neuroscience in the 1990s has continued to build momentum and bear fruit. New technologies have broadened our window to neural functioning; empirical discoveries have led us into new areas of exploration; and increasingly sophisticated theories have fueled our imaginations. Finally, the findings relevant to psychotherapy and mental health from all this new research continued to accrue and called out to be included in *The Neuroscience of Psychotherapy*.

This second edition contains a few new chapters that focus on attachment, epigenetics, and the construction of consciousness. There is also a discussion of some of the evolutionary shortcomings of the human brain that make us so susceptible to psychological distress. You will notice that this second edition embodies a shift in perspective toward social neuroscience, and the recognition that the human brain is a social organ. Reflecting this shift is the change in the book's subtitle from *Building and Rebuilding the Human Brain* to *Healing the Social Brain*: Less mechanistic and grandiose perhaps, and also more human. I hope you enjoy the fruits of this labor of love.

I want to thank Lauren Harb, Tehniat Mirza, Vanessa Streiff, Denise Duval, and Nazanin Moali for their assistance in the preparation of this manuscript. Thanks also to Andrea Costella and Deborah Malmud for being highly competent and compassionate rocks at the center of the storm. And finally, thanks to my family, friends, clients, students, and colleagues for their caring, support, energy, and love.

Louis Cozolino
Los Angeles, September 2009

# The Neuroscience of Psychotherapy

## Second Edition

# PART I.

# Neuroscience and Psychotherapy: An Overview

# Chapter 1
# The Entangled Histories of Neurology and Psychology

*We must recollect that all of our provisional ideas in psychology will presumably one day be based on an organic substructure.*
—Sigmund Freud

How does the brain give rise to the mind? Where do the brain and mind meet, and by what means do they interact with one another? These are difficult questions—so difficult, in fact, that the common reaction is to focus on either the mind or the brain and act as if the other is irrelevant (Blass & Carmeli, 2007; Pulver, 2003). The problem with this approach is the barrier it creates to understanding that the human experience of brain and mind is essentially a unified process (Cobb, 1944). Neurology and psychology are simultaneously pushed apart by academic and intellectual politics while being drawn together by their common psychobiological foundation. The entangled histories of neurology and psychology reflect the push and pull of these powerful opposing forces (Ellenberger, 1970; Sulloway, 1979).

Freud started out as a rebel, a neurologist curious about the mind. I suspect he was frustrated with the mind–brain partisanship of medical school, and longed to work with others who shared his interests. At the age of 29, Freud won a traveling fellowship to spend the fall and winter of 1885 at the Salpêtrière Hospital on the left bank of Paris. The choice of the Salpêtrière was based on the reputation of Professor Jean-Martin

Charcot, a man considered an expert on both mind and brain. In Charcot, Freud sought a teacher who was well established, confident, and unafraid of the no-man's-land between mind and brain. One can imagine Freud's excitement as he walked the streets of Paris on his way to meet the great man, a possible kindred spirit.

Charcot specialized in patients suffering from what was then called *hysteria*. These patients had symptoms, such as seizures or paralysis, that mimicked neurological illnesses but were without apparent physical cause. A classic example is a condition called *glove anesthesia*, in which feeling is lost in one or both hands beginning at the wrist. In these patients, the hands appear to take on symbolic significance; perhaps they have been used to commit some taboo act that triggered overwhelming guilt or fear. It was believed that a conflict within the mind was converted into a bodily symptom.

The 1880s were also a time when the ability of the subconscious mind to control behavior (as demonstrated through hypnosis) burst into popular awareness. Charcot used hypnosis during clinical demonstrations to illustrate his emerging theories about mind–body interactions. The months Freud spent at Salpêtrière with Charcot had a profound effect on him. He came to believe that hidden mental processes do indeed exert powerful effects on consciousness, and that hysterical symptoms result not from malingering or feigning illness, but from the power of the unconscious mind embedded within the neural structures of the brain. Hysteria, from this perspective, reflected the capacity of traumatic experience to reorganize the brain and disrupt conscious experience. Dissociative splits between consciousness and behavior demonstrated to Freud that the brain is capable of multiple levels of conscious and unconscious awareness. In the decades to come, he would explore the use of language, emotion, and the therapeutic relationship to reconnect them. Freud returned to Vienna in February 1886, and opened his own clinical practice 2 months later. Despite his entry into the medical establishment, he continued his rebellion later that year with the presentation of a paper on the existence of hysteria in males. Deeply fascinated by the unconscious, Freud remained its most ardent explorer until his death in 1939.

In the years following his residency at Salpêtrière, Freud expanded on Charcot's thinking in many significant ways. He placed the unconscious in a developmental context by tracing the genesis of hysterical symptoms to childhood experiences. He came to believe that hysterical patients suffered from the unconscious emotional aftereffects of repressed childhood memories. Furthermore, Freud connected the development of the individual to the evolution of the species. Influenced by the ancient idea that we contain within us the biological history of our primitive ancestors, he included the importance of instinctual drives such as sexuality, rage, and envy in his developmental theories. Freud believed that beneath our civilized exteriors, there exists within us a more primitive being, accounting for many of the contradictions of modern "civilized" behavior.

Freud argued that in order to understand who and what we are, we need to understand the primal unconscious elements of experience. He called this the *id*—the primitive and uncivilized life energy that we share with our reptilian and mammalian ancestors. This concept was met with understandable hostility by Freud's repressed and rational contemporaries. At that time, physicians were pillars of European culture, highly invested in their superiority over the animal kingdom and steadfast in their right and obligation to subjugate the "primitive" people of the world. Needless to say, linking civilized humans to animals (to say nothing of his idea that children have sexual desires) made Freud and his theories scandalous in respectable circles.

## Freud's Abandoned Project

*The seemingly irreconcilable dichotomies and paradoxes that formerly prevailed with respect to mind vs. matter . . . become reconciled in a . . . unifying view of mind, brain, and man in nature.*
—Roger Sperry

In the late 1800s, the doors to the microscopic world of the nervous system opened for the first time. Technical improvements in the microscope and newly developed staining techniques led to the discovery of both neurons and the synapses through which they communicate. The existence of synapses revealed that the nervous system is not a single structure, but instead is made up of countless individual processing units. Furthermore, that humans shared these neurons with all other living creatures supported the Darwinian idea of our common ancestry with other animals. Around this same time, the work of Wernicke and Broca showed that specific areas of the brain were responsible for different aspects of language. The dual neuroanatomical notions of synaptic transmission and the localization of specific functions to different areas of the brain provided rich theoretical soil for new ways of understanding the brain.

Inspired by Darwin, Charcot, and the opening of the microscopic neural world to investigation, Freud wrote *The Project for a Scientific Psychology* (Freud, 1968). In *The Project*, he postulated that what we witness of conscious and unconscious behavior is organized by and stored within the brain's neural architecture. As part of this work, he drew simple sketches of interconnecting neurons to represent human impulses, behaviors, and psychological defenses. These sketches depicted the interactions among drives, the organs of the senses, and mechanisms of inhibition. According to his colleagues, Freud became obsessed with the idea of constructing a neurobiological model of the mind (Schore, 1997b). Despite his enthusiasm, Freud realized that his dream for psychology to be based in an understanding of the nervous system was far ahead of its time, and at odds with prevailing religious beliefs and medical dogma. For these and other reasons, he suppressed the publication of *The Project* until his death.

Perhaps Freud kept the *Project* to himself because he feared that it would be relegated to the same sort of obscurity as the case of Phineas Gage. Gage, a 19th-century railroad foreman, had a metal bar pass completely through his head as a result of an accident, causing the destruction of the middle portions of his frontal cortex. This particular area of the brain has since been shown to be involved with judgment, planning, and emotional control. Although Gage had no specific motor or language deficits, those who knew him said that "Gage was no longer Gage" (Benson, 1994). His emotionality, relationship abilities, and the quality of his experience were all dramatically altered. Because Gage's symptoms involved his personality and emotions, the publication reporting his case received little attention for most of the 20th century. Not only was it outside the realm of behaviors that neurologists felt comfortable addressing, but there was also a bias against relating human personality to neurobiological mechanisms (Damasio, 1994).

Freud, the neurologist, became all but forgotten as his psychological theories moved further and further from their biological roots. He chose instead to utilize the more palatable and accessible metaphors of literature and anthropology to provide the primary vocabulary for psychoanalysis. Unfortunately, Freud's shift from the brain to metaphors of mind opened psychoanalysis to all sorts of criticism throughout the 20th century. Metaphors such as the Oedipal and Electra complexes were seen as contrived fictions, shielding them from scientific evaluation. Perhaps Freud anticipated that in the future, psychoanalysis would eventually be integrated with its neurobiological substrates. This would only happen when the time was right for a synthesis based in an equal partnership of both sciences (Pribram & Gill, 1976).

The time for such an integration has arrived, and respect for psychological processes have taken a strong enough hold within both the scientific community and general culture that we can avoid a reduction of the mind to basic biochemical processes. On the contrary, an appreciation for the structures and functioning of the brain by nonneurologists has become the norm. It is in this spirit that we turn our attention to ways of thinking about the brain that enhance our understanding of human experience. We begin with a model of the brain that provides a bridge between the fields of neuroscience, evolution, and the origins of the unconscious.

## The Triune Brain

*He who joyfully marches in rank and file . . . has been given a large brain by mistake, since for him the spinal cord would suffice.*
—Albert Einstein

In the 1970s, the neuroscientist Paul MacLean presented a theory that emphasized the conservation of more primitive evolutionary structures within the modern human brain (MacLean, 1990; Taylor, 1999). MacLean called his idea the *triune brain*. Very much in line with the theories of Darwin and Freud, it provides an evolutionary explanation that may account for some of the contradictions and discontinuities of human consciousness and behavior.

MacLean described the human brain as a three-part system that embodies our evolutionary connection to both reptiles and lower mammals. Think of it as a brain within a brain within a brain, with each successive layer devoted to increasingly complex functions and abilities. At the core is the *reptilian brain*, relatively unchanged through evolutionary history, responsible for activation, arousal, homeostasis, and reproductive drives. The *paleomammalian brain* (or *limbic system*), which is central to learning, memory, and emotion, wraps around the reptilian brain. The highest layer, the *neomammalian brain* or cerebral cortex, organizes conscious thought, problem solving, and self-awareness (MacLean, 1985).

MacLean suggested that our three brains don't necessarily communicate or work well together because of their differing "mentalities" and the fact that only the neomammalian brain is capable of consciousness and verbal communication (MacLean, 1990). This is a fundamental issue that connects evolution, neuroscience, and psychotherapy. What Charcot and Freud called dissociation and hysteria could well have been the result of inadequate integration and coordination among these different, cohabiting brains. MacLean's description of the nonverbal reptilian and paleomammalian brains unconsciously influencing processing in the neomammalian brain roughly parallels Freud's distinction of the conscious and the unconscious minds.

The model of the triune brain serves the valuable function of providing a connective metaphor among the artifacts of evolution, the contemporary nervous system, and some of the inherent difficulties in the organization of human experience. This conservation of our evolutionary history alongside our modern neural networks confronts the therapist with the challenge of simultaneously treating a human, a horse, and a crocodile (Hampden-Turner, 1981).

## Ah, If Only It Were So Simple!

*The large brain, like large government, may not be able to do simple things in simple ways.*

—Donald Hebb

A superficial reading of MacLean's work might lead us to the idea that each layer of the triune brain evolved independently and sequentially, and that they all cooperate in a hierarchical fashion like a military chain of command. This is clearly not the case. In reality, the reptilian and paleomammalian brains have continued to evolve alongside the neomammalian brain. Earlier structures are not conserved "as is" from past generations, but also undergo a process of *exaptation*—the modification of earlier evolving brain structures for new applications in networks dedicated to alternative or more complex functions (Cacioppo & Berntson, 2004). Thus, all three layers continue to evolve along with the emergence of ever more complex vertical and horizontal neural networks. This conservation and modification of neural networks has led to an amazingly complex brain capable of a vast array of functions from monitoring respiration to performing mathematical computations. This makes understanding functional neuroanatomy from a study of the contemporary brain quite a challenge.

An example from space exploration may prove useful in understanding the neuroanatomist's dilemma. When *Apollo 13* approached the moon, difficulties with the air supply system left the crew with just a few hours of oxygen (Lovell & Kluger, 1994). In the face of this crisis, scientists on earth removed nonessential components from a mock spacecraft and constructed a new air supply system. Pieces of upholstery, plastic bags, duct tape, and electrical wiring were used in innovative ways to serve new functions. The instructions on how to build this makeshift device were then conveyed to the *Apollo 13* crew. This scenario is much closer to the crafting of the modern brain than imagining an engineer sitting down with a blank sheet of paper. An engineer of the future presented with this bootstrapped air purification system would have a difficult time figuring out what it is and why it was built the way it was. Although there are obvious differences between the *Apollo 13* scenario and natural selection, both are examples of a pragmatic adaptation with existing materials to an environmental crisis.

The multiple roles played by the cerebellum offer a prime example of both neural conservation and exaptation. The cerebellum is a primitive brain structure. At its core is the vermis, centrally involved in balance. In fish, the vermis helps them to swim upright. In humans, it coordinates vestibular functioning and helps us to sit up and walk without falling. During evolution, as our brains and bodies became more complex, the cerebellum expanded to coordinate gross and then fine motor movements—a logical development for a structure initially at the core of the ability to swim. In an interesting and surprising twist, the later-evolving portions of the cerebellar lobes are involved in the organization and coordination of language, memory, and reasoning (Schmahmann, 1997). It appears that the cerebellum's ability to process, sequence, and organize vast amounts of sensory-motor information was utilized by the evolving brain as part of the neural infrastructure of higher cortical processes.

Just as balance and motor behavior require constant monitoring of posture and the inhibition of unnecessary and distracting movements, so, in their own ways, do attention, concentration, memory, and language. The same timing mechanisms involved in locomotion seem to have been conserved for sequential processing in thought and language. Although the cerebellum is considered a primitive brain structure, its evolution involved vertical networking with most of the cortex, suggesting that the vertical networks that connect the horizontal layers of the triune brain may serve as clues to its evolutionary history (Alexander, DeLong, & Strick, 1986; Cummings, 1993).

In addition to horizontal and vertical networks, evolution has also selected for increasing differentiation between the left and right hemispheres. Certain areas of the brain have become specialized for specific skills, such as language and spatial abilities. Still other areas, such as those in the prefrontal cortex, serve to organize and control the activity of multiple other regions. Keep in mind that the brains of men and women also have many differences and that the brain changes as we grow up and grow older (Cozolino, 2008). Many of these differences are especially important to the processes of attachment and affect regulation so central to psychotherapy.

Neural networks relevant to psychotherapy exist throughout the brain—some are evolutionarily primitive, others developing more recently. Some are fully functional from birth, while others take decades to mature. This is why an understanding of both evolution and development is vital in capturing the full picture of human experience.

## The Interpersonal Sculpting of the Social Brain

> *It is difficult to give children a sense of security unless you have it yourself. If you have it, they catch it from you.*
> —William Menninger

The theory that ontogeny recapitulates phylogeny refers to the concept that the evolution of the species is recreated in the gestation and development of each individual. To use MacLean's terms, we pass through the reptilian and paleomammalian stages before we develop into a fully human being. Although the theory of recapitulation is in most ways incorrect (Gould, 1977), some interesting parallels exist between our evolutionary history and the process of human development.

At birth, the reptilian brain is fully functional and the paleomammalian brain is primed and ready to be organized by early experiences. The cortex, on the other hand, continues to slowly grow into the third decade and matures throughout life. Thus, much of our most important emotional and interpersonal learning occurs during our early years when our primitive brains are in control. The result is that a great deal of learning takes place before we have the necessary cortical systems for explicit memory, problem solving, or perspective. Consequently, many of our most important socioemotional learning experiences are organized and controlled by reflexes, behaviors, and emotions outside of our awareness and distorted by our immature brains. To a great extent, psychotherapy owes its existence to these artifacts of evolution and development.

The slow development of the cerebral cortex maximizes the influence of experience in building the brain. That so much of the brain is shaped after birth is both good and bad news. The good news is that the individual brain is built to survive in a particular environment. Culture, language, climate, nutrition, and parents shape each of our brains in a unique way. In good times and with good-enough parents, this early brain building will serve the child well throughout life. The bad news comes into play when factors are not so favorable, such as in times of war or in the case of parental psychopathology or separation (Benes, Taylor, & Cunningham, 2000). The brain is then sculpted in ways that assist the child in surviving childhood but may be maladaptive later in life. It is in these instances that a therapist attempts to restructure neural architecture in the service of more adaptive behavior, cognition, and emotion. Building the human brain is vastly complex. Rebuilding it is a difficult and fascinating challenge.

A portion of the brain called the *anterior cingulate*—centrally involved with maternal behavior, nursing, and play—appears in the evolution of early mammals (MacLean, 1985). Before this, animals had to be prepared to survive on their own at birth. Good examples are newborn sea turtles that hatch from their eggs high on a beach and make a mad instinctual dash toward the ocean. With the evolution of maternal care, children are allowed to develop more slowly within a supportive, scaffolding environment. In the course of evolution, primates have experienced increasingly longer periods of maternal dependence. This luxury allows for the evolution and development of more complex brains, as well as an increasing impact of parenting and early experiences on how the brain is built.

Konrad Lorenz (1991) found that geese imprint (bond to attachment figures) during a limited period of time soon after birth. If baby geese saw Lorenz first, they would follow him as if he were their mother. Lorenz also found that when these geese reached sexual maturity 2 years later, they would "fall in love" with the kinds of geese they had been exposed to during their imprinting period. He even noted that a baby goose, which originally imprinted on him, fell in love with a human girl from the next town when he reached sexual maturity and would fly there to see her. These early experiences seemed to be permanently etched into the brains of Lorenz's geese.

This principle of imprinting can be seen in humans in the more flexible and complex form of attachment schema. The early interpersonal environment may be imprinted in the human brain by shaping the child's neural networks and establishing the biochemical set points in circuitry dedicated to memory, emotion, safety, and survival. Later, these structures and processes come to serve as the infrastructure for social and intellectual skills, affect regulation, and the sense of self.

Prolonged dependence in childhood has allowed for the development of a neocortex so complex that we have become capable of spoken and written language, self-consciousness, and the construction of both private and social selves. Although these abilities create tremendous possibilities, brainpower does have its downside. We are now also capable of becoming anxious about things that will never happen, depressed by imagined slights, and saddened by potential losses. Our imaginations can simultaneously create exciting new worlds, as well as the fears that prevent us from living in them. It is obvious that despite the evolution of consciousness and rationality, our primitive emotional brains and their early development continue to exert a great deal of influence over us.

## Summary

Although Freud began his career attempting to create a brain-based psychology, the theories and technology available to him did not allow him to carry out this project. Various ways of thinking about the brain (like MacLean's), although limited, provide models that bridge the gap between psychology and neurology. Evolution's legacy is a complex brain, vulnerable to a variety of factors that can disrupt the growth and integration of important neural networks. The field of psychotherapy has emerged because of the brain's vulnerability to these developmental and environmental risks. But how can psychotherapists synthesize and incorporate both the mind and the brain into our work? The following chapter presents a model of neural networks, how they develop, and how we attempt to alter them during treatment. It is from this perspective that we will then examine the relevance of the nervous system to our work.

# Chapter 2

# Building and Rebuilding the Brain: Psychotherapy and Neuroscience

*I know of no more encouraging fact than the unquestionable ability of man to elevate his life by a conscious endeavor.*
—Henry David Thoreau

Although psychotherapy originally emerged from neurology, differences in language and worldview have limited collaboration among the two fields for most of the 20th century. While psychotherapists developed a rich metaphoric language of mind, neurologists built a detailed database of brain–behavior relationships. As we approached the 21st century, neuroscience began providing us with tools to explore what happens in the brain during early development, and later in psychotherapy. A return to Freud's *Project* of a biological psychology is finally at hand.

At the heart of the interface of neuroscience and psychotherapy is the fact that human experience is mediated via two interacting processes. The first is the expression of our evolutionary past via the organization, development, and functioning of the nervous system—a process resulting in billions of neurons organizing into neural networks, each with its own timetable and requirements for growth. The second is the contemporary shaping of our neural architecture within the context of relationships. The human brain is a "social organ of adaptation" stimulated to grow through positive and negative interactions with others. The quality and nature of our relationships become encoded within the neural infrastructure of our brains. It is through this translation of experience into neurobiological structures that nature and nurture become one.

At the heart of psychotherapy is an understanding of the interwoven forces of nature and nurture, what goes right and wrong in their developmental unfolding, and how to reinstate healthy neural functioning. When one or more neural networks necessary for optimal functioning remain underdeveloped, underregulated, or underintegrated with others, we experience the complaints and symptoms for which people seek therapy. We now assume that when psychotherapy results in symptom reduction or experiential change, the brain has, in some way, been altered (Kandel, 1998).

How does psychotherapy change the brain? How is memory stored and how can the quality of experience change? Before we can address these questions we have to first get an idea of how the brain is organized and how it performs some of its many functions. We will discuss the building and rebuilding of neural networks, the role of enriched environments, and the part played by stress in changing the brain. We will also explore the central role of the therapeutic relationship in this change process, as well as the importance of the expression of emotion and the therapeutic use of language.

## Neural Networks

*A forest of these trees is a spectacle too much for one man to see.*
—David Douglas

So far we have used the term *neural networks* in a general way; I would like now to get a bit more specific. *Neurons* are the microscopic processing units that make up all parts of the nervous system. When we talk of the frontal cortex, amygdala, or hippocampus, we are literally talking about large numbers of individual neurons organized to perform a set of functions. The neurons within these systems need to be able to organize and reorganize in such a way as to allow us to learn, remember, and act as we adjust to different situations. Because each neuron is limited to either firing or not firing, the diverse capabilities of the nervous system come from the complex interaction of individual neuronal signals. A simplistic analogy is an old-fashioned billboard consisting of rows and columns of thousands of light bulbs. Although each individual bulb is

FIGURE 2.1
The Feedforward Neural Network

*A depiction of sixteen neurons in a simple feedforward circuit*

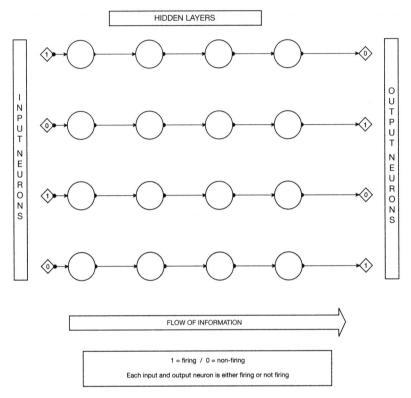

limited to being either on or off, the pattern created by these lights can spell out words, form images, and through precise timing, create the illusion of movement. In a similar fashion, patterns of neural firing come to represent specific information within the brain and throughout the nervous system.

To accomplish the complexity required for behavior, neurons organize into neural networks. A neural network can range from just a few neurons in a simple animal to trillions of neural interconnections in brains such as our own. Neural networks encode and organize all of our behaviors from basic reflexes, such as pulling our hand away from a hot stove, to our ability to simultaneously comprehend the visual, emotional, and political significance of Picasso's *Guernica*. Neural networks can interconnect with multiple other networks, allowing for interaction

## FIGURE 2.2
## The Feedforward and Feedback Neural Network

*A slightly more complex model in which information is fed backwards and each neuron can communicate with all of its neighbors.*

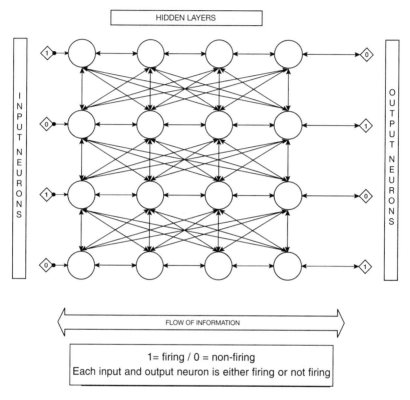

HIDDEN LAYERS

INPUT NEURONS

OUTPUT NEURONS

FLOW OF INFORMATION

1= firing / 0 = non-firing
Each input and output neuron is either firing or not firing

and integration. Because we will be referring to neural networks throughout the chapters to come, it is important to keep a good visual image in our minds as we proceed.

Figures 2.1 and 2.2 depict simple neural networks, with each circle representing an individual neuron. Starting with Figure 2.1, you will notice that the flow of information moves from left to right across the four columns of neurons. On the left, some of the *input neurons* are firing in response to some stimulus (1 = firing/0 = nonfiring). In turn, their firing stimulates the activation of some set of neurons within the *hidden layers* of processing, which leads to the firing of a set of *output neurons*, which results in a particular experience or behavioral reaction. Figure 2.2 represents a step toward a more accurate model, with information flow-ing in both directions and an increased level of interaction among neurons. Each of the connections will have either an excitatory or inhibitory effect on other neurons. This mosaic of firing patterns, the network's *instantiation*, will determine which set of output neurons fire. Making things slightly more complicated, instead of 16 neurons there are millions, each of which can be connected to thousands of others.

Instantiations are sculpted by experience and encode all of our abilities, emotions, and experiences into one or more forms of memory. It is the consistency of these firing patterns that results in organized patterns of behavior and experience. Once these neural patterns are established, new learning modifies the relationship of neurons within these networks. At other times, new learning may occur when we shape one neural network to inhibit the activation of another. When we talk of building and rebuilding the brain, neurons are our basic building blocks and neural networks are the structures that we build and sculpt.

Learning within neural networks occurs as a result of trial and error. Feed-forward and feedback information loops form complex patterns of excitation and inhibition among neurons within the hidden layers. This process eventually leads to consistent and adaptive output. This is demonstrated in a soon-to-be toddler, who repeatedly tests and refines her balance, leg strength, and coordination with each new attempt to walk. Her brain drives her to keep trying while recording her successes and failures within neural networks responsible for balance, motor coordination, and visual tracking. In this same way, neural networks organize behaviors, emotions, thoughts, and sensations that are shaped throughout life.

I remember being surprised to find a table of random numbers in an appendix of my college statistics textbook. At first, I thought this to be a waste of paper, assuming that anyone could generate random numbers on their own. When I shared my thoughts with the professor, he assured me that much research had gone into demonstrating that we are incapable of generating random numbers. He said that as hard as we might try, we cannot avoid generating specific patterns of numbers. This finally makes sense to me based on neural network organization: We are unable to engage in random actions because our behaviors are guided by patterns established through previous learning to which we automatically return. And while not being able to generate random numbers is of little consequence to us in our day-to-day lives, the tendency to make the same mistakes again and again is cause for a great deal of human suffering. This tendency to repeat patterns of thought and behavior is what led the psychoanalyst Wilhelm Reich to say that people tend to remain sick because they continue to find the same wrong solutions to the problems they hope to change.

## Neural Network Growth and Integration

*Plasticity then, in the wide sense of the word, means the possession of a structure weak enough to yield to an influence, but strong enough not to yield all at once.*

—William James

The growth and connectivity of neurons is the basic mechanism of all learning and adaptation. Learning can be reflected in neural changes in a number of ways, including changes in the connectivity between existing neurons, the expansion of existing neurons, and the growth of new neurons. All of these changes are expressions of *plasticity*, or the ability of the nervous system to change in response to experience. Although the first two forms of plasticity have been recognized in humans for decades, the birth of new neurons (*neurogenesis*) was only recently discovered in regions involved with ongoing learning, such as the hippocampus, the amygdala, and the frontal and temporal lobes (Eriksson et al., 1998; Gould, Reeves, Graziano, & Gross, 1999; Gould, Tanapat, Hastings, & Shors, 1999; Gross, 2000).

Existing neurons grow though the expansion and branching of the dendrites they project to other neurons in reaction to new experiences and learning (Purves & Voyvodic, 1987). This process is reflected in the connectivity among neurons in our simple schematic diagrams. Neurons interconnect to form neural networks, and neural networks, in turn, integrate with one another to perform increasingly complex tasks. For example, networks that participate in language, emotion, and memory need to become integrated in order for us to recall and tell an emotionally meaningful story with the appropriate words, correct details, and proper affect.

Association areas within the cortex serve the roles of bridging, coordinating, and directing the multiple neural circuits to which they are connected. Although the actual mechanisms of this integration are not yet known, they are likely to include some combination of communication between local neuronal circuits and the interactions among functional brain systems (Trojan & Pokorny, 1999). Changes in the synchrony of activation of multiple neural networks may also play a role in the coordination of their activity and the emergence of conscious awareness (Crick, 1994; Konig & Engel, 1995).

## Genetic Inheritance and Gene Expression

*Evolution consists of the gradual transformation of organisms from one condition of existence to another.*

—Ernst Mayr

Now that most of science has gotten beyond the basic debate of nature versus nurture, we can acknowledge that the growth and organization of the brain reflects a complex yet subtle blending of genetic and environmental influences. Toward this end, it is much more helpful to think of genes in terms of serving both a *template* and a *transcription* function (Kandel, 1998). As templates, genes provide the organization of the uniform structures of the brain, which are generally unaffected by environmental influences, except in cases of prenatal genetic abnormalities. These structures and functions, such as the general layout of the nervous system and basic reflexes, are inherited via our DNA and shared by all healthy members of our species. This is the aspect of genetic inheritance traditionally thought of as "nature."

On the other hand, the expression of many genes depends on experiences that trigger their transcription (Black, 1998). Transcription genetics controls the more subtle aspects of the brain's organization, such as the specific sculpting of later developing neural networks and the levels of specific neurotransmitters available to different brain systems. In fact, the majority of our cortex is added after birth in an experience-dependent fashion through this transcriptional process. Nurture, therefore, influences brain development via the selective activation of genes that shape the experience-dependent aspects of development. How does this happen?

Experience results in the expression of certain genes which trigger the synthesis of proteins that build neural structures. Through genetic transcription, existing neurons grow different kinds of receptors, expand their dendritic structures, and adjust their biochemistry. For example, although identical twins raised in the same household may have identical genes for schizophrenia, only one may develop the illness. This is believed to be the result of the expression of different genes based on the unique interactions between each child and his or her environment. The transcription function of genes allows for ongoing neural plasticity throughout life and provides the basis for enriched experiences (like psychotherapy) to benefit both the adolescent and adult brain. In a later chapter we will explore the links between maternal nurturance and the early building of the brain that result in different levels of learning, emotional regulation, and attachment behavior.

## The Role of Enriched Environments

*It is always with excitement that I wake up in the morning. . . . It's my partner.*

—Jonas Salk

The brain is not a static organ; it continually changes in response to environmental challenges. Because of this, the neural architecture of the brain comes to embody the environment that shapes it. You could also think of our neural architecture as a tangible expression of our learning history. The early research on neural plasticity began by exploring the impact of different types of environments on brain development. In these studies done primarily with rats, enriched environments took the form of more diverse, complex, colorful, and stimulating habitats, while impoverished environments were relatively empty monochromatic enclosures. It was found that animals raised in enriched environments had more neurons, more synaptic connections among neurons, a greater number of blood capillaries, and more mitochondria activity (Diamond, Krech, & Rosenweig, 1964; Kempermann, Kuhn, & Gage, 1997, 1998; Kolb & Whishaw, 1998; Sirevaag & Greenough, 1988). These findings demonstrate that a brain which is challenged comes to be more complex, active, and robust. Subsequent research with humans has yielded similar results for individuals with more education and more complex and challenging occupations.

For humans, enriched environments include the kinds of challenging educational and experiential opportunities that encourage us to learn new skills and expand our knowledge. Higher levels of education, practicing skills, and continued engagement in mental activities all correlate with more neurons and neural connections (Jacobs & Scheibel, 1993; Jacobs, Schall, & Scheibel, 1993). Higher levels of education and reading ability have also been shown to correlate with a diminished impact of dementia later in life (Schmand, Smit, Geerlings, & Lindeboom, 1997). Interestingly, brain regions dedicated to certain skills can actually hijack cells in adjacent neural areas to serve their needs to develop skills like playing an instrument or learning Braille (Elbert, Pantev, Wienbruch, Rockstroh, & Taub, 1995). There is no doubt that the human brain grows in response to challenge and new learning.

Psychotherapy can be thought of as a specific type of enriched environment that promotes social and emotional development, neural integration, and processing complexity. The way the brain changes during therapy will depend upon the neural networks involved in the focus of treatment.

## Learning and Stress

*Every stress leaves an indelible scar, and the organism pays for its survival after a stressful situation by becoming a little older.*
—Hans Selye

Mild to moderate stress (MMS) activates neural growth hormones supportive of new learning (Cowan & Kandel, 2001; Gould, McEwen, Tanapat, Galea, & Fuchs, 1997; Jablonska, Gierdalski, Kossut, & Skangiel-Kramska, 1999; Myers, Churchill, Muja, & Garraghty, 2000; Pham, Soderstrom, Henriksson, & Mohammed, 1997; Zhu & Waite, 1998). Thus, MMS may be utilized to enlist naturally occurring neurobiological processes in the service of new learning. Although we use the term *stress* in animal research, humans also demonstrate arousal in the form of curiosity, enthusiasm, and pleasure. Humans can also be motivated to learn new skills and take on new challenges to relieve discomfort and stress. These motivational states have all been recognized for their role in successful outcomes from psychotherapy.

Dissociation is a common result of the high levels of stress associated with traumatic experiences. Characterized by a disconnection among thoughts, behaviors, sensations, and emotions, dissociation demonstrates that the coordination and integration of these functions is an active neurobiological process. Because all of these functions are seamlessly and unconsciously interwoven during normal states of awareness, it is easy to overlook the fact that their integration is a central component of mental health.

The power of mild to moderate levels of stress to trigger neural plasticity is a key element in the success of psychotherapy or any learning situation. As opposed to traumatic experiences, the controlled exposure to stress during therapy enhances new learning and increases neural integration. As therapists, we intuitively work to regulate stress and integrate neural networks, a process that is essentially the opposite of the dissociation observed in reaction to trauma. Healthy functioning requires proper development and functioning of neural networks organizing conscious awareness, behavior, emotion, and sensation.

As in early development, the repeated exposure to stress in the supportive interpersonal context of psychotherapy results in the ability to tolerate increasing levels of arousal. This process reflects the building and integration of cortical circuits and their increasing ability to inhibit and regulate subcortical activation. Affect regulation, especially the modulation and inhibition of anxiety and fear, allows for continued cortical processing in the face of strong emotions, allowing for ongoing cognitive flexibility, learning, and neural integration.

In this process the therapist plays essentially the same role as a parent, providing and modeling the regulatory functions of the social brain. As affect is repeatedly brought into the therapeutic relationship and successfully managed, the client gradually internalizes these skills by sculpting the neural structures necessary for autoregulation. As in childhood, the repeated cycle of attunement, rupture of the attunement,and its reestablishment gradually creates an expectation of reconnection (Lachmann & Beebe, 1996). The learned expectation of relief in the future enhances the ability to tolerate more intense affect in the midst of the stressful moment.

As a therapist, one of my primary goals is to shift my clients' experience of anxiety from an unconscious trigger for avoidance to a conscious cue for curiosity and exploration. One of my patients described it metaphorically as using anxiety as a compass to help guide him to and through his unconscious fears. Becoming aware of anxiety is then followed with an exploration and eventual understanding of what we are afraid of and why. The next step is to move toward the anxiety with an understanding of its meaning and significance. In this way, anxiety becomes woven into a conscious narrative with the possibility of writing a new outcome to our story. This process reflects the integration of cortical linguistic processing with conditioned subcortical arousal in the service of inhibiting, regulating, and modifying maladaptive reactions.

As we will see later when discussing the building of the social brain, biological and environmental factors during childhood can result in long periods of dysregulation. Early deprivation or chronic stress increase the chances of damage to the brain, deficits in memory and reality testing, and the prolonged utilization of primitive defenses (Brown, Henning, & Wellman, 2005; Radley et al., 2006; Sapolsky, 1985). With increased nurturance and support, stress hormone levels decrease; physical comfort and soothing talk with caretakers helps the brain to integrate experience.

## Emotional Tolerance and Affect Regulation

*Few things are brought to a successful issue by impetuous desire, but most by calm and prudent forethought.*
—Thucydides

Although we usually think of the cortex as a giant hard drive capable of storing huge amounts of data, another primary role of the cortex is inhibition. Take for example the grasping reflex we are all born with. This powerful grip allowed our ancestors to hold onto their mothers as they moved through trees and over land. During the early months of life this grasping reflex is soon inhibited by descending cortical circuitry. The inhibition of this and other reflexes allow for a cortical takeover of these functions during development. So we sacrifice the grasping reflex for the finger dexterity necessary to manipulate digits, write, and use tools. Later in life if we have the misfortune of succumbing to dementia, this and other early reflexes begin to reappear as our cortex gradually loses its inhibitory ability. In a similar fashion, our prefrontal cortex is shaped by experience to inhibit and control subcortical functional activation, which eventually results in our ability to regulate our emotions. Early attachment relationships establish the experiences that shape these neural networks and allow us to regulate our emotional experience.

Assistance with experiencing increasing levels of positive and negative affect is a vital component of both parenting and psychotherapy. The gradually increasing tolerance for stress builds our brains, expands neural organization of emotional and cognitive integration, and creates networks of descending control to help inhibit and regulate affect (Schore, 1994). Emerging from childhood with an ability to experience a range of emotions and tolerate stress serves both as a means of brain growth and continued development throughout life.

During our first few years, we have the repeated experiences of going from a comfortable, regulated state to a state of dysregulation. We become frightened, cold, wet, and hungry, and show our displeasure with facial expressions, bodily postures, vocalization, and crying. In the presence of good-enough parenting, our signals are attended to, the source of our displeasure diagnosed, and we are helped back into a regulated state. Across thousands of these temporal-emotional experiences, we go from regulation to dysregulation to reregulation. These experiences shape secure attachment and the expectation of positive outcomes. The summation of these experiences, stored throughout our nervous system, becomes the sensory-motion-emotional background of our experience.

In the absence of adequate assistance in regulating affect or making sense of emotions, the brain organizes a variety of defensive coping strategies. These defenses vary in the degree to which they distort reality in order to achieve their goal of reducing anxiety. This distortion is accomplished in circuits of unconscious memory that control anxiety and fear (Critchley et al., 2000). The neural connections that result in defenses shape our lives by selecting what we approach and avoid, what our attention is drawn to, and the assumptions we use to organize our experiences. Our cortex then provides us with rationalizations and beliefs about our behaviors that help keep our coping strategies and defenses in place, possibly for a lifetime. These neural and psychic structures can lead to either psychological and physical health, or illness and disability.

## Psychopathology and Neural Network Integration

*In a structure as complex as the human brain a multitude of things can go wrong. The wonder is that for most people the brain functions effectively.*
—Seymour Kety

If everything we experience is represented by instantiations within neural networks, then by definition, psychopathology of all kinds—from the mildest neurotic symptoms to the most severe psychosis—must also be represented within and among neural networks. In line with this theory, psychopathology would be a reflection of suboptimal development, integration, and coordination of neural networks. Patterns of dysregulation of brain activation found in disorders such as depression and obsessive-compulsive disorder support the theory of a brain-based explanation for the symptoms of psychopathology.

Difficulties in early caretaking, genetic and biological vulnerabilities, or trauma at any time during life can result in the lack of integration among networks. Unresolved trauma can cause ongoing information processing deficits that disrupt integrated neural processing. For example, dissociative symptoms following trauma—reflecting the disconnection among networks of behavior, emotion, sensation, and cognition—predict the later development of posttraumatic stress disorder (Koopman, Classen, & Spiegel, 1994; McFarlane & Yehuda, 1996). Children victimized by psychological, physical, and sexual abuse have a greater probability of demonstrating electrophysiological abnormalities in executive regions of the brain vital to neural network integration (Ito et al., 1993; Teicher et al., 1997).

In general, psychological integration suggests that the conscious cognitive functions of the executive brain have access to information across networks of sensation, behavior, and emotion. A primary focus of neural integration in traditional talk psychotherapy is between networks of affect and cognition. Dissociation between the two occurs when high levels of stress inhibit or disrupt the brain's integrative abilities among the left and right cerebral hemispheres as well as among the cortex and limbic regions. The integration of the left and right hemispheres can be disrupted while the circuits of the reptilian and paleomammalian brains can be unlinked from the conscious neomammalian cortex.

This unlinking may not be an evolutionary accident. As valuable as language can be for humans, evolution appears to have selected for the shutdown of language (and a decrease in cognitive processing) when confronted with threat. The resulting disruption of information processing may be the most common cause of neural network dissociation. Cortical networks responsible for memory, language, and executive control (in its many forms) become inhibited and underperform during times of overwhelming stress. The very way that the brain has evolved to success-fully cope with immediate threat appears to have created a vulnerability to longer term psychological distress: Enter psychotherapy.

Applying this model, psychotherapy is a means of creating or restoring coordination among various neural networks. Research has demonstrated that successful psychotherapy correlates with changes in activation in areas of the brain hypothesized to be involved in disorders such as obsessive compulsive disorder and depression (Baxter et al., 1992; Brody, Saxena, Mandelkern, et al., 2001; Brody, Saxena, Schwartz, et al., 1998; Schwartz, Stoessel, Baxter, Martin, & Phelps, 1996). The return to normal levels of activation and homeostatic balance results in reestablishing positive reciprocal control among relevant neural structures and networks.

## Psychotherapy and Neural Network Integration

*The only thing they (neural connections) can do . . . is to deepen old paths or to make new ones.*

—William James

A basic assumption of both neuroscience and psychotherapy is that optimal functioning and mental health are related to increasingly advanced levels of growth, integration, and complexity. On a neurological level, this equates to the integration and communication of neural networks dedicated to emotion, cognition, sensation, and behavior and a proper balance between excitation and inhibition. On an experiential level, integration is the ability to live life—love and work—while employing a minimum of defensiveness. Growth and integration are optimized by a positive early environment, including stage-appropriate challenges, support, and parents who are capable and willing to put feelings into words. These factors lead to positive affect regulation, biological homeostasis, and a quiet internal milieu allowing for the consolidation of the experience of subjectivity and a positive sense of self.

From the perspective of neuroscience, psychotherapy can be understood as a specific kind of enriched environment designed to enhance the growth of neurons and the integration of neural networks. The therapeutic environment is individually tailored to fit the symptoms and needs of each client. I propose here that all forms of therapy, regardless of theoretical orientation, will be successful to the degree to which they foster appropriate neuroplasticity. Further, I also propose that neural plasticity, growth, and integration in psychotherapy are enhanced by:

1. The establishment of a safe and trusting relationship.
2. Mild to moderate levels of stress.
3. Activating both emotion and cognition.
4. The co-construction of new personal narratives.

Although psychotherapists do not generally think in "neuroscientific" terms, stimulating neuroplasticity and neural integration is essentially what we do. We provide information to clients about our understanding of their difficulties in the form of psychoeducation, interpretations, or reality testing. We encourage clients to engage in behaviors, express feelings, and become conscious of aspects of themselves of which they may be unaware. We dare them to take risks. We guide them back and forth between thoughts and feelings, trying to help them establish new connections between the two. We help clients alter their description of themselves and the world, incorporating new awareness and encouraging better decision making. With successful treatment, the methods being used are internalized so that clients can gain independence from therapy and we do this all in the context of a warm, supportive, committed, and consistent relationship. These same factors are at play across psychodynamic, systems, and cognitive-behavioral approaches to treatment.

The broad context in which these processes can successfully occur is one of increasing levels of *affect tolerance and regulation* and the development of *integrative narratives* that emerge from the client–therapist relationship. In the context of empathic attunement within a safe and structured environment, clients are encouraged to tolerate the anxiety of feared experiences, memories, and thoughts. In this process, neural networks that are normally inhibited become activated and available for inclusion into conscious processing (Siegel, 1995). Interpretations in psychodynamic therapy, exposure in behavioral therapies, or experiments in differentiation from a systems perspective all focus on this goal. Through the activation of multiple cognitive and emotional networks, previously dissociated functions are integrated and gradually brought under the control of cortical executive functions. Narratives co-constructed with therapists provide a new template for thoughts, behaviors, and ongoing integration.

## Pathways of Integration

*It is the harmony of the diverse parts, their symmetry, their happy balance; in a word it is all that introduces order, all that gives unity.*
—Henri Poincaré

Given that information flows simultaneously in multiple directions through many neural networks, optimal neural integration likely involves maximizing the flow and flexibility of energy through neural networks (Pribram, 1991). Using this model, psychopathology can be caused by difficulties not just in a specific region of the brain, but also in the interactions among participating systems (Mayberg, 1997; Mayberg et al., 1999). Numerous processing networks combine affect, sensation, behavior, and conscious awareness into an integrated, functional, and balanced whole—the neural substrate for what Freud called the ego. The ego is essentially shorthand for how the organization of the self comes to be expressed in dimensions such as personality, affect regulation, coping styles, and self-image.

The primary directions of information flow relevant to psychotherapy are top-down (cortical to subcortical and back again) and left-right (across the two halves of the cortex). Keep in mind that these information loops need to communicate with each other as well as with many other processing systems. *Top-down* or *bottom-up integration* would include MacLean's linkup among the three levels of the triune brain and the unification of the body, emotion, and conscious awareness. This is called top-down because these circuits form loops that go from the top of our head down into the depths of the brain and back up again. Top-down integration includes the ability of the cortex to process, inhibit, and organize the reflexes, impulses, and emotions generated by the brainstem and limbic system (Alexander et al., 1986; Cummings, 1993). Frontal lobe disorders often result in a disinhibition of impulses and movements normally under its control such as obsessive-compulsive and attention deficit disorders. Within this category I include what has been referred to as *dorsal-ventral integration*, connecting cortical with limbic processing (Panksepp, 1998; Tucker, Luu, & Pribram, 1995).

*Left-right* or *right-left integration* involves abilities that require the input of both the left and right cerebral cortex and lateralized limbic regions for optimal functioning. For example, adequate language production requires an integration of the grammatical functions of the left and the emotional functions of the right. Left-right integration allows us to put feelings into words, consider feelings in conscious awareness, and balance the positive and negative affective biases of the left and right hemispheres (Silberman & Weingartner, 1986). A balance among the left and right prefrontal cortices is also necessary for the proper balance of affect and emotion. Alexithymia (the inability to put words to feelings) and somatization disorder (the conversion of emotional conflicts into bodily illness) may reflect left-right dissociation (Hoppe & Bogen, 1977). There is also evidence that depression and mania correlate with dysregulation of the balance of activation between the left and right prefrontal cortices (Baxter et al., 1985; Field, Healy, Goldstein, Perry, & Bendell, 1988).

The right hemisphere is more highly connected with the body and the more primitive and emotional aspects of functioning. The left hemisphere is more closely identified with cortical functioning, whereas the right is more densely connected with limbic and brainstem functions (Shapiro, Jamner, & Spence, 1997). For example, states of stress, anxiety, and fear result in increased activation in the right cortex and subcortical structures (Rauch et al., 1996; Wittling, 1997). This bias is also relevant to the organization of social emotional attachment patterns, transference, and affect regulation (Minagawa-Kawai et al., 2008). Much of the integration of top-down and left-right systems is mediated through interactions among regions of the frontal cortex, our primary executive system.

Due to the interconnectivity between left-right and top-down neural networks, examining integration from either the vertical or horizontal dimension alone is overly simplistic. Studies of metabolic activity in specific areas of the brain in pathological states reveal differences in both cortical and subcortical structures on both sides of the brain. This research suggests that restoring neural integration requires the simultaneous reregulation of networks on both vertical and horizontal planes. It is also important to remember that although we are discussing brain functioning from the perspective of neural networks, an equally meaningful discussion could focus on the impact of pharmacological agents on the modulation and homeostatic balance of these same networks (Coplan & Lydiard, 1998). This perspective helps us to understand why both psychotherapy and medication can result in shifts of neural activity and symptom reduction and why together they may work better than either one alone (Andreasen, 2001).

Neural network integration can also be accomplished through the activation of conscious language production (top and left) with more primitive, emotional, and unconscious processes (down and right) that have been dissociated due to stress or trauma. Depending on their theoretical orientation, therapists facilitate the process of network integration by supplying challenges of all kinds. An analyst may use interpretations to enhance awareness of inhibited, repressed, or dissociated thoughts and emotions. A cognitive-behavioral therapist will expose a client to a feared stimulus combined with relaxation training, allowing normally inhibited cortical circuitry to integrate with the subcortical circuitry that controls fear. Research across all forms of psychotherapy supports the hypothesis that positive outcomes are related to utilizing both support and challenge in the combined engagement of thought and affect (Orlinsky & Howard, 1986). Both the quality of the interpersonal connection and creating the proper learning environment appear essential.

## Psychotherapy and Parenting

*Parents are like shuttles on a loom. They join the threads of the past with threads of the future and leave their own bright patterns as they go.*
—Fred Rogers

We have talked a little about the parallels between positive parenting and successful psychotherapy; these similarities reflect the commonality of the conditions required for building and rebuilding the brain. Mutual eye gaze and escalating positive emotional interactions between parent and child stimulate the growth and organization of the brain. In the future, we may discover scientific evidence that the interpersonal experience of psychotherapy impacts the neurobiological environment of the brain in ways that stimulate neural plasticity and neurogenesis. Although the various schools of therapy tend to accentuate their differences, the therapeutic relationship itself may be the most powerful curative agent.

The warmth, acceptance, and unconditional positive regard demonstrated by Carl Rogers's work embodies the broad interpersonal environment for the initial growth of the brain and continued development later in life (Rogers, 1942). Having spent a brief period of time with Dr. Rogers as a student, I can attest to the power of his interpersonal style and therapeutic technique. I am sure he left many, including myself, with the fantasy of being available for adoption.

Primary goals of parenting include providing a child with the capacity for self-soothing and the ability to form positive relationships. This allows the child to face the challenges of life and benefit from healing life experiences. The successful mastery of challenges throughout life leads to taking on even more complex challenges that will promote increasingly higher levels of neural network development and integration. When internal or external factors prevent an individual from approaching challenging and stressful situations, neural systems will tend to remain underdeveloped or unintegrated.

In a review of hundreds of studies examining the outcome of psychotherapy, Orlinsky and Howard (1986) looked for those factors that seemed to relate to success. They found that the quality of the emotional connection between patient and therapist was far more important than the therapist's theoretical orientation. Patients who are motivated to change and are able to work collaboratively with their therapists also do better. Therapists' professional experience was positively related to success, as were the use of interpretation, a focus on transference, and the expression of emotion. The continual involvement of both cognitive and emotional processing during treatment seems essential for positive change.

Psychotherapy, like parenting, is neither mechanical nor generic. Each therapist–client pair creates a unique relationship resulting in a particular outcome. The importance of the unconscious processes of both parent and therapist is highlighted by their active participation in the co-construction of new narratives of their children and patients. As we will see in research on attachment, each parent's unconscious plays a role in the creation of the child's brain, just as the therapist's unconscious contributes to the context and outcome of therapy. This underscores the importance of proper training and adequate personal therapy for therapists, who will be putting their imprint on the hearts, minds, and brains of their clients.

## Summary

In this chapter we have explored some initial concepts in the integration of psychotherapy and neuroscience based on common principles within both fields. We have equated psychological health with optimal neural network growth and integration. Both the brain and the self are built in a stepwise manner by experience. The nervous system is made up of millions of neurons while human experience is constructed within countless moments of learning. The psychological difficulties for which patients seek psychotherapy are a function of inadequate growth and integration within and between these same networks. The aspects of development that foster positive brain development and those in therapy that promote positive change are emotional attunement, affect regulation, and the co-construction of narratives.

In the following chapter, we turn our attention to major models of psychotherapy in use today. By examining their theories and techniques, we will see how they have been shaped by underlying principles related to the growth and integration of neural networks. It is my belief that the development of psychotherapy has always been implicitly guided by the principles of neuroscience. All forms of therapy are successful to the degree to which they have found a way to tap into processes that build and modify neural structures within the brain.

Chapter 3

# Neural Integration in Different Models of Psychotherapy

*The techniques of behavior therapy and psychotherapy have relied on the principles of brain plasticity, generally without realizing it, for nearly one hundred years.*
—Nancy Andreasen

Like other scientific discoveries, psychotherapy developed from a combination of trial-and-error learning, the intuition of its founder, and plain luck. Each school of psychotherapy offers an explanation of mental health and illness as well as why its strategies and techniques are effective. Fortunately, the effectiveness of an intervention does not depend on the accuracy of the theory used to support it. For example, there was a time when psychoanalysts attributed the success of electroshock therapy to the need of a depressed person to be punished. The treatment worked and still works despite the lack of a solid understanding of its mechanisms of action.

Although each approach to psychotherapy is experienced as a fundamental truth by its disciples, all modes of therapy are actually *heuristics*. Heuristics are interpretations of experience or ways of understanding phenomena. The value of a heuristic lies in its ability to organize, explain, and predict what we observe. Neuroscience is another heuristic, one that we are using in the present discussion to explain the mechanisms of action of psychotherapy; in other words how and why it works.

It is my belief that neuroscience is a helpful heuristic that will lead us to a fuller understanding of the process of psychotherapy and may also serve as a rational means of selecting, combining, and evaluating treatment modalities.

In this chapter we examine, in broad strokes, some of the primary approaches to psychotherapy. These overviews are presented in order to provide a context in which to understand and organize the neuroscientific concepts in the coming chapters. In taking a sample of general theoretical approaches to psychotherapy, we will look for common elements among them, and how these elements may relate to neural network development and change. Remember, from the perspective of neuroscience, psychotherapists are in the brain-rebuilding business.

## Psychoanalytic and Psychodynamic Therapies

*Being entirely honest with oneself is a good exercise.*
—Sigmund Freud

Freud's psychoanalysis, the original form of psychodynamic therapy, has spun off countless variants in its century-long existence. Ego psychology, self-psychology, and schools of thought connected to names such as Klein, Kernberg, and Kohut have all attracted considerable followings. Despite their differences, psychodynamic forms of therapy share theoretical assumptions such as the existence of the unconscious, the power of early childhood experiences, and the existence of defenses that distort reality in order to reduce anxiety and enhance coping.

The exploration of the unconscious and its connection to our evolutionary past may be Freud's greatest legacy. He remained true to Charcot by exploring the multiple levels of human awareness and designed many techniques to bring the unconscious into conscious awareness. The power of trauma, especially during childhood, and its ability to shape the organization of the mind were also examined in great detail. Freud theorized that early attachment and relational difficulties, neglect, or trauma result in developmental arrests or "fixations" that delay or derail the adult's potential to love and work. From the standpoint of neurobiology, most of Freud's work addressed the discontinuities and dissociations between networks of conscious and unconscious processing. Freud focused on the role of overwhelming emotion as the cause of unintegrated neural processing.

Freud's psychic self contains the primitive drives (id), the demands of civilization to conform for the benefit of the group (superego), and those parts of the self (ego) that attempt to negotiate the naturally occurring conflicts between the two. In its role as a diplomat in the fight between id and superego, the ego utilizes many elaborate defenses to cope with reality. Ego strength, or our ability to navigate reality with a minimum of defensiveness, reflects the integration of neural networks of emotion and thought, and the development of mature defenses. The more primitive or immature the defense mechanism, the more reality is distorted and the more functional impairment occurs. Sublimation, for example, enables us to convert unacceptable impulses into constructive and prosocial goals. Mature defenses, like sublimation or humor, allow us to assuage strong feelings, keep in contact with others, and remain attuned to a shared social reality.

Less mature defenses, such as denial and dissociation, result in greater distortion of reality and difficulties in both work and relationships. Defenses are often invisible to their owners because they are organized by hidden layers of neural processing that are inaccessible to conscious awareness. What Freud called defenses can be seen as ways in which neural networks have adapted to cope with emotional stress. People seek treatment when their defense mechanisms cannot adequately cope with repressed emotions, or when symptoms become intolerable.

Despite a conscious awareness that something may be wrong, the hidden layers of neural processing continue to organize the world based on the prior experiences that shaped them. As we will see in later chapters, the neural circuitry involved with fear has a tenacious memory and can invisibly influence conscious awareness for a lifetime. Part of psychodynamic therapy is an exploration and uncovering of this unconscious organization of experience. Freud's *projective hypothesis* described the process by which our brains create and organize the world around us. As the clarity of a situation decreases, the brain naturally generates structure and projects it onto the world. The way we organize and understand ambiguous stimuli gives us clues about the architecture of the hidden layers of neural processing (how our unconscious organizes the world). From the projective hypothesis came the invention of projective tests such as Rorschach's ink blots, free association, and an emphasis on the importance of dreams as the "royal road to the unconscious."

As part of the projective hypothesis, psychodynamic therapists often provide minimal information about themselves, allowing the client to project onto them implicit (unconscious) memories from past relationships. This form of projection, *transference*, results in the client placing expectations and emotions from earlier relationships on the therapist, which allows them to be experienced and worked through firsthand. It is through this transference that early relationships for which we have no conscious recollection are brought fully into therapy. Freud felt that the evocation and resolution of the transference was a core component of a successful analysis. In Freud's words, only transference renders "the invaluable service of making the patient's buried and forgotten love emotions actual and manifest" (Freud, 1975, p. 115).

Resistance represents aspects of implicit memory presented by the client that it is up to the therapist to decipher. Early experiences of rejection, criticism, or neglect from parents result in shame, which can evolve into a child's negative self-image. The resultant self-criticism (superego) manifests in disrespect for anyone who shows the child love or respect. An example of this is expressed in the Groucho Marx line, "I'd never join a club that would have me as a member." In therapy, this may manifest as a strong distrust of the therapist's intentions or his or her ability to be of help.

*Interpretations* are one of the psychodynamic therapist's most important tools. Sometimes called the "therapist's scalpel," interpretations attempt to make the unconscious conscious. Based on observations of all levels of the client's behavior, the therapist attempts to bring the processing of the hidden layers to the client's attention. Repeated and skillful attention to unconscious material via interpretations, confrontations, and clarifications results in a gradually expanding awareness of unconscious processes and the integration of dissociated top-down and right-left processing networks.

Accurate, successful interpretations are sometimes accompanied by feelings of disorganization, anger, or depression. This is because when defenses are made conscious and are exposed for what they are, they lose their effectiveness, leading to a disinhibition of the emotions that they have been successfully defending against. In other words, the networks containing the negative emotions become disinhibited and activated. For example, if intellectualization is being used to avoid the shame and depression related to early criticism, recognition of the defense will bring these feelings and related memories to awareness.

Emotions play a central role in the success of psychodynamic therapies. The neural networks that organize emotions are often shaped to guide us away from thoughts and feelings for which we were punished or abandoned. Unconscious anxiety signals continue to shape our behavior, leading us to remain on tried-and-true paths and avoid situations that trigger our unremembered past. An emphasis on the evocation of emotion and cognition is an important contribution of psychoanalysis and reflects fundamental underlying neurobiological processes of health and illness.

Across psychodynamic forms of therapy, conscious awareness is expanded, emotions are explored, and the expression of repressed or inhibited emotions is encouraged. Feelings, thoughts, and behaviors are repeatedly juxtaposed, combined, and recombined in the process of *working through*. The assumptions and narratives from the past are edited based on new information, and those about the present and future are reevaluated. The overall goal is combining emotion with conscious awareness and rewriting the story of the self. These processes, when successful, enhance the growth, integration, and flexibility of neural networks and human experience.

## Rogerian or Client-Centered Therapy

*The curious paradox is that when I accept myself just as I am, then I can change.*

—Carl Rogers

Against the dominant background of psychoanalysis, Carl Rogers (1942) emerged with a form of therapy he referred to as "client-centered." In stark contrast to a theory-based analysis of the patient, Rogers emphasized creating a relationship that maximized the individual's opportunity for self-discovery. Rogers's approach gained rapid acceptance in the nonmedical community and by the 1960s came to be the dominant form of counseling (Gilliland & James, 1998).

When different approaches to therapy are compared for effectiveness, the general agreement is that the perceived quality of the client–therapist relationship has the highest correlation with reported treatment success. Some have gone as far as saying that the curative element is the therapeutic relationship itself, rather than any specific techniques. This would certainly have been Rogers's belief, for he believed that the curative aspects of therapy were the therapist's warmth, acceptance, genuineness, and unconditional positive regard. His emphasis on interpersonal congruence foreshadowed the focus on emotional resonance and empathic attunement in later-emerging forms of psychotherapy such as object relations and intersubjectivity (Kohut, 1984; Stolorow & Atwood, 1979).

Over the last century, the therapist attributes suggested by Rogers and what we have come to think of as the best possible attitudes for optimal parenting have become essentially identical. Rogerian principles lead to a minimized need for defensiveness and shame while maximizing expressiveness, exploration, and risk taking. Rogers was likely describing the best interpersonal environment for brain growth during development and neural plasticity in psychotherapy when he stated that client-centered therapy "aims directly toward the greater independence and integration of the individual rather than hoping that such results will accrue if the counselor assists in solving the problem. The individual and not the problem is the focus. The aim is not to solve one particular problem, but to assist the individual to grow, so that he can cope with the present problem and later problems in a better-integrated fashion" (Rogers, 1942, p. 28).

During my training in client-centered therapy, I was struck by the power of Rogers's approach. I found it immensely difficult to maintain his supportive stance, and often struggled to keep myself from directing my clients, giving advice, and pushing them to change. To my astonishment, I found that providing clients with a supportive relationship led to insights on their part that mirrored the interpretations I struggled to suppress. Clients often expressed a mixture of sadness and appreciation when they realized how much they longed to be listened to without fear of judgment and shame.

What might be going on in the brain of a client in client-centered therapy? In the Rogerian interpersonal context, a client would most likely experience the widest range of emotions within the ego scaffolding of an empathic other. The activation of neural networks of emotion makes feelings and emotional memories available for reorganization.

Rogers's nondirective method activates clients' executive networks and their self-reflective abilities. Supportive rephrasing and clarification of what clients say may also enhance executive functioning. This simultaneous activation of cognition and emotion, enhanced perspective, and the emotional regulation offered by the relationship may provide an optimal environment for neural change. Clients, scaffolded by the therapist's support and stimulated by his or her words, can then work to rewrite their stories.

We know that social interactions early in life result in the stimulation of both neurotransmitters and neural growth hormones that participate in the active building of the brain. By recreating a positive parenting relationship, it is likely that the empathic connectedness promoted by Rogers actually stimulates biochemical changes in the brain capable of enhancing new learning. For example, studies with birds have demonstrated that the ability to learn their songs is enhanced when exposed to live singing birds versus tape recordings of the same songs (Baptista & Petrinovich, 1986). Other birds are actually unable to learn from tape recordings and require positive social interactions and nurturance in order to learn (Eales, 1985). We will see later how maternal contact and nurturance in rats protect the brain from the damaging effects of stress (Meaney, Aitken, Viau, Sharma, & Sarrieau, 1989; Plotsky & Meaney, 1993).

Studies such as these demonstrate that social relationships have the power to stimulate the neural plasticity required for new learning. The interpersonal and emotional aspects of the therapeutic relationship, referred to as a *nonspecific factor* in the psychotherapy outcome literature, may be the primary mechanism of therapeutic action. As we will see in a later chapter, these nonspecific factors are, in fact, quite specific, as early maternal care has been linked to increased neural plasticity, emotional regulation, and attachment behavior. In other words, those who are nurtured best survive best within a positive and safe environment. Unfortunately, the social isolation created by certain psychological defenses reinforces the rigidity of neural organization as the client avoids the interpersonal contexts required to promote healing. In these instances, the therapeutic relationship may serve as a bridge to once again connect with others.

## Cognitive Therapies

*It's not what happens to you, but how you react to it that matters.*
                                                           —Epictetus

Cognitive therapies highlight the centrality of a person's thoughts, appraisals, and beliefs in guiding his or her feelings and actions. They emphasize that negative thoughts, skewed appraisals, and erroneous beliefs can create psychological problems. Cognitive therapy focuses on the identification and modification of dysfunctional thoughts with the ultimate goal of improved affect regulation (Beck, Rush, Shaw, & Emery, 1979; Ellis, 1962). The primary targets of cognitive-behavioral therapy have been depression, anxiety, obsessive-compulsive disorder, phobias, and panic disorders.

Depressed patients tend to evaluate their world in absolute terms, take details out of context, and experience neutral comments and events as negative. Common depressive thoughts include the expectation of failure despite many past successes, and thoughts that one is alone despite being surrounded by friends and family. In cognitive therapy, the patient is educated about these common distortions and encouraged to engage in reality testing and self-talk designed to counteract negative reflexive statements.

In anxiety disorders, fear comes to organize and control the patients' lives. High levels of anxiety inhibit and distort rational cognitive processing. Cognitive interventions with these patients often include educating them about the physiological symptoms of anxiety such as a racing heart, shortness of breath, and sweaty palms. These patients are taught that feelings of dread are secondary to autonomic symptoms and should not be taken as seriously as they feel. A focus on understanding normal biological processes usually redirects the client away from catastrophic attributions that serve to increase anxiety.

With clients suffering with phobias or PTSD, *psychoeducation* is combined with *exposure* and *response prevention*, in which the client faces the feared stimulus (e.g., venturing outside or thinking about a negative event) without being allowed to retreat back to the safety of home or a state of denial. Exposure is usually systematic, gradual, and paired with *relaxation training* used to aid in the downregulation of physiological arousal. This process combines increased cortical processing (thought) with subcortical activation (emotion) to allow for integration with cortical circuitry in order to permit habituation, inhibition, and eventual extinction via descending cortical networks.

How does this translate into what is going on in the brain during cognitive therapy? Research has demonstrated that disorders of anxiety and depression correlate with changes in metabolic balance among different brain regions. For example, symptoms of depression correlate with activation imbalance within the prefrontal cortex—lower levels of activation in the left and higher levels in the right (Baxter et al., 1985; Field et al., 1988). This supports the hypothesis that mental health correlates with the proper homeostatic balance between neural networks. Symptoms of obsessive-compulsive disorder correlate with changes in activation in the medial (middle) portions of the frontal cortex and a subcortical structure called the *caudate nucleus* (Rauch et al., 1994). Posttraumatic flashbacks and states of high arousal correlate with higher levels of activation in right-sided limbic and medial frontal structures. Importantly, high arousal also correlates with decreased metabolism in the expressive language centers of the left hemisphere (Rauch et al., 1996).

Of all the different types of therapy, specific links have been found between successful cognitive-behavioral therapy and changes in brain functioning. As described in the last chapter, changes in brain functioning and symptomatology in both obsessive-compulsive disorder and depression have been found after successful psychotherapy (Baxter et al., 1992; Brody, Saxena, Mandelkern, et al., 2001; Brody, Saxena, Schwartz, et al., 1998; Schwartz et al., 1996). These findings strongly suggest that therapists can utilize cognition to alter the relationship among neural networks in a way that impacts their balance of activation and inhibition. In striving to activate cortical processing through conscious control of thoughts and feelings, these therapies enhance left cortical processing, inhibiting and regulating right hemispheric balance and subcortical activation. The reestablishment of hemispheric and top-down regulation allows for increases in positive attitudes and a sense of safety that counteract the depressing and frightening effects of right hemisphere and subcortical (amygdala) dominance (Ochsner & Gross, 2008).

Although cognitive-behavioral therapy is carried out in an interpersonal context of collaboration and support, it places far less emphasis on the therapeutic relationship than do Rogerian and psychodynamic approaches. The inherent wisdom of this approach with depressed and anxious patients lies in the fact that disorders of affect need activation of cortical executive structures. Given that emotions are contagious, a deeper emotional connection might result in the therapist attuning to dysregulated states and sharing in the patient's depressed, anxious, and panicky feelings. While emotional attunement with these feelings is helpful, it has been my experience that after the working relationship is established, challenging thoughts and encouraging new behaviors can often be far more beneficial to the therapeutic process than empathy alone. The structured aspect of cognitive-behavioral therapy may protect both therapist and patient from the power of negative affect.

## Systemic Family Therapy

*We must not allow other people's limited perceptions to define us.*
—Virginia Satir

There is increasing evidence that neural networks throughout the brain are stimulated to grow and organize by interaction with the social environment. Early relationships become encoded in networks of sensory, motor, and emotional learning to form what dynamic therapists call *inner objects*. These inner objects have the power to soothe, arouse, and dysregulate, depending on the quality of our attachment experiences with significant others. These unconscious memories organize our inner worlds when we are with others and when we are alone. Thus, we constantly experience ourselves in the context of others.

This is one reason systems therapists question the validity of diagnosing and treating people in isolation. They believe that in our day-to-day experience we simultaneously exist in two realities: our present families and our multigenerational family histories. This perspective is especially relevant when working with children who have yet to form clear ego boundaries between themselves and their family. Some adult patients who have not successfully individuated also demonstrate unclear boundaries between their own thoughts and feelings and those of family members. Regardless of age, however, the basic principles are the same.

Murray Bowen, a prime contributor to systems thinking, presented a model that is compatible with an exploration of the underlying neuroscience of psychotherapy. His perspective is based on the recognition that a family provides both emotional regulation and a platform for differentiation. He defines *differentiation* as the development of *autonomy*—a balance between the recognition of the needs of self and others. Differentiation involves the regulation of anxiety and a balance of integration of affect and cognition. Bowen would say that anxiety is the enemy of differentiation. That is, the more frightened people are, the more likely they are to dissociate and the more dependent and primitive they become in their interaction with others (Bowen, 1978).

When this regression occurs, family members try—consciously and unconsciously—to shape the family in a manner that reduces their own anxiety. The alcoholic needs the problem to go unmentioned, while the family needs to put on a good front to the outside world. Dysfunctional family patterns such as this one sacrifice the growth and well-being of one or more members (often the children) to reduce the overall level of anxiety in the family. The cognitive, emotional, and social world of an alcoholic family is shaped by the avoidance of feelings, thoughts, and activities that expose their shameful secret to conscious awareness and the outside world. The development of the children becomes distorted by the adaptations necessary for their survival within the pathological system. Unfortunately, the roles and rules of the family designed to decrease anxiety maintain the pathologies of some and create new pathologies in others.

Over time, the dysfunction becomes embedded in the personality and neural architecture of everyone in the family and they collude to maintain the system, because they now all require the status quo in order to feel safe. These experiences become embedded into their neural architecture and are carried forward into adult relationships. As a result, many of us re-create the dysfunction from our family of origin in our choice of partners and how we shape the families we build as adults. Each family's problems are determined by the multigenerational, unconscious shaping of both neural structure and behavior. The functioning of brains and family dynamics reflects how they have been organized. The dysfunctional brain, like the dysfunctional family, is shaped by the avoidance of thoughts and feelings, resulting in the dissociation of neural systems of affect, cognition, sensation, and behavior, as well as a lack of human differentiation.

As in other forms of psychotherapy, the goal of systems therapy is to integrate and balance the various cortical and subcortical, left and right hemisphere processing networks. This process requires a decrease in anxiety from high to low or moderate levels. High levels of affect block thinking, whereas moderate levels enhance neuroplastic processes, which in turn support cognition and emotion. In essence, Bowen is highlighting that the simultaneous activation of cognition and emotion leads to neural integration. Increased differentiation of individuals within a family will decrease the overall rigidity of the system. This process also allows family members to become more responsive to the needs of others and less reactive to their own inner conflicts.

The first step in systems therapy is to educate the family about these concepts and to explore the history of both sides of the family through the past few generations. In the context of systems theory and family history, the problems brought into relief often become more understandable. Uncovering family secrets and reality testing around the myths and projections of each family member allow for cortical processing of primitive and unconscious defenses. The process of family therapy involves a series of experiments with increasingly higher levels of differentiation. Communication skills, assertiveness training, and exercises in new forms of cooperation can all increase cortical involvement with previously reflexive or regressive emotions and behaviors. Often the person with the symptoms needs to take more responsibility, while pathological caretakers must learn to accept nurturance. Each member of the family needs to achieve a balance between autonomy and interdependence. Ultimately, psychological, interpersonal, and neural integration are different levels and manifestations of the same process.

## Reichian and Gestalt Therapy

*I am not in this world to live up to other people's expectations, nor do I feel that the world must live up to mine.*
                                                                    —Fritz Perls

Wilhelm Reich, one of Freud's early disciples, felt that memory and personality are shaped and stored not just in the brain but throughout the entire body. Because of this, Reich not only paid careful attention to his clients' musculature, posture, and breathing, but also encouraged them to express themselves physically during analysis. By beating their fists, stomping their feet, and using exaggerated breathing techniques, they attempted to release normally inhibited emotions. Reich highlighted the importance of the therapist's interpretation of the nonverbal messages of the body, making them available for conscious consideration. His theories led to the development of Rolfing (which uses deep body massage to evoke and process memories) and Gestalt therapy (which focuses on drawing attention to nonverbal aspects of communication and increased self-awareness).

Reich (1945) believed that the major focus of psychotherapy should be the analysis of the character, something he saw as similar to Freud's notion of ego. While Freud focused on verbal communication, Reich's major contribution was to draw more attention to the nonverbal and emotional aspects of the therapeutic interaction. He contended that the problems people bring to therapy are embedded in their *character armor*, shaped during development as an adaptation against real or imagined danger. Character armor forms as a result of misattunement, neglect, or trauma at the hands of caretakers. This armor is preverbal and organizes during the first years of life. According to Reich, early defenses take shape at all levels of the nervous system, become encoded in our entire being, and are, like the air we breathe, utterly invisible to us. The defenses identified by Reich reflect emotional memories from early preverbal experiences that are stored in sensory, motor, and emotional networks of early memory. Because character armor is invisible to its owner, the therapist's job is to make the client aware of its existence, expression, and meaning.

Gestalt therapy is a unique expression of Reichian theory that is particularly relevant to the notion of neural integration. *Gestalt*, a German word meaning "whole," reflects the orientation of bringing together an awareness of conscious and unconscious processes; in other words, seeing the whole picture. Gestalt therapy's charismatic founder, Fritz Perls, used the term *safe emergency* for the experience that psychotherapists strive to create in treatment (Perls, Hefferline, & Goodman, 1951). A safe emergency is a challenge for growth and integration in the context of guidance and support. It is also a wonderful way to describe an important aspect of good parenting. Therapists create this emergency by exposing clients to unintegrated and dysregulating thoughts and feelings while offering them the tools and nurturance with which to integrate their experiences. Safety is provided in the form of a supportive and collaborative therapeutic relationship, often in the context of a group. The emergency is created by an unmasking of defenses, making unacceptable needs and emotions conscious, and by bringing into awareness dissociated elements of consciousness.

The stories a patient tells about his or her problems are often seen, in the Gestalt context, as self-deceptions. They serve to keep from awareness those feelings that are relevant to healing but less acceptable. Unconscious gestures, facial expressions, and movements are first brought to awareness, then exaggerated, and finally given a voice with the purpose of understanding and integrating experience. The therapist points out contradictions, such as making positive statements while shaking the head "no," or smiling while talking about a painful experience. These contradictions are explored as indications of internal conflicts to be brought into awareness. Again, the focus is on bringing to conscious (cortical) awareness the automatic, nonverbal, and unconscious processes primarily organized in right hemisphere and subcortical neural networks.

Gestalt therapy emphasizes the identification and exploration of projection, identifying it as an avenue for discovering aspects of the self that have been difficult or impossible to accept. In the popular "empty chair" technique, patients alternately play the role of different parts of themselves to fully articulate the different sides of inner conflicts. The Gestalt therapist believes that maximizing awareness of all aspects of the self—including cognition, emotion, behavior, and sensation—will result in increased maturation and psychological health. This process depends on the integration of the neural networks responsible for each of these functions.

## Common Factors

*My work as a psychoanalyst is to help patients recover their lost wholeness and to strengthen the psyche so it can resist future dismemberment.*
—C. G. Jung

In reviewing these different psychotherapeutic modalities, a number of principles emerge that unify the various therapeutic schools. The first is that psychotherapy values openness, honesty, and trust. Each form of psychotherapy creates an individualized experience designed to examine conscious and unconscious beliefs and assumptions, expand awareness and reality testing, and encourage the confrontation of anxiety-provoking experiences. Each perspective explores behavior, emotion, sensation, and cognition in an attempt to increase awareness of previously unconscious or distorted material. The primary focus of psychotherapy appears to be the integration of affect, in all its forms, with conscious awareness, and cognition.

Intellectual understanding of a psychological problem in the absence of increased integration with emotion, sensation, and behavior does not result in change. All forms of treatment recognize the need for stress, from the subtle disruption of defenses created by the compassion of Carl Rogers to the exposure to feared stimuli in exposure therapies. There is a recognition that the evocation of emotion coupled with conscious awareness is most likely to result in symptom reduction and personal growth. Whether it is called symptom relief, differentiation, ego strength, or awareness, all forms of therapy are targeting dissociated neural networks for integration.

When theories of neuroscience and psychotherapy are considered side by side, a number of working hypotheses emerge. First, given that the human brain is a social organ, safe and supportive relationships are the optimal environment for social and emotional learning. *Empathic attunement* with the therapist provides the context of nurturance in which growth and development occur. By activating processes involved in secure attachment, empathic attunement likely creates an optimal biochemical environment for neural plasticity.

Second, we appear to experience optimal development and integration in the context of a mild to moderate level of arousal or what we might call *optimal stress*. Suboptimal affect regulation during development can result in symptoms, maladaptive defenses, and psychopathology. Optimal stress will create the most favorable neurobiological environment for neural plasticity and integration. Although stress appears important as part of the activation of circuits involved with emotion, states of mild to moderate arousal seem ideal for consolidation and integration. In states of high arousal, sympathetic activation inhibits optimal cortical processing and disrupts integration functions. The ebb and flow of emotion over the course of therapy reflects the underlying neural rhythms of growth and change.

Psychodynamic therapies alternate confrontations and interpretations with a supportive and soothing interpersonal environment (Weiner, 1998). The systematic desensitization of cognitive-behavioral therapy pairs exposure to feared stimuli with psychoeducation and relaxation training in the presence of a coach and ally (Wolpe, 1958). Bowen's family systems approach focuses on pairing anxiety reduction with experiments in increasing levels of independent and differentiated behavior (Bowen, 1978). All forms of successful therapy strive to create safe emergencies in one form or another.

A third hypothesis is that the involvement of affect and cognition appears necessary in the therapeutic process in order to create the context for integration of neural circuits with a high vulnerability to dissociation. It has been said that, in psychotherapy, "understanding is the booby prize." It is a hollow victory to end up with a psychological explanation for problems that remain unchanged. On the other hand, catharsis without cognition does not result in integration either. The ability to tolerate and regulate affect creates the necessary condition for the brain's continued growth throughout life. Increased integration parallels an increased ability to experience and tolerate thoughts and emotions previously inhibited, dissociated, or defended against. Affect regulation may be the most important result of the psychotherapeutic process across orientations, because it allows for a reconnection with the naturally occurring salubrious experiences in life.

Repeated simultaneous activation of networks requiring integration with one another most likely aids in their integration. Repetitive play in children and the phrase "working through" in therapy best reflect this process. This concept parallels the principle from neuroscience that "neurons that fire together, wire together" (Hebb, 1949; Shatz, 1990). The simultaneous activation of neural circuits allows them to stimulate the development of connections within association areas to coordinate and integrate their functioning.

Fourth, the co-construction of narratives between parent and child or therapist and client provides a broad matrix supporting the integration of multiple neural networks. Autobiographical memory creates stories of the self capable of supporting affect regulation in the present and the maintenance of homeostatic functions into the future. Memory, in this form, may maximize neural network integration as it organizes vast amounts of information across multiple processing tracks. Thus, language is an important tool in both neurological and psychological development.

## Sam and Jessica

*The deepest principle in human nature is the craving to be appreciated.*
—William James

Being human mean communicating with others. Humans have many channels of communication, including touch, eye contact, tone of voice, and words. Through our interactions we have the power to impact one another at every level. One of my most powerful experiences of the truth of this fact did not take place in a seminar or consulting room, but rather at the home of a friend. I had volunteered to watch his two young children for a few hours while he ran some errands. I had known Jessica and Sam, 4 and 6 years old, all their lives. I was someone on an outer ring of their universe, an attractive combination of familiar and new, and completely unprepared for what was about to happen. The minute their father left, they shifted from low to medium to high gear and I found myself in the midst of a frenzy of excitement.

Toys began flying out of closets and storage containers; games were begun and tossed aside; videos were started, stopped, and replaced—a succession of Indian princes, mermaids, lion kings, ladies, and tramps. After what felt like hours, I glanced at my watch to find only 15 minutes had passed! Four more hours at this pace? I wasn't sure I could survive. I kept trying to refocus Sam and Jessica's activity, to no avail. At one point, as we dashed from bedroom to den to living room, I sank to the floor in the hall, and propped myself up against the wall. When they realized that I wasn't right behind them, they ran back to find me.

They stood panting, one on either side of me, wondering what new game I had concocted. My suggestion that we sit and talk for awhile passed unnoticed. After a few seconds, Sam looked at his sister and yelled, "Show Lou how you burp your dolly!" Both let out a scream and Jessica soon returned with an adorable squishy doll. As I reached for the doll to hold and admire it, Jessica threw the doll on the floor face first and drove her fists into its back. As Jessica and Sam took turns crushing the doll into the carpet, I watched in horror, completely identifying with the doll. I had to hold back my urge to save the poor thing from her vicious attackers.

I quickly reminded myself that I was feeling sorry for a ball of cotton and that I should turn my attention back to the children. I also realized that rescuing the doll would be scolding Sam and Jessica for their behavior, which I did not want to do. I struggled to make sense of what was happening and asked myself if there might be some symbolic message in the way they were treating this doll. Jessica and Sam had experienced a great deal of stress in their brief lives in the forms of severe physical illness, surgery, drug addiction in the family, and an understandably overwhelmed support system. The frantic activity I was witnessing may have reflected the accumulated anxiety from all they had gone through, mixed with normal childhood exuberance. But how might knowing this be helpful to these two beautiful children?

As I reflected on these things I was hit by the notion that perhaps the doll represented both Sam and Jessica. This doll needed to be burped. It needed the help of an adult to alleviate its discomfort and regain a sense of comfort and equilibrium. Perhaps Sam and Jessica were showing me that when they needed to be comforted, they were met with more pain, or, at the very least, insufficient understanding and warmth. Might their behavior be a message? "Please, we need nurturance and healing!" Their world seemed chaotic and unsafe, a whirlwind; these were the same feelings they had created within me during the last half hour. Was their behavior a form of communication?

They had each taken a number of turns "burping" the doll and I suspected that their attention would soon turn to me. What to do or say? I didn't want to burp the baby their way, and my thoughts about what was happening would be meaningless. I could feel my anxiety growing when finally, they both turned to me and cried in unison: "Your turn!" I hesitated. The chant of "Burp the baby, burp the baby" began to rise. I looked at both of them and said, "I know another way to burp a baby. Here's how my mom burped me." A cheer went up. I suspect they assumed that I was going to set the doll on fire or put it in the microwave.

I gently picked up the doll and brought it to my left shoulder. Rubbing its back in a circular motion using my right hand, looking down at it with tenderness, I quietly said, "This will make you feel better, little one." A silence fell over the hallway. I looked up to find Jessica and Sam transfixed, as if hypnotized. Their eyes followed the slow circles of my hand, heads tilted like puppies. Their bodies relaxed, their hands limp at their sides, calm for the first time.

After following the movement of my hand for about 30 seconds, Jessica looked up at me and softly asked, "Can I have a turn?" "Of course you can," I told her. At first I thought she meant that she wanted a turn burping the baby. But then carefully, almost respectfully, she took the doll from me and placed it on the floor with its back against the wall. She stepped over to me, climbed over my crossed legs and put her head on my shoulder where the doll's head had been. She turned to me and almost inaudibly said, "I'm ready now." As I rubbed Jessica's back, I felt her growing more and more limp as she melted into my shoulder and chest. I half expected Sam to tear her off, climb on himself, and turn it into a wrestling match. When I looked over to him, I could see that he was in the same posture and state of mind he had been in watching me burp the doll. He eventually looked up at me and asked, "Can I have a turn?" Before I could answer, Jessica lifted her head slightly and told him, "In a minute."

After a while, she gave up her spot on my shoulder and Sam had his turn being "burped." It felt wonderful to hold them in this way and give them something they seemed to need so badly. After a few turns for each of them, we went into the den, curled up on the sofa, one of them under each of my arms, and watched a movie. Actually, I watched the movie— they dozed off after only a few minutes. While my eyes followed the frenetic animation on the screen, my breathing paced theirs and I shared the peace they seemed to be feeling.

I marveled at how they managed to communicate their pain and confusion by creating these same feelings in me. Emotion is truly contagious and a powerful source of human connection. By having them set the initial pace of our play, I told them I respected their way of coping. Through the use of the doll, they communicated that when they needed soothing their anxiety was often met with more of the same. When I burped their doll in a caring and loving way, I showed them that I was capable of soothing them if they were feeling bad. By asking me to burp them, they told me I was trusted. In falling asleep, they said, "We feel safe and we know you will watch over us while we rest." While none of this was spoken, the communication was clear.

Our interactions with the doll changed Sam and Jessica's state of mind and body as well as my own. I believe that it not only impacted their attitudes and behaviors that afternoon, but may have also changed their brains in some small but perhaps permanent way. I could see this reflected in their faces and hear it in the tone of their voices; something fundamental had changed that affected their entire beings. I provided them with a metaphor through which they could reorganize their experience, have their needs met, and regulate their emotions. Together, the three of us co-constructed a new narrative for them to use as a way of soothing themselves and each other.

Were this process to be repeated enough times, their brains could reorganize around this metaphor of nurturance and holding and enhance communication between networks of cognitive and emotional processing. Perhaps Sam and Jessica could internalize a model of self-holding and nurturance that would help them navigate future challenges. This kind of interaction is at the heart of all forms of psychotherapy, regardless of philosophy or technique. All forms of therapy have their own versions of integrative metaphors, serving to reorganize neural networks and alter human experience, hopefully, for the better.

## Summary

In this chapter we have discussed some of the basic principles connecting the historical and conceptual connections between psychotherapy and neuroscience. Four common factors related to the nature of social relationships, optimal stress, the activation of affect and cognition, and the co-construction of narratives emerge from the review. In the chapters to come, we will explore the components and organizing principles of the nervous system. These basic concepts will help us understand the neural mechanisms of the building and rebuilding of the brain.

Part II.

# How the Brain Works:
# The Legacy of Evolution

# Chapter 4

# The Human Nervous System: From Neurons to Neural Networks

*All functions of mind reflect functions of brain.*
                                        —Eric Kandel

Studying the human brain is a daunting task. In fact, the human brain is so vastly complex that it would take tens of thousands of pages to do justice to what is known about its structure and function. But how much do we really need to know about the brain to help us in our work as therapists? My belief is that a basic understanding of the nervous system, without getting lost in the details, would be very helpful. With this as our goal, we will move through a thumbnail sketch of the basic structures, functions, and development of the nervous system. Keep in mind that this is a skewed look at the human nervous system biased toward those structures, processes, and theories that will be relevant to the chapters to come.

## Neurons

> *It is impossible, in principle, to explain any pattern by invoking a single quantity.*
> —Gregory Bateson

The basic unit of the nervous system is the *neuron,* which receives and transmits signals via chemical transmission and electrical impulses.

There are an estimated 100 billion neurons in the brain, with between 10 and 100,000 synaptic connections each, creating limitless networking possibilities (Nolte, 2008; Post & Weiss, 1997). Neurons have fibers called *axons* covered with *myelin*, an insulator that enhances the efficiency of communication. Because neurons myelinate as they develop, one way of measuring the maturity of a neural network is to measure its degree of myelinization. Multiple sclerosis—a disease that breaks down myelin—results in a decrease in the efficiency of neural communication, negatively impacting cognition, affect, and movement (Hurley, Taber, Zhang, & Hayman, 1999). The *white matter* of the brain is white because myelin is white (or at least light in color). *Gray matter* consists primarily of neural cell bodies.

When a neuron fires, information is carried via an electrical charge that travels down the length of its axon. Neurons communicate with one another across *synapses* (the spaces between neurons) via chemical messengers called *neurotransmitters*. The combination of these two complementary processes creates the brain's *electrochemical* system. Many neurons develop elaborate branches, called *dendrites*, which form synaptic connections with thousands of dendrites from other neurons. The relationships formed among these dendrites organize the complex networking of the nervous system.

## Glia

*Complex, statistically improbable things are by their nature more difficult to explain than simple, statistically probable things.*
—Richard Dawkins

Although the focus of neuroscience research is usually on neurons, they make up only half the volume of the cerebral cortex. The other half of our brain is made up of approximately one trillion cells known as *glia*. One reason we know so much more about neurons is that they are approximately 10 times larger than glial cells. It has long been known that glia play an important supportive role in the construction, organization, and maintenance of neural systems. More recently, it has become apparent that they are also involved in neural network communication and plasticity (Allen & Barres, 2005; Pfrieger & Barres, 1996; Sontheimer, 1995; Vernadakis, 1996). *Neural plasticity* refers to the ability of neurons to change the way they are shaped and relate to one another as the brain adapts to the environment through time.

*Astrocytes*, the most abundant kind of glia, have been shown to participate in the regulation of synaptic transmission and to be involved in the coordination and synchronization of synaptic activity (Fellin, Pascual, & Haydon, 2006; Newman, 1982). There now appears to be glial as well as neural transmission. There is also the distinct possibility that astrocytes both shape and modulate synapses (Halassa, Fellin, & Hayden, 2007). Through evolution, the ratio of glial cells to neurons has steadily increased, leading some to believe that our expanding cognitive sophistication is, in part, related to the participation of astrocytes in information processing (Nedergaard, Ransom, & Goldman, 2003; Oberheim, Wang, Goldman, & Nedergaard, 2006). We will revisit this in a later chapter when we discuss Einstein's glial cells and his exceptional imaginal abilities.

## Neurogenesis

*What we teach today is part biology and part history . . . but we don't always know where one ends and the other begins.*
—J. T. Bonner

*Neurogenesis*, the birth of new neurons via cell division, occurs in the lower regions of the ventricles, the fluid-filled cavities within our brains. Some fish and amphibians, which demonstrate ongoing neurogenesis, possess nervous systems that continue to grow in size throughout life (Fine, 1989). During evolution, it appears that primates may have traded much of their capacity for neurogenesis to continue building existing neural networks in order to retain past learning and develop expert knowledge. In other words, if instead of being replaced, neurons are retained and continually modified through the branching of their dendrites in reaction to new experience, more refined learning may result (Purves & Voyvodic, 1987). Neurons do not appear to have a life span, but die off either as a function of normal apoptosis or because their biochemical environment becomes inhospitable. High levels of cortisol, a lack of blood flow, or the buildup of harmful free radicals can all lead to neuronal death.

The traditional wisdom concerning neurogenesis in vertebrates, and especially primates, has been that new neurons are no longer created after early development (Michel & Moore, 1995; Rakic, 1985). Despite considerable evidence to the contrary, this dogma held sway through most of the 20th century. However, research continues to demonstrate that new neurons are formed in the brains of adult birds (Nottebohm, 1981), tree shrews (Gould et al., 1997), primates (Gould, Reeves, Fallah, et al., 1999), and humans (Gould, Reeves, Graziano, et al., 1999). Further, neurogenesis is regulated by environmental factors and experiences such as stress and social interactions (Fowler, Liu, Ouimet, & Wang, 2002).

Humans have maintained the ability to create neurons in areas involved with new learning, such as the hippocampus, the amygdala, and the cerebral cortex (Eriksson et al., 1998; Gould, 2007; Gross, 2000). The importance of these discoveries and the abandonment of the old dogma cannot be underestimated. Nobel-prize-winning neuroscientist Eric Kandel referred to Nottebohm's discovery of seasonal neurogenesis in birds as having resulted in one of the great paradigm shifts in modern biology (Specter, 2001).

## Neural Systems

> *I believe in God, only I spell it Nature.*
> —Frank Lloyd Wright

As the brain develops and matures, neurons organize in more and more complex neural networks tailored to carry out the numerous functions of the nervous system. The two most basic divisions of the nervous system are the *central nervous system* (CNS) and the *peripheral nervous system* (PNS). The CNS includes the brain and spinal cord, whereas the PNS is comprised of the *autonomic nervous system* and the *somatic nervous system*. The autonomic and somatic nervous systems are involved in the communication between the CNS and the sense organs, glands, and the body (including the heart, intestines, and lungs).

The autonomic nervous system has two branches, called the *sympathetic* and *parasympathetic* nervous systems. The sympathetic system controls the activation of the nervous system in response to a threat or other form of motivation. The parasympathetic system balances the sympathetic system by fostering conservation of bodily energy, immunological functions, and repair of damaged systems. A third system referred to as the *smart vagus* operates in parallel to the parasympathetic branch of the autonomic nervous system and is dedicated to fine-tuning bodily reactions, especially in social situations (Porges, 2007). These three systems will be of particular interest in later chapters, when we discuss attachment and the effects of stress and trauma.

Although MacLean's formulation of the triune brain is seen as too simplistic by most neuroscientists, many still recognize the tripartite division of the brain into the cerebral cortex, the limbic system, and the brainstem. Each layer is thought of as having different responsibilities. The *brainstem*—the inner core of the brain—oversees the body's internal milieu by regulating temperature, heart rate, and basic reflexes such as blood flow and respiration. The structure and functions of the brainstem were shaped during our genetic history and are fully formed and functional at birth. The reflexes we see in the newborn who grasps her mother, suckles her breast, and knows to hold her breath when put under water are genetic memories retained from our tree-dwelling ancestors.

The outer layer of the brain, the *cerebral cortex*, is first organized by, and then comes to organize, our experiences and how we interact with the world. As we grow, the cortex allows us to form ideas and mental representations of ourselves, other people, and the environment. Distinct from the brainstem, the cortex is experience dependent, which means that it is shaped through countless interactions with our social and physical worlds. In this way we grow to adapt to the particular niche into which we are born.

The two halves of the cerebral cortex have gradually differentiated during primate evolution to the point where each has developed areas of specialization, referred to as lateral dominance or specialization. Language is the best-understood example of lateral specialization. The two cerebral hemispheres communicate with each other primarily via the *corpus callosum*, which consists of long neural fibers that connect the two. Although the corpus callosum is the largest and most efficient mode of communication between the hemispheres in adults, there are a number of smaller cortical and subcortical interconnections between the two halves of the brain (Myers & Sperry, 1985; Sergent, 1986, 1990).

The cortex has been subdivided by neuroanatomists into four lobes: frontal, temporal, parietal, and occipital (Figure 4.1). Each is represented on both sides of the brain and specializes in certain functions: the *occipital* cortex comprises the areas for visual processing; the *temporal* cortex for auditory processing, receptive language, and memory functions; the *parietal* cortex for linking the senses with motor abilities and the creation of the experience of a sense of our body in space; and the *frontal* cortex for motor behavior, expressive language, executive functioning, abstract reasoning, and directed attention. The term *prefrontal* cortex is often used to refer to the foremost portion of the frontal lobe. Two additional cortical lobes, the *cingulate* and *insula* cortices, are gaining increasing recognition as distinct and important areas of the cortical-subcortical interface. They are involved in the integration of inner and outer experience, linking the rest of the cortex with somatic and emotional experience.

### FIGURE 4.1
### The Four Lobes of the Cerebral Cortex

*The four lobes of the cerebral cortex as seen from the left side of the brain.*

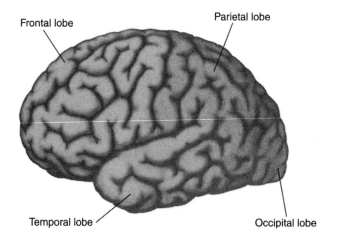

Frontal lobe

Parietal lobe

Temporal lobe

Occipital lobe

Between the brainstem and the cortex lies a region referred to as the limbic system, which is involved with learning, motivation, memory, and emotion. Because this book focuses on development and psychotherapy, you will notice repeated references to two limbic structures. The first is the *amygdala*, a key component in neural networks involved in attachment as well as the appraisal and expression of emotion throughout life (Cheng, Knight, Smith, & Helmstetter, 2006; Phelps, 2006; Strange & Dolan, 2004). The other is the *hippocampus*, which organizes explicit memory and the contextual modulation of emotion in collaboration with the cerebral cortex (Ji & Maren, 2007).

## Neurotransmitters and Neuromodulators

*Brains exist because the distribution of resources necessary for survival and the hazards that threaten survival vary in space and time.*
                                                                —John Allman

Recall that, within the nervous system, neurons communicate with each other via chemical messengers called neurotransmitters. Different neural networks tend to utilize different sets of neurotransmitters, which is why certain *psychotropic* medications impact different symptoms. Chemicals that serve as neurotransmitters include monoamines, neuropeptides, and amino acids. Neuromodulators (e.g., the hormones testosterone, estrogen, cortisol, and other steroids) regulate the effects of the neurotransmitters on receptor neurons. *Amino acids* are the simplest and most prevalent neuromodulators. *Glutamate* is the major excitatory amino acid in the brain and central to neural plasticity and new learning (Cowan & Kandel, 2001; Malenka & Siegelbaum, 2001). Interactions with one of its primary receptors, *N*-methyl-*D*-aspartate (NMDA), regulates long-term potentiation and long-term depression, thereby shaping the relationship between neurons (Liu et al., 2004; Massey et al., 2004; Zhao et al., 2005).

The *monoamines*—including dopamine, norepinephrine, and serotonin—play a major role in the regulation of cognitive and emotional processing (Ansorge, Zhou, Lira, Hen, & Gingrich, 2004). All three are produced in different areas of the brainstem and are carried upward via ascending neural networks to the cortex. *Dopamine*, produced in the substantia nigra and other areas of the brainstem, is a key neurotransmitter in motor activity and reward reinforcement. Too much dopamine can result in mood changes, increased motor behavior, and disturbed frontal lobe functioning, which, in turn, can cause depression, memory impairment, and apathy. Parkinson's disease results from damage to the substantia nigra and a consequent loss of dopamine. Many believe that schizophrenia is caused by too much dopamine, which overloads sensory processing capabilities and creates hallucinations and delusions.

*Norepinephrine*, produced in the locus coeruleus and other brain regions, is a key component of the emergency system of the brain and is especially relevant for understanding stress and trauma. High levels result in anxiety, vigilance, symptoms of panic, and a fight-flight response. Norepinephrine also serves to enhance memory for stressful and traumatic events. *Serotonin*, generated in the raphe nucleus, is distributed widely throughout the brain and plays a role in arousal, the sleep–wake cycle, and the mediation of mood and emotion (Fisher et al., 2006). Popular antidepressant medications such as Prozac and Paxil cause higher levels of available serotonin in the synapses and higher levels of neurogenesis (Encinas, Vaahtokari, & Enikolopov, 2006).

The group of neurotransmitters known as *neuropeptides* includes endorphins, enkephalins, oxytocin, vasopressin, and neuropeptide-Y. These compounds work together with neuromodulators to regulate pain, pleasure, and reward systems. The endorphins tend to modulate the activity of monoamines, making them highly relevant for understanding psychiatric illnesses. *Endogenous endorphins* (endorphins produced by the body) serve as an analgesic in states of physical pain. They are also involved with dissociation and self-abusive behavior, as we will discuss in a later chapter on trauma. The relationship between the monoamines and neuropeptides is vitally important to the growth and organization of the brain.

## Glucocorticoids/Cortisol

*We're lousy at recognizing when our normal coping mechanisms aren't working. Our response is usually to do it five times more, instead of thinking; maybe it's time to try something new.*
                                    —Robert Sapolsky

Cortisol, the most important glucocorticoid, is often referred to as the "stress hormone." It is produced in the adrenal glands in response to a wide variety of everyday challenges. The term glucocorticoid comes from the fact that it was first recognized for its role in glucose metabolism. With further study, however, many more functions of cortisol were uncovered. Glucocorticoid receptors (GRs) are found in almost all of the tissues of our bodies. At normal levels and over short periods, cortisol enhances memory, mobilizes energy, and helps to restore homeostasis after stressful situations. Glucocorticoids stimulate gluconeogenesis and the breakdown of lipids and proteins to make energy available to us for emergencies. If we have to fight or flee, we are going to need energy.

Cortisol evolved to be useful for periods of brief stress which, when resolved, allow GRs to signal the adrenal glands to shut down production. Prolonged cortisol release, on the other hand, can weaken the immune system by preventing T-Cell proliferation. In fact, the synthetic form of cortisol is called hydrocortisone and is used to treat inflammation and allergies by inhibiting natural immunological responses. Sustained high levels of cortisol disrupt protein synthesis, halt neural growth, and disturb the sodium-potassium balance to the point of neural death. Early and prolonged stress has been correlated with memory deficits, problems with affect regulation, and reduction of volume in brain regions including the hippocampus and amygdala (Buchanan, Tranel, & Adolphs, 2006).

It is believed that sustained high levels of glucocorticoids early in life can have a negative impact on brain development and make a child more vulnerable to subsequent stress. It has been shown that maternal behavior in rats stimulates the development of GRs in the brains of their pups. Greater density of GRs in the brain results in enhanced feedback to the adrenal glands, which serves to shut down cortisol production. This is one of the underlying neurobiological correlates associating maternal attention with resilience and positive coping later in life. The production and availability of these neurochemicals shape all of our experience, from bonding and affect regulation to cognitive processing and our sense of well-being. Regulation of these neurochemicals to control psychiatric symptomatology is the focus of the field of psychopharmacology (Gitlin, 2007; Stahl, 2008).

## Genetics and Epigenetics

*I am convinced that it will not be long before the whole world acknowledges the results of my work.*

—Gregor Mendel

At the forefront of the science of genetics is Abbot Gregor Mendel, who, in the garden of his ancient abbey, discovered many of the principles of inheritance that still hold true. It turns out that his discoveries with pea plants apply to animals and humans because the underlying mechanisms of heredity are similar for all complex life forms. As you probably remember, his findings included *dominant* and *recessive genes* and the principles of *segregation* and *independent assortment*.

With the benefits of modern technology, Mendel's observations of the natural world were later understood to be the effects of template genetics, or the way in which genes and chromosomes combine to pass along traits from one generation to the next. We now know that our genetic information is coded in four amino acid bases (adenine, thymine, guanine, and cytosine) that flow from DNA to messenger RNA (mRNA) to protein. Although this understanding was a huge leap forward in our knowledge of the underlying processes of genetic transmission, it accounts for only about 2% of genetic expression. The scientific term for the other 98% of genetic material was "junk," once thought to be accumulated debris of natural selection. It turns out, however, that some of this junk plays an important role in guiding introns and exons, which help determine whether specific elements of the genetic code get expressed or lie dormant.

Biologist C. H. Waddington coined the term *epigenetics* by combining the words genetics and epi, Greek for over or above. *Epigenesis* describes the transformation of cells from their original undifferentiated state during embryonic development into a specific type of cell. Thus, epigenetics is the study of how our genotype is orchestrated into our phenotype. Understanding the elements of epigenetics may help us grasp why identical twins with the same genes may differ in phenotype, that is, why one becomes schizophrenic and the other does not.

This gets us back to the old nature-nurture debate and the question: What do we inherit, and what do we learn from experience? Our best guess is that almost everything involves an interaction between the two. While we inherit a template of genetic material (genotype), what gets expressed (phenotype) is guided by noncoded genetic information that is experience dependent. Experience can include anything from toxic exposure to a good education; high levels of sustained stress to a warm and loving environment; feast to famine. Thus, many more genes are involved with the regulation of what is expressed than with the direct synthesis of protein. So while template genetics may guide the early formation of the brain during gestation, the regulation of gene expression directs its long-term development in reaction to ongoing adaptation to the social and physical worlds. Epigenetics is a term used to describe this change in the phenotypic expression of genes in the absence of a change in the DNA template.

An example of this process of particular relevance to emotional development and psychotherapy is the impact of early stress on the adult brain. Meaney and his colleagues (1991) believe that early environmental programming of neural systems has a profound and long-lasting effect on the hypothalamic-pituitary-adrenal (HPA) axis, which regulates an individual's responsivity to stress. Research with rats has demonstrated that the stress of early maternal deprivation downregulates the degree of neurogenesis and the response to stress during adulthood (Mirescu, Peters, & Gould, 2004; Karten, Olariu, & Cameron, 2005). Just as important for us, these processes are reversible later in life. As therapists, we attempt to reprogram these neural systems via a supportive relationship and the techniques we bring to bear during treatment. In other words, we are using epigenetics to change the brain in ways that enhance mental and physical well-being.

## Views of the Brain

*When considering the abilities and complexities of the brain, one is struck by the incredible efficiency and splendor expressed in gray and white matter.*

—Julian Paul Keenan

Throughout most of the history of neurology, the human brain was only examined after injury or death. The location of brain damage during autopsy was linked to the nature and severity of the patient's clinical symptoms during life. Brain development was studied by examining and comparing the brains of humans and animals at different ages. These brains were compared for size; the number of neurons, synapses, and dendrites; the degree of myelinization; and other aspects of neural maturation.

Newer techniques allow us to examine brain structure in living subjects. Through the use of *computerized tomography* (CT) and *magnetic resonance imaging* (MRI), we are able to see two- and three-dimensional pictures of the living brain. Both of these techniques provide a series of cross-sectional images of the brain through its many layers. CT scans do this via multiple X-rays. MRI scans utilize radio waves and a magnetic field to study the magnetic resonance of hydrogen molecules in the water present in different brain structures. In determining brain–behavior relationships, these measures need to be evaluated on the basis of whether they are causes or correlates of the disorder being studied (Davidson, 1999). In their present practical applications, radiologists learn to read these images for the presence and locations of tumors or lesions in order to assist surgeons in their work. These scans have become an indispensable tool in neurology.

The functioning of the brain can also be measured in many ways. Clinical and mental status exams, tests of strength and reflexes, and neuropsychological assessment all require a patient to perform physical or mental operations that are tied to known neurobiological systems. These clinical tests are supplemented by a number of laboratory tests that measure different aspects of brain functioning. The *electroencephalograph* (EEG) measures patterns of electrical activity throughout the cortex. There are characteristic brainwave patterns in different states of arousal and stages of sleep. Epilepsy or the presence of tumors will demonstrate characteristic alterations of normal electrical functioning, allowing EEGs to be used as diagnostic tools. EEGs can also be used to measure brain development, because neural network organization is characterized by the replacement of local erratic discharges with more widespread and constant wave patterns (Barry et al., 2004; Field & Diego, 2008b; Forbes et al., 2008).

The most exciting new tools in neuroscience are the various brain-scanning techniques providing us with a window to the brain in action. *Positron emission tomography*, *single photon emission tomography*, and *functional magnetic resonance imaging* measure changes in blood flow, oxygen metabolism, and glucose utilization, which tell us about the relative activity of different regions of the brain. Using these techniques, neuroscientists can now explore complex activation–deactivation patterns of brain activity in subjects performing a wide range of cognitive, emotional, and behavioral tasks (Drevets, 1998). Most of these newer scanning techniques are still somewhat experimental, and methodological standards regarding their use and interpretation continue to evolve. These methods, and those yet to be developed, will vastly enhance our understanding of the brain. As they grow increasingly more accurate and specific, so too will our knowledge of neural network functioning.

# Brain Development and Neural Plasticity

*Swiftly the brain becomes an enchanted loom, where millions of flashing shuttles weave a dissolving pattern—always a meaningful pattern—though never an abiding one*

—Sir Charles Sherrington

Experience sculpts the brain through selective excitation of neurons and the resultant shaping of neural networks. Paradoxically, the number of neurons decreases with age while the size of the brain increases. The surviving neurons continue to grow from what look like small sprouts into microscopic oak trees. This process of growth and connectivity is sometimes referred to as *arborization*.

In order for a neuron to survive and grow, it must wire with other neurons in increasingly complex interconnections. Just as we survive and thrive through our relationships with others, neurons survive and grow as a function of how "well connected" they are. Through what appears to be a competitive process referred to as *neural Darwinism*, cells struggle for connectivity with other cells in the creation of neural networks (Edelman, 1987). Cells connect and learning occurs through changes of synaptic strength between neurons in response to stimulation. Repeated firing of two adjacent neurons results in metabolic changes in both cells, which provides an increased efficiency in their joint activation. In this process, called *long-term potentiation* (LTP) or Hebbian learning, excitation between cells is prolonged, allowing them to become synchronized in their firing patterns and joint effectiveness (Hebb, 1949). LTP is believed to be a fundamental principle of neuroplastic learning. Underlying LTP is the constant reaching out of small portions of the dendrites in an attempt to connect with adjacent neurons. When these connections are made, neurons synthesize new protein to build more permanent bridges between them.

Through LTP, cell assemblies organize into functional neural networks that are stimulated through trial-and-error learning. This is only one small piece of a vastly complex set of interactions involving the connection, timing, and organization of firing within and between billions of interconnected neurons in the CNS (Malekna & Siegelbaum, 2001). Early in development, there is an initial overproduction of neurons that gradually decreases through the process of pruning, or apoptosis. Neural

Darwinism applies to both the survival of neurons and the synaptic connections among them. Synapses that are formed may be subsequently eliminated if they become inactivated or inefficient (Purves & Lichtman, 1980). In fact, elimination of synaptic connections in the cortex continues shaping neural circuitry through adolescence and into adulthood (Cozolino, 2008; Huttenlocher, 1994).

In contrast to the brainstem and limbic system, the cortex is immature at birth and continues to develop throughout adulthood. Because of this developmental timing, brainstem reflexes organize much of the infant's early behaviors and the behavior of a newborn is dominated by subcortical activity. The neonate will orient to the mother's smell, seek the nipple, gaze into her eyes, and grasp her hair. A good example of a brainstem reflex is the Moro reflex, by which the infant reaches out with open hands and legs extended, putting the infant into a position conducive to grasping and holding (Eliot, 1999). The child's eyes reflexively orient to the mother's eyes and face and a baby's first smiles are controlled by brainstem reflexes to attract caretakers. In fact, children born with a genetic malformation that results in having only a brainstem are still able to smile (Herschkowitz, Kegan, & Zilles, 1997). These reflexes enhance physical survival and jump start the attachment process by connecting parent and child, while enhancing their bond.

As anyone who has been pregnant can tell you, babies begin to engage in spontaneous activity of the arms and hands well before birth. While the baby is practicing using its arms and legs, parents-to-be grow increasingly excited as these signs of activity grow in frequency and strength. After birth, newborns continue to move all parts of their bodies, allowing them to discover their hands and feet as they pass in front of their faces. Although these movements may look random, they are the brain's best guess at which movements will eventually be needed. These reflexive movements jump start the organization of motor networks to build the skills the child will need later on (Katz & Shatz, 1996).

Through months and years of trial-and-error learning, these best guesses become shaped into purposeful and intentional behaviors that are reflected in the organization of underlying neural networks (Shatz, 1990). As sensory systems develop, they provide increasingly precise input to guide neural network formation for more complex patterns of behavior. As positive and negative values are connected with certain perceptions and movements—such as the appearance of the mother and reaching out to her—emotional networks will integrate with sensory and motor systems. In the development of these and other systems, we find the sequential activation of reflexive and spontaneous processes priming neural development, which comes to be shaped by ongoing experience.

## Cortical Inhibition and Conscious Control

*He who conquers others is strong; he who conquers himself is mighty.*
—Lao-Tzu

The gradual attenuation of neonatal reflexes and spontaneous behavior corresponds with rising levels of cortical activity and involvement in behavior. As the cortex develops, vast numbers of top-down neural networks connect it with subcortical areas. These top-down networks provide the pathways for inhibiting reflexes and bringing the body and emotions under increasing cortical control. An example of this is the development of the fine motor movements between the thumb and forefinger that are required to hold a spoon. Primitive grasping reflexes allow only for the spoon to be held in a tight fist, rendering it useless as a tool. The developing cortex enables the grasping reflex to be inhibited, while cortical networks dedicated to finger sensitivity and hand–eye coordination mature. Thus, a vital aspect of the development of the cortex is inhibitory—first of reflexes, later of spontaneous movements and even later of emotions and inappropriate social behavior.

Only through repeated trial-and-error learning are early clumsy movements slowly shaped into functional skills. Children and their brains intuitively know this and will resist being held back or helped too much. When we attempt to help, a child's impatient protest of "Let me do it!" reflects instinctual wisdom of the importance of trial-and-error learning in the growth of neural networks. This makes for many years of messes and boo-boos. Another good example of the process of brain maturation is our ability to swim. The newborn's brainstem reflex to hold its breath and paddle when dropped into water is lost (inhibited by higher brain circuitry) just weeks after birth. The skills involved with swimming need to be relearned as cortically organized skills in years to come. Motor networks need to be taught body movements, as breathing becomes timed and synchronized with each stroke.

Cortical inhibition and descending control are also central to affect regulation. The rapidly changing and overwhelming emotions displayed by very young children reflect this lack of control. As the middle portions of the frontal cortex expand and extend their fibers down into the limbic system and brainstem, children gradually gain increasing capacity to regulate their emotions and find ways to gain soothing, first through others, and eventually by themselves. When these systems are damaged or developmentally delayed, we witness symptoms related to deficits in attention, emotional regulation, and impulse control.

We see the changes in motor control and posture as a child moves from being able to sit upright without help at about 6 months, to crawling at about 9 months, and then to walking without help by about 1 year. At 2 years, a child will walk up and down stairs; by 3 she can peddle a tricycle. As these skills are shaped, so too are the brain systems dedicated to balance, motor control, visual–spatial coordination, learning, and motivation that control them. The growth, development, and integration of neural networks continue to be sculpted by environmental demands. In turn, neuronal sculpting is reflected in increasingly complex patterns of behavior and inner experience.

## Sensitive Periods

*The principal activities of brains are making changes in themselves.*
—Marvin L. Minsky

The brain continues to grow as long as we continue to learn, essentially until the day we die. Early brain development is highlighted by periods of exuberant neural growth and connectivity called *sensitive periods* triggered by the interaction of genes and experience. These sensitive periods are times of rapid learning during which thousands of synaptic connections are made each second (Greenough, 1987; ten Cate, 1989). The timing of sensitive periods varies across neural systems, which is why different abilities appear at different ages.

The most widely recognized sensitive period is the development of language. At 24 months, an average child understands and uses about 50 words; this increases to 1,000 words by 36 months (Dunbar, 1996). The extent of neural growth and learning during sensitive periods results in early experience having a disproportionate impact on our brains, minds, and experiences. As we learn of the brain's ability to create new neurons and retain plasticity throughout life, the importance of sensitive periods takes on new meaning. The question for therapists is: How amenable are these established structures to modification? This is a topic we will come back to again and again in later chapters.

The growth of neurons and the development of increasingly complex neural networks require large amounts of energy. Patterns of increasing glucose metabolism during the first year of life proceed in phylogenic order, meaning that the development of more primitive brain structures precedes those which evolve later (Chugani, 1998; Chugani & Phelps, 1991). Early sensitive periods account for the higher level of metabolism in the brains of infants compared to adults. Ever notice how warm a baby's head is? It has been estimated that in rats' brains, 250,000 synaptic connections are formed every second during the first month after birth (Schuz, 1978). Just imagine what the number must be for humans.

Networks dedicated to individual senses develop before the association areas that connect them to one another (Chugani, Phelps, & Mazziotta, 1987). The growth and coordination of the different senses parallel what we also witness in such behavioral changes as hand–eye coordination and the ability to inhibit incorrect movements (Bell & Fox, 1992; Fischer, 1987). As the cerebral cortex matures, a child at 8 months is able to distinguish faces and compare them to his or her memory of other faces. It is around this period that *stranger anxiety* and *separation anxiety* develop. As the brain matures, we witness increasing cortical activation and the establishment of more efficient neural circuitry firing in increasingly synchronous patterns.

Although both the left and right cerebral hemispheres are developing at very high rates during the early years of life, the right hemisphere appears to have a relatively higher rate of activity and growth during the earliest years (Chiron et al., 1997). During this time, vital learning in the areas of attachment, emotional regulation, and self-esteem are organized in neural networks biased toward the right hemisphere. Somewhere around age 3, this pattern of asymmetrical growth shifts to the left hemisphere.

## Summary

The maturation and sculpting of so much of the cortex after birth allows for highly specific environmental adaptations. The caretaker relationship is the primary means by which physical and cultural environments are translated to infants. It is within the context of these close relationships that networks dedicated to feelings of safety and danger, attachment, and the core sense of self are shaped. The first few years of life appear to be a particularly sensitive period for the formation of these networks. It may be precisely because there is so much neural growth and organization during sensitive periods that early interpersonal experiences may be far more influential than are those occurring later. The fact that they are preconscious and nonverbal makes them difficult to discover and more resistant to change. Because these neural networks are sculpted during early interactions, we emerge into self-awareness preprogrammed by unconsciously organized hidden layers of neural processing. The structure of these neural networks organizes core structures of our experience of self.

# Chapter 5

# Multiple Memory Systems in Psychotherapy

*To "do memory" is essentially to engage in a cultural practice.*
—Kenneth Gergen

The process of psychotherapy is totally dependent upon memory. From what we know of clients' past and current lives, to their ability to bring the lessons of therapy into practice, everything depends on their ability to learn and remember. Yet, despite its central role in our work, the majority of clinical psychologists, psychiatrists, family therapists, and social workers receive little or no training in the hows and whys of memory. In this chapter we explore various aspects of memory and their role in both mental illnesses and psychotherapy.

Psychotherapists have traditionally divided memory into the broad categories of conscious, preconscious, and unconscious. Conscious memory is expressed in recollections of the past, the content of previous therapy sessions, and reports of current day-to-day life. The preconscious contains memories that are not the focus of current attention but which can easily be brought into conscious awareness with a minimum of difficulty. Unconscious memory unavailable to conscious consideration can manifest in behaviors, attitudes, and feelings as well as in more complex forms such as defenses, self-esteem, and transference. Much of the training of psychodynamic therapists is the identification and deciphering of unconscious memory into a form that is accessible to the patient.

Freud believed that a fundamental goal of therapy is to make the unconscious conscious. From the perspective of rebuilding the brain, this goal can be described as increasing the interconnection and integration of neural networks dedicated to unconscious and conscious memory. This process makes understanding the evolution, development, and functioning of the various systems of memory crucial to conceptualizing and treating psychological distress and mental illnesses. It also aids in explaining to clients some of the paradoxes and confusion they experience based on the variety of ways their brains process information.

## Resistance to Therapy or Memory Deficit?

*Our sense of worth, of well-being, even our sanity depends upon our remembering. But, alas, our sense of worth, our well-being, our sanity also depend upon our forgetting.*

—Joyce Appleby

For almost a year, I treated a woman named Sophia who had experienced repeated traumas and chronic stress dating back to early childhood. Among the many issues she brought to treatment were family conflict, early sexual abuse, and current relationship problems. One of Sophia's long-standing complaints was severe memory difficulties, especially when it came to remembering names, dates, and appointments. In high school her teachers told her she was stupid because she was unable to recall what was said in class from one day to the next. Sophia was so embarrassed by her inability to remember names that she avoided parties and all but essential work gatherings. On the other hand, her memory for emotionally laden experiences was like a steel trap, continually evoking fear and sadness. Sophia was convinced that the part of her brain responsible for remembering shame was very different from the one that recalled names.

Sophia had gone to many therapists throughout her adult life, repeatedly missed appointments, and had been told she was resistant to treatment. Sophia found this very frustrating but had no explanation of her own. Based on her history, these therapists assumed that her problems with memory were caused by denial, avoidance, or repression, and encouraged her to face her fears. While each therapist offered their own interpretation of her defensiveness to treatment, none rang true, and she usually terminated therapy after just a few sessions. Certain that it was her fault, Sophia's treatment failures led her to feel increasingly hopeless about ever finding the help she needed. The annoyance and "criticism" she received from therapists also increased her feelings of shame. Although she feared our work together would meet the same fate, she was willing to give therapy one more try.

After learning her history, I shared a bit of neuroscience to help her better conceptualize her issues with memory. My mini lecture focused on the destructive role of early and prolonged stress on the development and well-being of the hippocampus and associated neural networks responsible for explicit memory. I suggested that we begin our work by studying memory together and exploring pragmatic ways to improve it. Along the way we experimented with the use of memory aids from the field of cognitive rehabilitation. Daytimers, watches with alarms, and personal digital assistants (PDAs) all proved useful. (The development of smart phones now allows us to carry all of these functions in one device, a real boon to many patients.)

For the first 2 months, Sophia and I scheduled telephone contact every other day for a few minutes. During these contacts, we exercised her memory, checked on the various strategies we had set up during our previous session, and reinforced her successes. Initially, Sophia needed help learning to remember to use her strategies that helped her remember. Utilizing her memory aids and checking them on a regular basis gradually became automatic even if, in the moment, she would forget why she was checking her book or calling me.

After 6 weeks, Sophia was consistently able to remember appointments. This success stimulated confidence in herself and in therapy. She began to see that her memory problems in no way meant she was stupid or harbored deep psychological problems. On the contrary, her self-respect increased as our discussions helped her to realize how much she had accomplished in her life despite her traumatic history and struggles with memory. Once memory-related issues were no longer an impediment to maintaining consistent contact, we shifted the focus of treatment to the impact of her life experiences on her relationships and career. The initial focus of therapy, using a formulation from neuroscience and cognitive rehabilitation, turned out to be a necessary first step in a sustained and successful therapeutic relationship. From this point, the therapy was characterized by a more traditional psychodynamic approach with regular memory checkups and adjustments to her strategies.

Many psychological disorders manifest a variety of memory deficits. Any disorder that results in substantial arousal and triggers the secretion of the stress hormone cortisol can damage neural networks of explicit memory. In fact, most psychiatric disorders reveal high rates of cortisol and smaller hippocampi, both of which are correlated with memory disturbances. In addition to problems with remembering, some illnesses serve to distort both learning and memory. Depression, for example, results in a negative bias in the recollection and interpretation of past, present, and future events (Beck, 1976). It also leads us to selectively scan the environment, which reinforces negative perceptions. Depression convincingly demonstrates the influence of emotional states in the organization of conscious memory, sometimes called *state-dependent memory*. Clients report that if they wake up depressed, everything looks worse than it did the day before, even though they know, intellectually, that nothing has changed.

The rapid (and unconscious) networks of emotion shape our understanding of the world microseconds before we become aware of our perception. Through similar mechanisms, our past experiences create our expectations for the future. Implicit, unconscious memories, created in dysfunctional situations years before, can repeatedly lead us to re-create unsuccessful but familiar patterns of thought, emotion, and behavior. Thus, our perception of the world is a creation based on past experience.

## Multiple Memory Systems

> *Memory . . . is the diary that we all carry about with us.*
> —Oscar Wilde

Research and clinical experience support the existence of multiple memory systems, each with its own domains of learning, neural architecture, and developmental timetable (Tulving, 1985). Learning within all systems of memory is dependent on the process of long-term potentiation in the Hebbian synapses we have already discussed, as well as the dendritic remodeling and changes in the relationships between neurons (Hebb, 1949; Kandel, 1998). The two broadest categories of memory are explicit and implicit. The concepts of explicit and implicit memory, although similar in some ways to Freud's concept of the conscious and unconscious, do not directly overlap.

*Explicit memory* describes conscious learning and memory, including semantic, sensory, and motor forms. These memory systems allow us to recite the alphabet, recognize the smell of coconut, or play tennis. Some of these memory abilities remain just beneath the level of consciousness until we turn our attention to them. *Implicit memory* is reflected in unconscious patterns of learning stored in hidden layers of neural processing, largely inaccessible to conscious awareness. This category extends from repressed trauma to riding a bicycle, to getting an uneasy feeling when we smell a food that once made us sick. Explicit memory is the tip of our experiential iceberg; implicit memory is the vast structure below the surface.

Many of our daily experiences make it clear that we have multiple systems of explicit and implicit memory. For example, moving your fingers over the keypad of an imaginary phone sometimes helps you recall a phone number. This process demonstrates that implicit systems of motor and visual memory can aid in the explicit recall of numbers. Another example is a phenomenon common among older adults, in which they have difficulty learning new information but easily recall stories from their youth. This may be because the networks involved in the storage of long-term explicit memory are distributed throughout the cortex and are more resistant to the effects of aging than those responsible for short- and medium-term memory (Schacter, 1996).

Thinking back to the triune brain, each tier is involved with different aspects of memory functioning. The reptilian brain contains instinctual memories, the lessons of past generations (genetic memory) that control reflexes, and inner bodily functions. The paleomammalian brain (limbic system) contributes to emotional memory and conditioned learning—a mixture of primitive impulses and survival programs sculpted by experiences. These two systems are nonverbal and comprise aspects of the Freudian unconscious. The neomammalian brain, although largely unconscious in its processing, contains networks responsible for explicit verbal memory biased toward the left hemisphere.

Because of the order in which they develop, implicit and explicit memory (detailed in Table 5.1) are referred to as early and late memory. Systems of implicit memory are active even before birth, as demonstrated in the newborn's instincts to orient to the sound of her mother's voice (de Casper & Fifer, 1980). During the first months of life, basic sensory memories combine together with bodily and emotional associa-

TABLE 5.1
Multiple Memory Systems

*A number of the basic distinctions between implicit and explicit systems of memory*

| IMPLICIT | EXPLICIT |
|---|---|
| Early Developing | Late Developing |
| Highly Functional at Birth | Matures later with Hippocampus and Cortex |
| Subcortical/Amygdala Bias | Cortical/Hippocampal Bias |
| Nondeclarative | Declarative |
| Emotional | Organized by Language |
| Visceral/Sensory-Motor | Visual Images |
| Context Free | Organized within Episodes and Narratives |
| Procedural Learning | Conscious Organization of Experience |
| Behavior Patterns and Manual | Construction of Narrative Self |

tions (Stern, 1985). These networks allow for the sight of one's father to be paired with raised arms, a smile, and a good feeling. Somatic, sensory, motor, and emotional experiences help sculpt neural networks during the first few years into a sense of a physical self.

The development of conscious memory parallels the maturation of the hippocampus and higher cortical structures over the first years of life (Fuster, 1996; Jacobs, van Praag, & Gage, 2000; LeDoux, 1996; McCarthy, 1995). *Childhood amnesia* or the absence of explicit memory from early life likely results from this maturational delay and other developmental changes in how our brains process information. In the absence of explicit memory, however, we learn how to walk and talk, whether the world is safe or dangerous, and how to attach to others. These vital early lessons, stored in networks throughout our brain, lack *source attribution*; that is, we do not remember how we learned them. Although many of us think we have explicit memories from the first years of life, these are most likely constructed later and attributed to an earlier time in our life.

Explicit memory can be sensory and linguistic, as we associate and remember sights, sounds, and smells with words and organize them in conscious memory. For most of us, words and visual images are the keys to conscious memory. Different types of semantic memory include episodic, narrative, and autobiographical, which can all be organized sequentially. Autobiographical memory maintains the perspective of the narrator at the center of the story. Stories about the self combine episodic, semantic, and emotional memory with the self-awareness needed for maximal neural network integration (Cabeza & St. Jacques, 2007). This form of memory is especially important for the formation and maintenance of emotional regulation, self-identity, and the transmission of culture.

Overall, the development of the different systems of memory reflects the early primacy of implicit memory for learning in sensory, motor, and emotional networks. These early-forming neural networks depend on the more primitive brain structures such as the amygdala, thalamus, and middle portions of the frontal cortex (Figure 5.1). As the cortex and the hippocampus continue to develop over the first few years of life, there is a gradual maturation of the networks of explicit memory. These systems provide for conscious, contextualized learning and memory that becomes more consistent and stable over time.

The various systems of memory are distributed throughout the brain and where a particular memory is stored depends on the type of mem-

### FIGURE 5.1
### The Amygdala and Hippocampus

*The right half of the brain viewed from the left side. The hippocampus and the amygdala are located on the inferior and medial aspects of the temporal lobes.*

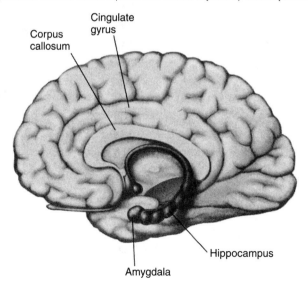

ory and how it is encoded (McCarthy, 1995). A good example of the distribution of memory comes from an experiment measuring cerebral blood flow while subjects were asked to name pictures of either animals or hand tools (Martin, Wiggs, Ungerleider, & Haxby, 1996). Naming both animals and tools resulted in increased activity in the temporal lobes and Broca's area. This makes sense, because the temporal lobes are known to be important for the organization of memory whereas Broca's area organizes verbal expression. More specifically, naming tools activated areas in the left motor cortex involved in the hand movements that would be used to control them (Martin et al., 1996). This suggests that part of our "tool memory" is stored in neural networks that utilize them. While there is overlap of activation during picture naming, the nature of the visual image triggers brain areas relevant to what is depicted. Thus, memory is a form of internal enactment of whatever is being recalled.

The portion of the visual system activated by pictures of animals is an area involved with very early stages of visual processing. This may be a reflection of how evolution has shaped the primitive areas of our visual brains to recognize and react quickly to threats from possible predators (animals chosen for this study happened to be a bear and an ape, both evolutionarily relevant based on their potential danger to us). Research has consistently demonstrated that the occipital lobe becomes activated when something is seen and, later, imagined. In the case of the imagined memory, the prefrontal area also becomes activated, reflecting its role in processing the instructions, staying on task, and accessing imagination. How neural networks in the prefrontal cortex know how to do this is as yet unknown (Ungerleider, 1995).

Although these studies focus primarily on cortical activity, psychotherapy often involves the retrieval of subcortical emotional memories. Emotional memories rely on subcortical structures such as the amygdala and hippocampus: both central to upcoming discussions of psychopathology and the impact of childhood experiences, stress, and trauma on adult functioning.

## Amygdaloid Memory Networks

*Nothing fixes a thing so intensely in memory as the wish to forget it.*
—Michel de Montaigne

The amygdala, the central hub of fear processing, is located within the limbic system and beneath the temporal lobes on each side of the brain. It is fully developed by the eighth month of gestation, so that even before birth, we are capable of experiencing intense physiological states of fear. During the first few years of life we are dependent on caretakers for external modulation of the amygdala until we are able to regulate it ourselves. In some ways the amygdala is our first cortex, playing a significant role in the networks involved in emotional learning (Brodal, 1992). Portions of the amygdala (the basolateral areas) have evolved in tandem with the expansion of the cerebral cortex in humans along with our abilities to assess the environment (Stephan & Andy, 1977).

The amygdala's neural connectivity supports its participation in the integration of the different senses within humans, with a special emphasis on vision (van Hoesen, 1981). It functions as an organ of appraisal for danger, safety, and familiarity in approach-avoidance situations (Berntson et al., 2007; Elliott, Agnew, & Deakin, 2008; Sarter & Markowitsch, 1985). In association with medial areas of the frontal cortex, it connects emotional value to the object of the senses based on both instincts and learning history, and translates these appraisals into bodily states (Davis, 1992; LeDoux, 1986). It is a central neural player in associating conscious and unconscious indications of danger with preparation for a survival response (Ohman, Carlsson, Lundqvist, & Ingvar, 2007). Most important for psychotherapy is that it plays a "behind the screens" role in creating emotional bias in conscious processing by spinning our experience in ways that make us, for example, see the glass as half empty or half full (Kukolja et al., 2008).

Two circuits of sensory input reach the amygdala in the adult brain. The first comes directly from the thalamus and the other first loops through the cortex and hippocampus before reaching the amygdala (LeDoux, 1994). The first system serves rapid responses during survival decisions based on a minimum of information. The slower second system adds cortical processing (context and inhibition) to appraise ongoing perceptions and behaviors. The amygdala's direct neural connectivity with the hypothalamus, limbic-motor circuits, and many brainstem nuclei allows it to trigger a rapid survival response. The emotional power of phobias and flashbacks is greatly enhanced by the activation of intense somatic arousal provided by this direct connectivity.

Thus, the amygdala is one of the key components of affective memory, not just in infancy but throughout life (Chavez, McGaugh, & Weinberger, 2009; Ross, Homan, & Buck, 1994). In a fully developed brain, the amygdala also enhances hippocampal processing of emotional memory by stimulating the release of norepinephrine and glucocorticoids via other brain structures (McGaugh, 2004; McGaugh et al., 1993). Through these chemical messages, the hippocampus is alerted to the importance of remembering what is being experienced—a key component of new learning. The activation of the sympathetic nervous system alters the chemical environment within and between neurons, enhancing LTP and neural plasticity. We will return to this topic in greater detail in later chapters, when we discuss the impact of stress and trauma on the brain.

## The Amygdala and Unusual Experiences

*The "uncanny" elements we know from experience arise either when repressed childhood complexes are revived by some impression, or when primitive beliefs that have been "surmounted" appear to be once again confirmed.*

—Sigmund Freud

Given the amygdala's early development and its unique role in learning and memory, abnormalities of amygdala functioning may be involved in some unusual human experiences. Electrical stimulation of the amygdala has been shown to result in a wide variety of bodily sensations, feelings of anxiety, déjà vu, and memory-like hallucinations (Chapman, Walter, Markham, Rand, & Crandall, 1967; Halgren, Walter, Cherlow, & Crandall, 1978; Penfield & Perot, 1963; Weingarten, Cherlow, & Holmgren, 1977). Because of its low seizure threshold, subtle seizure activity may trigger the amygdala to activate normally inhibited sensory and emotional memories that then break through into conscious awareness (Sarter & Markowitsch, 1985). These primitive memories may also become triggered by sensory cues of past fears and account for posttraumatic intrusions (van der Kolk & Greenberg, 1987). Individuals under stress may be particularly vulnerable to the intrusion of powerful but conscious memories, even from very early childhood (Cozolino, 1997).

Primary process thinking and dreamlike experiences are more likely to merge with conscious awareness in situations of decreasing contextual cues, as in near-sleep states or conditions of sensory deprivation (Schacter, 1976). Decreasing contextual cues lessen the ability of the cortico-hippocampal systems to utilize past learning to make sense of present experience and inhibit amygdala input to conscious awareness. This may account for the success of projective testing in tapping into unconscious processing. In attempting to make sense of ambiguous situations, subcortical circuits are more likely to guide conscious awareness.

Individuals with temporal lobe epilepsy (TLE) often experience extreme religiosity, suggesting that stimulation of the amygdala can infuse everyday experience with a sense of deep significance. In other words, its ability to inform the rest of the brain that we are experiencing something highly significant can be applied in an inappropriate manner leading to odd and delusional thinking. The central nucleus of the amygdala also has a high density of *opioid receptors*, which are biochemical mechanisms of bonding and attachment behavior (Goodman, Snyder, Kuhar, & Young, 1980; Herman & Panksepp, 1978; Kalin, Shelton, & Lynn, 1995; Kalin, Shelton, & Snowdon, 1993) that are also implicated in alterations of consciousness. This suggests that unregulated activation of the amygdala may be a neurobiological trigger for the religious preoccupations occurring in some individuals with TLE. The fact that hypergraphia (writing a lot) can also be a symptom of TLE has led many to speculate that some religious texts have been driven by unusual amygdala activation stimulated by seizure activity.

## Hippocampal Memory Networks

*A memory is what is left when something happens and does not completely unhappen.*

—Edward de Bono

The hippocampi, shaped like seahorses on either side of the human brain, are essential structures for the encoding and storage of explicit memory and learning (Zola-Morgan & Squire, 1990) and play a central role in the organization of spatial and temporal information (Edelman, 1989; Kalisch et al., 2006; O'Keefe & Nadel, 1978; Selden, Everitt, Jarrard, & Robbins, 1991; Sherry, Jacobs, & Gaulin, 1992). The hippocampus also participates in our ability to compare different memories and make inferences from previous learning in new situations (Eichenbaum, 1992). If damaged, it can prevent new learning from occurring, condemning the victim to forgetting everything a few seconds after it is experienced (Squire, 1987).

The hippocampus is noted for its late maturation, with the myelination of cortical-hippocampal circuits continuing into early adulthood (Benes, 1989; Geuze, Vermetten, & Bramner, 2005). The late development of the hippocampus and its connectivity with the cortex reflects both its delayed functional availability and prolonged sensitivity to developmental disruption and traumatic insult. It remains particularly vulnerable to hypoxia (lack of oxygen) throughout life. Mountain climbers and deep sea divers who may experience periods of decreased oxygen availability have been shown to have hippocampal damage and short-term memory deficits. Gradual atrophy of the hippocampus appears to be a natural component of aging, along with a corresponding decrease in explicit memory abilities (Gartside, Leitch, McQuade, & Swarbrick, 2003; Golomb et al., 1993).

Research suggests that sustained stress results in excessive exposure of the hippocampus to glucocorticoids (cortisol), released in response to acute stress (Sapolsky, 1987). Prolonged high levels of glucocorticoids can result in dendritic degeneration, cell death, increased vulnerability to future neurological insult, and inhibited hippocampal functioning (Kim & Diamond, 2002; Watanabe, Gould, & McEwen, 1992). Patients suffering from post-traumatic stress disorder (PTSD) secondary to childhood trauma or combat exposure, prolonged depression, temporal lobe epilepsy (de Lanerolle, Kim, Robbins, & Spencer, 1989), and schizophrenia (Falkai & Bogerts, 1986; Nelson, Saykin, Flashman, & Riordan, 1998) have also been shown to have hippocampal cell loss. Decreases in hippocampal volume have been shown to correlate with deficits of encoding short-term into long-term memory and an increased vulnerability to psychological trauma (Bremner, Scott, et al., 1993; Gilbertson et al., 2002). Given that chronic stress correlates with decreased hippocampal volume, and that so many patients in psychotherapy have experienced chronic stress, it is logical to assume that many patients (like Sophia) have difficulty in those functions which depend upon the hippocampus.

# Amygdaloid-Hippocampal Interaction

*The struggle of man against power is the struggle of memory against forgetting.*

—Milan Kundera

The relationship between the amygdala and hippocampus is extremely important to human experience and contributes significantly to top-down and left-right integration. The participation of the amygdala is biased toward both right and down systems, whereas the hippocampus plays a large role in left and top processing. Put another way, the amygdala has a central role in the emotional and somatic organization of experience, whereas the hippocampus is vital for conscious, logical, and cooperative social functioning (Tsoory et al., 2008). Their relationship will impact affect regulation, reality testing, resting states of arousal and anxiety, and our ability to learn emotional and more neutral information. The level and quality of the functional connectivity of the amygdala and hippocampus will be impacted by temperament, life stress, and epigenetic factors (Canli et al., 2006).

Douglas and Pribram (1966) suggested that the amygdala and hippocampus play opposite roles in an attention-directing process. By accentuating small differences among inputs, the amygdala heightens awareness of specific aspects of the environment (attention) whereas the hippocampus inhibits responses, attention, and stimulus input (habituation) (Douglas, 1967; Kimble, 1968; Marr, 1971). The amygdala is involved with generalization, while the hippocampus is involved with discrimination (Sherry & Schacter, 1987). In other words, the amygdala will make us jump at the sight of a spider, while the hippocampus will help us to remember that this particular spider is not poisonous, so we shouldn't worry. Their proper balance will also allow us to stay close to others even when they cause us upset.

We can immediately see the relevance of these two systems to psychotherapy. The amygdaloid memory system, organizing early shame experience, makes the patient with borderline personality disorder react to the perception of abandonment when little or none exists in reality. Therapy with this patient would utilize the hippocampal-cortical systems to test the reality of these amygdala-triggered cues for abandonment in order to inhibit inappropriate reactions. This reality testing helps us to distinguish real abandonment from innocent triggers such as someone showing up a few minutes late for an appointment and inhibit inappropriate emotional reactions. Remember, for a young primate, abandonment means death. The catastrophic reaction of borderline patients to abandonment is a result of the fact that, to them, it is experienced as life threatening.

Flashbacks, memories from traumatic experiences, likely reside in amygdaloid-driven memory networks. PTSD victims describe flashbacks as powerful and multisensory, often triggered by stress, and experienced as if they were occurring in the present (Gloor, 1978; LeDoux, Romanski, & Xagoraris, 1989; van der Kolk & Greenberg, 1987). These flashbacks also have the characteristic of being stereotyped and repetitive (van der Kolk, Blitz, Burr, Sherry, & Hartmann, 1984), suggesting that they are not subject to the assimilating and contextualizing properties of the cortex and hippocampus. A model of dual memory processing, paralleling the amygdala/hippocampal distinction made here, has been previously proposed as underlying mechanisms in both PTSD (Brewin, Dalgleish, & Joseph, 1996) and the reemergence of past fears and phobias (Jacobs & Nadel, 1985).

Given the reciprocal nature of amygdaloid and hippocampal circuits, impairment of the hippocampus should lead to an increased influence of the amygdala in directing memory, emotion, and behavior. This imbalance toward the amygdala would also disrupt affect regulation. Depressed patients are overwhelmed by their negative feelings and unable to engage in adequate reality testing. Indeed, Sheline and her colleagues noted both decreased hippocampal and amygdaloid volume in depressed patients (Sheline, Wang, Gado, Csernansky, & Vannier, 1996; Sheline, Gado, & Price, 1998). Dysregulation of hippocampal-amygdaloid circuits are likely involved in depressive symptomatology and disturbed reality testing (Pittenger & Duman, 2008). Research with rats has found that increased levels of serotonin leads to enhanced neurogenesis in the hippocampus (Jacobs et al., 2000). This suggests that Prozac and Paxil may be effective in treating depression because they boost hippocampal volume and its ability to moderate amygdala activation.

# The Intrusion of Early Implicit Memory Into Adult Consciousness

*All our knowledge has its origins in our perceptions.*
—Leonardo da Vinci

Early memories stored in circuits of the amygdala and right hemisphere can intrude into adult consciousness in a variety of ways. They become especially relevant to psychotherapy when they are the result of trauma and impact our ability to love and work. Children who suffer early abuse may enter their school-age years agitated, aggressive, and destructive. They may engage in fights, property damage, setting fires, or hurting animals, resulting in criticism, punishment, and social exclusion. Although these behaviors are expressions of their memories of abuse, others react with criticism and retaliation. This feedback, in combination with the emotional damages from their abuse, evolves into an ever-deepening negative self-image.

In the absence of an explicit memory of their early trauma, these children's behavior is not experienced by them as a reaction to a negative past event, but as an affirmation of their inner feelings of essential badness. Because these experiences date back to the formation of preverbal sensory, motor, and affective memory systems, victims often report feeling "evil to the core." This is common in children who grow up in cults or with highly authoritarian or abusive parents. The kids of soldiers, police officers, and ministers appear to be at particular risk for the internalization of a negative self-image. Children of parents with obsessive-compulsive disorder can also find they hold an extremely negative view of themselves. While a person with OCD needs order, cleanliness, and control, a newborn brings just the opposite into their life. The child's early implicit memories are likely to be centered around being a source of annoyance, anxiety, and disgust to their parents.

The formation of attachment schema (a key form of implicit memory) guides and shapes relationships throughout life. Given that so many clients come to therapy with relationship difficulties, this implicit memory system may be one of the most important to explore in psychotherapy. These same networks of social memory give rise to the phenomenon of transference, a process that brings these early unconscious memories into the consulting room as they are played out between client and therapist. Enactments in psychotherapy, involving the interplay between unconscious elements within the patient and the therapist, also activate these implicit memories.

We have all experienced having our buttons pushed by someone; many of these "buttons" are the emotional traces of personal experiences, stored in implicit systems of memory. Overreacting to something implies that the difference between an appropriate reaction and how we actually react is attributable to a sensitivity based on our learning history. The most common distortions based on the input of early memory are in the direction of shame, a primary socializing affect starting at about 12 months (Schore, 1994). Individuals who are "shame based" (Bradshaw, 1990) can find criticism, rejection, and abandonment in nearly every interaction, resulting in a life of chronic anxiety, a struggle for perfection, exhaustion, and depression.

Silence is an ambiguous stimulus that activates systems of implicit memory. Silence may be golden, but in therapy it evokes a variety of implicit memories. The reaction of clients to the silence teaches us something of their emotional history. During periods of silence, many clients assume that the therapist is thinking critical thoughts. They imagine the therapist thinks they are boring, stupid, a waste of time, or a bad client. These feelings usually mirror those based in problematic relationships with one or both parents. Furthermore, these feelings are deep seated and tenacious, often taking many years to make conscious, examine, and modify. On the other hand, some clients find silence to be a form of acceptance and a relief from the pressures of being articulate and communicative. These stark differences in client reactions to the similar situations are convincing evidence of the workings of implicit memory and their effects on conscious experience.

A similar phenomenon occurs in individuals who become uncomfortable when they try to relax without any distractions. The emotions, images, and thoughts that emerge in conditions of low stimulation (or the absence of distraction) may hold clues to the workings of our brains and the aftereffects of early learning. Defenses to escape negative feelings come to require constant action and distraction to keep us from becoming frightened or overwhelmed.

## The Malleability of Memory

*The only paradise is paradise lost.*

—Marcel Proust

The false memory debate of years past highlighted many shortcomings in the knowledge of therapists when it came to understanding the workings of memory. Highly publicized legal cases of repressed memory and clinician contribution to the co-construction of false memories have resulted in increased understanding and training focused on the processes of memory. Most therapists are now aware of the vulnerability of conscious memory to suggestion, distortion, and fabrication from both client and therapist (Loftus, 1988; Paz-Alonso & Goodman, 2008).

Research has demonstrated that memory can be implanted in experimental situations where the subject soon becomes certain that the false memories have actually occurred (Ceci & Bruch, 1993; Loftus, Milo, & Paddock, 1995). A therapist's belief that her client has been abused may influence that patient to unconsciously fabricate a memory that they both then come to believe is true. This process is a clear demonstration of both the malleability of memory and the power of co-constructed narrative in shaping experience (Alberini, 2005; Anderson, Wais, & Gabrieli, 2006; Dudai, 2006; Nielson, Yee, & Erickson, 2005).

Given that memory is encoded among neurons and within neural networks, the malleability of memory is an observable manifestation of the plasticity of these neural systems. This malleability is certainly a stumbling block to our justice system, which relies so heavily on eyewitness testimony. The hundreds of convictions that have been overthrown by new DNA methods attest to the inadequacy of our present standards of eye-witness evidence. But from the perspective of psychotherapy, this plasticity provides an avenue to the alteration of destructive memories. Revisiting and evaluating childhood experiences from an adult perspective often leads to rewriting history in a creative and positive way. The introduction of new information or scenarios to past experiences can alter the nature of memories and modify affective reactions.

## The Magic Tricycle

*The greatest weapon against stress is our ability to choose one thought over another.*

—William James

Sheldon was a man in his late 60s who came to therapy for help with his many anxieties and fears. As a child, his parents had hidden him from the Nazis in a storage room behind the home of family friends. One day, after finding out that she and Sheldon's father would soon be taken to the concentration camps, Sheldon's mother told him to be a good boy, said goodbye, and left. While the family friends were kind to him, he spent his days alone with few toys, his small tricycle, and some scraps of food. Describing these days, Sheldon recalled alternating states of terror and boredom, during which he would either sit and rock or ride his tricycle around in slow tight circles. The slightest noise would startle him and he feared that each passing siren might be the police coming for him. Each day, exhausted by fear, he would eventually fall asleep.

The intervening decades had not diminished the impact of his experiences during the war; 60 years later, he still found himself reflexively rocking or walking in small slow circles when he became frightened. His life felt like one long, fear-filled day. In repeatedly recalling these experiences in treatment, he sometimes mentioned how he wished he could have left the house where he was hidden and traveled down the narrow streets to his grandmother's house. Sheldon remembered long afternoons he spent there before the war, listening to stories of her childhood on her father's farm. His grandmother and his parents perished in the war, and he never saw them again.

One day, I asked him for permission to change his memories just a bit. After a few quizzical looks he agreed to close his eyes and tell me the entire story again, at which point I would interrupt him and make some suggestions. As he came to the part of the story where he rode around in circles, I asked him, "What would you do if this was a magic tricycle and it could take you through walls without getting hurt?" I felt Sheldon had sufficient ego strength to allow him to simultaneously engage in the role-play while staying fully in touch with present reality.

After some hesitation, Sheldon said, "I would ride right through the house and out onto the sidewalk."

"Fine," I said. "Let's go!" Sheldon had been primed for our imaginary therapy play because he had spent many enjoyable hours of storytelling, cuddling, and laughing with his grandchildren. I felt that an imaginative task like this was not only accessible to him but would also serve the purpose of bridging the positive affect from his grandchildren to his lonely and frightened experiences as a child. Imagining he was making up the story for his grandchildren might also help him cope with the embarrassment of doing this with another adult.

After some mild hesitation, he pedaled through the house. As he got close to the door, however, he said, "They'll see me and kill me."

"What if the magic tricycle has the power to make you invisible?" I asked.

"I think that'll do," said Sheldon, and he pedaled through the front of the house and out onto the sidewalk. Once he got out of the house, he knew what to do. He described the street to me as he pedaled toward his grandmother's house. The storekeepers, the neighbors, the park, his rabbi, even some of his young friends were all alive in his memories. Sure enough, when he finally got to his grandmother's house she was home and, as always, happy to see him. He told his grandmother about his invisible tricycle and how scared he was in his hiding place. He went on to tell her of the end of the war, his travels, and raising his family. Finally, almost like a prayer, Sheldon told her how, many years from now, she would have the most beautiful great-great-grandchildren living in freedom, redeeming her suffering.

Over the next few months, whenever Sheldon experienced his childhood fears and anxieties, we would revisit his story and modify different details. These changes seemed to grow more detailed and more vivid in his mind. His imagination gave him the power to master many of his past fears. Because memory is modified each time it is remembered, Sheldon's brain was able to gradually contaminate his painful childhood with his present safety and joy (Bruner, 1990). He even began to tell his grandchildren stories about a little boy with a magic tricycle who accomplished great things with his courage and wit. Sheldon was a very special man who was able to take advantage of the malleability of memory to make his inner world a safer place. Nothing had changed about his childhood except that now, when he remembered his hiding place, he also remembered his magic tricycle.

An important part of restructuring memory is something Freud called *Nachtraglichkeit*, which means the ability to reconceptualize a memory based on evolving maturity. This process requires being able to hold the memory in mind without being emotionally overwhelmed and simultaneously bringing it into the present, picturing it as it would look from the perspective of who we are and what we know today. Both Freud's idea and Sheldon's experiences highlight the fact that memory is an evolving process that is subject to positive influence.

The construction and reconstruction of autobiographical narratives requires that the semantic processing of the left hemisphere integrate with the emotional networks in the right. Storytelling also invokes participation of the body as we gesture and act out the events we are describing. As such, narratives are a valuable tool in the organization and integration of neural networks prone to dissociation. Because we can write and rewrite our own stories, new ones hold the potential for novel ways of experiencing. In editing our narratives, we change the organization and nature of our memories and, hence, reorganize our brains. This is a central endeavor in many forms of psychotherapy.

## Summary

As a boy in the early 1960s, I remember being fascinated by news stories of Japanese soldiers attacking tourists on tiny islands in the South Pacific. During World War II, the Japanese navy left soldiers on many islands throughout the Pacific but never retrieved them at the end of the war. Decades later, pleasure crafts would innocently land on these islands only to be attacked by soldiers who thought the war was still being fought. They had dutifully kept guns oiled and remained vigilant for decades in anticipation of an American attack. I was awed by their loyalty and saddened by the thought of the years they spent fighting a war that no longer existed.

Like these soldiers, early amygdala-based memory systems retain struggles, stress, and trauma from a time before conscious memory. We may grow and move on to new lives, yet our implicit memory systems retain old fears. While remaining vigilant for signs of attack for early attachment pain, approaching intimacy can set off all of the danger signals. Therapists are trained to be amygdala whisperers who land on these beaches, attempting to convince the loyal soldiers within implicit systems of memory that the war is over.

# Chapter 6

# Laterality: One Brain or Two?

*Though the brain is enclosed in a single skull, it is actually made of two separate lumps . . . which are designed to disagree with each other.*
—Jonah Lehrer

We now switch our focus from the multiple and diverse systems of memory to another realm of neural complexity—cortical laterality. As you know, the human cerebral cortex is divided into right and left hemispheres, each controlling the opposite side of the body. The term *laterality* refers to the specialization of certain tasks to one side of the brain or the other, and is reflected in how the hemispheres differ in their organization, processing strategies, and neural connectivity. Keep in mind also that laterality shows variability among individuals, and left- and right-handed people, as well as males and females.

Although most neural processing requires the contribution of both hemispheres, there are situations when the hemispheres not only think differently but also compete with one another. This struggle for dominance and control may be one cause of our psychological struggles, giving new meaning to why we sometimes feel "beside ourselves" or "of two minds." By the end of this chapter, you may be left wondering whether we in fact have one brain or two.

John Hughlings Jackson, the eminent 19th-century neurologist, believed that the left side of the brain was, for most people, the "leading" side. This seemed logical given Broca's finding that the left hemisphere was responsible for our ability to use semantic language. Jackson later suggested that the right hemisphere was the leading side of the brain in visual-spatial abilities.

Over the years, it has become clear that dividing the brain into two discrete halves is not the best approach. Given that most neural systems integrate circuitry from the left and right sides of the brain, research attempting to localize functions in one hemisphere or the other often results in "untidy" findings (Christman, 1994). When we speak of functions of the right or left brain, we are more accurately referring to functions that are either represented more fully or performed more efficiently in one hemisphere than the other. Over the past 40 years, much has been written about the artistic right brain and the logical left. Although this view may be appealing to the imagination, it is far too simplistic. Assigning specific functions to particular areas of the brain needs to be done with both caution and the recognition that our knowledge is still evolving.

## Evolution and Development

*A scientific truth does not triumph by convincing its opponents and making them see the light, but rather because its opponents eventually die and a new generation grows up that is familiar with it.*
—Max Planck

Lateral specialization is an evolutionary choice, and does not exist in all animals. Many birds and fish, for example, have identical hemispheres. These animals are able to sleep one hemisphere at a time, allowing them to keep swimming or flying to avoid predators, continue feeding, or rest during long migrations. Although redundant hemispheres provide certain benefits, such as a backup system in case of injury, hemispheric specialization via natural selection promotes neural complexity. Through human evolution, the right and left cerebral hemispheres have become increasingly dissimilar (Geschwind & Galaburda, 1985). Lateral dominance appears to have been delegated depending on the functional domain in question (Cutting, 1992; Goldberg & Costa, 1981; Semmes,

1968). For example, areas of the left and right cortices have become specialized in the organization of the conscious linguistic self in the left and the physical emotional self in the right.

During the first 2 years of life, the right hemisphere has a growth spurt that parallels the rapid development of sensorimotor, emotional, and relational capabilities (Casey, Galvan, et al., 2005; Chiron et al., 1997; Thatcher, Walker, & Giudice, 1987). The child learns hand–eye coordination, crawling, and walking while becoming attached to caretakers. An organized sense of the body in space and the embodied self form in subcortical and cortical networks involving the thalamus, cerebellum, and parietal cortex. At the same time, middle portions of the prefrontal cortex are maturing and integrating with subcortical structures to establish the basic structures of emotional regulation and attachment. During this period, the development of the left hemisphere is slowed a bit and reserved for later-developing functions (Gould, 1977).

In the middle of the second year, a growth spurt occurs in the left hemisphere and an explosion in language and locomotion launches children into the broader physical and social worlds. In the frontal lobes, there is a shift of development to the dorsolateral areas, linking back to other cortical regions, that sculpts the language network (Tucker, 1992) while connecting the movements of hands and eyes to visual stimuli and words. The corpus callosum begins to develop at the end of the first year, is significantly developed by age 4, and continues to mature past the age of 10. Because of this slow maturation, the two hemispheres at first function relatively autonomously, gradually gaining interconnection and coordination through childhood (Galin, Johnstone, Nakell, & Herron, 1979).

A great deal of what is known about the functions of the different hemispheres has been the result of the split-brain research of Sperry and his colleagues (Sperry, Gazzaniga, & Bogen, 1969). Split-brain patients are individuals suffering from medication-resistant epilepsy, who have their corpus callosum surgically severed to limit seizures to one side of the brain. Presenting information separately to each of their hemispheres has revealed divisions of awareness and specialization in a range of cognitive and emotional tasks, thereby expanding our knowledge of cortical laterality (LeDoux, Wilson, & Gazzaniga, 1977; Ross et al., 1994; Sperry, 1968).

## Lateral Asymmetry

*All organs of an animal form a single system . . . and no modification*
*can appear in one part without bringing about corresponding*
*modifications in all the rest.*

—George Cuvier

The earliest form of language was most likely hand gestures, which may explain why handedness and language functions are so closely linked in the brain. Most of us are right-handed (controlled by the left brain) and have semantic language lateralized in the left hemisphere. Neural networks for both spoken and sign language are located in the left hemisphere for most adults, and damage to the left hemisphere usually results in language disturbances such as aphasia (Corina, Vaid, & Bellugi, 1992). In left-handed or ambidextrous individuals, lateralization of language is somewhat less clear. As the semantic functions of the cortex expanded during evolution and language became more descriptive and useful, words gradually replaced gestures in importance. Our present use of hand gestures to augment spoken language may betray this evolutionary path. Our tendency to use hand gestures even when talking on the telephone suggests that they not only play a role in communication but also in organizing and supporting our thinking.

The left hemisphere appears to be more involved in conscious coping and problem solving than the right. This is most likely a function of its language skills and prosocial orientation. The left hemisphere functions best within the middle range of affect and is biased toward positive emotions and approach behaviors (Silberman & Weingartner, 1986). Strong affect, especially anxiety and terror, result in high levels of right hemisphere activation and appears to inhibit the left hemisphere and language—hence, the experience of stage fright and speechless terror.

It has been suggested that Wernicke's area in the left temporal lobe, known to be centrally involved in language comprehension, acts as a probability calculator for other forms of behavior as well as language (Bischoff-Grethe, Proper, Mao, Daniels, & Berns, 2000). Given the rapidity with which we process speech, Wernicke's area may process what is heard based as much on what it expects to hear as what is actually said. This would certainly help to explain why human communication can be so problematic and misunderstandings so common. Broca's area may have similar predictive functions, which allow us to speak faster than we think and even, at times, be surprised by what we hear ourselves saying (Nishitani et al., 2004). In fact, William James, one of the fathers of American psychology, said that he needed to hear himself talk to know what was on his mind.

For most individuals, the right hemisphere processes information in a holistic fashion and is densely connected to the limbic systems and the viscera (Nebes, 1971). The left hemisphere, on the other hand, processes information in a linear, sequential manner and has less connection with the body. The right hemisphere is heavily wired to the limbic system and is more directly involved in the regulation of the endocrine and autonomic nervous systems than the left (Wittling & Pfluger, 1990). It also contains centers within the parietal lobes that might contain a representation of the entire body.

The right hemisphere is generally responsible for both appraising the safety and danger of others and organizing a sense of the corporeal and emotional self (Devinsky, 2000). Appraisal simply means attaching a positive or negative association to a stimulus, while emotion is the conscious manifestation of this appraisal process (Fischer, Shaver, & Carnochan, 1990; Fox, 1991). The vast majority of appraisal occurs at an unconscious level. This is why the right hemisphere is more often associated with the unconscious mind, that is, what guides our thoughts and behavior outside of our awareness.

The bias against left-handedness across many cultures may reflect an intuitive understanding of the left hand's (right brain's) relationship to the dark, primitive aspects of our nature. These biases likely date back into prehistory, when the left hemisphere may have exerted less inhibitory control over the right. Think about the French word *gauche* and the Italian *sinestre* for left and all their tasteless and evil connotations. By offering the right hand in greeting, early humans may have been more likely to behave in a civilized manner, and less likely to act out selfish or violent impulses. An examination of cave drawings in Southern Europe suggests that the bias toward right-handedness has existed for at least the last 5,000 years (Coren & Porac, 1977).

Although the left hemisphere generally produces semantic language, it is unclear whether it has any advantage in language comprehension. The right hemisphere may, in fact, be better at comprehending the emotional aspects of language such as the tone of voice or the attitude with which words are said (Searleman, 1977). Emotions in general, the ability to evaluate emotional facial expressions, and visual-spatial and musical abilities are primarily right-hemisphere processes (Ahern et al., 1991). Damage to the right hemisphere results not only in an impairment of our ability to assess facial gestures, but also to comprehend other nonverbal aspects of communication such as hand gestures and tone of voice (Blonder, Bowers, & Heilman, 1991).

## Laterality and Emotion

> *When angry, count to four; when very angry, swear.*
> —Mark Twain

Evidence suggestive of a relationship between laterality and emotionality was first observed in cases of damage to the prefrontal cortex. Patients with damage to the left hemisphere appeared to be far more likely to have a depressive reaction than those with damage to the right (Gainotti, 1972; Goldstein, 1939; Sackheim et al., 1982). It was later found that the closer these lesions were to the prefrontal regions, the more severe the symptoms of depression (Robinson et al., 1984). Right brain-damaged patients were also found to describe experiences with less emotional intensity than left brain-damaged patients or normal controls (Borod et al., 1998).

Imaging studies have shown that people without brain damage who suffer from depression have lower levels of glucose metabolism and cerebral blood flow in the left prefrontal cortex (Galynker et al., 1998; Kalia, 2005; Mathew et al., 1980). In addition, people experiencing mania in the absence of brain damage demonstrate decreased right prefrontal activity (Al-Mousawi et al., 1996). These studies expand the association between laterality and emotion to the general population. An examination of Table 6.1 reveals that the left hemisphere is biased toward positive affect, safety, and positive social approach, as well as anger and aggression directed toward others. Overall, the left side of the brain appears to be in charge of the successful navigation of the social world.

TABLE 6.1
Laterality and Emotion

---

*Increased left hemisphere activation occurs in response to:*

Happy stimuli[1]

Positive pictures[2]

Positive affect in response to positive films[3]

Approach-related dispositional tendencies[4]

More positive disposition[5]

Smiling and facial expressions of enjoyment[6]

Reported well-being[7]

Infant smiling in response to mother approach[8]

Trait anger[9]

State anger[10]

State aggression[11]

*Increased right hemisphere activation occurs in response to:*

Facial expressions of disgust[12]

Tastes associated with disgust[13]

Negative pictures[14]

Avoidance behavior[15]

Negative affect in response to negative films[16]

Threat-related vigilance[17]

Stranger approach[18]

Maternal separation[19]

---

The intimate association between emotion and cognition has been demonstrated in many laterality studies. For example, sad faces are rated as relatively sadder when presented to the left visual field compared to the right (Sackheim et al., 1988). Negative stimuli are consciously perceived most often when presented to the right hemisphere (Smith & Bulman-Fleming, 2004). Research has shown that anesthesia of the left hemisphere results in greater expressions of negative emotions and less prosocial explanations of experience (Dimond & Farrington, 1977; Ross et al., 1994). Orienting eye gaze to the left (stimulating the right hemisphere) results in decreased optimism, while the opposite is true with rightward eye gaze (Drake, 1984; Thayer & Cohen, 1985). Right-hemisphere-biased neural processing correlates with low self-esteem (Persinger & Makarec, 1991).

Higher levels of left prefrontal activation have been associated with a resilient affective style, faster recovery following negative events, and lower levels of the stress hormone cortisol (Davidson, 2004; Jackson et al., 2003; Kalin, Larson, Shelton, & Davidson, 1998). While there appears to be an overall bias of positive left/negative right, the picture is more complicated. The hemispheres are also lateralized for social/private and approach/avoidance (left/right) behavior. These patterns of left/right activation suggest that health and happiness may be associated with general lateral balance as well as the ability to be aggressive and express anger biased toward the left and grief and shame biased toward the right.

## The Integration of the Body in the Right Hemisphere

*The body never lies.*

—Martha Graham

The parietal lobes, located above our ears toward the top of our heads, are at the crossroads of neural networks responsible for vision, hearing, and sensation. They serve as a high-level association area for the coordination and integration of these functions. The anterior (front) portion of the parietal lobes organizes tactile perception, while the posterior (back) portion interconnects the senses to organize sensory-motor with conceptual events (Joseph, 1996). Accordingly, cells in the parietal lobes respond to hand position, eye movement, words, motivational relevance, body position, and other factors relevant to the integration of experience.

The purpose of the association of all of these high-order processing networks is to provide a coordinated and integrated awareness of one's own body and its relation to the external environment (Ropper & Brown, 2005). This makes sense in that the parietal lobes evolved from the hippocampus, which, in lower mammals, serves as a cognitive map for external space (O'Keefe & Nadel, 1978). Part of the job of the parietal lobes is to organize an integrative map of our bodies in space, which is available for conscious reflection. Thus, damage to the parietal lobes, especially on the right side, results in a variety of disruptions in our experience of the self and the world around us.

Although the left hemisphere seems to contain a network to monitor attention on the right side of the body, the right hemisphere of right-handers has a specialized ability to direct attention bilaterally to both the right and left sides of "extrapersonal space" (Mesulam, 1981). *Hemineglect*, or the denial of the existence of the left side of the body, can result from lesions to the right parietal lobe. When neglect is severe, the patient behaves as if the left half of the world has ceased to exist. Patients with hemi-neglect will dress and put makeup only on the right side of their bodies while denying ownership of their left arm or leg. Asked to draw the face of a clock, they may put all 12 numbers on the right side or simply stop at 6 o'clock.

The phenomenon of hemi-neglect has also been shown to exist in imaginary space. Bisiach and Luzzatti (1978) examined two patients with right parietal injuries and left-sided neglect who were asked to describe the Piazza del Duomo in Milan. The piazza was very familiar to both patients. But when asked to imagine the piazza from one end, they could recall and describe the details on their imagined right side and not their left. Later, they were asked to reimagine the piazza from the other end. Looking back to where they previously pictured themselves sitting, they were now able to accurately describe what was on the right side but not on the left. In other words, once they imagined turning around 180 degrees, they now had access to memories that they were unable to remember just a short while earlier. Further, the information they provided previously was no longer accessible. This remarkable demonstration suggests neural networks that organize and attend to the body in space are also utilized in imagination.

In later research, Bisiach and his colleagues (Bisiach, Rusconi, & Vallar, 1991; Cappa, Sterzi, Vallar, & Bisiach, 1987; Vallar, Sterzi, Bottini, Cappa, & Rusconi, 1990) found that vestibular stimulation via cold water irrigation of the left ear (the caloric test) in patients with right parietal lobe lesions resulted in temporary remission of their left hemi-neglect. Putting cold water into the left inner ear stimulated areas within the right temporal lobe and caused the patients to orient toward the left (Friberg, Olsen, Roland, Paulsen, & Lassen, 1985). Although the mechanism of action is not certain, one possible explanation could be that activation of the right temporal lobe resulted in a reintegration of right and left hemispheric attentional processes, bringing the world temporarily into an organized whole (Rubens, 1985). This theory is supported by the fact that being shown fearful faces also appears to overcome the attentional neglect of these patients (Tamietto et al., 2007). The survival value of these faces may surpass a higher threshold established in the hemi-neglect phenomenon.

## The Language Network and the Left Hemisphere Interpreter

*All men are frauds. The only difference between them is that some admit it. I myself deny it.*

—H. L. Mencken

The left hemisphere language network relies on the convergence of auditory, visual, and sensory information from the temporal, occipital, and parietal lobes. Wernicke's area in the temporal lobe receives input from the primary auditory area and organizes it into meaningful bits of information. The convergence zone connects sounds, sights, and touch, so that cross-modal connections can be made, allowing us to name things we touch and hear without visual cues. It is also necessary for the development of sign language, where words take the form of gestures. This sophisticated and highly processed information projects forward to Broca's area where expressive speech is organized.

Neural networks linking language areas to the rest of the frontal lobes allow both spoken and internal language to guide behavior and regulate affect. Although the semantic aspects of language are usually lateralized to the left hemisphere, the right contributes the emotional and prosodic element of speech. The integrative properties of language may be unequaled by any other function of the brain. Creating and recalling a story requires the convergence of multisensory emotional, temporal, and memory capabilities that bridge all vectors of neural networks. In this way, language integrates, organizes, and regulates the brain, and is therefore used to great benefit in everyday storytelling as well as in psychotherapy.

Consistent findings across a variety of settings have led to a general acceptance that the verbal neocortex organizes conscious experience and embodies the social self as arbiter of rules, expectations, and social presentation (Nasrallah, 1985; Ross et al., 1994). Working with split-brain patients, Gazzaniga and his colleagues found that the left hemisphere could create an explanation of experience when right hemisphere information was unavailable (Gazzaniga, LeDoux, & Wilson, 1977). Gazzaniga (1989) later developed the concept of the *left hemisphere interpreter* that synthesizes available information and generates a coherent narrative for the conscious social self.

The strategy of filling in gaps in experience and memory, and making a guess at an explanation, parallels confabulatory processes seen in patients with psychosis, dementia, and other forms of brain damage. *Confabulation* appears to be a reflexive function of the left hemisphere interpreter as it attempts to make sense of nonsense, organize experience, and present the self in the best possible light. This phenomenon is likely related to Freudian defense mechanisms that distort reality in order to reduce anxiety.

A good example of this kind of confabulatory behavior was demonstrated by S.M., a 77-year-old suffering from parietal and temporal lobe atrophy in her right hemisphere. One day her son saw her using sign language in front of the mirror in her bedroom (Feinberg & Shapiro, 1989). When asked what she was doing, the patient told him that she was communicating with the "other S.M." She went on to tell him that there was another S.M. who was identical to her in appearance, age, background, and education who was always in the mirror. She and the other S.M. had gone to the same school, but did not know each other from that time. The other S.M. also had a son with the same name who looked just like him.

S.M. and her double were identical in every respect, except that the other S.M. had a tendency to talk too much and did not communicate as well as she did in sign language. If her son or the examiner appeared behind her in the mirror, she would correctly label that person's mirror reflection. Thus, the phenomenon of a double was only evident for her own image. When it was pointed out that this was her own image in the mirror, she would reply, "Oh sure, that's what you think" (Feinberg & Shapiro, 1989, p. 41). While S.M.'s comprehension and identification of herself and the world had been disrupted by her right hemisphere lesion, her left hemisphere interpreter remained intact. It is somewhat comical to think that she experienced her reflection in the mirror as talking too much and being less skilled than herself in sign language. Perhaps the left hemisphere interpreter may explain why we are all above average in our own minds.

This confabulatory and positive self-bias of S.M. versus her reflection is a perfect example of the left hemisphere interpreter at work. It also reflects the brain's basic instinct to engage in explanatory behavior for things it cannot understand. Some version of the interpreter concept has previously been used to explain the development of paranormal beliefs (Cozolino, 1997), schizophrenic delusions (Maher, 1974), and religious beliefs (Gazzaniga, 1995). The concept is especially relevant to psychotherapy, because the construction of reality is at work in the worldviews of patients with character disorders, the defense mechanisms of neurotics, and the day-to-day reality of healthy individuals. The left hemisphere interpreter is an internal press agent for the self, putting a positive spin on what is experienced and how it is presented to others. If the interpreter is not doing its job adequately, as in the case of left hemisphere damage or decreased activation of the left frontal cortex, we can become realistic, pessimistic, and depressed.

## Communication and Coordination Between the Hemispheres

*Is the brain, which is notably double in structure, a double organ, "seeming parted, but yet a union in partition"?*
                                                                                    —H. Maudsley

As our left and right hemispheres differentiated during evolution, each came to gain dominance for specific functions after failed experiments with transcortical democracy (Levy, Trevarthan, & Sperry, 1972). At the same time, the blending of the strengths of each hemisphere allows for the maximum integration of our cognitive and emotional functioning. When we are awake, the right hemisphere constantly provides information to the left. Nasrallah (1985) suggested that this input relates to intuition, feelings, fantasy, and visual images. The momentary bubbling up of feelings or images, which are then quickly lost, may reflect one aspect of the intrusion of right hemisphere processing into left hemisphere control. The filtration of right hemispheric processes may be necessary to allow us to remain focused on the tasks in which we are engaged, although it may not necessarily register, understand, or allow the information into consciousness.

What happens when the hemispheres find themselves disconnected from one another? Jason and Pajurkova (1992) reported a case of a 41-year-old right-handed man who suffered damage to the front portion of his corpus callosum and the medial portion of his frontal cortex. The most salient aspect of his behavior after his injury was that the two sides of his body seemed to be in conflict with one another. During neuropsychological testing, the patient's right hand would attempt to perform a task but the left would move in and disrupt what had been accomplished. When he would try to go down a set of stairs, his right foot would lead but then his left hand would grab the doorjamb and refuse to let him move forward. He found himself unable to do things that required the cooperation of both hands.

The patient said, "My left foot and my left hand want to do the opposite of what my right one does all the time" (Jason & Pajurkova, p. 252). On another occasion he stated, "My left hand doesn't go where I want it to" (p. 249). In each situation, the right hand and side (controlled by the left hemisphere) attempted to carry out the conscious will of the patient. But the left side (controlled by the right hemisphere) would have no part of it. The authors reported that it seemed as if the right hemisphere was acting like a spiteful sibling, competing for attention and control (Jason & Pajurkova, 1992). Although this conflictual behavior decreased over time, it was still evident 6 months after the injury. Similar left–right conflicts, usually resolving in the first few weeks after surgery, have also been reported in split-brain patients.

It is clear in these cases that the left hemisphere is experienced as the conscious self (ego) while the behavior of the right hemisphere is experienced as a force from outside the self (ego-alien). The experience and behavior of such patients suggests not only alternate ways of processing information in each hemisphere, but also two separate wills. The unconscious and oppositional quality of the behavior of this client's right hemisphere suggests that the left hand may have been acting out unconscious emotional reactions.

## Right-Left Integration and Psychopathology

*We use our brains too little and when we do, it is only to make excuses for our reflexes and instincts.*
                                                            —Martin Fischer

I postulated earlier that neural network integration should correlate with mental health, while dissociation or imbalance among neural networks should correlate with mental illness. If this is true, we can assume that integration between the right and left hemispheres is one element of optimal brain functioning. It turns out that anxiety, affective disorders, psychosis, alexithymia, and psychosomatic conditions have all been linked to deficits in the integration and balance among the cerebral hemispheres.

## Anxiety and Depression

*Anxiety is love's greatest killer . . .*

—Anaïs Nin

As mentioned earlier, each hemisphere has an emotional bias, and so it appears that the proper balance of right-left activation allows us to experience a healthy mix of positive and negative emotional experiences, as well as to regulate and manage anxiety (Silberman & Weingartner, 1986). The left hemisphere has a bias toward positive affect, prosocial behavior, and assertiveness, all of which help us to connect with others and find safety in the group, while the right hemisphere's bias toward suspiciousness and negativity keeps us vigilant and alert to danger.

Frontal lobe activation, when biased toward the right hemisphere, correlates with the signs and symptoms of depression (Nikolaenko, Egorov, & Freiman, 1997). The same phenomenon holds true for anxiety. Primates with extreme right frontal activity are more fearful and defensive, and have higher levels of stress hormones, than do those with activity biased toward the left hemisphere (Kalin et al., 1998). Adults with a history of childhood trauma demonstrate a significantly greater shift to right hemispheric processing when asked to think about unpleasant memories (Schiffer, Teicher, & Papanicolaou, 1995). Activation of many structures of the right hemisphere is also evident during posttraumatic flashbacks (Rauch et al., 1996).

If anxiety and depression are, in part, the result of a bias toward right hemisphere processing, then any form of successful treatment will enhance a rebalancing of these systems. Cognitive therapies for both anxiety and depression utilize rational thought that may work by activating left hemisphere processes to regain lateral balance. Symptomatic relief can also be achieved by a downregulation of the right hemisphere processes through relaxation training.

An unfortunate artifact of the evolution of laterality may be that the right hemisphere is biased toward negative emotions while also having primary control over emotional self-awareness (Keenan et al., 1999). In addition, because there is so much early, unconscious right hemisphere emotional learning, early negative experiences have a long-lasting yet hidden impact on our self-esteem, attitudes, and personalities. These aspects of laterality may create a bias toward shame, guilt, and pessimism while possibly explaining the neurobiological mechanism underlying Nietzsche's statement that "Man is the only animal who has to be encouraged to live."

## Alexithymia and Psychosomatic Illness

> It is precisely because a child's feelings are so strong that they cannot be repressed without serious consequences.
>
> —Alice Miller

Alexithymia—the inability to consciously experience and describe feelings—is characterized by deficits in the awareness and integration of right hemisphere functions. These patients are not prone to depression or mania but instead have a poverty of emotional expression and experience. They are able to recognize that others have feelings, but report being unable to locate any within themselves.

From a psychodynamic perspective, these patients seem trapped in secondary process thinking, disconnected from their inner physical and emotional worlds. Patients with alexithymia are described as having a concrete or stimulus-bound cognitive style, restricted imagination, and a lack of memory for dreams (Bagby & Taylor, 1997). They have difficulty benefiting from traditional modes of talk therapy because of their inability to bring emotions into the session, or to use imagination or role-playing to expand their thinking about themselves. Although the neurological correlates of this disorder are still unknown, alexithymia has been described as a "bidirectional interhemispheric transfer deficit" (Taylor, 2000). The resultant failure of the integration of affect and cognition leaves the conscious self of the left hemisphere with little input from the emotional, intuitive, and imaginative right.

Patients with other psychiatric disorders reveal patterns similar to those with alexithymia. Hoppe (1977) found that patients with psychosomatic disorders have characteristics similar to those with alexithymia such as impoverished dreams, a paucity of symbolic thinking, and trouble putting feelings into words. Similar difficulties were also found in Holocaust survivors, split-brain patients, and individuals with traumatic brain injuries. Hoppe and Bogen (1977) hypothesized that problems during development or underlying genetic processes could lead hemispheres to organize and function autonomously. The theory of such an "interhemispheric transfer deficit" was supported by research with patients suffering from PTSD and alexithymia who were found to have deficits in transferring sensorimotor information between hemispheres (Zeitlin, Lane, O'Leary, & Schrift, 1989).

## Psychosis

> *Reality is merely an illusion, albeit a very persistent one.*
> —Albert Einstein

Whereas normal states of awareness are comprised of an integration and balance of right and left hemisphere processing, psychosis may be a result of the intrusion of right hemisphere functioning into conscious awareness. Hyperactivation of the right hemisphere, or a decrease in the inhibitory capacities of the left, may diminish the ability to filter primary process input from the right hemisphere. This shift in right-left bias may occur for many reasons, including changes in levels of important neurochemicals such as dopamine, neuroanatomical abnormalities, or changing activation in subcortical brain areas such as the thalamus. Schizophrenic patients and their close relatives demonstrate reduced left hemisphere volumes in the hippocampus and the amygdala, which has been shown to correlate with thought disorder (Seidman et al., 1999; Shenton et al., 1992).

Auditory hallucinations, or hearing one or more voices talking, are a core symptom of schizophrenia. In fact, the term schizophrenia means split mind. These aberrant, intrusive, and ego-dystonic experiences may reflect right hemisphere language (related to primary process thinking and/or implicit memories) breaking into left hemisphere awareness. These voices, often heard as single words with strong emotional value, are experienced as coming from outside the self. For example, patients report hearing profanities or critical words (*jerk, idiot*) as people walk by them on the street. Command hallucinations to hurt oneself or others or to engage in dangerous behaviors have the same qualities. Schizophrenic patients appear to openly struggle with shameful aspects of their inner world (likely stored in the right hemisphere) that the rest of us are better able to inhibit, repress, and deny.

In psychosis, primary process thinking breaks into normal states of awareness to create what are diagnosed as deficits in reality testing and thought disorders. Patients describe this as a feeling of dreaming while awake and struggling to make sense of the simultaneous superimposition of primary and secondary process experiences. This attempt to make sense out of nonsense fires up the left hemisphere interpreter, leading to the elaboration of bizarre delusions (Maher, 1974). Although a hemispheric model of psychosis is still speculative, tests of lateral dominance (measured by a listening task) have shown that decreased lateral dominance in these patients correlates with more severe psychotic symptoms (Wexler & Heninger, 1979).

Inspired by both modern science and ancient texts, the neuropsychologist Julian Jaynes (1976) developed a theory of the evolution of human consciousness based on the increasing ability of the left hemisphere to inhibit input from the right. Jaynes argued that prior to 1000 B.C., the two halves of the human brain acted independently; the right hemisphere unconsciously controlled the body, while the left witnessed and described the social environment and actions of the body. This model of laterality may have reflected an intermediate evolutionary stage between having two modes of conscious awareness and our current bias toward right hemisphere inhibition.

Jaynes suggested that when our forebears were in situations of extreme stress, such as combat, the right hemisphere provided auditory commands to the left, which were experienced as coming from outside the self. This could reflect an internalized auditory memory of the tribal leaders and warriors, commands similar to those reported by modern-day schizophrenics. With the expansion of the corpus callosum and increasing dominance of the left hemisphere, a more unified sense of self grounded in the left hemisphere has become dominant and able to inhibit these inner voices. Jaynes felt that psychotic symptoms seen in patients in modern times may be the result of a breakdown of the left hemisphere's capacity to inhibit these messages from the right.

## Laterality and Psychotherapy

*Happiness is not a matter of intensity but of balance, order, rhythm and harmony.*

—Thomas Merton

The proper balance and integration of the right and left hemispheres does not appear to be a given in the course of development. I strongly suspect that left-right integration is an experience-dependent process that relies on adequate assistance with affect regulation through secure attachment. It is also dependent on the co-construction of narratives where a model is presented for the recognition and labeling of feelings, as well as integrating them into experience. Psychotherapy can serve as a means to reintegrate the patient's disconnected hemispheres through reality testing, emotional expression, and putting words to feelings in the context of a caring relationship.

Examples from psychiatry and neurology strongly suggest that psychological health is related to the proper balance of activation, inhibition, and integration of systems biased toward the left and right hemispheres. Genetic and neuroanatomical factors can combine with early neglect or trauma to interfere with the development of optimal neural network integration and regulation. The similarity between hemispheric specialization and Freud's notion of the conscious and unconscious mind has not been lost on psychotherapists. Right hemisphere functions are similar to Freud's model of the unconscious in that they develop first and are emotional, nonverbal, and sensorimotor (Galin, 1974). This nonlinear mode of processing allows the right hemisphere to contain multiple overlapping realities, similar to Freud's primary process thinking most clearly demonstrated in dreams. The linear processing of conscious thought in the left hemisphere parallels Freud's concept of secondary process, which is bound by time, reality, and social constraints.

When patients come to therapy, the left hemisphere interpreter tells its story. But something is usually wrong: the story does not fully account for what is happening in their lives. The narratives that organize their identities inadequately account for their experiences, feelings, and behaviors. The right hemisphere also speaks via facial expressions, body language, emotions, and attitudes. Thus, we listen to both stories for the congruence between the verbal narrative, and nonverbal and emotional communication. In this process, we analyze the integration and coherence of left-right and top-down neural networks. A primary tool across all models of therapy is editing and expanding the self-narrative of the left hemisphere to include the silent wisdom of the right.

Hopefully, the therapist will be better integrated than the client in a therapeutic relationship. This will allow the therapist to react to what is said with emotion, resonate with the client's emotions, and then share thoughts about those emotions with the client. Thus, the therapist's ability to traverse the colossal bridge between his or her own right and left hemispheres serves as a model and guide for the client.

Another way of describing therapy from the perspective of laterality is that we teach clients a method by which they can learn to attend to and translate right hemisphere processing into left hemisphere language. We teach them about the limitations and distortions of their own conscious beliefs presented by their left hemisphere interpreter. Many clients need to be suspicious of the ideas that their left hemispheres offer them. This is why reality testing is so important for treatment success. It is the therapist's job to hear what is not said, resonate with what the client is unable to consciously experience, and communicate it back to him or her in a way that will allow it to become integrated. This human process serves hemispheric integration.

## Summary

The integration of dissociated processing systems is often a central focus of treatment. Gradually, clients come to learn how the therapist gathers and interprets the information presented to them (Gedo, 1991). This process closely parallels what is done during positive interactions with parents during childhood. If the method taught during childhood is maladaptive, it leaves the child (and later the adult) in a state of limited self-awareness and neural network dissociation. The learning of these skills in therapy occurs in the context of emotional and cognitive integration, requiring the participation of both hemispheres, reflective language, feelings, sensations, and behaviors. In the language of neuroscience, we are integrating dissociated systems of memory and processing systems by teaching new strategies for integrating rational and emotional information. These processes aid in the construction of a more inclusive self-narrative, which, in turn, serves as a blueprint for ongoing neural integration.

# Part III.

# The Organization of Experience and the Healthy Brain

# Chapter 7

# The Executive Brain

*My own brain is to me the most unaccountable of machinery—always buzzing, humming, soaring roaring diving, and then buried in mud. And why? What's this passion for?*
                                                            —Virginia Woolf

Through countless adaptational challenges and the process of natural selection, we find ourselves with staggeringly intricate and sophisticated brains: Ferraris—not Fords. Ancient networks have been conserved, expanded, and reorganized, while new networks have emerged and combined to perform increasingly complex functions. In the process, some executive functions remained with earlier evolving networks, and some moved up to frontal and prefrontal regions, while still others were assumed by the mind and the social group.

The control of the vast majority of our bodily and mental functions is on automatic pilot. Under normal circumstances, we pay virtually no attention to breathing, walking, talking, and thousands of other complex processes. We can drive a car safely (and mindlessly) for hours while conversing and listening to music. All of this automaticity allows us to focus our conscious attention on just a small fraction of what is happening at any given moment.

The executive cortical areas in our prefrontal lobes are some of the latest neural systems to evolve and the slowest to develop during childhood and adolescence. In many respects these systems continue to develop throughout life, allowing the potential for increasing perspective, compassion, and wisdom. The executive brain contains the control mechanisms that enable us to attend to a particular activity, filter out distractions, make decisions, and act in an organized and purposeful way. If these functions are carried out successfully, we feel calm and safe enough to turn our attention inward for contemplation, imagination, and self-awareness. These capabilities, in turn, create the possibility for art, religion, philosophy, and other uniquely human endeavors.

Think for a moment of a large corporation with a CEO at the top of its executive hierarchy. Lower level managers, who specialize in particular areas of operation, are employed by the corporation to control thousands of diverse functions. Utilizing multiple lower level executives frees the CEO to monitor market forces, keep an eye on the competition, and plan for the future. Just as a CEO is freed from the everyday concerns of production, building maintenance, and bill paying, the executive areas of the cerebral cortex are freed from attention to basic bodily functions, well-learned motor behavior, and visual-spatial organization. The executive brain participates in more basic functions only in situations that are novel and problematic.

Although the executive areas of the brain are traditionally thought of as being responsible for our rational abilities, they actually combine sensory, motor, memory, and emotional information to shape ideas, plans, and actions. This broader view of executive functioning has been guided, in part, by an increasing appreciation of the contribution of emotion and intuition in decision making (Damasio, 1994). Because so much of brain functioning is unconscious, nonverbal, and hidden from conscious observation, the executive brain is also strongly influenced by nonconscious processes. Psychotherapy calls on the executive brain to update and reorganize the relationship among the conscious and unconscious networks they oversee in the service of mental and physical health.

For the purpose of the present discussion, we will focus primarily on the executive functions of the frontal and prefrontal cortices. What we know about these areas is based on a combination of primate and human research, naturalistic observations, and clinical evidence with human patients. Although the focus here is on the frontal and prefrontal cortices, we will return to the idea of multiple executive regions in a later discussion of the parietal lobes.

## The Frontal and Prefrontal Cortices

*The highest possible stage in moral culture is when we recognize*
*that we ought to control our thoughts.*

—Charles Darwin

The frontal and prefrontal cortices are the prime candidates for behavioral and emotional executive functioning in primates and humans. Their organization and connectivity provide for the integration of cognitive and emotional processing (Fuster, 1997). Because there are no primary sensory areas in the frontal cortex, they are entirely dedicated to the association of information that has already been highly processed in other neural systems throughout the brain (Nauta, 1971). For example, projections from the parietal regions contain integrated visual, motor, and vestibular information, whereas those from the temporal lobe have already combined sensory information with socioemotional appraisal.

Although the human frontal lobes initially evolved to organize complex motor behavior, the expansion of the prefrontal lobes added capacities for planning, strategy, and working memory. Neurons and neural networks within the frontal cortex organize our behavior through time (Fuster, Bonder, & Kroger, 2000) by sustaining a memory for the future (Ingvar, 1985) that keeps in mind the eventual consequences of behaviors about to be performed (Dolan, 1999; Watanabe, 1996). The ability to remember the past and predict the future is essential for survival. Broca's area, in the left frontal cortex, for example, which controls expressive speech, is located adjacent to the area of the motor cortex dedicated to the lips and tongue. This proximity reflects the coevolution and interdependence of spoken language and fine motor control. Because of the evolutionary links between motor behavior and cognition, some theorists consider cognition to be a derivative of motor behavior (Wilson, 1998). Support for this idea may exist in that much of our symbolic and abstract thinking is organized by the visceral, sensory, and motor metaphors that permeate our language (Johnson, 1987).

As we have seen, networks in both hemispheres feed highly processed sensory-motor information forward to the frontal cortex. Simultaneously, multiple hierarchical networks, which loop up and down through the cortex, limbic system, and brainstem, provide the frontal cortex with somatic and emotional information (Alexander et al., 1986). The convergence of all of these networks within the frontal and prefrontal lobes allows them to synthesize diverse information and coordinate our attention, emotions, and cognition with action.

The prefrontal cortex also participates in constructing ideas about the beliefs, intentions, and perspective of others in a process called *theory of mind* (Goel, Grafman, Sadato, & Hallett, 1995; Stuss, Gallup, & Alexander, 2001). Damage to the prefrontal cortex in early childhood usually results in deficits in the development of theory of mind, including learning social roles, perspective taking, and empathic abilities (Dolan, 1999). Damage in the same areas later in life can also result in deficits in these abilities, sometimes referred to as pseudopsychopathy (Meyers, Berman, Scheibel, & Hayman, 1992). Because empathy requires conceptual understanding, emotional attunement, and the ability to regulate one's own affect, damage to any area of the prefrontal cortex may impair different aspects of empathic behavior (Eslinger, 1998). Empathic thinking requires both cognitive flexibility and affect regulation in order to pull back from the environment, put our current needs aside for the moment, and imagine the feelings of others.

The act of murder is the ultimate expression of a lack of empathy. As a group, people who have committed murder demonstrate significantly lower glucose metabolism in both dorsal and orbital portions of the frontal areas. This finding exists in the absence of indications of brain damage or decreased metabolism in other areas of the brain (Raine et al., 1994). Although antisocial behavior is a complex phenomenon, correlations exist between deficits in affect regulation, impulse control, and the inability to relate to the experience of others.

The classic example of damage to the orbitomedial prefrontal cortex (ompfc) is the case of Phineas Gage (Harlow, 1868; Damasio, 1994). Mr. Gage was a young and well-respected New Hampshire railroad foreman who was known for his maturity and "well-balanced" mind. An accident on the job sent an inch-and-a-quarter-wide iron bar up through his head, obliterating much of his ompfc. Although free of any "neurobehavioral" deficits from the accident (such as aphasia, paralysis, or sensory loss), his workmates reported that Gage was "no longer Gage." After the accident he was unable to control his emotions, sustain goal-oriented behavior, or adhere to social conventions. He went from being a young man with a promising future to an aimless and unsuccessful drifter.

## The Cortex and Inhibition

*What a man's mind can create, man's character can control.*
—Thomas A. Edison

When we think of the human cerebral cortex, we may think of the accomplishments of music, art, and culture—products of cortical and especially prefrontal evolution. Although we focus on these visible and impressive products of the human brain, the hidden role of the cortex in inhibiting itself and other brain structures is a vital aspect of the brain's capabilities. Consider this example: we are born with a broad array of primitive brainstem reflexes conserved from our primate ancestors. One of these is the grasping reflex, which allows us to pick up infants by putting our index fingers in their palms and lifting. For the first few months of life infants can hold their own weight, after which they are no longer able to hold on.

It is believed that this grasping reflex is a holdover from a time when newborn monkeys had to hold onto their mothers' fur to free the mothers' hands to traverse branches and gather food. So although this behavior is no longer required for survival by humans, it has been conserved within our genetic blueprint. The only possible role it may play for us is to enhance the experience of bonding between newborn and parent. Many parents are captivated and enthralled by the fact that their infant grasps them and holds on so strongly. Over the first few months of life this reflex gradually diminishes as descending fibers from the cerebral cortex connect with the brainstem regions that trigger them. But why does the cortex make this inhibitory process such an early priority? After all there is so much to learn. The most likely reason is that before the cortical motor areas can begin to shape the dexterity of the hands and fingers, they need to be released from the control of this primitive reflex. In other words, before we can move each of our fingers independently and in coordination with each other, they need to be free from the tendency to act together for a single purpose.

Now fast forward to later in life, when this same child is 60, 70, or 80 years old. Her children notice that she seems forgetful and becomes disorganized from time to time, and wonder if there may be something wrong. The family doctor refers her to a neurologist who performs a series of clinical tests. In one of these tests, the doctor asks her to hold her arms out straight in front of her with her hands open and palms facing down. Extending his arms under hers with his palms up, the doctor slides his fingers under her arms from the elbows up towards her hands. As he reaches her wrists, he curls his fingers slightly and holds them rigid. As the doctor's fingers slide under the palms and then the fingers he is looking to see if the touch of his hand triggers her fingers to curl inward and grasp his own. If they do, he will try it again after telling her not to grasp his fingers. If it happens again, it is likely that the touch of his hand is triggering the same brainstem grasping reflex that she showed early in life. Why is this clinically significant?

It turns out that the reflexes in the newborn do not dissolve, but rather remain embedded within the brainstem throughout life, and are continually inhibited by descending fibers from the cortex. With diseases like dementia, the neurons in the cortex gradually die off and the cortex becomes increasingly compromised. So what the doctor is looking for are signs of compromise of cortical inhibitory functioning suggestive of a potential stroke, tumor, or the onset of dementia. Early reflexes that reemerge after damage to the brain in adulthood are referred to as *cortical release signs* (Chugani et al., 1987).

This inhibitory cortical function is not limited to primitive reflexes; it is in play when we are able to keep ourselves from reacting in games of Simon Says when Simon doesn't say, or hold our tongues in emotional situations where saying something would only make things worse. A major neurobiological component of secure attachment is the building of descending fibers from orbital and medial regions of the prefrontal cortex down to the amygdala and other limbic structures, which allow the child to first use parents as emotional scaffolding for the regulation of fear, and later to be able to regulate her own fear through self-talk, memory of positive outcomes, and proactive problem solving (Ghashghaei, Hilgetag, & Barbas, 2007).

## The Prefrontal Cortex

*One of the most remarkable aspects of an animal's behavior is the ability to modify that behavior by learning, an ability that reaches its highest form in human beings.*
—Eric Kandel

The prefrontal cortex is generally divided into two divisions; the first consists of the orbital and medial regions (ompfc) and the second comprises the dorsal and lateral areas (dlpfc). Although physically contiguous, the orbitomedial and dorsolateral prefrontal areas differ in their connectivity, neural architecture, biochemistry, and function (Wilson, O'Scalaidhe, & Goldman-Rakic, 1993). Research with primates has demonstrated that although both areas play a role in inhibition and control, the dlpfc is involved when the decision is attentional, and the ompfc when it involves emotional information.

The ompfc, first to evolve and first to develop during childhood, sits at the apex of the limbic system and is richly connected with subcortical networks of learning, memory, and emotion (Barbas, 1995). These connections, and their bias toward the right hemisphere, are associated with the extremes of emotional processing. Like the right and left hemispheres with which they are linked, the ompfc and dlpfc can demonstrate various degrees of integration and dissociation.

## TABLE 7.1
### Functions of the Prefrontal Lobes

**Orbital and Medial Regions**

| | |
|---|---|
| Attachment[1] | Estimating reward value and magnitude[8] |
| Social cognition[2] | Sensitivity to future consequences[9] |
| Thinking about a similar other[3] | Achieving goals[10] |
| Self-referential mental activity[4] | Stimulus-independent thought[11] |
| Appreciating humor[5] | Inhibitory control in emotional processing[12] |
| Encoding new information[6] | |
| Sensory-visceral-motor linkage[7] | Decisions based on affective information[13] |

**Dorsal and Lateral Regions**

| | |
|---|---|
| Cognitive control[14] | Learning motor sequences[20] |
| Directing attention[15] | Decisions based on complex information[21] |
| Organizing temporal experience[16] | |
| Organizing working memory[17] | Thinking about a dissimilar other[22] |
| Organizing episodic memory (right)[18] | The integration of emotion and cognition[23] |
| Voluntary suppression of sadness[19] | |

The cognitive and emotional intelligences in which they specialize have different developmental timetables and learning contexts. Orbital and medial prefrontal areas begin to organize emotional development—

in the context of interpersonal relationships—from the first moments of life. During the first 18 months of life, the ompfc shares a sensitive period of development with the right hemisphere. Dorsolateral areas exhibit an initial lag and then a growth spurt with the development of language and the exploration of our physical and conceptual worlds.

Our prefrontal cortex has two overarching and interwoven areas of function, the regulation of affect and attachments on the one hand, and the synthesis and coordination of cognitive and motor processes on the other. Although these two tasks seem quite different, each is dependent upon the other. Abstract thinking and problem solving are particularly dependent on adequate emotional regulation, which, in turn, can be accomplished by using rational thought and problem solving. The prefrontal cortex also appears necessary for *metacognition*—our ability to observe our stream of consciousness, revisit memories, and think about our thinking, which depends upon the integration of affect and cognition.

We can observe an array of functions in which the prefrontal lobes participate by examining the kinds of problems that emerge when they are injured (see Table 7.2). We can also see that different regions of the prefrontal cortex specialize in different functions. With most traumatic brain injuries, like the one suffered by Luis, whom you will soon hear about, all of these areas are negatively impacted. On the other hand, more localized lesions may result in some of these symptoms and not others. Each psychiatric illness, too, has its characteristic profile of cognitive distortions, difficulties with emotional regulation, and deficits of self-awareness and self-monitoring reflective of different patterns of frontal lobe involvement.

Problem solving—which requires emotional regulation, sustained attention, and cognitive flexibility—is a central executive function that can become impaired with frontal compromise. Some patients get stuck in a particular way of thinking (perseveration), while others have difficulty utilizing abstract concepts (concrete thinking). They may have difficulty in remembering the outcome of past behaviors and repeatedly apply the same unsuccessful solutions to new problems. Patients with frontal deficits often have a difficult time monitoring social interactions, such as keeping the listener's perspective in mind and abiding by social rules.

**TABLE 7.2**
**Manifestations of Prefrontal Compromise**

| Orbital and Medial Regions | Dorsal and Lateral Regions |
| --- | --- |
| *Social and Emotional Disinhibition* | *Loss of Executive Function* |
| Tactlessness or silly attitude | Forgetfulness |
| Decreased social concern | Distractibility |
| Sexual exhibitionism and lewd conversation | Decreased memory for the future |
| Grandiosity | Decreased anticipation |
| Flare with anger and irritability | Poor planning ability |
| Restlessness | Deterioration of work quality |
| *Apathy* | *Loss of Abstract Attitude* |
| Decreased attention | Concreteness |
| Loss of initiative | Stimulus bound |
| Lack of spontaneity | Loss of aesthetic sense |
| Indifference | Perseveration |
| Depression | Set stuckness |

## Luis

*The very essence of instinct is that it's followed independently of reason.*

—Charles Darwin

Luis was in a serious auto accident a few days after his 20th birthday. He and his parents came in to see me after his neurologist suggested they all might benefit from family therapy. At the time of their first appointment, I opened the door to find eight people packed tightly into my small waiting room. As Luis, his parents, and five younger siblings filed into my office, I noticed the scars and indentations across Luis's forehead and imagined the damage beneath them. I knew from talking with his neurologist that he had sustained severe injuries to his prefrontal cortex and that he had become impulsive, irritable, and occasionally violent. Luis now possessed limited inhibitory capacity, reasoning abilities, and almost no ability to be guided by social expectations.

After we all settled in my office, I turned to the father and asked how I could help him help his family. He immediately became tearful, shook his head slowly from side to side, and rubbed his hands together. "He drives too fast," he said quietly. "I don't!" exclaimed Luis. "Except for that one time!" Everyone in the family looked away and appeared embarrassed. It was immediately clear that talking back to his father was part of the problem. Although he had always been somewhat impulsive, his parents claimed that he was far worse than before the accident. I suspected that no matter how impulsive Luis might have been before the accident, this disrespectful behavior was new. This effect of Luis's accident was apparent just a few seconds into the session.

As the family discussed their situation, I found out that Luis's parents had moved to the United States from Mexico shortly before his birth, and had adapted well to their new home. Despite their successful acculturation, they remained true to traditional Mexican values of loyalty to the family and respect for elders. In this context, Luis's reflexive and loud contradiction of his father was a source of shame for everyone except Luis. His injury had damaged the networks that allowed him to monitor and control his own behavior and take into account the expectations of others. A year after the accident he returned to his auto repair job but was unable to focus on his work or get along with coworkers and customers. The descending networks of cortical inhibition had been compromised through the loss of so many prefrontal neurons.

Luis didn't remember anything about his accident and, in fact, had no memory for the weeks before or after the event. He read the police reports to discover that he had lost control of his car while street racing and crashed into a pole. His injuries were compounded by the fact that he was not wearing a seat belt and had installed a steel steering wheel without an airbag. Was this the foolishness of adolescence or evidence reflecting his lack of judgment prior to the accident? His mother reported that he spent most of his time at home with her, and that his behavior was erratic and sometimes frightening. At times he would cry for no reason, yell at her and the others, and jump in her car and race off. A few times, he went into a rage and threw furniture around the house. He had also made sexual statements and cursed using Jesus's name during the holidays, upsetting everyone in the family. Family members were confused and torn between their loyalty to Luis and their disgust with his behavior.

Automobile, industrial, and recreational accidents, as well as community and domestic violence, all contribute to the increasing number of people who experience traumatic brain injury. Because the frontal areas are located directly behind the forehead, they are also most likely to be damaged in fights and accidents. Although patients with head injuries come from all walks of life, young males are disproportionately represented. Their youthful impulsivity, risk taking, and lack of judgment, all dependent on prefrontal and frontal lobe functioning, make them more vulnerable to damaging these very regions. The massive reorganization of prefrontal brain areas along with biochemical and hormonal changes during adolescence likely contribute to these dangerous behaviors (Spear, 2000). Many of these young men may have already had frontal deficits or slowed frontal development prior to their accidents, amplifying more typical adolescent risk taking. In this way, frontal injuries often compound preexisting deficits of impulse control and judgment, complicating treatment and recovery.

Treatment with Luis and his family was multifaceted. I began by educating the entire family about the brain and Luis's particular injuries. The specific information was less important than labeling his behaviors as symptoms of his injury. I targeted in particular his cursing and sexual statements, which were, in their minds, connected to his character and spiritual health. By sharing case studies of others with them, I was able to show that Luis's symptoms were part of a pattern of pathological disinhibition related to his brain damage and not the result of moral lapses or bad parenting.

More specific interventions included enrolling Luis in an occupational therapy program to help him develop the instrumental and interpersonal skills needed to obtain and maintain employment. As the oldest son, it was important for him and the rest of the family that he be productive and regain a sense of self-worth. One of my goals was to reduce his resistance to taking medication that would help him with his anxiety and depression caused by his changed circumstances. I also worked with Luis and his family to develop skills related to stress reduction and anger management. We turned these exercises into family role-playing games that alleviated tension and allowed everyone to participate in helping Luis.

Over time, Luis was able to apply his knowledge of cars to a part-time job in an auto parts store. His occupational therapist helped him establish routines that allowed him to successfully use the computer. Antidepressants proved helpful with both his mood and irritability, and the role-playing games became woven into the family's everyday interactions. All of these improvements made the occasional outbursts more tolerable and more easily seen as part of his illness. Luis was so very fortunate to have the unquestioning love and support of a strong and involved family.

## The Orbitomedial Prefrontal Cortex

*Opinion is ultimately determined by the feelings, and not by the intellect.*

—Herbert Spencer

Tucked under and between the lobes of the frontal cortex and sitting directly above the eyes, the ompfc is densely connected to the anterior cingulate, amygdala, and other structures of the basal forebrain (Heimer et al., 2008; Zahm, 2006). These networks are of special interest to psychotherapists because they both generate and regulate emotion and attachment (Kern et al., 2008; Levesque et al., 2004; Rogers et al., 2004; Wager et al., 2008; Walton et al., 2003). The anterior cingulate—involved with attention, reward-based learning, and autonomic arousal—first appeared during evolution in animals demonstrating maternal behavior, nursing, and play (Devinsky, Morrell, & Vogt, 1995; MacLean, 1985; Shima & Tanji, 1998). Consequently, damage to either the ompfc or the anterior cingulate results in deficits of maternal behavior, emotional functioning, and empathy. As described earlier, disorders of emotional control are also seen with damage to these regions, including inappropriate social behavior, impulsiveness, sexual disinhibition, and increased motor activity (Price, Daffner, Stowe, & Mesulam, 1990).

The ompfc is vital for appraisal—interpreting complex social events and linking them with their emotional value via connections to the amygdala and other subcortical structures. A good example of this is the ability of the ompfc to modulate the amygdala's reaction to fearful faces based on the context in which the faces are presented (Hariri, Bookheimer, & Mazziotta, 2000). So while the amygdala will alert us to the sight of an angry face, the ompfc will include information about additional environmental variables and information based on past learning. If the ompfc recognizes the face as that of a feared predator, the fight-or-flight response will be activated. If the ompfc adds that it is the face of a distressed baby, we may approach the child to find out what is wrong and if there is something we can do to help. Damage to either the amygdala or ompfc at any time during life can result in an inability to organize vital social information in a useful manner, resulting in deficits in communication and connection.

Research has demonstrated that the ompfc also calculates the magnitude of reward or punishment value of our behavior such as approaching another for help and winning or losing money while gambling. Estimating reward value is a joint operation between the ompfc and the amygdala (Dolan, 2007; Gottfried, O'Doherty, & Dolan, 2003). Much of this analysis occurs out of conscious awareness and is commonly called *intuition*. Those of us who are good at "reading" people or gambling might just be aware of having a feeling about a particular decision. In actuality, basal forebrain and somatosensory areas work together to appraise huge amounts of information that provide us with this feeling about what to do even if it is sometimes contrary to our conscious logic (Damasio, 1994).

## The Dorsolateral Prefrontal Cortex

*Two things control men's nature, instinct and experience.*
—Blaise Pascal

The dorsal and lateral regions of the prefrontal cortex (dlpfc) integrate information from the senses, the body, and memory to organize and guide behavior. The dlpfc performs a variety of functions, including directing attention, organizing working memory, learning motor sequences, and organizing temporal experience (Fuster, 2004). The dlpfc is the latest developing region of the cortex and continues to mature into the third decade of life. This gradual maturation of neural networks is vital to attention and judgment. It can be tracked by looking at the increasing complexity of school curricula and later through the slow decline of automobile insurance rates from the teens into the 30s. The role of the dlpfc in interacting and coping with the environment is highlighted by the reduced spontaneity and flattened affect seen when they are damaged.

A component of the integration of top-down, cortical, and limbic processing occurs in the communication between the ompfc and the dlpfc. The bias of these regions toward the right and left hemispheres respectively allows them to also support the integration of the left and right cerebral cortices. In addition, the dorsal and lateral areas of the frontal cortex evolved to network with the hippocampus while the medial regions became densely interwoven with the amygdala. Thus, the communication among prefrontal regions provides pathways of integration for the hippocampal and amygdaloid memory systems described earlier.

Emotion and higher cognition can be integrated, i.e., at some point of processing, functional specialization is lost, and emotion and cognition conjointly and equally contribute to the control of thought and behavior. (Gray et al., 2002, p. 4115)

Like a tennis doubles team, the ompfc and the dlpfc depend on one another's performance for optimal functioning. If the ompfc is not doing an adequate job regulating amygdala activation, heightened levels of autonomic arousal will interfere with dlpfc-directed cognitive processes (Dolcos & McCarthy, 2006). This is why we may have difficulties in comprehending and solving even the most basic problems when we are frightened or distraught. On the other hand, if the dlpfc is not properly processing and managing environmental demands, the resultant anxiety will overtax and eventually disrupt emotional regulation. In essence, both inner and outer worlds need to be balanced and adequately regulated for optimal functioning.

## Attention-Deficit/Hyperactivity Disorder

*Thinking is the momentary dismissal of irrelevancies.*
                                        —Buckminster Fuller

Jimmy, an elfin 8-year-old, was referred to me to assess whether or not he had attention-deficit/hyperactivity disorder (ADHD). Before meeting him, I read notes from his parents, teachers, and soccer coach that described his behavior. All agreed he was more distracted and energetic than other children his age. His coach noted Jimmy's inability to stay focused on the game; one teacher described him as a bundle of energy; his father wrote, in big letters, "Exhausting!" Jimmy's restlessness and impulsivity made it difficult for other kids to interact with him, and his mother felt he was becoming isolated as his peers sought calmer company.

I walked into the testing room to find Jimmy's mother slumped in a chair with her face in her hands. She did not react when I entered the room and I wondered if she might be crying. I scanned the room, looked behind the chair and small sofa, but could not see Jimmy anywhere. Before I could speak, Jimmy shouted, "I'm up here!!" Startled, I looked up and saw him perched on top of a six-foot storage unit. I saw his mother momentarily pick up her head, roll her eyes, and lower it back down into her hands. She wasn't crying, just overwhelmed. It was clear that while making a diagnosis might not be difficult, getting through the assessment process would require stamina and patience.

Jimmy did have ADHD, with the same symptoms his father had when he was a boy. ADHD does sometimes run in families. Apparently, his father still suffered from many symptoms of distractibility and restlessness that created difficulties in his work and relationships. After many failed career attempts, he found considerable success in real estate. The constant movement and transient relationships utilized his energy and personality, while his choice of a business partner—who excelled at handling the details of his sales—protected him from his deficits in attention. Being a stable husband and father, however, proved more problematic.

The treatment for Jimmy included behavioral therapy to help with his attention and social skills, martial arts classes, and stimulant medications. These and other interventions were designed to boost frontal functioning through biochemical and behavioral interventions (social skills and teaching him to stop and think), and by giving him constructive avenues through which to channel his considerable energy. Individuals like Jimmy who suffer from ADHD are characterized by an inability to sustain attention and inhibit extraneous impulses, thoughts, and behaviors. These individuals can be easily lost in daydreams or be in constant motion. They are also in danger of leaping before they look. In fact, Jimmy had been injured a year earlier when he raced into a neighbor's backyard and jumped into the pool before noticing it had been drained for repair.

Since Satterfield and Dawson (1971) first pointed to a dysfunction of frontal-limbic circuitry, ADHD has been understood to be a disorder of executive control. The common explanation from psychiatrists to parents is that their children have a lag in frontal lobe development that results in a disinhibition of impulses from lower in the brain and difficulties with tasks which require sustained attention. They are also told that there is a good chance their child will "grow out of it" as the frontal lobes mature. In the meantime, stimulant medications will turbocharge these lagging frontal regions, allowing for more functional behavior. While this is a good anecdotal explanation, the underlying mechanisms and the etiology of ADHD are likely much more complicated.

Functional imaging research comparing ADHD to non-ADHD subjects reveals a variety of patterns of higher and lower levels of activation throughout the brain. And like most psychiatric disorders, ADHD is heterogeneous and emerges from a spectrum of genetic, biological, and interpersonal factors (Sun et al., 2005). It is likely that the explanations of the causes and treatments of the disorder lie within hierarchical networks between the attentional and inhibitory circuitry of the frontal and parietal cortex, and subcortical networks in the striatum and cerebellum that trigger and organize motor behavior. It is unwise, however, to necessarily posit these deficits in the frontal lobe because complex behaviors rely on far-reaching circuitry that can demonstrate similar dysfunctions regardless of where in the network the problems exist (Seidman, Valera & Makris, 2005; Willcutt et al., 2005).

Stimulant medications (such as Ritalin) may be working on the frontal lobes, the striatum (Vaidya et al., 1998), the cerebellum (Anderson et al., 2002), or more systemically by boosting general levels of dopamine and norepinephrine (Arnsten, 2000; Arnsten & Li, 2005). All we can be sure of is that it is rebalancing this hierarchical circuitry in a way that decreases motor agitation while enhancing attention. Because the brain works in interactive networks, the safest working hypothesis at this point is that there is a problem in the hierarchical neural networks that both activate and regulate behavior and attention (Durston et al., 2003; Lee et al., 2005; Rubia et al., 1999).

Think of playing a game of Simon Says. Simon Says tests our abilities to respond to the command while monitoring and inhibiting our behavior based on whether or not Simon says. The winner will be someone with well developed, balanced, and integrated bottom-up networks of motor responses and top-down networks of inhibitory control. When we hear a command in the absence of the words, "Simon says," we feel our body react and the tension of inhibition as we exert control to stop ourselves. The popularity of this game with small children reflects the development of these systems as well as a way to exercise voluntary control over impulses. When individuals with ADHD engage in tasks similar to Simon Says, they show a lower level of activity in the usual cortical areas dedicated to inhibition and instead rely on a more diffuse and less effective group of neural structures as compensatory mechanisms (Durston et al., 2003; Schulz et al., 2004; Zang et al., 2005).

Children with ADHD have difficulties in organizing their behavior when they are confronted with situations that require them to inhibit motor responses and sustain attention to addressing complex tasks.

Thus, they have difficulties in learning, which requires attending to and recalling verbal material, complex problem solving, and planning. They require much more motivation to maintain attention, and so they often excel at video games, which capture their attention and for which their ability to shift attention serves them well.

Our understanding of the brains of individuals with ADHD is still limited, and a variety of findings have emerged from research using various imaging techniques (Bush, Valera, & Seidman, 2005). Table 7.3 lists some of the studies that point to an array of differences between ADHD and non-ADHD individuals using different measurement methods. The

TABLE 7.3
Attention-Deficit/Hyperactivity Disorder

### Functional Magnetic Resonance Imaging (fMRI)

*Decreased Activation In*
Parietal attentional systems[1]
Anterior-mid cingulate cortex[2]
Supplemental motor area[3]
Right middle prefrontal cortex[4]
Right inferior frontal cortex, left sensorimotor cortex and bilateral
   cerebellum lobes and vermis[5]

*Increased Activation In*
Left temporal gyrus[6]
Basal ganglia, insula, cerebellum[7]
Right anterior cingulate cortex[8]

### Regional Cerebral Blood Flow (rCBF)

*Hypoperfusion or Decreased Activation*
White matter regions of the frontal lobes and caudate nuclei[9]

*Hyperperfusion or Increased Activation*
Right striatum and somatosensory area[10]

### Brain Morphology

Smaller cerebral and cerebellar volume[11]
Smaller right prefrontal and caudate volume[12]
Reduction of left cortical convolutional complexity in boys[13]
Cortical thinning in adults in right parietal, dorsolateral, and anterior
   cingulate areas—all involved with attentional control[14]
Loss of cerebellar volume[15]
Decreased frontal and cerebellar white matter density[16]

best guess at this point is that individuals diagnosed with ADHD likely reflect a number of subgroups with different types of brain involvement. They suffer from a number of different processes reflected in the size, shape, and function of their brains. The usual cortical systems of attentional control and inhibition appear compromised while other networks attempt to compensate. Subcortical structures involved in motor movements are also affected in ways that result in greater but less organized impact on experience and behavior.

Lastly, I want to mention a phenomenon I have witnessed repeatedly over the years—children who are diagnosed with ADHD and treated with medication but are better described as using a manic defense to cope with overwhelming anxiety. An assessment of the psychological state of the household—parental relationship, parental psychopathology, emotional context of siblings and extended family, external stressors, and so on, can all go a long way in sorting out a proper diagnosis. Chronic stress negatively impacts frontal lobe functioning and can result in memory impairment, poor impulse control, and deficits of attention (Birnbaum et al., 1999).

## Summary

Executive functioning is a complex evolutionary accomplishment that we are still in the process of understanding. Many regions across the prefrontal regions and throughout the cortex contribute to our abilities to focus, organize our thoughts, regulate our emotions, and create the experience of self. Head injury, ADHD, and other psychiatric illnesses provide selective insight into the results of dysregulation or loss of neural networks central to executive processing. As our knowledge of neural networks expands, perhaps we gain a greater understanding of how the mind emerges from the wetware of the brain.

# Chapter 8

# Consciousness and Reality

*People are accustomed to look at the heavens and to wonder what happens there. It would be better if they would look within themselves . . .*

—Kotzker Rebbe

At the heart of psychotherapy are two interwoven processes; the first is the way in which our brains and minds construct reality, while the second is our ability to modify these constructions to support mental health and well-being. In other words, why are we so vulnerable to constructing distorted realities, and how can we learn to counterbalance these distortions? People come to therapy because one or more aspects of their lives are not how they would like them to be. Most often our clients know what they should be doing differently but cannot bring themselves to make changes. They come in with a feeling that something within them is holding them back. The answers to their questions can usually be found in the architecture of the hidden layers of neural processing—those networks within the brain that construct our reality, guide our experience, and shape our identity.

Prior to my training as a clinical psychologist, I spent many years studying the beliefs and practices of Eastern religions. One of the first things I discovered was that Buddhism is less akin to Western religious traditions than to the analytic introspection of William James or the self-analysis of Sigmund Freud. At the core of Buddhist teachings is the belief that the experience of world and self are illusions (Maya) and that our minds and senses fool us into attributing significance to things that are, in themselves, devoid of meaning. In other words, "reality" is a construction of the mind which we take to be an external truth. So, at the heart of both dynamic psychotherapy and Buddhism is the fundamental belief that our conscious experience is a creative fiction subject to distortion.

Although controversial, the way in which the brain generates consciousness, including its many distortions, may have been subject to the pressures of natural selection. That is, our creative fictions may be sculpted to enhance survival rather than to maximize perceptual accuracy. While the way in which our brains construct consciousness and reality may have some survival advantages, we turn our focus here to those aspects which impair our relationships and limit self-insight. You will soon see that the take-home message from psychoanalysis, Buddhism, and neuroscience is to be a skeptical consumer of the offerings of your mind.

## Beware of Maya

*We don't see things as they are; we see things as we are.*

—Anaïs Nin

Let's begin by taking a look at some of the illusions of consciousness through which we construct reality. The first is that our conscious awareness comes together at some specific location within our heads and is presented to us on a screen. This Cartesian theater—an homage to Descartes's articulation of mind–body dualism—creates the subjective illusion of self as a nonphysical spirit inhabiting the body as opposed to being one with it (Dennett, 1991). This spirit, some religions believe, can leave the body upon death, go to heaven, or occupy a new body in the next life.

A second illusion is that our experience occurs in the present moment and that conscious thought and decision making precede feelings and actions. In fact, our brains react to internal and external stimuli in as little as 50 milliseconds, yet it takes more than 500 milliseconds for conscious awareness to occur. During this half-second, hidden layers of neural processing shape and organize these stimuli, trigger related networks, and select an appropriate presentation for conscious awareness (Panksepp, 1998). Although we tend to think of our brains as processing information from the environment, the vast majority of the input to the cerebral cortex comes from what is already inside the brain. And because our senses are shaped by experience, they are also silent contributors to the construction of reality (Gibson, 1966).

The projection onto the screen of our Cartesian theater is actually generated within the hidden layers of our neural architecture prior to conscious awareness. This leads us to assume that the world of our experience and the objective world are one and the same. We also tend to believe that we have all the necessary information we need to make choices. In truth, we often have little or no access to the information or logic upon which we base our decisions. In addition, we possess a powerful reflex to confabulate in the absence of knowledge (Bechara, Damasio, Tranel, & Damasio, 1997; Lewicki, Hill, & Czyzewska 1992). What we call intuition is likely the result of rapid and unconscious processing that can be so surprising to us that it is often attributed to occult knowledge or psychic powers.

A third illusion, which relies on the first two, is that our thoughts and behaviors are under conscious control (Bargh & Chartrand, 1999; Langer, 1978). This hubris leads us to consistently overestimate the authority we have over an outcome, while underestimating the role of chance, unconscious influences, and outside forces (Taylor & Brown, 1988). So although we may feel as if we are at the wheel of our lives, it might be more accurate to say that most of us are trying to steer our lives with the rearview mirror.

The illusions of the Cartesian theatre, living in the present moment, and being in total control of our actions can be successfully exposed on cognitive and neurological grounds. Yet the ubiquity of many perceptual and cognitive distortions in everyday human interaction, provides convincing evidence for the existence of nonconscious processing (Levy, 1997). And unlike bothersome psychological symptoms, these illusions and distortions are invisibly woven into the warp and woof of our perception, memory, and character (Reich, 1945).

By definition, hidden layers of neural processing cannot be directly observed. Like black holes, we are made aware of their existence by their effects upon the visible world. Hidden layers can make the same situation a source of pleasure or dread, acceptance or rejection, pride or shame. They will highlight some aspects of experience while diminishing others, orient us to certain aspects of the environment, and completely block awareness of others. Our hidden layers translate past experience into an anticipated future, converting past trauma into a self-fulfilling prophecy of future suffering (Brothers, 1997; Freyd, 1987; Ingvar, 1985). This carryover of past learning into the present where it may be irrelevant or destructive is certainly one of the contemporary human brain's major design flaws.

## Perceptual Biases and Self-Deception

*The most erroneous stories are those we think we know best—and therefore never scrutinize or question.*
—Stephen Jay Gould

The consistency of many perceptual and cognitive biases across individuals reflects our shared neural organization and functioning. Some of these biases are the result of natural limits to our perspective and judgment, while others may have evolved to help us cope with living in an uncertain and dangerous world. Although many of our perceptual biases appear to serve us, they can also lead to the kinds of problems that often become the focus of psychotherapy.

Social psychologists have identified a number of consistent errors in human judgment that can be especially damaging to relationships among individuals, groups, and nations. Our tendency to explain the behavior of others based on aspects of their character, while explaining our own behaviors as a result of external factors, is referred to as the *fundamental attribution error* (Heider, 1958). In other words, others flunk tests because they are not smart enough or are too lazy to study; we fail because the test wasn't fair or because the professor wasn't very good. An extension of this attributional bias leads to a phenomenon called *blaming the victim*, where individuals victimized by crime or poverty are believed to have done something to create their misfortune (Ryan, 1971).

While individual perspectives are limited and incomplete, this does not stop us from assuming that we possess the true view of the world. This *egocentric bias* leads us to reflexively believe that anyone who sees the world differently from ourselves is misguided or dull-witted. Unfortunately, it also leads mortal enemies to both believe that God is on their side. While an egocentric bias is reflexive and self-evident, maintaining a balanced perspective requires sustained mindful effort.

Another bias organized within our hidden layers is called *belief perseverance*—the tendency to attend to facts supportive of existing beliefs while ignoring others (Lord, Ross, & Lepper, 1979). The hidden layers are conservative, holding onto thoughts, feelings, and behaviors that have been associated with past survival (Janoff-Bulman, 1992). Thus, we scan for examples that prove preexisting beliefs and ignore ones which contradict them. This tendency is likely driven by the tenacity of fear memories stored within the amygdala and our desire to avoid the possibility of danger in the unknown. This may explain why prejudices continue to persist in the face of conflicting evidence.

One reason that our abilities of self-deception may have been selected during evolution is because they aid in the deception of others. The more we believe our own deceptions, the less likely we are to give away our real thoughts and intentions via nonverbal signals. In fact, it requires considerable more brain power to lie than to tell the truth, and even more to convince others that we are being honest with them when we are lying (Ganis et al., 2003). Good poker players raise the skill of social deception to an art by keeping a poker face while learning the "tells" of their opponents. Actions and beliefs that are the opposite of our true desires can be quite effective in deceiving others. It has also been noted that "people are remarkably reluctant to consider impure motives in a loud moralist" (Nesse & Lloyd, 1992, p. 611) despite the repeated and well-publicized downfall of one moral crusader after another. In fact, the best con artists are often so convincing that their victims refuse to accept that they have been cheated at all.

The distortions of the psychodynamic unconscious—reflected in defense mechanisms such as reaction formation, denial, humor, and intellectualization—are thought to keep thoughts and feelings out of conscious awareness to help us regulate negative emotions. Defense mechanisms may enhance survival by reducing shame, minimizing anxiety, and decreasing awareness of depressing and demoralizing realities. Some defenses also support social cooperation and lead us to either overlook or put a positive spin on the bad behavior of family and friends. Freud recognized that we can see the workings of defense mechanisms and other aspects of the unconscious in the way that we organize and understand ambiguous stimuli. In a condition of reduced external structure, our hidden layers organize the world, make predictions, and highlight certain thoughts and feelings while ignoring others. You may remember that Freud referred to this phenomenon as the projective hypothesis.

Therapists employ the projective hypothesis to explore the architecture of their clients' unconscious. Some try to remain as neutral as possible to allow clients to project feelings and thoughts onto them in a process referred to as transference. In a similar manner, projective tests like the Rorschach present ambiguous stimuli to evoke idiosyncratic perceptions of the material. Finally, because of their uninhibited nature, Freud was impressed with the value of dreams in providing us with insight into hidden layers, calling them "the royal road to the unconscious."

Most forms of psychotherapy attempt to shine the light of conscious awareness on belief perseverance and attribution biases, and undermine the conservative nature of the hidden layers. Others engage in a deep exploration of the dynamic unconscious, defenses, and primitive emotional states. By encouraging clients to be open to new ideas, explore the connections within their hidden layers, and take responsibility for positive change, we challenge them to reorganize the neural networks of their hidden layers.

## Searching for the Still Point

> *Men are disturbed not by things, but by the view which they take of them.*
> —Epictetus

By now it is clear that our brains are in the business of constructing rather than conveying reality. This perspective is in sharp contrast to the modern Western notion of the brain as a combination camera, tape recorder, and computer. If our electronic equipment really did function like our brains, we would replace them at the first opportunity. But I'm sure you would agree that, imperfect as they are, we would take our brains over a machine any day. Few of us would want to sacrifice feelings of love, inspiration, and passion for the sake of accuracy or efficiency.

Once we wake up to how our brains work, what do we do? How can we overcome or at least cope with our distortions, impulses, and unconscious drives in constructive and healthy ways? Fortunately, our brains contain structures and networks that allow us to counteract some of the more problematic workings of our hidden neural layers. Let's begin an exploration of the evolution of consciousness with ice cream.

I'm a person who has been on a diet all my life with limited success. I could do well all day—eat properly and exercise—but at night, I would seem to have no self-control. I would go into each day feeling bad about the night before and vow to do better, only to fail again. Years into therapy I mentioned this in a session and was given the following suggestion: "Pay attention to your thoughts, feelings, and fantasies during the transition from doing well to your loss of control." It turned out that, depending on the day, I felt exhausted, stressed, lonely, or dissatisfied with one thing or another on these evenings. When my therapist asked what I did with these negative and painful feelings, I was stumped. I didn't remember doing anything with them—they seemed to just dissolve. As I struggled to make sense of this process, I recalled a vivid memory.

I was a young boy of 5 or 6 standing in my grandmother's kitchen and had just expressed being upset about something. I could feel my unhappiness expressed in the muscles of my face and recall my grandmother's face mirroring mine. Without saying a word she pivoted around, opened the freezer, took out a large box of Neapolitan ice cream (chocolate, vanilla, and strawberry in three neat rows), tore off the cardboard tab holding the lid closed, buried a spoon in the ice cream, and handed me the entire box. Also without a word I went to the sofa, lay down, put the quart of ice cream on my chest and began eating. In fact there were no words at all. There was no memory of discussing how I felt. Whatever bad feelings I may have been having quickly dissolved in a haze of glucose.

The similarity of this memory to my experience in my adult life was striking. My hidden layers had learned a pattern—feel tired, sad, stressed, or disappointed; get lots of calories; watch TV; and the feelings pass. These early memories were encoded in hidden layers and guided my behavior when triggered by similar states of mind. Being the first grandchild in an extended family that had experienced a great deal of sadness and loss, I realize in retrospect that no one could cope with my sadness. I was the hope for a better future where there would be no pain. Having no language with which to process my feelings, I could only deal with them through actions. As long as I continued to act this process out without awareness of what was happening, it continued in a stereotyped manner much like a posttraumatic flashback.

What is it that allows us to become self-aware, generate explanations, and modify long-standing ways of being? How do we expand conscious awareness in ways that allow us to change? Obviously, something has to change in the way our brains process information when we benefit from psychotherapy. Let's explore two central regions involved in awareness and change—the prefrontal and parietal cortices.

Because behavior is easily observable, neurologists have traditionally focused on the manifest results of brain injury such as deficits in language, motor behavior, and memory. At the same time, there has been significant confusion and misunderstanding when it comes to changes in subjective experience. I have worked with many clients who perform within normative ranges on objective tests of memory and intellect, but complain that their inner worlds are no longer the same. Some use the metaphor of a house and say that some rooms are no longer accessible to them. Others have described blackboards they could use to work out problems that have been lost. These subtle and elusive aspects of human experience have received little attention from neurologists. What is even more difficult for clients is to perform well on objective tests of memory and problem solving, and be told that they have fully recovered, when in fact they know better. Their use of three-dimensional metaphors like houses and blackboards to describe inner experience may be telling. Is the house as an archetype for the self (as Carl Jung suggested) more than myth?

How does the brain achieve conscious awareness? Where is the seat of consciousness? The answer to both of these questions is that we don't yet know. At this point, we must be satisfied with discovering pieces of this complex puzzle of consciousness that will be assembled sometime in the future. Because executive problems often arise after damage to the prefrontal areas, it is generally assumed that consciousness and self-awareness reside within these regions, but the key to understanding consciousness extends beyond the frontal lobes. We can be somewhat confident that consciousness emerges from the coordination of many processes throughout the brain and that the prefrontal lobes are major players. I would suggest that another major contributor to our conscious experience is our parietal lobes. Let me explain why.

## The Parietal Lobes

*The soul never thinks without a mental picture.*

—Aristotle

You may remember that the parietal lobes evolved from the hippocampus which, in lower mammals and humans, organizes an internal three-dimensional map of the external environment (Joseph, 1996; O'Keefe & Nadel, 1978). This is especially useful in navigating a habitat for foraging, storing, and retrieving food. The hippocampi of mother rats actually increase in size when they have babies, in preparation for having more mouths to feed. The hippocampi of cab drivers in London are larger than those of other Londoners, because of their need for a detailed inner map of a large and complicated city (Maguire, Woollett, & Spiers, 2006). It seems that the parietal lobes developed a parallel capacity for constructing and navigating a map of internal, imaginal space.

Curiously, some studies of primate brain evolution suggest that expansion of the parietal and not the frontal lobes is most characteristic of the transition to the human brain (von Bonin, 1963). Could the fact that we don't think of the parietal lobes as a component of the executive brain reflect a cultural bias of equating individuals with their external behavior rather than the quality of their inner experiences? The parietal lobes' interconnections with the rest of the cortex allowed for the integration of working visual memory, attentional capacities, and bodily awareness necessary for these imaginal abilities. This suggests that our self-awareness was likely built in a stepwise manner during evolution through a series of overlapping "maps"—first of the physical environment, then of self in environment, and later of self as environment. Thus, the growth of imaginal abilities allowed us to create an increasingly sophisticated inner topography.

The lower parts of the parietal lobes develop through the first decade of life in parallel with our increasing abilities in reading, calculations, working memory, and three-dimensional manipulation (Joseph, 1996; Klingberg, Forssberg, & Westerberg, 2002; Luna, 2004). Cells in these inferior parietal regions respond to hand position, eye movement, words, motivational relevance, body position, and many other components of the integration of physical experience in space. Left parietal damage disrupts mathematical abilities while damage to the right parietal lobe results in disturbances of body image and the neglect of the left side of the body. Despite these florid and debilitating symptoms, patients are either oblivious to or deny the significance of their deficits, which suggests that the parietal lobes serve an executive role in the organization of self-awareness. Damage to the parietal lobes disrupts the experience of location, self-organization, and identity—in other words, who and where we are (see Table 8.1).

TABLE 8.1
Manifestations of Parietal Compromise

*Left Parietal Compromise Results In*

Gerstmann syndrome, which includes the following symptoms:
  Right-left confusion
  Digital agnosia (inability to name the fingers on both hands)
  Agraphia (inability to write)
  Acalculia (inability to calculate)[1]
The symptoms of Gerstmann syndrome are linked through a unitary deficit in spatial orientation of body—sides, fingers, and numbers[2]

*Right Parietal Compromise Results in Deficits Of*

| | |
|---|---|
| Mental imagery and movement representations[3] | Detecting apparent motion[9] |
| Visual-spatial awareness[4] | The analysis of sound movement[10] |
| Visual-spatial problem solving[5] | Spatial-temporal abnormalities[11] |
| Temporal awareness and temporal order[6] | Contralateral neglect of the body and external space[12] |
| Spatial perception[7] | Denial of hemiparalysis and neglect[13] |
| Somatosensory experience[8] | |

The posterior parietal regions weave together sensory information about our physical environment with networks of organized motoric actions and intentions which (along with the frontal lobes) create goal-directed action plans (Anderson, Snyder, Bradley, & Xing, 1997; Colby & Goldberg, 1999; Medendorp, Goltz, Crawford, & Vilis, 2005). In combination with episodic and working memory, this would provide a work space for decision making about whether or not to perform an action—should I eat the ice cream or is something else going on that I should pay attention to? Utilizing these abilities, a frontal-parietal network could support the integration of perception and action over time (Quintana & Fuster, 1999).

Parietal activation occurs during a wide variety of cognitive tasks, suggesting that high-level association areas involved in the coordination of sensory and motor processing underlie what we experience as abstract (nonphysical) processes (Culham & Kanwisher, 2001; Jonides et al., 1998). It is likely that evolution has used these core visual-spatial networks to serve as an infrastructure for language and higher cognitive processes (Klingberg et al., 2002; Piazza et al., 2004; Simon et al., 2002). The parietal lobes participate in our conscious awareness of visual experience, voluntary actions, and a sense of agency during actions (Chaminade & Decety, 2002; Decety et al., 2002; Rees, Kreiman, Koch, 2002; Sirigu et al., 2003). The multimodal representation of space in the posterior parietal areas integrates our goal-directed behavior and attention with higher cognitive functions (Andersen et al., 1997; Bonda et al., 1996; Corbetta & Shulman, 2002; Culham & Kanwisher, 2001).

Like the frontal lobes, areas of the parietal lobes become activated by novelty and appear to be involved in coding intentions and calculating the probability of success (Platt & Glimcher, 1999; Snyder, Batista, & Andersen, 1997; Walsh, Ashbridge, & Cowey, 1998). These findings point to the fact that the parietal lobes are far more than sensory-motor association areas, but are involved in the deployment of attention, understanding the environment, and constructing the experience of self (see Table 8.2).

The medial parietal area can be conceptualized as the central structure for self-representation, self-monitoring, and a state of resting consciousness (Lou et al., 2004). Damage at the junction of the parietal and temporal lobes correlates with out-of-body experiences and a variety of other disturbances of identity and self (Blanke & Arzy, 2005). There is also evidence to suggest that the parietal lobes participate in the creation of internal representations of the actions of others within us (Shmuelof & Zohary, 2006). In other words, we internalize others by creating representations of them in our imaginations. This allows us to both learn from others and carry them with us when they are absent. These inner objects, as described in psychoanalysis, likely serve as the infrastructure of the construction and maintenance of our experience of self (Macrae et al., 2004; Tanji & Hoshi, 2001).

TABLE 8.2
**Functions of the Parietal Lobes**

| Hemisphere | Function |
|---|---|
| Right | Analysis of sound movement[1] |
| | General comparison of amounts[2] |
| | Attention[3] |
| | Self-face recognition[4] |
| Left | Verbal manipulation of numbers[5] |
| | Mathematics[6] |
| | Multiplication[7] |
| | Motor attention[8] |

**Bilateral Findings**

| | |
|---|---|
| Visual-spatial work space[9] | Controlling attention to salient event and maintaining attention across time[17] |
| Visual-spatial problem solving[10] | Preparation for pointing to an object[18] |
| Visual motion[11] | Grasping[19] |
| Construction of a sensory-motor representation of the internal world in relation to the body[12] | Movement of three-dimensional objects[20] |
| Internal representation of the state of the body[13] | A sense of "numerosity" defined as nonsymbolic approximations of |
| Verbal working memory[14] | quantities (l)[21] |
| Retrieval from episodic memory[15] | Processing of abstract knowledge[22] |
| Sequence and ordering of information in working memory[16] | Perspective taking (r)[23] |
| | Processing of social information (r)[24] |
| | Taking a third-person perspective (r)[25] |

(l) left hemisphere (r) right hemisphere

Some sort of frontal-parietal network appears to be essential to our experience of self. Neural fibers connecting the middle portions of these two areas appear to serve a general integrative function of linking right and left hemispheres, limbic and cortical structures, as well as anterior and posterior regions of the cortex (Lou et al., 2004). Frontal-parietal networks work together to analyze the context and location of specific variables, work to interrupt ongoing behavior, and direct attention to new targets (Corbetta & Shulman, 2002; Peers et al., 2005). Frontal-parietal circuits are also involved in the sustained focus and updating of information in working memory (Edin et al., 2007; Sauseng et al., 2005). They may together give rise to a global work space or central representation allowing for conscious working memory and self-reflection (Baars, 2002; Cornette, Dupont, Salmon, & Orban, 2001; Taylor, 2001).

The frontal-parietal network may be primarily responsible for the construction of the experience of self (Lou, Nowak, & Kajer, 2005). A properly functioning frontal-parietal network allows for the successful negotiation of our moment-to-moment survival and the ability to turn our attention to inner experience. A compromised or poorly developed prefrontal cortex can ensnare us in "a noisy and temporally constrained state, locking the patient into the immediate space and time with little ability to escape" (Knight & Grabowecky, 1995, p. 1368). Without the ability to reflect on and sometimes cancel reflexive motor and emotional responses, there is little freedom (Schall, 2001). A similar phenomenon can occur with anxiety, as in obsessive-compulsive disorder. When the medial frontal lobes are incapable of adequate affect regulation, victims become "stuck" to the environment or "stimulus bound" and unable to override reflexive reactions (Brown et al., 1994).

## Constructing a Self

*I never came to any of my discoveries through the process of*
*rational thinking.*
                                                    —Albert Einstein

Creating a quiet internal world allows for private thought, self-reflection, and traveling through time via episodic memory. Quiet moments can then serve as the grounds for mentalization, creativity, and consolidating the self (Winnicott, 1958). Victims of frontal brain injury lose this ability and are constantly distracted by sensory and emotional experience, are unable to maintain focus, and suffer deficits of imagination. These individuals become trapped in time, unable to disengage from the constant stream of sensations, emotions, and demands of their inner and outer worlds. Although they retain consciousness, for them, attention, concentration, affect regulation, and motivation become problematic, while higher level metacognitive processes become impossible.

Winnicott (1962) suggested that the ego and one's sense of self consolidate during the periods of quiescence when children feel safe and calm in the presence of their parents. Good-enough parenting scaffolds the child, allowing him or her to go "inside" and rest in imagination and the experience of self (Stern, 1985). This may serve as an important mechanism of the transmission of neural organization from parent to child. It is rare to find a child who is able to be still and centered and feel safe in the presence of chaotic adults. We believe that early caretaking builds and shapes the cortex and its relationships with the limbic system, which supports emotional regulation, imagination, and coping skills. To this we now must add the development of the parietal lobes in the construction of internal space.

As a child I had an imaginary retreat. I would close my eyes and picture the back of my grandmother's closet, always piled high with shoe boxes. Behind these boxes was a hidden door just large enough for me (but not an adult) to squeeze through. Once through the door, there was a flight of stairs leading up to a large room resembling a medieval laboratory, the kind with a resident sorcerer. This was a safe place for me—quiet and private—where I could imagine other worlds, reflect on life, and fantasize about the future. The evolution and expansion of the parietal lobes were likely essential to the emergence of this kind of imaginal self.

One study has shown that when experienced meditators engage in meditation, the frontal lobes become less active while the parietal lobes become more active, reflective perhaps of a shift from outer to inner attention (Newberg et al., 2001). Other studies have shown a shift to left hemisphere activation and stronger immune response with meditation (Davidson, Kabat-Zinn, et al., 2003). Interestingly, inferior regions of the right parietal lobe become activated when we witness others being still. This may explain how meditating on inanimate objects or statues of a tranquil Buddha may help us feel centered within ourselves (Federspiel et al., 2005). This may also be a part of internalizing calm parents as a model for self-reflection.

Johnson (1987) asserts that the experience of our bodies provides the internal basis for meaning and reasoning with our sense of numbers, quantity, and space growing out of bodily experience. The brain's ability to take our physical experience and use it metaphorically is the basis of imagination. For example, jumping down a slide may serve as a sensory-motor metaphor for falling in love. The child's experience of emerging from under the covers into the light of day provides a metaphor for religious enlightenment later in life. The balance provided by the vestibular system may be the model for psychological and emotional stability, and ultimately for leading a more balanced life (Frick, 1982). Physical metaphors provide a contextual grounding in time and space that helps us grasp our experience and may serve as an infrastructure of higher cognitive processes.

Albert Einstein, who did poorly in math during his formal education, went on to solve some of the universe's most complex mysteries. He intuited relationships between time, matter, and energy, which contributed to the development of atomic energy and brought us a step closer to understanding the workings of the universe. I remember my seventh grade math teacher praising us with the phrase "Little Einstein." As you can imagine, many neuroscientists were interested in having a look at Einstein's brain to see if and how it differed from yours and mine. In comparison to 91 other brains, Einstein's was different only in the size of the inferior parietal lobe (Witelson, Kigar, & Harvey, 1999). A subsequent examination of the same region revealed lower ratios of neurons to glial cells when compared to other areas of Einstein's brain as well as to the brains of other people (Diamond et al., 1966; Diamond, Scheibel, Murphy, & Harvey, 1985). It is highly likely that this enhanced neural-glial relationship enhanced neuronal activity and led to superior visual-spatial abilities (Nedergaard et al., 2003; Oberheim et al., 2006; Taber & Hurley, 2008).

These neuroanatomical findings are especially interesting in light of Einstein's reported use of mental imagery to solve complex conceptual problems. Einstein described translating numerical equations into images that he would manipulate in imagination, come up with solutions, and translate back into equations. This ability to conceptualize and manipulate three-dimensional objects in imagination appears to separate us from other primates and may be a uniquely human evolutionary accomplishment (Orban et al., 2006; Vanduffel et al., 2002). Based on his description of his problem-solving strategies and the findings concerning his brain, it is possible that Einstein's unusual parietal lobes may have been central to his genius.

Einstein's difficulty in navigating the simple demands of day-to-day life was notorious, making him the archetypical absent-minded professor. Interestingly, one study has shown that the volumes of the frontal and parietal lobes demonstrate significant negative correlation (Allen,

Damasio, & Grabowski, 2002). Being absent-minded may have been the price he paid for an overdeveloped parietal lobe. Research suggests that inner imaginal space enhances the possibility for creative problem solving, empathy, and compassion. Perhaps this is one of the reasons that Einstein turned his attention to world peace and other humanitarian concerns later in life.

## The Executive Brain in Psychotherapy

*All of our final decisions are made in a state of mind that is not going to last.*

—Marcel Proust

As stated earlier, the brain is an organ of adaptation, a process that continues for as long as we live. Given their role as high-level association areas sculpted by ongoing experience, the frontal and parietal lobes likely retain a great degree of neural plasticity. This plasticity and their joint roles in the synthesis of physical, social, and emotional information make these regions primary targets of psychotherapy. In line with this, psychotherapy requires that we step away from reflexive behavior and the immediate demands of the environment to reflect upon our experiences in sophisticated ways. Acting in instead of acting out provides us with the interpersonal and intrapsychic space to try on new truths. Consider my client, Sandy, who found herself trapped in a mysterious cycle of changing attitudes and moods.

Sandy came to therapy in her mid-40s with the usual concerns about relationships, family, and career. Although her mood was generally upbeat and positive, she occasionally came to sessions feeling irritable, deflated, and hopeless, leading me to think that she might be suffering from bipolar disorder. When I mentioned her fluctuating moods, she was distressed that they were noticeable to others. She told me that she had discounted their importance because they didn't seem to relate to events in her life, "just hormones I guess."

Once Sandy began to focus her attention on these moods, she reaffirmed that they seemed to come out of nowhere and disappear just as mysteriously. When she was down, she felt like a fraud, and planned to quit her job and leave her husband. "When I feel this way," she said, "I just lose the will to live." On further reflection she realized that these mood states had been part of her life for as long as she could remember—recalling instances as far back as elementary school.

We monitored and discussed her experiences through a number of mood cycles and engaged in considerable speculation about their origin. Her father was prone to moodiness and she had a maternal aunt who had a "nervous breakdown" decades earlier, which made us consider a genetic inheritance or modeling behaviors that she saw as a child. Sandy struggled to find thoughts, feelings, or events in her life that would precipitate them and discovered that they did not coincide with anything related to her work, family, menstrual cycle, exercise, or diet. All serious medical conditions were ruled out, her only physical complaint being her allergies and frequent sinus infections. On the outside chance there was some relationship between her use of antihistamines and her mood changes, we created a mood chart that included her use of medication.

Although we did not find any connection between mood and medication, it did turn out that she consistently lost her will to live a day or two before suffering a sinus infection. Her mood would then improve shortly after the onset of her respiratory symptoms and headaches. Once we made this connection, we waited for the next dip in mood to see if it would again be followed by a sinus infection. Sure enough, the same pattern emerged. Although we still did not know what affected her mood, the timing did suggest that it was related to the cycle of her allergies and sinus infections. Up to this point, our work together depended upon Sandy's ability to reflect on her experiences, analyze her reactions to situations, and think about her thinking. Now it was time to develop Sandy's memory for the future, and create some experiments focused on alternative plans and actions.

We decided to anticipate her next dip in mood with a new plan. We agreed that she would stop evaluating her life on days that she lost her will to live. She was not allowed to think about leaving her husband or her job, or assess her worth as a person. Instead, the mood dip would be a cue for her to go to the health food store, buy vitamin C and zinc tablets, and rearrange her schedule to reduce stress. She also made an appointment with a new allergist. In essence, her assignment was to remember the future in the present. Sandy had to remain mindful of the possibility that what she experienced as negative emotions was really a result of biological changes related to a physical illness and not a collapse of character or impending global catastrophe. We worked on developing a safe internal place for her to retreat to at these times, where she could soothe and comfort herself and focus on healing.

Over time, the association between sinus infections and mood changes held up—we had created a new narrative with far more explanatory power than the one it replaced. For some unknown reason, Sandy's biochemistry reacted to infection with a sharp drop in mood, most likely related to drops in serotonin and dopamine. The psychological depression experienced as a result of these changes led her to reinterpret, in a negative way, the value of all aspects of her existence. How she dealt with these feelings was neither pleasant nor adaptive. By being mindful of this process and using her frontal and parietal executive functions to associate experiences with new meanings, she was able to engage in different behaviors and create a better outcome. We had converted what usually led to an existential crisis into a trigger for enhanced self-awareness, self-care, and medical management.

Sandy needed to learn how to pay attention to her feelings, reflect on them with past experiences in mind, and follow a new plan of action contrary to old reflexive patterns. These important frontal functions allowed Sandy to escape from automatic and detrimental behaviors. She was able to modify stimulus-response connections by escaping the present moment both in therapy and then in her day-to-day life, first imagining and then executing a new scenario. As Sandy learned to understand the functioning and fluctuations of her brain, she was able to utilize executive functions and an imaginal self to gain insight, perspective, and change dysfunctional patterns of behavior.

## Summary

The exploration of human consciousness is a vast new frontier for neuroscience where there may always be more questions than answers. We know consciousness exists; we just have no idea of how it emerges from the functioning of the brain. An inherent challenge to this exploration will always be the conflict of interest involved when something is studying itself with all the bias and distortion that interferes with objective observation. There is no easy way around this.

# Chapter 9

# From Neural Networks to Narratives: The Quest for Multilevel Integration

*There is no greater agony than bearing an untold story inside you.*
—Maya Angelou

It appears that nature has retained a fundamental strategy of connecting things—be they neurons, neural networks, or individual people—into more complex organizations. As we zoom in to look at groups of neurons and zoom out to look at groups of people, the same basic principles of connectivity and homeostatic balance appear to hold true. As we learn about the necessary synergistic connectivity of neural networks, we are also coming to understand the relationship between network imbalance and mental distress. From extreme PTSD to everyday neurosis, we all exhibit a pattern of integration and dissociation reflective of our adaptational history and the health of our brains. At the level of the experience of self, networks dedicated to sensation, perception, and emotion seamlessly integrate into the emergence of conscious experience (Damasio, 1994; Pessoa, 2008; Fox et al., 2005). Let's take a look at the impact of a somewhat simple breakdown of neural network integration on the experience of self.

A few years ago, a young man in his late teens came in for a therapy session. The previous September, Craig had left home to attend his first year of college, but by mid-December, something had gone haywire. His parents were called by the dean and told that Craig had not been going to classes for weeks. They were also informed by the resident advisor that 5 days earlier, Craig had locked himself in his room, thrown all of his and his roommate's possessions out of the window, and was listening to the same song 24 hours a day. His parents raced to campus to find him in the middle of an acute psychotic episode.

Craig had been released from the hospital where I worked just a few weeks earlier and it was good to see him once again independent and active. As he walked across my office, I could see his movements were slowed by the medications that were keeping his hallucinations at bay. I had seen Craig in individual and group therapy for approximately a month. His symptoms had slowly cleared and he was released to his parents' care a week earlier. This was his first session since being discharged. After he settled in, I asked him how things had been going since he left the hospital. Slowly, and in a soft voice, he told me that life was pretty good and that he enjoyed playing his guitar and working on some new songs. He wasn't feeling paranoid or hearing voices like he had been weeks ago, his sleep and appetite were okay, and he felt like he was ready to return to school. "There's only one problem, Doc. I don't feel comfortable at home because my parents and brother have been replaced by doubles."

"Doubles?" I asked him. "What do you mean, doubles?"

Craig started by saying that he had gotten a strange feeling about his parents and brother when they came to visit him in the hospital, but he figured he was off because of the medication. But once he got home, he discovered the reason for his strange feelings. "After a while I realized that they've been replaced by doubles!" I gave him my best quizzical therapist expression and asked what made him think they were doubles. Craig described how they were excellent copies and well prepared to trick him. He asked them scores of questions he thought only his parents and brother could answer and, sure enough, they got them right. "Whoever is doing this to me is good!" he said with nervous admiration. When I asked him again how he could be so sure they were replacements, he replied with annoyance, "Don't you think I would know my own parents?"

This syndrome of suspecting impostors, called Capgras syndrome, can occur alone but usually appears in tandem with some other brain dysfunction such as schizophrenia, temporal lobe epilepsy, or head injury (Serieux & Capgras, 1909). Although the neurobiology of Capgras syndrome is not definitively understood, there has been ongoing speculation that it is a disconnection syndrome that somehow separates networks of perception, emotion, and conscious analysis (Alexander, Stuss, & Benson, 1979; Merrin & Silberfarb, 1979). An EEG study found "abundant and severe EEG abnormalities" in 21 Capgras patients in the area of the temporal lobes. This led the authors to suggest that the delusion of impostors may be caused by a "dysrhythmia" of brainwaves in networks responsible for matching faces with emotional familiarity (Christodoulou & Malliara-Loulakaki, 1981).

Capgras syndrome does not affect the neural networks responsible for recognizing familiar faces. Craig could see that these people he took for imposters were physically identical to his parents and brother. But Craig's experience was that they no longer felt like his parents—the emotional "glow" of recognition of loved and familiar people was missing (Hirsten & Ramachandran, 1997). We can hypothesize that a disconnection or lack of coherence occurrs between the circuits of the temporal lobes responsible for face recognition and the ompfc-amygdala axis, which would add the emotional reaction of seeing a loved one. With this connection somehow disrupted, Craig's still intact left hemisphere explanatory circuitry created a delusion of imposters; an explanation that is logical if you accept the experiential premise. The people in Craig's home looked and acted like his family, but without the usual input from the emotional circuitry responsible for the feeling of familiarity, his left hemisphere interpreter concluded that they must be imposters.

Most of us have felt the firing of these familiarity circuits in an exaggerated form when we unexpectedly run into a friend in an unusual place. Our shock of recognition leads to the inevitable, "Oh my God, what are you doing here?" Craig was experiencing what amounts to the opposite of this experience. He expected to have the feeling of recognition but didn't. This is probably what he was referring to when he said, "Don't you think I would know my own parents?" Capgras syndrome may well be the opposite of a déjà vu experience, where something which is actually new is paired with a feeling of familiarity. Déjà vu is likely a random firing of familiarity circuits in an unfamiliar setting. The fact that strong déjà vu experiences are often reported by patients with temporal lobe epilepsy suggests that their out-of-control electrical firing is activating the amygdala, which is deep within the temporal lobes.

The delusion of impostors generated by the left hemisphere interpreter may be similar to the attributions made about déjà vu experiences such as past lives, clairvoyance, and other paranormal beliefs. This very normal impulse to make sense of nonsense is also seen in schizophrenics, who attempt to create a logical explanation for their bizarre sensory experiences (Maher, 1974). In the face of experiencing thoughts being inserted in their heads, patients ask themselves, "Who would have the technology to do such a thing?" When I worked in Boston, patients pointed the finger at MIT, while the people I treated in Los Angeles suspected Cal Tech. Delusional beliefs can become quite central to a client's life as well as tenacious and difficult to dislodge. For example, when three patients, each of whom believed they were Christ, were housed together, each came to believe that the other two were delusional (Rokeach, 1964).

## Pathways of Integration

*All organs of an animal form a single system . . . and no modification can appear in one part without bringing about corresponding modifications in all the rest.*

—George Cuvier

The long and circuitous path of brain evolution has not provided us with a brain that is simple in function or straightforward in design. We have already seen how the brain consists of different memory systems, two hemispheres with different processing capabilities, and multiple executive systems controlling different skills and abilities. We have also explored how, when these systems get out of sync, psychotherapy attempts to reconnect and balance them.

Although we are just beginning to understand functions and the complexities of our neural pathways, some consistent findings are beginning to emerge. As we discussed in an earlier chapter, the two main pathways to consider are top-down and left-right. It is also important to always keep in mind that they are not independent of one another because top and left areas have developed certain special connections, as have the bottom (subcortical) and the right hemisphere. Another important point to keep in mind is that these top-down and left-right systems involve multiple structures along the way, each with its own unique contribution and potential role in network functioning. We should also add two more specific pathways, the relationships between regions within the frontal lobes (the ompfc and the dlpfc), and between the hippocampus and amygdala. These systems also have particular associations with both top-down and left-right integration.

Let's review the general map of the brain's pathways of integration. In Table 9.1, notice the alignment of these four pathways. Top-down, left hemisphere, dlpfc, and the hippocampus are aligned on the left because they tend to be connected more heavily with one another than with those in the column on the right. They also tend to be involved with conscious, rational, and language-based functions. Bottom-up processing, the right hemisphere, the ompfc, and the amygdala appear to have more dense connectivity among themselves and are more likely to be involved with unconscious, somatic, and emotional functions. So, for example, Capgras syndrome may reflect a disconnection of bottom-up emotional processing involving the amygdala and right hemisphere from the top-down and left hemisphere cognitive analysis of sensory experience.

### TABLE 9.1
### Pathways of Integration

| | |
|---|---|
| Top (cortical) | Bottom (subcortical) |
| Left hemisphere | Right hemisphere |
| dlpfc | ompfc |
| Hippocampus | Amygdala |

There is presently a great deal of research focused on breaking down these functional networks into finer and more precise distinctions and generating models of processing paths and organizational patterns. Separating the roles of each region of the brain in each hemisphere is also under exploration, as is the mapping of patterns of activation (instantiations) for different symptoms and diagnostic groups (Dougherty et al., 2004). As with all of this research, we have to keep in mind that age, gender, and life experiences all play a role in how these networks organize and function in each individual. For our present purposes, I have chosen to focus on these general categories because of their obvious applicability to psychotherapy and mental health.

## Top-Down–Bottom-Up

*The complexity of the nervous system is so great, its various association systems and cell masses so numerous, complex and challenging, that understanding will forever lie beyond our most committed efforts.*
—Ramon y Cajal

Although there are many vertical circuits that cut across the horizontal strata of the brain, important top-down networks for psychotherapists are those connecting the ompfc and amygdala. The ompfc and the amygdala are connected by dense bidirectional networks that feed physiological and emotional information upward to the cortex while allowing the ompfc to modulate the output of the amygdala to the autonomic nervous system (Ghashghaei & Barbas, 2002; Ghashghaei et al., 2007; Hariri et al., 2000, 2003). Think of the amygdala as a primitive structure designed to link immediate threat with a rapid survival response. Think of the ompfc as having the ability to gather and update information and use it to predict potential outcomes and shape behavior (Dolan, 2007; Rosenkranz, Moore, & Grace, 2003). Perhaps a good analogy is a squad of soldiers trained to fight and survive (amygdala and anatomic nervous system) and a general who is an expert strategist who continues to keep an eye on the entire battlefield, update his strategy, and adjust long-range goals (ompfc).

In the normally functioning brain, the balance of ompfc–amygdala activation reflects a dynamic moment-to-moment balance of focused attention and emotional arousal (Simpson, Drevets, et al., 2001; Simpson, Snyder, et al., 2001). When faced with a psychosocial stress, we see elevated cortisol levels along with increased activation in the amygdala and lower levels of activation in the ompfc (Kern et al., 2008). Higher levels of ompfc activity are believed to reflect an inhibition of affective processes and an enhanced focus on the outside world, while a decrease suggests a shifting of attention to internal processes. As negative affect decreases, so does amygdala activation, while activation in the ompfc increases (Urry et al., 2006). It is now believed that each of us has a unique homeostatic balance of this circuitry which shapes our emotional regulation and affective style (Davidson, 2002).

Let's think about what happens in the human brain during public speaking. For most individuals, getting up in front of a group to speak results in increased cortical activation. This makes sense because we need our cortex to process the cognitive demands of giving a talk. But when socially phobic individuals get up to speak, there is a decrease in cortical activity and an increase in amygdala firing along with bodily symptoms of anxiety and panic (Tillfors et al., 2001). This may help us understand the phenomenon of stage fright, where people either forget their lines or find it impossible to speak when faced with an audience. High levels of cortisol, dopamine, and bottom-up inhibition from the amygdala can all take the prefrontal cortex "off-line" during stress (Arnsten & Goldman-Rakic, 1998; Bishop, Duncan & Lawrence, 2004). This "amygdala hijack," as it is called in the self-help literature, is the takeover of executive functioning by the amygdala and other subcortical systems (Goleman, 2006).

The balance and integration of the ompfc and amygdala are influenced by everything including past trauma, current stress, and serotonin levels (Hariri, Drabant, & Weinberger, 2006; Heinz et al., 2005). When people suffer from symptoms of depression or anxiety, there is a general decrease in cortical activation and an increase in anterior regions of the cingulate and insula (Kennedy et al., 2007; Mayberg et al., 1999). This balance reverses as mood lightens with or without treatment (Kennedy et al., 2001). It has also been found that pretreatment metabolism in these and other regions predicts response to antidepressant medication (Davidson, Irwin, et al., 2003; Pizzagalli et al., 2001; Saxena et al., 2003; Whalen et al., 2008; Wu et al., 1999).

As we saw earlier, sadness and depression also reflect a left-right imbalance. Left-biased prefrontal activation downregulates negative affect in nondepressed individuals while depressed individuals show bilateral frontal activation (Johnstone et al., 2007). These findings highlight the fact that the modulation of mood is likely to occur simultaneously on multiple planes of homeostatic balance—top-down, left-right, and so on. Thus, a shift away from depression may reflect a dual regulatory shift from right and down to top and left activation. Keep in mind that conflicting results have also been found, so our understanding of these processes is still just developing (Holthoff et al., 2004).

Within this broad top-down system there are likely numerous subsystems involved in emotional regulation. Different studies have demonstrated a variety of activation patterns in broad top-down networks in tasks of affect regulation and the voluntary suppression of emotions (Anderson & Green, 2001; Beauregard, Lévesque, & Bourgouin, 2001; Phan et al., 2005). For example, the coordination of activity between the amygdala and the anterior cingulate has been shown to be correlated with trait anxiety and a susceptibility to depression (Pezawas et al., 2005). Suppressing cigarette craving correlates with increased activation in the cingulate cortex and an inhibition of sensory and motor regions as subjects respond to smoking-related stimulus cues (Brody et al., 2007).

The anterior cingulate, amygdala, and insula are modulated by the processing of internal somatic experience during biofeedback training while the anterior insula is involved with the interaction between the accuracy and sensitivity of the feedback (Critchley et al., 2002). This may be the same circuitry activated during therapy as we integrate conscious awareness with somatic, emotional, and memory processing. Simultaneous top-down and left-right inhibition is likely responsible for what Freud called repression. As prefrontal and anterior cingulate regions are inhibiting conscious recall of explicit memories, left frontal networks can be simultaneously inhibiting negative somatic and emotional memories stored in right-biased systems (Anderson & Green, 2001). The result would be a lack of conscious recall of a threatening experience and a dissociation of experience from conscious awareness.

### Left Hemisphere–Right Hemisphere

> *The interpretive mechanism of the left hemisphere is . . . constantly looking for order and reason, even when there is none—which leads it continually to make mistakes.*
>
> —Michael Gazzaniga

As we saw in an earlier chapter, left-right integration is required for proper language functioning, bodily awareness, emotional regulation, and many other essential human processes. As we will soon discuss, the emergence of storytelling and narrative structure as universal aspects of human culture may have emerged, in part, to assist in the integration and coordination of the two very different brains.

A greater left-hemisphere advantage in verbal processing has been shown to be a predictor of a more favorable outcome in cognitive-behavioral therapy (Bruder et al., 1997). This suggests that those individuals with more left-lateralized language abilities may also have stronger inhibitory capacities over emotional experience stored in the right. It has been shown that good readers have less interhemispheric connectivity and are better at processing rapidly changing sensory input (Dougherty et al., 2007). For some tasks, less integration and cooperation are an advantage, especially when speed or focus of attention are factors. Having the input of both hemispheres may be quite adaptive when we are solving complex social and emotional problems, but is likely to slow us down and make us stumble if we need to engage in fast and automatic behavior (Cozolino, 2008).

A form of treatment used to readjust right-left balance is transcranial magnetic stimulation (TMS). TMS is a noninvasive, painless technique for the stimulation and inhibition of neural firing. A coil of wires is placed on the scalp that generates a magnetic field strong enough to penetrate the skull. This magnetic field is transformed into current flow in the brain that temporarily excites or inhibits select areas, which can be applied either as a single pulse or repetitively (rTMS). Depending on its frequency, it either increases or decreases cortical excitability—fast rTMS increases activation while slow rTMS decreases it (Daskalakis, Christensen, Fitzgerald, & Chen, 2002).

In several studies, patients with treatment-resistant depression experienced symptomatic improvement after a series of fast rTMS treatments applied to the left prefrontal cortex (Pascual-Leone et al., 1996; George et al., 1997; Figiel et al., 1998; Teneback et al., 1999; Triggs et al., 1999). These repeated magnetic pulses to the left hemisphere may have increased activity and shifted the balance of mood in a more positive direction. Slow rTMS applied to the right prefrontal cortex resulted in similar improvements in depressive symptoms (Klein et al., 1999; Menkes et al., 1999). Slower frequency rTMS to the right prefrontal cortex was thought to inhibit right frontal functioning and have less adverse side effects (Schutter, 2009).

Studies of rTMS and depression lead us to the conclusion that the technique's ability to both stimulate the left hemisphere and inhibit the right hemisphere may prove equally useful in depressed patients. Current views take the position that restoring the balance between left and right prefrontal cortex activity is more important in treating depression than establishing clear increases in left-sided activity. If rTMS can have a positive effect on depressive symptoms, might it work in the reverse manner for mania? Studies in this area are less extensive, but findings do suggest some effectiveness of rTMS in the treatment of mania when it is applied at high frequency to the right prefrontal cortex (Belmaker & Grisaru, 1999; Grisaru et al., 1998; Michael & Erfurth, 2002; Saba et al., 2004). The procedure has been approved by Health Canada for clinical use but not in the United States, where its application is limited to clinical research.

## Dlpfc–Ompfc

*Modern Psychology takes completely for granted that behavior and neural function are perfectly correlated, that one is completely caused by the other. . . . It is quite conceivable that some day this assumption will have to be rejected.*

—Donald Hebb

As a whole, the prefrontal cortex sculpts experience and behavior through a complex array of inhibitory and excitatory activities (Knight, Staines, Swick, & Chao, 1999). You will recall that the prefrontal cortex is divided into four regions and that the dorsal and lateral regions tend to engage in coordinated activity as do the orbital and medial areas. Because of these connections they are often referred to as the dlpfc and ompfc. The location of prefrontal activation varies depending on the emotional salience of the task; the more emotional the task, the more ompfc activation—the more cognitively demanding a task, the more the dlpfc takes center stage (Goel & Dolan, 2003; Northoff et al., 2004; Schaefer et al., 2002). As the cognitive demands of a task increase, there is a decrease in activation not only in the ompfc, but also in the amygdala and anterior cingulate, which are closely linked to the ompfc (Pochon et al., 2002; Rushworth & Behrens, 2008). This is likely the reason why engaging in cognitive tasks, like word or math problems, often reduces anxiety.

The dlpfc exerts control over neural processing based on higher order rules (environmental context, prediction, etc.) while the ompfc does the same from the perspective of lower order rules (impulse, drives, emotions, etc.). From this we get the sense that top-down and bottom-up processing is interwoven with the balance of activation between the dlpfc and ompfc, respectively. Interestingly, when people make decisions congruent with implicit racial and gender biases, the ompfc and amygdala become more active, while the dlpfc shows more activity when we express beliefs that are incongruent with prejudice (Knutson, Mah,

Manly, & Grafman, 2007). This reflects what we already know—more primitive impulses drive prejudice while education and expanded perspective allow us to go beyond our reflexive limitations.

Experiencing the world from a first-person perspective and tasks of self-regulation activate ompfc regions while situation-focused regulation activates dlpfc systems (Ochsner et al., 2004). The ompfc becomes involved in diverse tasks that require differing kinds and degrees of self-referential knowledge (Ochsner et al., 2005). Within the ompfc, the decoding of the mental states of others based on observable cues such as facial expressions may rely on the right ompfc while reasoning about their mental states may be lateralized to the left ompfc (Sabbagh, 2004). When we consider the types of issues brought into psychotherapy, it is likely that we are working to build, integrate, and balance the ompfc and dlpfc.

Consider what we do when we assist clients in shifting from their own perspective to looking at a situation from another point of view, to thinking about the situation once again from a more objective perspective. We are calling upon the ompfc and dlpfc in different ways as we attempt to guide them to a more holistic perspective of a life situation. This process most likely enhances the growth of ompfc and dlpfc systems, while building new brain networks to bridge the two for higher level awareness. Optimal functioning necessitates coordination, flexibility, and complementarity between these modes of functioning. When the ompfc and dlpfc are in proper balance, they create the possibility of true cognitive-emotional integration (Gray et al., 2002). In situations of stress and trauma the ompfc and dlpfc are capable of either mutual dissociation or inhibition (Roberts & Wallis, 2000). An inability of the ompfc to modulate stress will result in a decrease of activation in the dlpfc during a cognitive memory task and cause a performance deficit (Dolcos & McCarthy, 2006; Drevets & Raichle, 1998). Building strong connections between ompfc-dlpfc circuits creates resilience to stress and a hedge against resorting to dissociation, as well as greater affect tolerance and ego strength.

## Hippocampus–Amygdala

*Emotions have taught mankind to reason.*
—Marquis De Vauvenargues

The hippocampus and amygdala both play central roles in learning and memory. The amygdala (in connection with the ompfc) organizes emotional experience and (in moderate states of arousal) signals the hippocampus about what is important to learn. On the other hand, the hippocampus (along with the dlpfc) participates in the cognitive evaluation of situations that will inform the amygdala when to ramp up or back down on its emotional reaction. In other words, I can see that the dog is wagging his tail so perhaps I don't need to be as afraid of being bitten. Since the activation of emotion and the cognitive analysis of experience are both necessary for normal functioning, the proper regulatory balance of the hippocampus and amygdala is vital.

The hippocampus is necessary for forming new explicit memories while the amygdala organizes highly stressful and traumatic learning. At low levels of arousal, amygdala activation supports hippocampal learning by boosting the biochemical aspects of neural plasticity. At higher levels of arousal, the amygdala stimulates HPA activation, which interrupts hippocampal learning while supporting fear-based amygdala learning (Kim, Koo, Lee, & Han, 2005; Kim, Lee, Han, & Packard, 2001). In essence, during states of high arousal, hippocampal and amygdala networks become dissociated, resulting in a disconnection between visceral-emotional (amygdala) and declarative-conscious (hippocampal) processing (Williams et al., 2001). Thus, optimal learning requires a balance of amygdala and hippocampal participation.

Many people, perhaps even the majority of clients in psychotherapy, do not come for treatment of a major psychiatric illness. Most clients who are somewhat "less ill" have so far not been included in extensive (and expensive) outcome research that includes brain imaging studies. Many people seek psychotherapy simply because, as they often say themselves, life has somehow gotten out of balance. This may mean that their fears and worries have taken control of their lives and limited their ability to function or find happiness in the world. Others find themselves devoid of emotion and without empathy for others, leading them to seek therapy to save their marriages and relationships with their children. Many have the sense that they are not living up to their potential or get in their own way when it comes to worldly success and emotional satisfaction.

These clients are often referred to as the "worried well," implying that they should somehow get over themselves and get on with life. My sense is that this group of patients, in which I would include myself, also suffer various versions of a homeostatic imbalance. An exaggerated reliance on intellectual defenses, overemotionality, or a negative attachment experience can become established as self-perpetuating patterns that lead to social isolation and underperformance. All of these suboptimal lifestyles are most likely reflected in biased patterns of neural activation, which become the focus of psychotherapy. While psychotherapy is a relatively recent and culture-specific development in human history, talking to one another, seeking out advice, and exchanging stories likely go back to the first humans. Thus, the talking cure exists within a matrix of beings who share the gift of gab. I suggest to you that the evolution of the brain and the development of narratives have gone hand in hand.

## From Neural Networks to Narratives

*[Words] leave finger marks behind on the brain, which in the twinkling of an eye become the footprints of history.*
—Franz Kafka

The evolution of the human brain is inextricably interwoven with the expansion of culture and the emergence of language. Thus, it is no coincidence that human beings are storytellers. Through countless generations, humans have gathered to listen to stories of the hunt, the exploits of their ancestors, and morality tales of good and evil. It has long been supposed that these stories support the transmission of culture while promoting psychological and emotional stability. Stories connect us to others, prop up our often fragile identities, and keep our brains regulated. Thus, I believe that both the urge to tell a tale and our vulnerability to being captivated by one are deeply woven into the structures of our brains.

Narratives perform an array of important functions including:

- Grounding our experience in a linear sequential framework
- Remembering sequences of events and steps in problem solving
- Serving as blueprints for emotion, behavior, and identity
- Keeping goals in mind and establishing sequences of goal attainment
- Providing for affect regulation when under stress
- Allowing a context for movement to self-definition.

For most of human history, oral communication and verbal memory were the medium and repository of our accumulated knowledge. The ongoing value of stories to each of us is highlighted in today's world by the energy we invest in television, movies, magazines, and everyday gossip. The drive of older folks to repeatedly tell the same stories is matched by the desire of young children to hear them again and again. This interlocking conduit of culture across generations carries memories, ideas, and ideals through time. The importance of narratives in human evolution is further underscored by the fact that our ability to remember and recall stories is essentially limitless. In fact, the astonishing abilities of memory experts rely on placing discrete pieces of information into narratives that expand the capacity of working memory to the limits of their imagination.

Although stories may appear imprecise and unscientific (Oatley, 1992), they serve as powerful tools for high-level neural network integration (Rossi, 1993). The combination of a linear storyline and visual imagery woven together with verbal and nonverbal expressions of emotion activates and utilizes dedicated circuitry of both left and right hemispheres, cortical and subcortical networks, the various regions of the frontal lobes, and the hippocampus and the amygdala. The cooperative and interactive activation involved in stories may be precisely what is required for sculpting and maintaining neural network integration while allowing us to combine our sensations, feelings, and behaviors with conscious awareness. Further, stories link individuals into families, tribes, and nations and into a group mind linking each individual brain. It is likely that our brains have been able to become as complex as they are precisely because of the power of narratives and the group to support neural integration.

Much of neural integration takes place in the association areas of the frontal, temporal, and parietal lobes, which serve to coordinate, regulate, and direct multiple neural circuits. They are our conscious switchboard operators, able to use language and stories to link the functioning of systems throughout the brain and body. An inclusive narrative structure provides the executive brain with the best template and strategy for the oversight and coordination of the functions of mind. A story well told, containing conflicts and resolutions, gestures and expressions, and thoughts flavored with emotion, connects people and integrates neural networks.

## A Story Well Told

*Man's mind, once stretched by a new idea, never regains its original dimensions.*

—Oliver Wendell Holmes

Have you have ever watched the faces of small children as they listen to a gifted storyteller? You can see the unfolding drama reflected in their eyes, on their faces, and throughout their bodies. Listeners will experience a range of drastically shifting emotions, be absorbed in every detail, and even shout out warnings to characters in danger. Narratives allow us to place ourselves within alternate points of view and increase our understanding of the experience of ourselves and others. We can escape our bodies in imagination to other possible selves, ways of being, and worlds that have yet to be created.

Through stories we have the opportunity to ponder ourselves in an objective way across an infinite number of contexts. In life and in therapy, we can use stories to imagine our problems happening to someone else or view ourselves at a distance (externalization). We can share versions of possible selves and receive input from others. Finally, we can experiment with new emotions, actions, and language to edit the scripts of our lives (Etchison & Kleist, 2000). Our ability to edit narratives summons us to try on new ways of being. (Recall the case of Sheldon and his magic tricycle.)

What makes for a good story? Why can I sit through *Pretty Woman* or *A Few Good Men* over and over again, even though I know exactly how they end? If you take a screenwriting class you learn that there is a formula for successful narrative structure. Every story needs a hero, a protagonist with whom we can identify. The protagonist is facing an external challenge and possesses an inner wound that causes him persistent pain. For both Richard Gere and Tom Cruise, this pain came from their emotional estrangement from their fathers. At first the hero either avoids the challenge or fails, leading him to question his ability to succeed or even his desire to change. The challenge confronting the hero is at first resisted, then rejected, and eventually accepted. During the journey, the hero leaves behind old definitions of self and travels into uncharted territory. Some inner transformation takes place that allows him to face his demons, succeed in his worldly challenge, and solidify his identity. Richard Gere accepts Julia Roberts and Tom Cruise faces down Jack Nicholson.

This is essentially the universal Myth of the Hero, describing the transition from adolescence to adulthood (Campbell, 1949). Redemption—a word commonly used for this transition—can happen at any age. The adolescent struggling to attain adult status, the emotionally shut-down Scrooge faced with his history of loss, or a client trying to make sense of early deprivation have, at their core, a wound that needs healing. My explanation would be that what we share in common—brain, culture, language, and the fight for growth and survival—are the underlying motives of the heroic narrative. Another way of saying this is that what we share in our common struggle for survival and meaning is deeper and more powerful than those things which make us appear different.

## Narratives and Emotional Regulation

*Good psychiatry is a blend of science and story.*
—Jeremy Holmes

As the language areas of the left hemisphere enter their sensitive period during the middle of the second year of life, grammatical language in the left integrates with the interpersonal and prosodic elements of communication already well developed in the right. As the cortical language centers mature, words are joined together to make sentences and can be used to express increasingly complex ideas flavored with emotion. As the frontal cortex continues to expand and connect with more neural networks, memory improves and a sense of time slowly emerges and autobiographical memory begins to connect the self with places and events, within and across time. The emerging narratives begin to organize the nascent sense of self and become the bedrock of our sense of self in interpersonal and physical space.

As our experience of self and the stories we tell about ourselves become interwoven, self-identity becomes the center of narrative gravity (Dennett, 1991). As children we are told by others, and gradually begin to tell others, who we are, what is important to us, and what we are capable of. These self-stories are shaped by culture and co-constructed with parents and peers. And although it does sometimes seem that children are little scientists discovering the world, what we often miss is that they are primarily engaged in discovering what the rest of us already know, especially about them (Newman, 1982). This serves the continuity of culture from one generation to the next as we reflexively strive to recreate ourselves.

The role of language and narratives in neural integration, memory formation, and self-identity makes them a powerful tool in the creation and maintenance of the self (Bruner, 1990). Stories are powerful organizing forces that serve to perpetuate both healthy and unhealthy forms of self-identity. There is evidence that positive self-narratives aid in emotional security while minimizing the need for elaborate psychological defenses (Fonagy, Steele, Steele, Moran, & Higgitt, 1991). In the same way, anxious and traumatized parents pass along their negative experiences in the stories they tell. The recognition of the negative power of personal narrations containing negative self-statements stimulated the development of rational and cognitive-based therapies (Ellis, 1962). Let's look at the role of a positive narrative for a young boy.

Seven-year-old Trevor was brought to see me because his parents were concerned that he might have "something troubling him." He was very close to his grandfather who had passed away 6 months earlier, but he didn't seem to have a reaction to this loss. While his parents felt they had done everything they could to encourage him to talk about his feelings, he didn't have that much to say. Trevor seemed to be a normal kid with interests in science, video games, and computers. As he became comfortable, we hung out, played, and talked about all kinds of things. During our second session, he mentioned that he liked doing puzzles, so I purchased a few and brought them to the office.

Before our session, I spread one of the puzzles out on my desk. I put together a few pieces to give him a jump start and had to quell my own compulsive impulse to keep going. He was excited when he noticed it and asked if he could help me work on it. "Certainly," I said, and we sat down to a session of puzzling. It didn't take long for me to realize that he was having difficulty and I wondered if I had chosen one that was too difficult for him. The last thing I wanted to do was to give him a failure experience.

I offhandedly suggested that we didn't have to work on the puzzle if he would prefer to do something else. "Maybe this one is too hard for us," I said. "No," he replied, "don't give up. We'll get it." Impressed by his determination, we continued to move pieces around in search of colors and patterns. Every once in a while, I would leave a piece in front of him that I knew would fit with something he was holding. I became more and more amazed at his patience and dedication. Many boys his age would move on to something else or just clear the table with the swipe of an arm.

After a while, I heard Trevor mumbling under his breath. He was repeating something over and over like a song or mantra. I leaned over, slowly putting my ear closer and closer to him so I could make out his words. Finally I could hear, "I think I can, I think I can." He was chanting the theme of "The Little Engine That Could." He was the little train that kept on keeping on. I immediately felt my eyes well up and had to resist the urge to hug him. Sure enough, he slowly got the hang of it and made lots of progress.

I later found out from his parents that the Little Engine was his favorite story and one his grandfather loved to tell him. They told me he wanted to hear it exactly the same way each time and if they made a mistake on any word he would stop and correct them. It was clear that this Little Engine was a kind of hero to him, and he used it when he was stressed by a challenging situation to regulate his anxiety and keep himself moving ahead. Part of this heroic story was likely the memory of a loving grandfather whom he carried inside of him. The Little Engine became a way for us to share about his grandfather. Trevor was showing me the power of a story to soothe and inspire. I came to realize that his grandfather had done a wonderful job of becoming part of Trevor's experience of himself and preparing him for his death. I learned that Trevor's loss was complicated because, in many ways, he still had his grandfather with him. I believe that Trevor's ability to use narrative in this way and his internalization of his grandfather's love bode well for his healing.

To serve their important role in emotional regulation, narratives need to have a brief summary or hook that can be held in mind in the present moment. This summary, which can be a word, a phrase, a visual image, or even a gesture, can instantaneously evoke the beginning, middle, and end of the narrative, and especially its message. In Trevor's case, it was the phrase "I think I can." This decreased his anxiety, enhanced his problem solving, and allowed him to discover his true competence.

Putting feelings into words (affect labeling) has long served a positive function for many individuals suffering from stress or trauma. Labeling emotions correlates with decreased amygdala response and an increase in right prefrontal activation (Hariri et al., 2000). It has also been found that amygdala–right frontal activation are inversely correlated and that this homeostatic balance is mediated by the ompfc (Lieberman et al., 2007). This suggests that the labeling process may require both the lateral and medial prefrontal regions in order for cognitive processes to have a modulatory impact on our emotional activation (Johnstone et al., 2007). The narrative, which simultaneously activates an array of networks, enhances metabolic activity and neural balance.

The perception of control has been shown to reduce emotional arousal and stress. It is likely that cognitive processes involved in prediction and control activate frontal functioning and downregulate amygdala activation. In other words, thinking we have some control puts us in a state of mind that prepares us to think and activates prefrontal functioning, which reduces our emotionality. As a self-fulfilling prophecy, believing you are an efficacious person stimulates frontal activation, making you a more efficacious person (Maier et al., 2006).

Even writing about your experiences supports top-down modulation of emotion and bodily responses. In a large series of studies, James Pennebaker (1997) and others have instructed subjects to journal about emotional issues of personal importance, especially experiences related to close personal relationships. These studies have revealed increased well-being including a reduction in physical symptoms, physician visits, and work absenteeism (Pennebaker & Beall, 1986; Pennebaker, Kiecolt-Glaser, & Glaser, 1988). This sort of journaling has also been found to correlate with greater T-helper response, natural killer cell activity, and hepatitis B antibody levels as well as lower heart rate and skin conductance levels (Christensen et al., 1996; Petrie et al., 1995; Petrie, Booth, & Pennebaker, 1998). Journaling about emotional issues likely increases prefrontal activation, downregulating the negative emotional activation of the amygdala (Dolcos & McCarthy, 2006). Our ability to tame the amygdala (and the HPA axis) in this way results in a cascade of positive physiological, behavioral, and emotional effects.

## Levels of Language and Self-Awareness

*The less men think, the more they talk.*
                              —Baron de Montesquieu

Language is not one entity used for a single purpose. During the evolution of culture, types and uses of language expanded along with the sophistication of the brain. Through self-reflection, most of us become aware that we seem to shift back and forth among different perspectives, emotional states, and ways of using language. Introspection provides us with a window to shifts in states of mind that reflect the activation and integration of different neural networks. I am aware of at least three levels of language processing that take place within my clients and myself during these shifting states of mind; a reflexive social language, an internal dialogue, and a language of self-reflection.

*Reflexive social language* (RSL) is a stream of words that services the maintenance of ongoing social relatedness and communication. Primarily a function of left hemisphere processing, RSL mirrors activity within the interpersonal world and is designed to grease the social wheels. Verbal reflexes, clichés, and overlearned reactions in social situations provide a loose but meaningful web of connections. Most of us experience this whenever we automatically say something positive to avoid conflict, or tell people we are fine regardless of what's troubling us. The natural clichés of RSL are as automatic to us as walking and breathing. This level of language serves the same purpose as grooming in most types of primates.

In addition to RSL, we are also aware of the conversations we seem to carry on with ourselves inside our heads. This *internal dialogue* often departs in content and tone from what we express to others. And while RSL is driven by social cooperation, internal dialogue is shaped by personal emotions and is usually experienced as a conversation between two aspects of the self. Internal dialogue may have evolved on a separate track from social language to allow for private thought as well as deceiving others. It may also be one of the primary ways in which right hemisphere processing participates in conscious awareness. RSL and internal dialogue are like overlearned motor skills that serve to maintain preexisting attitudes, behaviors, and feelings. Like RSL, internal dialogue is primarily reflexive and based on semantic routines and habits reflecting our learning history. We hear in our heads the supportive or critical voices our parents implanted early in life. So while RSL keeps us in line with the group, internal dialogue keeps us in line based on early programming.

When we find ourselves reflecting on RSL and internal dialogue, a new level of language seems to emerge, one of self-reflection. In this state of mind, our thoughts and words focus on the reflexive thoughts, feelings, and behaviors we usually engage in. This third level of language is less a mechanism of social control than a vehicle of thoughtful consideration and potential change. It employs executive function and serves to develop a theory of our own mind. Much of therapy consists of uncovering and exploring reflexive social language and internal dialogue, both of which reflect unconscious aspects of the self. In this process we develop the *language of self-reflection*, learning that we are not only our social reflexes plus the voices that haunt us but are also the one that can observe, listen, and judge what we hear these voices say.

As the language of self-awareness is expanded and reinforced, we learn we are capable of evaluating and choosing whether to follow the expectations of others and the mandates of our childhoods. The language of self-reflection, when contrasted with RSL and internal dialogue, most likely reflects a higher level of integration. In this language, cognition is blended with affect so that there can be feelings about thoughts and thoughts about feelings. At a very deep level, this language leads us to meditation, where we learn to quiet our thoughts and move beyond words.

Therapy attempts to create this metacognitive vantage point from which the shifting states of mind that emerge during day-to-day life can be thought about. This is accomplished by interweaving the narratives of client and therapist and hopefully leading them in a more healthful direction. You begin by making clients aware of one or more of the narrative arcs of their life story and then help them understand that change is possible and offering alternative story lines. As the editing process proceeds, new narrative arcs emerge, as do possibilities to experiment with new ways of thinking, feeling, and acting. The importance of the unconscious processes of both parent and therapist is highlighted by their active participation in the co-construction of the new narratives of their children and patients. This underscores the importance of the proper training and adequate personal therapy for therapists who will be putting their imprint on the hearts, minds, and brains of their clients.

In essence, therapists hope to teach their clients that they are more than their present story but can also be editors and authors of new stories. When we evolved the capacity to examine our narratives (metacognition) and see them as one option among many, we also gained the ability to edit and modify our lives (White, 2001). The narrative process allows us to separate story from self. It is like taking off your shirt to patch a tear and then putting it back on. This allows us to have the experience of a self that is separate from our behaviors, feelings, actions, and problems. The fact that someone can say, "I'm not myself today," implies the capacity for self-reflection and comparison between a current state of mind and our everyday self-narrative. The ability to take other perspectives also enhances our empathy for others.

## Abbey

> *Do not dwell in the past, do not dream of the future, concentrate the mind on the present moment.*
>
> —Buddha

Like most things, our narratives are both good and bad. Unexamined, they keep us in negative patterns. Seen and understood, they provide a means of change. Thus, unraveling all of the conscious and unconscious material that supports a narrative arc can take considerable time and bring many challenges. Here is an example.

Abbey, an extremely bright and charismatic woman, came to my office with tears in her eyes and a smile on her face. Even before she sat down, Abbey launched into a description of all the positive events that had happened to her and her family over the last week. Seeing the pain in her eyes and the rigidity of her body, my face must have reflected the sadness I was feeling. My expression seemed to make Abbey avoid my eyes and speak even faster. From time to time, I would attempt to break in and ask her what she was feeling.

Abbey ignored my questions, talking at an ever faster pace. She reminded me of how, as a child, I would cover my ears and hum when my mother was about to say, "Bedtime!" I soon realized that all I could do was sit, listen, and wait. I sat across from her and tried to remain true to my feelings, allowing them to show in my eyes and facial expressions. Eventually her speech slowed and she became quiet and hung her head. Her feelings seemed to have finally caught up with her, the impulsive stream of reflexive social language finally coming to a halt.

I was considering what to say when she spoke: "I caught myself blabbing on." It was good to see that Abbey could employ her language of self-reflection and share her observations with me. I asked her what she had been thinking about while sitting in silence. Abbey replied, "I was thinking of what an idiot I am and how I must bore you with endless prattle about my stupid life." Now she was sharing the content of her internal dialogue, likely programmed early in life. She seemed deflated, depressed, and ashamed of herself. As a reaction against her own shame, she attacked. "What a stupid job you have, sitting in this office every day, listening to people's problems. Why don't you get out of here and get a life?" Abbey soon lowered her face into her hands and began to sob. I could see that not only was she sharing with me the voices in her head and her fears and doubts, but she was also projecting onto me her anger, confusion, and frustration. Her internal dialogue was hurting her and she wanted me to know how she felt. I said, "Being criticized can be really painful." She instantly knew I was talking about the victimization by her inner voices now, and by her parents as a child.

When she spoke again, she told me of the emptiness she felt from the loss of her husband a few months earlier (until this point she had denied its having much impact on her). It had become clear to her over the last few minutes that she had been coping with her sadness by burying herself in a flurry of words, social activities, and taking care of others. After a few minutes of silence and deep sighs, Abbey began to talk about how much she missed his hugs, good advice, and the feeling of safety of having him around. Abbey was now speaking in the language of self-reflection. She was able to mourn the death of her husband in this state of mind.

When clients shift to the language of self-reflection, the changes in their tone, manner, and mood are palpable. I imagine at this moment that clients have the clearest perspective on their thoughts, behaviors, and feelings. They speak more slowly because the organization of sentences takes time when they no longer rely on clichés and semantic habits. Emotions bubble up and clients feel safe enough to express them in a process that enhances affect regulation. This is when I feel most confident about a client's ability to join me as a collaborator in the therapeutic process. These states are usually fleeting and often not supported by family, friends, or the day-to-day demands of modern life. Therapy sometimes needs to become somewhat subversive and conspiratorial as client and therapist attempt to work against all the forces of habit and social momentum that keep us consistently unhealthy. It has been said that the challenge of increased self-awareness is remembering we are more than our reflexes and defenses (Ouspensky, 1954).

## Summary

The focus on integration exists at each level of nature's complexity from neurons to narratives to nations. As systems become more complex, it takes more sophisticated mechanisms and increasing amounts of energy to support their continuing interconnection and homeostatic balance. In this chapter we have explored the axes of neural integration as well as the narratives that help us coordinate the government of systems that comprise our brains and construct our conscious experience. Although psychotherapy deals in stories, it turns out that they emerged from brain evolution to serve the purposes of increasing complexity, coordination, and connectivity between us. This is one of the many connections between interpersonal relationships and brain functioning that make psychotherapy a neuroscientific intervention.

Part IV.

# The Social Brain

# Chapter 10
# The Social Brain

*Our brains and bodies are designed to function in aggregates,*
*not in isolation.*

—John Cacioppo

Using evolution as an organizing principle, we begin with the assumption that our highly social brains have been shaped by natural selection because banding together in groups enhances survival. The more tightly interwoven we are as a group, the more eyes, ears, hands, and brains we have available to us. We know that the expansion of the cortex in primates corresponds to increasingly large social groups and the development of language, problem-solving, and abstract abilities. Our larger and more complex brains not only allow for a greater variety of responses to challenging situations and across diverse environments, but also process the vast amount of social information needed to support communication and group coordination.

Increasingly sophisticated social groups allowed for task specialization such as hunting, gathering, and prolonged and dedicated caretaking. Caretaking specialization, in turn, allowed for longer postnatal development and brains built not by genetic preprogramming but by lived experience. So, while many animals need to be immediately prepared upon birth to take on the challenges of survival, human infants have the luxury of years of total dependency as they learn the complexities of the group. With the expanding size of primate groups, the grooming, grunts, and hand gestures adequate in small groups were gradually shaped into spoken language. As social groups grew even larger, more cortical geography was needed to process increasingly complicated social information. This coevolution of relationships, language, and brain allowed for the development of higher levels of symbolic and abstract functioning. In other words, early caretaking and intimate relationships are a fundamental building block in the evolution of the human brain.

Despite the fact that our brains are social organs, Western science studies each individual as a single, isolated organism rather than one embedded within the human community. This way of thinking leads us in the West to search for technical and abstract answers to human problems instead of looking at day-to-day human interactions. Take, for example, how physicians responded to the high mortality rate among children in orphanages during the last century. Assuming that microorganisms were to blame, they separated children from one another and ordered their handling to be kept to a minimum to reduce the risk of contamination. Despite these mandates, the children continued to die at alarming rates, leading staff to fill out admissions forms and death certificates during intake for the sake of efficiency. It was not until children were held and played with by consistent caretakers and allowed to interact with one another that their survival rate improved (Blum, 2002).

The notion of the brain as a social organ emerged in neuroscience during the 1970s as animal researchers slowly began to appreciate that neuroanatomy, neurochemistry, and social relationships are inextricably interwoven. The notion that primates possess neural networks specifically dedicated to social cognition was initially proposed by Kling and Stecklis (1976), who found that damage to certain brain structures in primates resulted in aberrations of social behavior and a decline in group status. Since then, scientists have been exploring the varied neural terrain activated during social interactions. Subsequent research in the expanding field of neuroscience has uncovered multiple sensory, motor, cognitive, and emotional processing streams that contribute to interpersonal intelligence (Karmiloff-Smith et al., 1995).

Many of these findings have led to the growing realization that the lessons learned during a century of dynamic psychotherapy may have important neuroscientific implications. The most basic is that we are born into relationships and come to our individual identity while resting upon social connectivity. Another is that social interactions affect everything from our biology to our intellectual abilities. Neuroscience researchers are slowly coming to the realization that the scope of their scientific observation needs to expand to include relationships.

Neuroscientists already possess the perfect model for understanding interdependency—the individual neuron. We know that neither the individual neuron nor the single human being exist in nature. Without mutually stimulating interactions, people and neurons wither and die. In neurons, this process is called apoptosis, while in humans, it is called anaclitic depression. From birth until death, each of us needs others who seek us out, show interest in discovering who we are, and help us to feel cared for and safe. Relationships are our natural habitat, while the isolated brain is an abstract concept. Thus, understanding the brain requires knowledge of the person embedded within a community of others. Therapists, teachers, and parents intuitively grasp this profound reality just as laboratory scientists often do not. We are now in a position to help research scientists know where to look as they explore how the brain grows, learns, and changes throughout life.

## The Social Synapse

*Life is the continuous adjustment of internal relations to external relations.*
—Herbert Spencer

As we discussed earlier, individual neurons are separated by small gaps called synapses. These synapses are inhabited by a variety of chemical substances engaged in complex interactions that result in neural transmission. This activity stimulates neurons to survive and modify themselves and each other. Over vast expanses of evolutionary time, synaptic transmission has grown increasingly intricate to meet the needs of a more complex brain. A parallel process has also been occurring in the evolution of the social synapse.

The social synapse is the space between us. It is also the medium through which we are linked together into larger organisms such as families, tribes, and societies. When we smile, wave, and say hello, these behaviors are sent through the space between us via sights, sounds, odors, and words. These electrical and mechanical messages received by our senses are converted into electrochemical impulses within our brains. These signals stimulate new behaviors, which, in turn, transmit messages back across the social synapse. From the moment we are born, our very survival depends upon connecting to those around us through touch, smell, sights, and sounds. If we are able to connect with nurturant others whose brains are primed to accept us as an extension of themselves, then we can bond, attach, and survive.

The band of communication across the social synapse is extremely broad and includes unconscious messages sent via posture, facial expression, eye gaze, pupil dilation, and even blushing. As we grow increasingly interdependent, our inner experience becomes more visible through these and other means of communication, in order to enhance the strength of our attachments (Cozolino, 2006). Contact with others across the social synapse stimulates neural activation, which influences the internal environment of our neurons. This activation in turn triggers the growth of new neurons as well as the transcription of protein, which builds neurons as they expand, connect, and organize into functional networks. A basic assumption is that loving connections and secure attachments build healthy and resilient brains, while neglectful and insecure attachments can result in brains vulnerable to stress, dysregulation, and illness.

Early bonding experiences not only strengthen the networks of the social brain, they also promote the building of the brain as a whole by stimulating metabolic arousal. Physical and emotional interactions between mother and child result in a cascade of biochemical processes, enhancing the growth and connectivity of neural networks throughout the brain (Schore, 1994). Face-to-face interactions activate the child's sympathetic nervous system and increase oxygen consumption and energy metabolism. Higher levels of activation correlate with increased production and availability of norepinephrine, endorphins, and dopamine, enhancing the child's pleasure during positive connections (Schore, 1997a). The vital importance of these early interactions to the building of the entire brain may help to explain the death of institutionalized children deprived of interaction and love (Spitz, 1946).

You may remember from an earlier chapter that a sensitive period is a window of time when exuberant growth and connectivity occur in specific neural networks. The onset and conclusion of these periods are genetically and environmentally triggered, and correspond with the rapid development of skills and abilities organized by each network.

Thus, early experiences have a disproportionately powerful role in sculpting the networks of attachment and affect regulation due to the strength of learning during these sensitive periods (Ainsworth, Blehar, Waters, & Wall, 1978). Just as positive experiences equip us with feelings of self-assurance and optimism, suboptimal bonding experiences become stored within implicit memory, carried into adulthood, and become woven into our adult relationships. Nowhere are these organizing principles more evident than in psychotherapy.

## Attunement and Reciprocity

*Mirror neurons show how strong and deeply rooted is the bond that ties us to others.*
　　　　　　　　　　　　　　—G. Rizzolatti and C. Sinigaglia

Attunement and reciprocity are aspects of the attachment process that reflect mutual awareness, turn taking, and emotional resonance. Mother–infant emotional attunement during the first year is predictive of the toddler's self-control at 2 years, even when temperament, IQ, and maternal style are controlled for (Feldman, Greenbaum, & Yirimiya, 1999). A mother's ability to resonate with her infant's internal states and translate her feelings into words will eventually lead to the child's ability to associate feelings with words. As the child grows, the pairing of feelings with words enhances the integration of vertical and horizontal networks dedicated to language and emotions. Early emotional regulation, established via mother–infant synchrony, contributes to the organization and integration of neural networks and the eventual development of self-regulation in the child.

Stage-appropriate attunement maximizes the possibility of neural growth, network coherence, and secure attachment. The combined sense of safety, freedom from anxiety, and excitement generated via attunement provides the affective background for the experience of vitality and spontaneous expression. For the newborn, attunement may be communicated via stroking and cuddling; for a 4-year-old, it means helping him or her learn to share with a sibling. A 16-year-old, on the other hand, may need assistance with creating and staying focused on goals for the future, while a 30-year-old will benefit from financial advice and some free babysitting. This safe emotional background created by proper attunement, reciprocity, and loving kindness parallels an optimal educational and psychotherapeutic relationship.

The building of the social brain during the first 2 years is driven by the attunement between the right hemispheres of the parent and the child (Schore, 2000). It is through this connection across the social synapse that the unconscious of the mother is transferred to the unconscious of the child. The right-hemisphere-biased circuits of the social brain come online at birth and appear to have their sensitive periods during the first 2 years of life (Chiron et al., 1997). The mother seems to regress to a state of preoccupation with her infant in the last months of pregnancy, and continues in this state for a number of months after giving birth (Winnicott, 1963). This maternal preoccupation involves an increased sensitivity to the visceral and emotional experience of the child in order to attune to his or her primitive means of communication. The mother's purposeful regression allows her to lend her capacity to translate bodily states into words and actions that are soothing to the infant.

## Jump-starting Attachment

*A mother understands what a child does not say.*
—Jewish proverb

Even before birth, mothers and children engage in complex and reciprocal interactions. Communication occurs through sound, movement, and touch, while their shared biochemical environment informs the child about his or her mother's state of mind and body. Prior to the formation of cortically organized social neural networks, we possess a number of primitive reflexive behaviors that jump-start and stimulate the development of the more sophisticated forms of attachment behavior to come. These reflexes reach across the social synapse and allow us to become quickly integrated with our parents. The process of transmitting the communication style of the mother, family, and culture begins immediately at birth.

Within the first hours after birth, newborns open their mouths and stick out their tongues in imitation of adults, and after 36 hours they are able to discriminate among happy, sad, and surprised facial expressions (Field, Woodson, Greenberg, & Cohen, 1982). Seeing happy faces causes newborns to widen their lips, while sad faces elicit pouting, and surprised expressions result in wide-open mouth movement. Infants look primarily at the mouth for happy and sad faces, whereas they alternate between the eyes and mouth in response to expressions of surprise, suggesting they are capable of selecting different visual targets based on the types of information presented to them (Field et al., 1982).

Over 20 involuntary reflexes have been identified in the newborn. Some—like the rooting and sucking reflexes—help the infant obtain nurturance, while the palmar grasp (automatic hand grasp) and the Moro reflex (reaching out of the arms) help the child hold onto the caretaker. These early reflexes, controlled by the brainstem, are gradually inhibited by the cortex and replaced by conscious, flexible, voluntary behavior. Reflexes such as these increase the newborn's chances of survival by enhancing his or her physical and emotional connection to mother and father. The old image of the infant as a passive recipient of stimulation has been replaced with a view of the infant as a competent participant in the social environment.

One of my clients told me of his first interaction with his son: "A few seconds after he was born, the nurse handed him to me and told me to put him in a small bed under a heat lamp. I dutifully crossed the delivery room and gently placed him under the lamp. The light was very bright and he squinted hard, making his face look like a bunch of wrinkles. I put my hand over his face to shield his eyes and he instinctively reached up and took my thumb in his left hand and my pinky in his right and pulled my hand onto his cheek. He was now about 90 seconds old and had become my son. I felt the glow of pride about how clever he was, while simultaneously feeling a surge of protectiveness. This was obviously a very intelligent child with a bright future." In this way, reflexes provide the dual function of creating physical connection and ensuring the emotional investment of the adults upon whom the infant relies.

Although specific words are meaningless, the tone and prosody of the parents' voices hold center stage. Even strangers will instinctively raise the pitch of their voice when talking with babies to match their hearing abilities. A mother reflexively holds her baby against her body after birth, maximizing skin contact and helping the infant's hypothalamus establish a set point for temperature regulation. The infant and mother gaze into each other's eyes, linking their hearts and brains, while nursing establishes the lifelong relationship between nutritional and emotional nurturance (food equals love).

The warm and happy feelings associated with holding, touching, and nursing, the pain of separation and the joy of reunion, are all stimulated through a variety of primitive neurochemicals that support bonding and attachment. Through this biochemical cascade, mother–child interactions stimulate the secretion of oxytocin, prolactin, endorphins, and dopamine, resulting in warm, positive, and rewarding feelings. These biochemical processes, in turn, stimulate neural activation and the structural maturation of the brain while shaping attachment circuitry (Fisher, 2004; Panksepp, 1998).

The secretion of endogenous endorphins results in feelings of well-being and elation. It actually does feel better when a loved one kisses your boo-boo because endorphins are also natural analgesics. These opiates are strongly reinforcing and serve to shape our preferences from early in life (Kehoe & Blass, 1989). Research with primates suggests that the activation of the opioid systems of mother and child propels and regulates the attachment process. When parent–child primate pairs engage in touching and grooming behavior, endorphin levels increase in both (Keverne, Martens, & Tuite, 1989). During separation, the administration of nonsedating morphine has the same soothing effect on the infant as does the reappearance of the mother. When naltrexone (a drug that blocks the effects of endogenous opioids) was administered to infant primates, rodents, and dogs, proximity seeking increased (Kalin et al., 1995; Knowles, Conner, & Panksepp, 1989; Panksepp, Nelson, & Siviy, 1994).

Reflexively orienting the head to the sound of the mother's voice increases the possibility of eye contact while the instinct to seek circles and complex figures directs the baby's attention toward the mother's eyes and face. Prolonged mutual gazing stimulates metabolic activity and neural growth, while reflexive smiling evokes positive feelings and expressions in caretakers, further stimulating the infant's brain.

Close examination of the bidirectional *protoconversation* between a mother and her baby demonstrates that infants have far more influence on their mothers than previously thought (Bateson, 1979). A baby does not simply react to its mother, but instead learns how to affect her feelings and behaviors. Both mother and infant adjust to each other's gestures, behaviors, and sounds in a sort of lyrical song and dance (Trevarthen, 1993). It is through this language of intersubjectivity that children learn from their mothers about the fundamental safety or dangerousness of the world. Protoconversation over the first year of life serves as the interpersonal and emotional scaffolding into which semantic language and narratives will gradually emerge. The growth spurt of the right hemisphere provides the neural substrate for the development of the emotional components of language.

## The Importance of Eyes

*There is a road from the eye to heart that does not go through the intellect.*
—G. K. Chesterton

The eyes are a primary point of orientation for infants. They play a significant role in bonding and social communication. Throughout the animal kingdom, eyes play a crucial role in determining the safety or danger posed by others. Gaze aversion (visual cutoff) is an important social behavior that indicates dominance hierarchy in both primates and humans. Direct eye gaze is a threat signal in primates (De Waal, 1989), and the recognition that we are being looked at results in increased heart rate and amygdala activation (Nichols & Champness, 1971; Wada, 1961). What must it be like for primates trapped in zoos who have hundreds of human primates filing by and staring at them each day? Robert De Niro's "Are you lookin' at me?" monologue in *Taxi Driver* is a dramatic example of the relationship between eye gaze, threat, and dominance.

Learning the language of eyes provides us with valuable information about our environment and what might be on the minds of others. We reflexively look up when we see other people doing so; in these situations, the eyes serve as a source of social communication about possible threats in our environment. Elaborate neural circuits have evolved to monitor the direction of eye gaze of potentially dangerous others in order to anticipate their next move. On the other end of the spectrum, the connection among the eyes, the visual system, and emotion can be easily witnessed in the delight a child takes in a game of peek-a-boo. Thanks to the neurochemistry of bonding, the smiles and laughter elicited from a child during peek-a-boo are just as addicting for adults. There is a surge of good feelings in both children and caretakers with each reappearance of the eyes. Similarly, consider the way two people in love can stare endlessly into each other's eyes, constantly recharging feelings of happiness.

During infancy, mutual gaze between caretaker and child is a primary mechanism for promoting brain growth and organization. In their exploration of the environment, toddlers regularly check back to see the expression on their parent's face. If the parent looks calm, the child will feel confident to explore further. A frightened look from the parent may result in the child seeking proximity and decreasing exploration. This use of the eyes and facial expressions to encourage or inhibit toddler activities is referred to as *social referencing* (Gunnar & Stone, 1984).

In therapy, the way a patient experiences your gaze (as caring or threatening) is an aspect of transference that may provide important cues to early bonding experiences. An identical expression will, for some patients, lead to a request that the therapist not stare at them, while it will make others feel attended to and cared for. Although some patients prefer to lie down and look away from the therapist, others want to keep an eye on you. These reactions reflect the eyes' ability to elicit emotions from the patient's interpersonal history stored within networks of implicit memory. Thus, exploring the clients' reaction to your gaze may yield valuable information.

## Recognizing Faces and Reading Facial Expressions

*Laughter is the sun that drives winter from the human face.*
—Victor Hugo

A vital function of the social brain is to recognize faces and assign a value to them; in other words, are they familiar or strange, friend or foe—should I stay or should I go? This involves both determining identity (who is this?) and using facial expressions to guess the other person's emotional state and intentions (what are they up to?). The first part of this process involves the complex task of recognizing a face from all possible angles, an analysis that is easy for a child but continues to elude the fastest computers. Although the recognition of faces involves both hemispheres, it is a function most suited to the visual-spatial mechanisms and holistic processing strategies of the right hemisphere.

Research with primates has demonstrated that a particular region of the temporal cortex contains cells that are responsive to faces, their identity, and various facial expressions (Perrett et al., 1984). Neurons activated specifically by faces have also been detected in the amygdala connecting the reading of others' faces to our own autonomic reactions, emotions, and behaviors (Leonard, Rolls, Wilson, & Baylis, 1985; Perrett, Rolls, & Caan, 1982). The temporal cortex contributes its abilities for complex recognition tasks (i.e., the countless combinations of facial features), while the amygdala and the ompfc add the emotional elements to processing social information. Together they give us the ability to approach friendly faces and make us wary of potential enemies.

Our temporal lobes contain neurons dedicated to faces that are essential to our ability to relate to others. Besides being able to recognize faces and the behaviors of others, we need to experience other people as being different from inanimate objects. You are probably familiar with autism and Asperger syndrome; both disorders are characterized by profound deficits in the ability to relate to others. In interacting with individuals suffering from these disorders, I have been left with the feeling that, to them, I am no different from any other object in the room. Not surprisingly, research has demonstrated that individuals with autism process faces in an area of the right temporal lobe normally used to process objects (Schultz et al., 2000). This finding reflects one of the many neuroanatomical mechanisms underlying profound disorders of relationship.

## Mirror Neurons

*Behavior is the mirror in which everyone shows their image.*
—Johann Wolfgang von Goethe

Another way in which we link up across the social synapse is with the help of what are called *mirror neurons*. Let me first describe how they were discovered. Using microsensors, neuroscientists are able to record the firing of single neurons in monkeys' brains. This recording can take place while they are aware, alert, and interacting with other monkeys. Through such methods, neurons were discovered in the premotor areas of the frontal cortex that fire when another primate or the experimenter is observed engaging in a specific behavior, such as grasping an object with a hand (Jeannerod, Arbib, Rizzolatti, & Sakata, 1995). Some of these neurons are so specific that they only fire when an object is grasped in a certain way by particular fingers (Rizzolatti & Arbib, 1998). What is even more interesting is that these very neurons fire when the monkey itself performs the same action (Gallese, Fadiga, Fogassi, & Rizzolatti, 1996).

These neurons have been dubbed mirror neurons because they fire both in response to an observation of a highly specific relationship between an actor and some object and when the action is performed by the observer. Thus, mirror neurons serve to connect our visual and motor systems with frontal systems responsible for goal-directed behavior. For obvious reasons, the same sort of studies are not possible in healthy human subjects. However, noninvasive scanning technologies have been used to extend these findings to human brains. One such study demonstrated that areas in our brain analogous to those containing mirror neurons in primates are activated during both the observation and the execution of hand actions (Nishitani & Hari, 2000). Support for the relationship between these areas in the monkey and Broca's area in humans comes from positron emission tomography studies showing activation in Broca's area during the active or imagined carrying out of hand movements (Bonda, Petrides, Frey, & Evans, 1994; Decety, 1994; Grafton, Arbib, Fadiga, & Rizzolatti, 1996).

The fact that mirror neurons fire when the same action is observed or performed leads to some interesting hypotheses about their role in learning and communication. It has always been known that both humans and primates can learn by observation. Because mirror neurons activate for both observation and action, they may be the mechanism for one-trial learning. Also, because these neurons have been found in Broca's area in humans, mirror neurons may be involved in the imitation, learning, and expression of language (Gallese et al., 1996). Shared actions and turn taking may have been the genesis of protoconversation and semantic language. Some language learning may be jump-started by these mirror neurons within Broca's area, as the sounds and lip movements of caretakers are imitated. The alternation of mirroring and turn taking seen in mother–infant interactions may be a contemporary reflection of the early evolution of language (Iacoboni, 2008; Rizzolatti & Sinigaglia, 2008).

The most interesting application of mirror neurons to psychotherapy is that the facial expressions, gestures, and posture of another will activate circuits in the observer similar to those which underlie empathy. Seeing a sad child cry makes us reflexively frown, tilt our heads, say "aawwhhhh," and feel sad too. Watching an athlete walk off the field with his head held high and chest pushed out can lead us to feel energized and proud. In these and other ways, mirror neurons may bridge the gap between sender and receiver, helping us understand one another and enhance the possibility of empathic attunement (Wolf, Gales, Shane, & Shane, 2000). The internal emotional associations linked to mirror circuitry are activated via outwardly expressed gestures, posture, tone, and other pragmatic aspects of communication. Thus, our internal emotional state—generated via automatic mirroring processes—can become our intuitive "theory" of the internal state of the other. These structures are at the core of our ability to develop intimate relationships, be attuned to one another, and aid our children in shaping a healthy and balanced sense of self.

## Winnicott and the Emergence of the Person

*Many patients need us to be able to give them a capacity to use us.*
—Donald Winnicott

Donald Winnicott, an English pediatrician and psychoanalyst, developed some basic principles that provide a helpful way of thinking about the social processes which shape these neural structures. His work with mothers and children led him to coin terms such as good-enough mothering, holding environment, and transitional object, which have become part of the basic lexicon of child development. His ideas have been highly influential both because of their relevance to everyday experience and their freedom from obscure jargon.

Winnicott described the core of mothering as providing a *facilitating and holding environment*, which requires both the mother's empathic abilities and respect for the autonomy of the child. A mother's devotion to her child allows her to offer an expanding scaffolding that constantly adapts to her child's changing needs and abilities. Winnicott defined the early and intense focus on the baby as *primary maternal preoccupation*, and understood it to include the mother's absorption into and attunement to the experiences with her baby's primitive developmental state. In this process, she utilizes the biochemistry of attachment and the circuits of the social brain to bridge the social synapse between herself and her child. The *good-enough mother*, in Winnicott's thinking, is a mother who does an adequate job in this difficult, complex, and constantly shifting process of adaptation (Winnicott, 1962).

Winnicott believed that to talk of an infant separate from its mother was a theoretical abstraction. What actually exists is a symbiotic infant–

mother dyad within which the child is nurtured and its social brain is formed, and from which the infant eventually emerges as an individual psychological being. Because an internalized mother and the representation of the mother–infant dyad remain as organizing principles of the social brain, they continue to impact us throughout our lives. In this way, an adolescent or adult with good-enough mothering is never really alone.

A central component of development from Winnicott's perspective depends on the mother's ability to mirror her child. *Mirroring* is the process by which a mother attunes to her child's inner world and gives form to his or her formless fantasies, thoughts, and needs. Mirroring serves the purpose of taking the disorganized processes within the child, naming them, and making them a part of the relationship. The child then learns about his or her inner world through the relationship. Although many decades before their discovery, Winnicott was describing a process that relies on mirror neurons to support this deep attunement between mother and child.

It is not uncommon for women in the third trimester of their pregnancy or in the first months after giving birth to report that they feel they have lost IQ points. Although these changes are often attributed to the effects of hormones and sleep deprivation, they may also be related to a shift in bias to the right hemisphere. A shift away from logical and orderly left-hemisphere thinking to right-hemisphere-biased processing may allow the mother an increased level of emotional and physiological sensitivity that enhances the intuitive elements of attachment. A shift of brain coherence toward the right hemisphere would explain the decrease in linear semantic processing and memory abilities reported by new mothers and mothers-to-be. Although such a shift might be very useful for attunement with an infant, it could be detrimental to functions best performed by the left, such as finding the right words, remembering appointments, and following logical arguments. Many new mothers report an increasing need during the first year to get out into the world of adults or back to work. This need may parallel a shift back to previous levels of left-right hemisphere balance.

As the mother gradually recovers from a deep preoccupation with her infant and again becomes interested in other areas of life, the child is forced to come to terms with some of his or her own limitations. In an appropriately attuned parent, a graduated failure of adaptation will parallel the infant's increasing abilities, frustration tolerance, and affect regulation. Winnicott used the term *impingement* to describe the impact on the child of maternal misattunements. These can take the form of not appropriately anticipating the child's needs, interfering with the need for quiet and calm, and even underestimating his or her abilities. Parents have to fail to adapt in different ways in order for their children to face the challenges necessary for adequate development.

Minor impingements are challenges that create moderate and manageable levels of stress which the child is able to cope with and master. These experiences likely promote and may even maximize brain growth and neural network integration. Major impingements overwhelm the child's ability to cope and integrate experience in a cohesive manner, resulting in dissociated networking and functional disabilities. Gradual minor impingements force the infant to grow, whereas major impingements can result in derailment of positive adaptation and the solidification of defense mechanisms. Minor impingements are learning-enhancing experiences, whereas major impingements result in decreased neural integration and hamper the child's development.

One of Winnicott's most clinically useful concepts has been the idea of the development of a true and false self. Secure attachments and a sense of a safe world create the context for the development of the *true self*, which represents those aspects of the self that develop in the context of manageable (minor) impingements, support, encouragement, and proper meaning by the caretaker. Respect for the autonomy and separateness of the child motivates the parent to discover the child's interests, instead of imposing his or her own upon them. The true self reflects our ability to tolerate negative feelings and integrate them into conscious awareness and to seek out what feels right for us in our activities, ourselves, and our relationships with others. Winnicott's true self is obviously one in which neural network development has been maximized, affect is well regulated, and emotions and cognition are well integrated. The true self reflects an open and ongoing dialogue among the heart, the mind, and the body.

What Winnicott called a *false self* results from major impingements for which the child is unprepared. Prolonged impingements can result in chronic emotional dysregulation. For example, neglect, abuse, or continuous states of shame can overwhelm the child's natural development and lead to the dominance of emotional defenses. These stressful relationships will also inhibit neurogenesis and proper brain development (Stranahan,

Kahlil, & Gould, 2006). When self-involved or pathological parents use children for their own emotional needs, the child can become compulsively attuned to the parents, creating a false self designed to regulate the parents' needs. Without appropriate assistance in developing his or her self-reflective capacity, such children live through reflexive social behavior and never learn that they have feelings and needs of their own that should be expressed and nurtured. Winnicott understood therapy most generally as a process of controlled regression to a childhood state with the purpose of succeeding in developing a true self in the present which was thwarted in early life (St. Clair, 1986).

## Shame

*Every word, facial expression, gesture, or action on the part of a parent gives the child some message about self-worth. It is sad that so many parents don't realize what messages they are sending.*
—Virginia Satir

During the first year of life, healthy parent–child interactions are primarily positive, affectionate, and playful. Due to their limited mobility, infants stay in close proximity to caretakers, who provide for their many bodily and emotional needs. As the infant transforms into a toddler, a parent's role comes to include protecting the child from danger such as falling down stairs, being bitten by stray dogs, or drinking fabric softener. The emergence of normal, incessant exploratory behavior in toddlers is driven by the brain's intense need for stimulation and growth. Due to the toddler's increasing motor coordination and exploratory drive, parents find themselves protectively saying "no" beginning at about 18–24 months (Rothbart, Taylor, & Tucker, 1989). Affection and attunement, experienced as unconditional during the first year, come to be tied to limit setting, control, and early attempts at discipline.

Shame, appearing early in the second year of life, is both a powerful inhibitory emotion and a mechanism of social control. Thus the positive face-to-face interactions that stimulated excitement and exhilaration during the first year come to include expressions of disapproval and anger. Shame is represented physiologically by a rapid transition from a positive to negative affective state and from sympathetic to parasympathetic dominance. This shift is triggered by the expectation of attunement to a positive state, only to receive negative emotions from the care-taker (Schore, 1994). While it may be hard to believe, toddlers expect their parents to be just as excited as they are about covering the floor with milk or plopping their toys in the toilet. Parental reactions of disapproval or anger are, at first, confusing and difficult to comprehend but soon come to shape the biology and psychology of the child.

Behaviorally, people in a shame state look downward, hang their head, and round their shoulders. This same state (submission) is shown by your pet dog when he hunches over, pulls his tail between his legs, and slinks away as you upbraid him for some canine faux pas. Similarly, this posture in humans reflects social exclusion, loss, and helplessness. During early socializing experiences, shame is the emotional reflection of a lost attunement with the caretaker, drawing its power from the child's primal need to stay connected for survival. Prolonged and repeated shame states result in physiological dysregulation and negatively impact affect regulation, attachment, and the development of networks of the social brain (Schore, 1994).

The return from a state of shame to attunement results in a rebalancing of autonomic functioning, supports affect regulation, and contributes to the gradual development of self-regulation. Repeated and rapid return from shame to attuned states also consolidates into an expectation of positive outcomes during difficult social interactions. These repairs are stored as visceral, sensory, motor, and emotional memories, making the internalization of positive parenting a full-body experience. Thus, the continual experience of attunement, misattunement, and reattunement creates a kind of body memory which becomes an expectation of a positive outcome for relationships and life. Children left in a shamed state for long periods of time may develop permanently dysregulated autonomic functioning along with depression, hopelessness, and despair. As the child graduates into increasingly complex peer group relations, these same physiological processes are connected to popularity, social status, and dominance within groups at school and on the playground.

Because shame is a powerful, preverbal, and physiologically based organizing principle, the overuse of shame in the process of parenting can predispose children to developmental psychopathology related to affect regulation and identity (Schore, 1994; Schore & Schore, 2008). As part of his therapeutic programs, John Bradshaw (1990) refers to "inner child work" as addressing the long-standing power of these early shame experiences, which he calls "toxic shame." Shame needs to be differentiated from the later-occurring phenomenon of guilt. Guilt is a more complex, language-based, and less visceral reaction that exists in a broader psychosocial context. Guilt is related to unacceptable behaviors, whereas shame is an emotion about the self that is internalized before the ability to distinguish between one's behavior and one's self is possible. If guilt is "I did something bad," then shame is "I am bad." We see this often, in individuals who spend their lives taking care of others and doing good deeds in an attempt to make up for some "sin" that they cannot recall.

## The Consolidation of the Self

> *Never be afraid to sit awhile and think.*
> —Lorraine Hansberry

In Winnicott's view, too many impingements prevent the infant from experiencing what he called *formless quiescence*: those moments of safety and calm that teach the child the world can be a safe place. It is in these quiet moments that the experience of self is consolidated, neural networks integrate, and fantasy and reality are gently combined. In essence, good-enough parenting results in the belief in a benign world where one is safe to build an internal experience of self (Winnicott, 1958). Thus, Winnicott felt that a major achievement of early attachment was the capacity to be alone, an ability learned by being alone in the presence of a competent caretaker. These experiences create enough security to allow feelings in the child to spontaneously bubble up with the confidence that they will be manageable and understandable. In this state of mind, the need to employ defenses to cope with external threat and inner emotions is at a minimum. At the same time, parietal-frontal systems involved in imagination and the creation of an inner sense of self become activated.

The manic defenses we often see in our clients result from the lack of the capacity to be alone. Impulsive behaviors and thoughts, disconnected from self-reflective processes, serve to inhibit emotions because to these individuals, to feel is to feel bad (Miller, Alvarez, & Miller, 1990). Slowing down stimulates discomfort, sadness, isolation, and shame, which become background affect throughout life. If manic defenses are chronically employed, they can become a way of life and keep children and adults from constructing inner imaginal experience and a sense of self. Sadly, many children with manic defenses are mistakenly diagnosed with ADHD. They are medicated to help them cope, while the real problem goes unresolved.

People with manic defenses often mask their inability to be alone by stirring up a constant whirlwind of activities, social interactions, and phone calls. Despite their outward success, and their narcissistic and grandiose attitudes, they often have great difficulties in relationships and report feelings of despair and emptiness. Exploration of their histories usually points to patterns of insecure attachments in which achievement served as the currency for acceptance. Constantly escalating levels of activity are reinforced by praise from others and the avoidance of the negative feelings that bubble up when the patients are quiet or alone. These people often have a hard time relaxing or taking a vacation because the lack of distractions leaves them open to the intrusion of uncomfortable feelings for which they have no effective coping skills.

The inability to be alone is seen most clearly in individuals with borderline personality disorder, who have a catastrophic reaction to real or imagined abandonment. For these people, separation is experienced as a threat to their very survival in much the same way as an infant reacts to the absence or loss of a parent. Their catastrophic reaction in adulthood is likely the activation of an implicit memory of overwhelming abandonment fears from a time before object constancy or self-regulation. It is as if the child within these patients is in a holding pattern, awaiting proper parenting. The extremely emotional life-and-death reactions in borderline patients may be our best window to the chaotic and often frightening emotional world of early childhood.

## Summary

The brain is a social organ connected to other brains via the social synapse. Primitive reflexes jump-start the attachment process and are gradually replaced by voluntary behaviors. The motivation to stay connected is driven by biochemical systems we share with our primitive ancestors. While there are multiple channels of communication between us, vision is an important link across the social synapse and the expressive face a focal point of social information. Theories of psychological development by Winnicott, Freud and others provide us with models for the development of mind embedded in these more basic neurobiological processes. The development of a sense of self requires periods of freedom from external threat and inner turmoil. It also requires the development of frontal-parietal systems responsible for inner imaginal space. Children constantly buffeted by external chaos can remain trapped in a "selfless" state where they are witness to internal impulses and external behaviors with little or no ability to either understand or control what they are doing.

Chapter 11

# Building the Social Brain: Shaping Attachment Schemas

*Experience is a biochemical intervention.*

—Jason Seidel

While Winnicott observed and worked with mother–infant pairs in his consulting office, John Bowlby was performing naturalistic observations of primates in the wild and children in orphanages. He was especially interested in mother–child bonds, the importance of exploratory behavior, and the impact of separation and loss on healthy development. His experiences led him to develop the concepts of *attachment figures*, *proximity seeking*, and a *secure base* (Bowlby, 1969). Bowlby's observations and the subsequent scientific findings in attachment research are easily integrated with Winnicott's theories of bonding and attachment.

Bowlby's work, which highlighted the importance of specific caretakers to a child's sense of security, resulted in a major shift in the care of institutionalized children. To encourage bonding, children who had previously been cared for by whomever was available, were now assigned consistent caretakers. In addition, this change in attitude changed the role of nurses and caretakers from only custodians of small babies into emotional attachment figures. In essence, they were told that becoming attached should not be avoided. Subsequently, Mary Ainsworth and her student Mary Main developed research methods to test Bowlby's theories. Decades of attachment research followed, providing us with some fascinating tools to study the sculpting of the social brain during childhood, as well as the long-term impact of early experiences later in life.

Bowlby suggested that early interactions create *attachment schemas* that predict subsequent reactions to others. Schemas are implicit memories that organize within networks of the social brain, based on experiences of safety and danger with caretakers during early sensitive periods. A secure attachment schema enhances the formation of a biochemical environment in the brain conducive to regulation, growth, and optimal immunological functioning. Insecure and disorganized attachment schemas have the opposite effect, and correlate with higher frequencies of physical and emotional illness.

Bowlby believed attachment schemas to be a summation of thousands of experiences with caretakers that become unconscious, reflexive predictions of the behaviors of others. Attachment schemas become activated in subsequent relationships and lead us to either seek or avoid proximity. They also determine whether we can utilize intimate relationships for physiological and emotional homeostasis. These implicit memories are obligatory; that is, they are automatically activated even before we become conscious of the people with whom we are about to interact. They shape our first impressions, our reaction to physical intimacy, and whether we feel relationships are worth having. They trigger rapid and unconscious moment-to-moment approach-avoidance decisions in interpersonal situations. Attachment schemas are especially apparent under stress because of their central role in affect regulation. Attachment is mediated by the regulation of the autonomic nervous system by the social brain, and a cascade of biochemical processes that create approach and avoidance reactions as well as positive and negative emotions. Schemas shape our conscious experience of others by activating rapid and automatic evaluations hundreds of milliseconds before our perceptions of others reach consciousness.

Empirical research into attachment schemas began with Ainsworth's naturalistic in-home observations of mothers interacting with their children (Ainsworth et al., 1978). These mothers were found to fall into three categories: available and effective (free autonomous), dismissing and rejecting (dismissing), and anxious and inconsistent in their attentiveness (enmeshed/ambivalent). The belief was that these different caretaking styles would create differing coping and interpersonal styles in their children. So the next step was to determine whether the children of mothers in each category displayed differences in their attachment behaviors, especially when stressed or frightened.

The method developed to study the children's attachment behavior is called the infant strange situation (ISS). The ISS consists of placing an infant and its mother in a room, then having a stranger join them. After a period of time, the mother exits the room, leaving the child alone with the stranger. Another brief period follows, and then the mother returns. Children's *reunion behavior*, or how they respond to the return of their mother, is rated to determine their attachment style. This situation was chosen because of Bowlby's observation that being left alone with an unknown other evokes distress calls in young primates. The attachment schema of the child, or the expectation of being soothed by the mother, should be aroused by the stress of the situation and reflected in his or her reunion behavior. Does the child seek comfort from the mother or ignore her? This research was begun with a number of questions: Does the child have a hard time being comforted? Does the child soon feel safe and return to play, or is he or she anxious, clingy, or withdrawn? These and other behaviors are the focus of the ISS scoring system and are thought to reflect the child's experience and expectation of the mother's soothing capacity.

Four categories of the infants' reactions to their mothers' return have been derived from the ISS: *secure, avoidant, anxious-ambivalent,* and *disorganized.* Furthermore, a relationship was found between ISS categories and the maternal behavior originally derived from in-home observations. The general findings were as follows: children rated as securely attached sought proximity with the mother upon her return, were quickly soothed, and soon returned to exploratory or play behavior. These children, comprising approximately 70% of the sample, seemed to expect that their mothers would be attentive, helpful, and encouraging of their continued autonomy. Securely attached children appeared to have internalized their mothers as a source of comfort, using them to feel safe. These mothers were seen as effective in their interactions with their children and had become "a background context for seeking stimulation elsewhere" (Stern, 1995, p. 103).

Avoidantly attached children tended to ignore their mothers when they returned to the room. They would glance over to the mother as she came in, or shun contact altogether. These children tended to have dismissing and rejecting mothers and appeared to lack an expectation that she would be a source of soothing and safety. Avoidantly attached children behaved as though it was easier to regulate their own emotions than seek comfort from their mothers, whose misattunement or dismissal might well compound their stress.

Children rated as anxious-ambivalent sought proximity but were difficult to soothe and slow to return to play. Anxious-ambivalent children, who often had enmeshed or inconsistently available mothers, may have their stress worsened by their mothers' distress. Their slow return to play and emotional regulation may be a reflection of their mothers' anxiety and lack of internalized safety. These children tended to cling more and explore their environment less.

Finally, there was a group of children who engaged in chaotic and even self-injurious behaviors. On reunion with their mothers, they demonstrated odd behavior such as turning in circles or falling to the ground. They would freeze in place or be overcome by trancelike expressions. During later research, these children were included in a fourth category called disorganized attachment. These chaotic behaviors were demonstrated in conjunction with secure, avoidant, and anxious-ambivalent behaviors and were often present in children whose mothers suffered from unresolved grief or trauma. Parents of children in this category demonstrate frightened and frightening behavior to their children, inducing an alarm state in the child. In this biological paradox, the child's brain has an innate drive to move toward the mother. However, since the parent is also a source of alarm, the child is faced with an approach-avoidance conflict. The resulting inner turmoil dysregulates the child to the point that his or her adaptation and coping skills—even motor abilities—appear to become disorganized. The fear and chaos of the mothers' internal worlds can be observed in their children's behavior.

The transmission of trauma from parent to child is both powerful and insidious. A traumatized mother who creates alarming experiences for her child leaves the child no choice but to stay with and depend on the source of the alarm. The child's safe haven is replaced with repetitive *trauma by proxy* and emotional dysregulation (Olsson & Phelps, 2007). This process creates a new generation of victims. In research with Holocaust survivors, indications of parental trauma were found to be reflected in the biochemistry of their nontraumatized children (Yehuda et al., 2000; Yehuda & Siever, 1997). Further compounding the child's dysregulating environment, the trauma-related behaviors of victims will lead them to be avoided by other children in normal social interactions. It is not surprising that children with avoidant and disorganized attachment schema are also shown to have higher levels of stress hormones and other biological markers of trauma and sustained stress (Spangler & Grossman, 1993).

## Parents Talk of Their Childhoods

*A Freudian slip is when you say one thing but mean your mother.*
—Unknown

The relationships discovered between attachment schemas and parenting style raised the question of whether a parent's early attachment experiences influenced parenting style decades later. While it was assumed that the parenting styles of adults are somehow shaped by childhood experiences, there was no empirical support for this transfer from one generation to the next. Because implicit memory is inaccessible to our conscious mind, and explicit memories of childhood are shaped by so many emotional factors, a measure was needed that could bypass the usual distortions of memory and all of our defense mechanisms. An extremely interesting research tool that appears to have succeeded in this task is the Adult Attachment Interview (AAI) (Main & Goldwyn, 1998).

The AAI consists of a series of open-ended questions about childhood relationships and early experiences such as these:

- I'd like you to try to describe your relationship with your parents as a young child . . . if you could start from as far back as you can remember.
- Choose adjectives that reflect your relationship with your mother, father, and so on.
- Which of your parents did you feel closest to and why?

Although the AAI gathers information about what individuals remember of their childhood, it also provides the data for a linguistic analysis of the coherence of the narrative's organization and presentation. Coherence analysis is conducted based on what are called Grice's maxims and include an examination of both the logic and understandability of the narrative based on the following four principles:

1. Quality: Be truthful, and have evidence for what you say.
2. Quantity: Be succinct, and yet complete.
3. Relevance: Stick to the topic at hand.
4. Manner: Be clear, orderly, and brief.

Scoring takes into account the integration of emotional and experiential materials, gaps in memory and information, and the overall quality of the presentation (Hesse, 1999).

The AAI bypasses the left hemisphere interpreter by examining the quality of the brain's synthesis of the various cognitive and emotional components of explicit and implicit memory. Siegel (1999) proposed that the coherence of the AAI narrative parallels the level of neural integration attained during childhood, providing a window to early attachment experiences and emotional regulation. In essence, the AAI gets at how individuals put feelings into words, resolve traumatic experiences, and integrate the various networks of information processing across emotion, sensation, and behavior in making sense of their lives. It does all of this while simultaneously bypassing the problems inherent in self-report measures about the past.

Four categories emerge from the AAI that appear to correspond to the findings of the in-home observations and the infant strange situation. Mothers and fathers with securely attached children tended to have more detailed memories, as well as a realistic and balanced perspective of their parents and childhood. Adhering well to Grice's maxims, they were able to describe these experiences in a coherent narrative that was understandable and believable to the listener (Main, 1993). This group, called *autonomous*, demonstrated an integration of cognitive and emotional memories, had processed their negative experiences, and was therefore more fully available to their children.

The second group of parents, associated with avoidantly attached children, demonstrated a lack of recall for childhood events and large gaps in memory for their childhood. This lack of recall is believed to reflect a disruption of the integration of cognitive and emotional elements of autobiographical memory. This could be due to trauma, chronic stress, or a lack of assistance in learning to regulate affect from their own parents early in life. They also demonstrated an overall dismissing attitude toward the importance of their early relationships, just as they were dismissive of their own children now. The narratives of these parents were incoherent both due to missing information and a tendency to either idealize or condemn their parents. They gave the impression that they were defending against fully acknowledging their histories through denial and repression.

A third group of parents, rated as *enmeshed* or *preoccupied*, tended to have anxious-ambivalently attached children. Their narratives contained excessive, poorly organized verbal output that lacked boundaries between the past and present. They appeared preoccupied, pressured, and had difficulty keeping the perspective of the listener in mind.

Last, the *unresolved/disorganized* group of parents had highly incoherent narratives disrupted by emotional intrusions and missing or fragmented information. Their narratives not only reflected the disorganization of verbal and emotional expression, but also the devastating impact early stress had on the development and integration of their neural networks. The content of their narratives confirmed chaotic and frightening childhood experiences which we can assume were devastating to the integration and homeostatic balance of both body and brain. See Table 11.1 for a summary of attachment findings.

TABLE 11.1
Summary of Attachment Findings

| In-Home Observations of Mothers | Infant Strange Situation Interview | Adult Attachment |
|---|---|---|
| **Free autonomous** Emotionally available Perceptive and effective | **Secure** Infant seeks proximity Easily soothed/returns to play | **Autonomous** Detailed memory Balanced perspective Narrative coherency |
| **Dismissing** Distant and rejecting | **Avoidant** Infant does not seek proximity Infant does not appear upset | **Dismissing** Dismissing/denial Idealizing Lack of recall |
| **Enmeshed-ambivalent** Inconsistent availability | **Anxious-ambivalent** Infant seeks proximity Not easily soothed  Not quick to return to play | **Enmeshed-preoccupied** Lots of output Intrusions, pressured, preoccupied Idealizing or enraged |
| **Disorganized** Disorienting Frightening or frightened | **Disorganized** Chaotic Self-injurious | **Unresolved/disorganized** Disoriented Conflictual behavior Unresolved loss Traumatic history |

The power of the relationship between parent and child attachment patterns was demonstrated by Fonagy and his colleagues when they administered AAIs to expectant first-time parents (Fonagy, Steele, & Steele, 1991a). Over a year later, when the children reached their first birthday, their attachment patterns were assessed using the ISS. In 75% of these cases, the child's attachment pattern was predicted by the coherence of the parent's narrative and attachment style many months before birth. Parents of infants who came to be securely attached were able to provide a fluid narrative with examples of interactions, had few memory gaps, and presented little idealization of the past. These parents did not seem to have significant defensive distortions, were able to express negative feelings without being overwhelmed, and listeners tended to believe what they were saying. It is not a big stretch to see that these parents were best able to provide the kind of good-enough social environment providing a balance between safety and challenge, attunement and autonomy.

We now have some evidence that parents' capabilities for attachment to an infant begin to take shape in their own childhoods. Their skill as parents will depend on their empathic abilities, emotional maturity, and neural integration: in essence, how they were parented as children. As a child, a young girl may begin to imagine someday having children of her own. The shaping of her virtual children will be influenced by both her fulfilled and unfulfilled needs. The empathy and care each parent received as well as the assistance they experienced in articulating and understanding their inner worlds will influence future parenting abilities. A mother's childhood can determine whether she is prepared to emotionally provide for her newborn or if she will unknowingly require her child to give her the attention she failed to receive when she was young (Miller, 1981).

Because attachment schemas are part of implicit memory, this level of caretaking occurs automatically and connects our unconscious childhood experiences across the generations. In this way, a parent's unconscious is a child's first reality. Interestingly, negative events in childhood are not necessarily predictive of an insecure or disorganized attachment schema or future parenting style. Working through, processing, and integrating early experiences, and constructing coherent narratives, are more accurate predictors of a parent's ability to be a safe haven for his or her children. This *earned autonomy*, through the healing of childhood wounds, appears to interrupt the transmission of negative attachment patterns from one generation to the next.

The inference that parents who are rated as autonomous have higher levels of neural integration is based on the fact that they are able to access and connect cognitive and emotional functioning in a constructive and useful manner. They do not appear to be suffering the effects of unresolved trauma or dissociative defenses and have attained a high degree of affect regulation, as demonstrated by their ability to meet the demands of parenting with ongoing grace. They are able to remember and make sense of their own childhoods and are available to their children both verbally and emotionally. Their children develop attachment schemas that make them secure in the expectation that their parents are a safe haven and will soothe and assist them when threats arise. Not surprisingly, parents' emotional insight and availability to themselves appears to parallel their emotional availability to their children.

The three nonsecure patterns of attachment research all reflect lower levels of psychological and neurological integration. They also correlate with the use of more primitive psychological defenses associated with disconnections among streams of processing within the brain. The lack of recall and black-and-white thinking of the dismissing parent likely reflect blocked and unintegrated neural coherence. This brain organization then results in decreased attention and emotional availability to the child. The enmeshed parent has difficulty with boundaries between self and others, as well as between past memories and present experiences. These internal and interpersonal issues then lead to inconsistent availability and a flood of words that dysregulate the child. Thus the child, who is also anxious and ambivalent, will seek proximity but have a difficult time returning to play because of the unpredictable availability, as well as the confusing and emotionally dysregulating nature of the parent's messages and emotions. The internalized mother, instead of being a source of security and autonomic regulation, becomes organized as a destabilizing state of mind and body.

Maternal and paternal instincts—in fact all caretaking behaviors—are acts of nurturance that depend upon the successful inhibition of competitive and aggressive impulses. Too often, however, that inhibition is incomplete and some of us are unable to be good-enough parents. When a parent abuses, neglects, or abandons a child, the parent is communicating to the child that he is less fit. Consequently, the child's brain may become shaped in ways that do not support his long-term survival. Nonloving behavior signals to the child that the world is a dangerous place and tells him to not explore, discover, or take chances. When children are traumatized, abused, or neglected, they are taught that they are not among the chosen. They grow to have thoughts, states of mind, emotions, and immunological functioning that are inconsistent with well-being, successful procreation, and long-term survival. With all due respect to the old adage, we could also say that what doesn't kill us makes us weaker.

The tragedy of this lies in the fact that early experiences have such a disproportionately powerful impact on the development of the infrastructure of the brain. As highly adaptive social organs, our brains are just as capable of adjusting to unhealthy environments and pathological caretakers as they are to good-enough parents. While our brains become shaped to survive early traumatic environments, many of these adaptations may impede health and well-being later in life. Negative interpersonal experiences early in life are a primary source of the symptoms for which people seek relief in psychotherapy.

Secure attachments represent the optimal balance of sympathetic and parasympathetic arousal, whereas their imbalance correlates with insecure attachment patterns such as fight or flight and splitting (Schore, 1994). The balance of these two systems becomes established early in life and translates into enduring patterns of arousal, reactivity to stress, and possible vulnerability to adolescent and adult psychopathology. Poor attachment patterns lead to long-lasting emotional and physical over- or underarousal throughout the body and the brain.

Secure and insecure attachment schemas are quite different. Securely attached children do not produce an adrenocortical response to stress, suggesting that secure attachment serves as a successful coping strategy. On the other hand, those with insecure attachment schemas do show a stress reaction, demonstrating that insecure attachment is better described by a model of arousal rather than of successful coping (Izard et al., 1991; Nachmias, Gunnar, Mangelsdorf, Parritz, & Buss, 1996; Spangler & Grossman, 1993; Spangler & Schieche, 1998). In other words, the behavior of insecurely attached individuals is an expression of the state of their autonomic arousal in response to fear.

## Narrative Co-construction

*The wise man must remember that while he is a descendant of the past, he is a parent of the future.*

—Herbert Spencer

Parent–child talk, in the context of emotional attunement, provides the ground for the co-construction of narratives. These narratives, in time, become the mass of our inner experience and the parameters of our personal and social identities. When verbal interactions include references to sensations, feelings, behaviors, and knowledge, they provide a medium through which the child's brain is able to integrate the various aspects of its experience in a coherent manner. The organization of autobiographical memory that includes input from multiple neural networks enhances self-awareness and increases the ability to solve problems, cope with stress, and regulate affect. This integrative process is what psychotherapy attempts to establish when it is absent.

Co-constructed narratives form the core of human groups, from primitive tribes to modern families. The combined participation of caretakers and children in narrating shared experiences organizes memories, embeds them within a social context, and assists in linking feelings, actions, and others to the self. The creation and repetition of stories help children to develop and practice recall abilities and have their memories shaped in relationships (Nelson, 1993). This mutual shaping of memory between child and caretaker can serve both positive and negative ends. Positive outcomes include teaching the importance of accuracy of memory, imparting of cultural values, and shaping the child's view of herself based on her role in the story. Negative outcomes include the transfer of the caretakers' fears and anxieties into the child's narratives so that they become central themes in the experience of the child (Ochs & Capps, 2001).

When caretakers are unable to tolerate certain emotions, they will be excluded from their narratives or shaped into distorted but more acceptable forms. The narratives of their children will come to reflect these editorial choices. At the extreme, parents can be so overwhelmed by the emotions related to unresolved trauma that their narratives become disjointed and incoherent. On the other hand, narratives that struggle to integrate frightening experiences with words can serve as the context for healing by simultaneously creating cortical activation and increasing descending control over subcortically triggered emotions. Parental narratives, both coherent and incoherent, become the blueprint not only for the child's narratives, but for the organization and integration of their neural circuitry. As it turns out, there appears to be a relationship among the complexity of a child's narratives, self-talk, and the security of the child's attachment.

Main and her colleagues (Main, Kaplan, & Cassidy, 1985) studied a group of 6-year-old children who, at 1 year, were assessed in the infant strange situation. They discovered that securely attached children engaged in self-talk during toddlerhood and spontaneous self-reflective remarks at age 6. They also tended to make comments about their thinking process and their ability to remember things about their history. These processes of mind, which insecurely attached children often lack, reflect the utilization of narratives in the development of self and self-identity. They also point to a more sophisticated ability to metacognize (think about thinking), that represents a high level of neurolinguistic self-regulation. What we are witnessing appears to be the internalization of their parents' self-regulatory mechanisms. As you might expect, child abuse correlates with less secure attachment patterns in children and a decreased ability to talk (or think) about their internal states (Beeghly & Cicchetti, 1994).

Fonagy, Steele, Steele, Moran, et al. (1991) studied the relationship between infant security and reflective self-functioning in mothers and fathers. They found a strong correlation between measures of self-reflection and narrative coherence. In fact, when reflective self-function was controlled for in the statistical analysis, coherence no longer related to infant security. This suggests that the relationship between coherence and reflective self-functioning is powerful, and that the ability to reflect on the self plays an important role in the integration of multiple processing networks of memory, affect regulation, and organization. In discussing these results, the researchers suggested, "The caregiver who manifests this capacity at its maximum will be the most likely to be able to respect the child's vulnerable emerging psychological world and reduce to a minimum the occasions on which the child needs to make recourse to primitive defensive behavior characteristic of insecure attachment" (p. 208).

When the parents' inability to verbalize internal and external experiences leaves the child in silence, the child does not develop a capacity to understand and manage his or her own inner and outer world. The ability of language to integrate neural structures and organize experience at a conscious level is left unutilized. When children with nonhealing parents experience trauma early in life, the stress of each new developmental challenge is multiplied. In the same way, language, in combination with emotional attunement, is a central tool in the therapeutic process, creating the opportunity for neural growth and neural network integration.

A child who is able to achieve this ability with the help of someone other than the primary caretaker, may be able to earn a higher level of integration and security than would be predicted by his or her parents' rating on the Adult Attachment Interview. This may come from other significant people in the child's environment who are able to attune to the child's world and assist in the child's articulation of his or her emotional life. This might explain some of the earned autonomy seen in parents with negative childhood experiences but with coherent narratives and the ability to provide a safe haven for their children. Earned autonomy is convincing evidence that early negative experiences can be reintegrated and repaired later in life. Personal growth has the ability to heal because the social brain remains plastic.

Attachment patterns formed in childhood can be relatively stable into adulthood and have been shown to impact romantic love, interpersonal attitudes, and psychiatric symptoms (Brennan & Shaver, 1995; Hazan & Shaver, 1990). Adult children of anxious parents repeatedly return to them throughout life, still seeking comfort and a safe haven. Many of these children become parents to their parents, taking care of the people they wish would and could care for them. They continue to return to an empty well; each time the bucket is lowered there is the hope that it will contain the nurturance they need. Each returning empty bucket reinforces their lack of safety.

## Child Therapists

*Treat people as if they were what they ought to be and you help them to become what they are capable of being.*
                                                                    —Goethe

A question that commonly arises among therapists, adoptive parents, and mental health legislators is, "When is it too late?" At what age do the negative effects of early abuse, trauma, and neglect become permanent? Getting to the heart of the issue, the true question becomes: Who is worth seeing as a client, adopting as a child, or investing public funds in for rehabilitation? In my mind, these are moral rather than scientific questions. I have become very skeptical of "experts" who think they have found answers to any issue in neuroscience. My bias is to trust in plasticity and our own ingenuity to discover new solutions to these problems. Here is a study that may give us some guidance as we consider these issues.

To test the impact of maternal deprivation, Harry Harlow isolated newborn monkeys not only from their mothers, but from any and all contact with other monkeys. Beyond minimal contact related to taking care of their basic needs, these young monkeys were left alone in a cage with a few toys and little else. Pictures of these isolate monkeys are heartbreaking—they huddle in corners, rock, bite themselves, and stay curled up in a fetal position. It is as if they are trapped in an autistic hell waiting to be born into the social world.

When these isolated monkeys are then introduced into a standard monkey colony at 6 months of age, they are understandably terrified. They don't seem to understand what is going on, retreat from curious others, and do their best to avoid interaction. At first it was tempting to think of this 6-month period as a cutoff point for attachment plasticity. Perhaps attachment circuitry had gone through a hard-wired critical period and, by 6 months, it was too late to learn how to be social. But as with every conclusion in neuroscience, there needs to be caution.

Harlow and Suomi (1971) wondered if therapy could help these isolate monkeys overcome their fear and allow them to join the social world of the colony. But how do you do therapy with a monkey? Would you choose Gestalt, cognitive-behavioral, or psychoanalytic treatment? Ultimately what was chosen was a combination of play and attachment therapy. The "therapists" chosen for the job were normal 3-month-old monkeys, who were selected because they were smaller, craved playful contact, were less aggressive, and probably less threatening than same-aged peers.

Therapy consisted of three 2-hour sessions per week for 4 weeks—a total of 24 hours of "treatment." When the "therapists" arrived for the session, the isolates were terrified and retreated. The therapists approached, touched, and climbed on their older clients. The isolates tried to retreat while their anxiety and self-stimulating behavior increased. Again the therapists engaged, touched, climbed on, and got in the face of their clients. Apparently, when it comes to play and social engagement, a 3-month-old monkey won't take no for an answer. As the sessions continued it was reported that the isolates gradually came to habituate and accept their therapists' interventions. These interactions interrupted autistic, self-stimulating behavior, and the clients eventually began to initiate physical contact and interact with their younger therapists. Therapy was so successful that the authors stated, "By 1 year of age, the isolates were scarcely distinguishable from the normal therapists in terms of frequencies of exploratory, locomotive, and play behavior" (p. 1537).

After a course of treatment, when these former isolates were introduced to the colony, they did much better, and were able to find a role within the group and social hierarchy. Were they impaired? Most likely, early deprivation had a long-lasting impact, but it appeared to the researchers that they had attained a functional social recovery. These results surprised Harlow and Suomi because of their prior assumptions about critical periods. They also help remind me to keep an open mind, and remember that giving up on a child or client is not something I am ever willing or prepared to do.

## Summary

Neuroscience suggests that an important aspect of love is the absence of fear. If therapists and adoptive parents can create an environment that minimizes fear and maximizes the positive neurochemistry of attachment through human compassion, attachment circuitry can be stimulated to grow in ways which are not only healing, but that allow victims of abuse and neglect to risk forming a bond with another.

Because the process of attachment is, at heart, a way in which social animals initially regulate fear, and later their affective lives, modifying insecure attachment, first and foremost, requires the establishment of a safe and secure relationship. Therapists work diligently to establish this type of relationship for each client and to create an experience similar to what the 3-month-old monkeys were able to give their senior isolates: the experience of social connection in the absence of threat or rejection.

There are probably thousands of studies supporting what we all intuitively know—childhood experience affects emotional and physical health later in life. While there are plenty of psychological and social theories that attempt to explain this relationship, we are beginning to put together the biological mechanisms of action of these findings. The general question is, how do early social experiences shape our neurobiology in ways that can influence us decades later?

# Chapter 12

# The Neurobiology of Attachment

*Offspring inherit, along with their parents' genes, their parents, their peers, and the places they inhabit.*
—Leon Eisenberg

Reflected in the architecture of each of our brains is the coming together of our evolutionary history, the generations preceding our birth, and our unique relationship with our parents (Eisenberg, 1995). Hundreds of studies have demonstrated the ways in which early experience is correlated with physical and emotional health later in life. Research in psychoanalysis, epidemiology, developmental psychology, and psychiatry have all supported what we think of as common sense: A good childhood is better than a bad one; positive parental attention is important; and less stress early in life is a good thing. Of course, each field explains these findings from its own theoretical model and tends to see other perspectives as secondary.

Recent research in molecular biology offers us a groundbreaking view into the underlying mechanism of the effects of early experience on genetic expression, that is, how early experience triggers gene expression to guide our brains onto particular adaptational trajectories. In contrast to the correlations found in other fields of study, this new work explores causal biological links between maternal behavior and the building of the brains of children.

When we think about having an internalized mother, our thoughts usually stray to images of a kind smile, a warm hug, feeling safe, and being loved. Depending on the culture, you may remember your mom serving Thanksgiving dinner, stirring tomato sauce, or frying chicken. Those of us who are less fortunate may have images of rageful behavior, endless criticism, or a mother passed out on the couch after a long day of drinking. These conscious autobiographical memories are but one layer of an internalized mother. Another level, deeper and just as meaningful, is how these early experiences shaped the neurobiological processes of our brains.

In this chapter we climb up and down the evolutionary ladder from humans to rats and back again to humans. It turns out that we have learned a great deal by exploring how the behavior of mama rats influences the brains of their pups. The conservation of structures and functions during evolution provides us with a good animal model of the effects of maternal behavior on the brain. Although this research has yet to be done with humans, the behavioral and neurobiological parallels between rats and humans are striking, making rats very helpful in understanding the interpersonal aspects of neurobiology. We also explore networks of the human brain that rely on similar shaping during early experience, as well as some other ways in which epigenetics factors may impact everything from the timing of menopause to human longevity. In places, this chapter is heavy on the science, so be prepared to read certain sections over a few times. I have put most of the specific data in tables to act as an overview and guide to particular studies for those who wish to do follow-up reading.

## The Evolution of Complexity

*Who takes the child by the hand takes the mother by the heart.*
—German proverb

Let's set the stage to look at these studies with the assumption that our social brains have been shaped by natural selection because being social enhances survival. Our best guess is that larger and more complex brains allow for more diverse responses in challenging situations and across diverse environments. Our brains allow us to fashion clothing, build houses with heating systems, and create sophisticated farming techniques that allow us to expand our habitats and sources of food. But does this explain why we have relationships?

We know that the expansion of the cortex in primates correlates with increasingly large social groups. The benefit of living in a tribe is not just in the safety of numbers, but also in the ability of groups to have task specialization such as hunting, gathering, and caretaking. So, while many fish and reptiles need to be born immediately prepared to take on the challenges of survival, human infants have years of total dependency during which their brains can grow and adapt to very specific environments. This larger window of time for adult–child interactions allows for increasingly sophisticated postnatal brain development and increased investment in each child (Kaplan & Robson, 2002). This expanded social investment enhances the child's chances of survival, which in turn increases the chances of our genes surviving into the next generation (Allen, Bruss, & Damasio, 2005; Charnov & Berrigan, 1993). Thus, the development of the brain, group organization, caretaking, and social communication co-evolved in a mutually interdependent manner.

There are many interesting theories about how humans evolved to be the complex social creatures we are. The big story probably goes something like this:

- Larger group size enhanced the probability of survival, but required bigger and more complex brains to process social information, and so larger brains were selected.
- More complex brains require longer periods of development and result in prolonged periods of child dependency.
- Longer periods of dependency require more attention and dedication to nurturance, caretaking specialization, and social structures that can support this specialization.
- As the size of primate groups expanded, grooming, grunts, and hand gestures became inadequate and were gradually shaped into spoken language.
- Complex social structures encouraged the development of more sophisticated communication, leading to the development of oral and written language.

- As social groups grew in size and language became more complex, a larger cortex was needed to process increasingly complex information.
- Language and culture provide our expanding brains the ability to record and accumulate history and information, and develop technology.
- The accomplishments of culture allow for even greater group size and more sophisticated brains.

It is very likely that some version of this evolutionary narrative shaped the contemporary human brain. But despite some remarkable advances, we have continued to be governed by the basic biological principles of homeostasis, fundamental approach-avoidance choices, and flows of electrical and chemical information throughout our brains and bodies. Like every living system, from a single neuron to complex ecosystems, the brain depends on interaction with other brains for its survival. Because increasing complexity requires greater interdependency, our brains have come to exist more and more profoundly within a matrix of other brains.

At birth, the human brain is dependent on caretakers for its survival and growth. The prolonged and sophisticated parenting that has evolved in primates scaffolds an increasing amount of postnatal growth and development. This allows each human brain to be a unique blending of nature and nurture as it builds its structures through interactions and molding itself to its environment. Parents' nonverbal communications and patterns of responding to the infant's basic needs also shape the baby's perceptions of the world and its sense of self. Because the first few years of life are a period of exuberant brain development, early experience has a disproportionate impact on the development of neural systems.

Genes first serve to organize the brain and trigger sensitive periods, while experience orchestrates genetic transcription in the ongoing adaptive shaping of neural systems, so that experience becomes the actual hardware of our brains. This structure, in turn, organizes other brains, allowing experiences to be passed through a group and carried forward across generations. While being embedded in a group comes with many challenges, it also comes with an ability to interactively regulate each other's internal states and assist in neural integration.

## Environmental Programming

*The group consisting of mother, father, and child is the main*
*educational agency of mankind.*
                              —Martin Luther King Jr.

The transduction of bonding experiences into neurobiological structure
is a fascinating area of study. It carries deep implications for how relationships throughout life impact our experience and thereby shape our
brains. Michael Meaney and his colleagues have been studying this question in great depth for many years. Their work has taken advantage of
naturally occurring variation in the maternal behavior of mother rats
(dams) to explore the impact of their ministrations on the brains of their
pups. Mother rats lick, nurse, and retrieve their pups when they roll out
of the nest. These three behaviors are easily observed and counted by
willing undergraduates, and correlated with behavioral and biological
variables in the brains of both mothers and children.

The work of Meaney and others has provided us with ample evidence
that mother rats pass on their genes through DNA and shape genetic
expression through their behavior. *Environmental programming* is a
term used to describe this orchestration of epigenetic factors during
development (Fish et al., 2004; Meaney & Szyf, 2005; Sapolsky, 2004).
Thus, two mechanisms of inheritance exist: slow changes across many
generations through mutation and natural selection, and rapid changes
in genetic expression during each generation (Clovis et al., 2005;
Cameron et al., 2005; Meaney & Szyf, 2005; Zhang, Parent, Weaver, &
Meaney, 2004). Their research has thus far revealed three primary ways
in which maternal behavior impacts variations in brain structure—learning and plasticity, the ability to cope with stress, and later maternal
behavior in adulthood. A mother's impact on the way her daughter will
mother her children serves as a parallel channel of inheritance that is
highly sensitive to environmental conditions.

Genetic expression is programmed by experience through the alteration of the chromatin structure and the methylation of DNA (Szyf,
Weaver, & Meaney, 2007). In effect, the genome is like a keyboard while
these processes select the notes to be played. Methylation is a process by
which a methyl group is added to DNA. This has been shown to be a
reversible but stable modification to DNA that is passed along to daugh-

ter cells and can lead to long-term gene silencing. Low licking/grooming mothering results in increased glucocorticoid receptor methylation, decreased glucocorticoid receptor (GR) expression, and an increased stress response. Licking/grooming decreases methylation, increases GR expression and downregulates the stress response (Weaver et al., 2007). So as we show affection and kindness to our children, we may be building more resilient brains, an expression of genetic variation that would likely have made Lamarck smile.

Three different research methods have been employed to study the effects of maternal behavior on genetic expression. In the first model, the amount of attention is measured and the behaviors and brains of pups in high- and low-attention groups are compared. The second examines the effects of periods of maternal deprivation, while the third uses handling of the pups by human researchers as the experimental manipulation. Because it has been found that human handling stimulates more maternal attention, the first and third categories may turn out to be one and the same (Garoflos et al., 2008).

Levels of maternal attention have been shown to either stimulate or silence gene expression in the domains of neural growth and plasticity, modulation of hypothalamic-pituitary-adrenal (HPA) activity, and programming of future maternal behavior (Szyf, McGowan, & Meaney, 2008). Neural growth is stimulated via the activation of brain-derived neurotrophic factor (BDNF), cFos, and messenger RNA expression in a variety of brain areas, processes tied to the biochemistry of neuroplasticity and learning. Stress reactivity is controlled via levels of benzodiazepine, oxytocin, and glucocorticoid receptors in many regions of the brain. Higher levels of maternal attention result in more of these receptors being formed, allowing for the dampening of fear and anxiety and an increase in exploratory behavior. Maternal behavior is governed by the growth and activation of medial optic areas (the rats' version of our ompfc) as well as the regulation of oxytocin and estrogen receptors (Neumann, 2008). See Table 12.1 for some of the specific findings in each area of study.

In essence, rats who receive more maternal attention have brains that are more robust, resilient, and nurturing of others. They are able to learn faster and maintain memories longer. They are less reactive to stress and are thus able to use their abilities to learn at higher levels of arousal and across more difficult situations. They will also suffer less from the dam-

TABLE 12.1
The Impact of Maternal Attention

| Maternal Action | Study Findings |
| --- | --- |
| | **Neural Growth and Plasticity** |
| Licking | Increased synaptic density, longer dendritic branching, and increased neuronal survival[1] |
| Licking | Increased neuronal survival in the hippocampus[2] |
| Licking | Fos expression in the hippocampus and parietal and occipital cortex[3] |
| Licking/nursing | Increased NMDA and BDNF expression and increased cholinergic innervation of the hippocampus[4] |
| | **Modulation of HPA Activity** |
| Licking | Increased medial PFC dopamine in response to stress and increased startle inhibition[5] |
| Licking/nursing | Decreased fear reactivity[6] |
| Licking/nursing | Increased epigenetic expression of glucocorticoid receptor gene promoter in the hippocampus[7] |
| Licking/nursing | Increased mRNA expression in medial prefrontal cortex, hippocampus, and the basolateral and central regions of the amygdala[8] |
| Licking/nursing | Increased levels of benzodiazepine receptors in the lateral, central, and basolateral regions of the amygdala and the locus coeruleus as well as increased levels of alpha 2 adrenoreceptor density and decreased CHR receptor density in the locus coeruleus[9] |
| | **Modulation of Future Maternal Behavior** |
| Nursing call | Enhanced metabolic activation in precentral medial cortex, anterior cingulate cortex, and lateral thalamus[10] |
| Licking | Elevated levels of estrogen mRNA and more maternal behavior later in life[11] |
| Licking/nursing | Increased levels of oxytocin and estrogen receptors in medial preoptic areas (and increased maternal behavior when they have their own pups)[12] |
| Licking | Less sexual behavior in females and less likely to become pregnant after giving birth[13] |

aging effects of cortisol by downregulating it sooner after a stress response. And finally, females growing up with more attentive mothers pass these positive features on to their children. The mechanisms for the association in humans between early secure attachment and healthier minds and bodies is likely similar but far more complex.

Maternal attention stimulates the expression of BDNF, the most abundant neurotrophins in the brain. Among its many functions, BDNF modulates glutamate-sensitive NMDA receptors which, in turn, regulate both long-term potentiation, long-term depression, and neuroplasticity (Alonso et al., 2002; Bekinschtein et al., 2008; Monfils, Cowansage, & LeDoux, 2007). While cortisol inhibits the production of BDNF (and new learning), higher levels of BDNF appear to both buffer the hippocampus from stress and encourage ongoing plasticity (Pencea et al., 2001; Radecki et al., 2005; Schaaf, de Kloet, & Vregendenhil, 2000). And because the production of BDNF (and other neurotrophins) are under epigenetic control, physical, emotional, and interpersonal experience all influence their production and availability (Berton et al., 2006; Branchi et al., 2004; Branchi, Francia, & Alleva, 2006).

Many researchers have found correlations between hippocampal volume and symptoms of depression. While most stressful illnesses correlate with reductions in hippocampal volume, there is speculation that depression may be a result rather than a cause of hippocampal reduction. In other words, the symptoms of depression are an experiential expression of a shutdown of neuroplasticity. Thus, if our neurons become depressed, so do we. Since depression is often a natural consequence of prolonged stress, one mechanism of action linking the two may be the catabolic impact of high levels of cortisol on the neurons within the hippocampus. It is suspected that antidepressant SSRIs and physical activity work to reverse the negative impact of cortisol in the hippocampus by triggering BDNF synthesis (Fernandes et al., 2008; Russo-Neustadt et al., 2000; Warner-Schmidt & Duman, 2006). Direct administration of BDNF has also been shown to have long-lasting antidepressant effects (Hoshaw, Malberg, & Lucki, 2005).

While more maternal attention results in increased growth and enhanced functioning throughout the pups' brains, separation from mothers proves to have the opposite effects. The same three areas that are upregulated with more maternal attention are all downregulated by her absence. Deprivation of maternal attention increases neural and glial death, while reducing gene expression, impairing their ability to learn. Maternal separation also results in reduced inhibitory (GABA) receptors in the locus coeruleus, increasing adrenaline secretion in reaction to stress while reducing the antianxiety properties of benzodiazepine receptors in the amygdala. Decreased cortisol receptors in the hippocampus also impair the inhibitory feedback to the stress system to shut down cortisol production. See Table 12.2 for the specific studies from which this information is taken. So again we see results that parallel findings with human subjects where early maternal deprivation through separation or depression results in decreased brain functioning, higher levels of anxiety, and difficulty with subsequent attachment (Brennan et al., 2008; Tyrka et al, 2008).

### TABLE 12.2
### The Impact of Maternal Separation

*Neural Growth and Plasticity*

Increased neuronal and glial death[1]

Decreased neurotrophin levels in ventral hippocampus[2]

Decreased glial density[3]

*Modulation of HPA Activity*

Reduced GABA receptors in the locus coeruleus

Decreased GABA receptor maturity

Reduced benzodiazepine receptors in the central and lateral amygdala and increased mRNA expression in the amygdala[4]

Increased anxiety, fearfulness, and response to stress[5]

Increased LTP and LTD in amygdalo-hippocampal synapses[6]

Decreased exploratory behavior, avoidance of novelty, and greater vulnerability to addiction[7]

Reduced gene expression[8]

Greater cortisol secretion in response to mild stress and increased startle response and startle-induced sounds[9]

Reduced somatic analgesia and increased colonic motility mimicking irritable bowel syndrome in humans[10]

Upregulation of glutamate receptors[11]

*Modulation of Future Maternal Behavior*

Decreased synaptic density in the medial prefrontal cortex

Decreased cell survival in maternal neural networks[12]

Decreased activation in the Bed nucleus of the stria terminalis and nucleus accumbens[13]

The evidence from the handling studies is essentially the same as for highly attentive mothers in neural health and the modulation of anxiety, supporting the idea that they may both represent the effects of greater amounts of maternal attention. More glucocorticoid receptors, lower cortisol levels, and greater brain activity reflect a brain geared toward less anxiety, helplessness, and fear. In turn, these pups are more resilient, engage in more complex exploratory behavior, and are better learners than their nonhandled siblings. Similar results have also been discovered in parrots and pigs (see Table 12.3).

TABLE 12.3
**The Impact of Human Handling on Rats, Pigs, and Parrots**

*Modulation of HPA Activity*

**Rat pups**

Increased concentrations of glucocorticoid receptors in the hippocampus and frontal lobes[1]

Increased glucocorticoid receptor binding capacity in the hippocampus[2]

Increased corticotrophin-releasing factor mRNA and greater CRF levels[3]

Decreased inhibitory avoidance and increased object recognition[4]

Lower levels of stress in reaction to a predatory odor[5]

Increased neurotrophin-3 expression and neuronal activation in hippocampus and parietal lobes[6]

Low cortisol secretion in response to stress/high exploratory behavior[7]

Protection against age-related neuroendocrine and behavioral decline with age[8]

Decreased helplessness behaviors[9]

**Baby pigs**

Lower basal and free plasma levels of cortisol[10]

**Amazon parrots**

Decreased serum cortisol levels in response to stress[11]

These and other studies support the belief that the reaction of the brain to maternal attention is not an abstract theory but a well-documented phenomenon. The consistency of behavioral, emotional, and biological findings across species is too powerful to be discounted. In fact, over 900 genes have been discovered that are differentially expressed based on the amount of maternal behavior (Rampon et al., 2000; Weaver et al., 2006). And there is no reason to believe that the maternal control of epigenetic expression has not been conserved in primates and humans.

Rhesus monkeys deprived of maternal contact demonstrate reduced transcriptional efficiency of serotonin and its receptors in the brain (Bennett et al., 2002). We do know that low levels of caring maternal behavior in humans correlate with more fearful behavior, less positive joint attention, and right-biased frontal activation, all of which are related to higher levels of stress and arousal (Hane & Fox, 2006). Self-esteem and locus of control have been found to correlate with hippocampal volume, which we know is tied to cortisol regulation (Pruessner et al., 2005). In my mind, the parallels as well as the tendency for evolution to conserve such mechanisms form a strong case for the theory that what Meaney and his colleagues are finding in rats is at work in humans.

In an exciting twist, it has been found that biological interventions and enriched social and physical environments can reverse the effects of low levels of maternal attention and early deprivation on both HPA activity and behavior (Bredy et al., 2004; Francis et al., 2002; Hood, Dreschel, & Granger, 2003; Szyf et al., 2005; Weaver et al., 2005). Unfortunately, chronic stress or trauma in adolescence and adulthood can also reverse the positive effects of higher levels of attention earlier in life, shaping a brain that resembles one that was deprived of early maternal attention (Ladd, Thrivikraman, Hout, & Plotsky, et al., 2005). These studies all support the notion that our brains are capable of continual adaptation in both positive and negative directions and that successful psychotherapy, one that establishes a nurturing relationship, may well be capable of triggering genetic expression in ways that can decrease stress, improve learning, and establish a bridge to new and healthier relationships.

Keep in mind that the amount of attention that a mother rat shows her pups exists in a broad adaptational context. Highly stressed mothers demonstrate lower rates of licking and grooming, which prepare her pup's brains for living in a stressful environment. In other words, under adverse conditions, maternal behavior decreases, which programs her offspring for enhanced reactivity to stress. This likely increases the probability of survival while simultaneously elevating the risk of physical and emotional pathology later in life (Diorio & Meaney, 2007). The impact of neonatal handling is also different for male and female pups, reflecting their divergent adaptational roles and contributions to the survival of their species (Park, Hoang, Belluzzi, & Leslie, 2003; Ploj et al., 2001; Stamatakis et al., 2008). All of this suggests that the level of maternal behavior is interwoven into a matrix of adaptation choices that vary based on external factors. The fact that processes that are set in motion early in life can be modified by subsequent experience demonstrates the ability to adapt to a changing environment.

This work with rats has established guidelines for future exploration into environmental programming in humans. There are obvious limitations to research with humans that requires physical examination of the brain. We will have to rely on samples of opportunity and utilize careful methodological controls to be certain of the quality of results. One such study compared the brains of suicide victims with normal controls and found lower mRNA levels of BDNF and trkB in the suicide victims, both of which are involved in neuronal health and plasticity. These data raise the possibility that early environmental programming may have made them susceptible to depression and suicide (Dwivedi et al., 2003). A more recent study compared the brains of suicide victims with and without histories of child abuse and found that those with histories of early abuse demonstrated decreased levels of glucocorticoid receptor mRNA, receptor expression, and growth factor transcription when compared to those without abuse (McGowan et al., 2009). These studies are highly supportive of our ability to apply animal research to humans.

## Attachment and the Human Brain

*What I do and what I dream include thee, as the wine must taste of its own grapes.*
—Elizabeth Barret Browning

It turns out that gene expression in response to close contact is a two-way street. Giving birth and exposure to children changes the brains of parents and caretakers in ways that support bonding, attachment, and nurturance. A primary discovery in mother rats has been the remodeling and expansion of the hippocampus in preparation for locating, storing, and retrieving greater amounts of food (Pawluski & Galea, 2006). Contact with her pups causes increased growth in the medial preoptic area, basolateral amygdala, and parietal and prefrontal cortex as the brain expands to incorporate these new beings into the self-experience of the mother (Fleming & Korsmit, 1996; Kinsley et al., 2006; Lonstein et al., 1998). Even virgin rats who are given pups to care for experience increased dendritic growth and neuronal excitation in superoptic areas (Modney, Yang & Hatton, 1990; Modney & Hatton, 1994; Salm, Modney, & Hatton, 1988). Thus, just as in children, interpersonal contact changes the brains of parents.

It has been shown that when human mothers hear their infants cry, there is an increase in activity in their right medial prefrontal cortex and anterior cingulate—regions known to mediate maternal response (Lorberbaum et al., 1999). Watching a video of their own infant will stimulate activity in the right anterior temporal pole, left amygdala, and both right and left ompfc (Minagawa-Kawai et al., 2008; Nitschke et al., 2004; Ranote et al., 2004).

It is likely that just as maternal attention triggers epigenetic factors in children, caring for children may also change genetic expression in their caretakers. The *grandmother gene hypothesis* suggests that human women experience early menopause to be available to help nurture their grandchildren and avoid the risks inherent in mating and childbirth, which rise with age for both mother and child (Lee, 2003; Rogers, 1993; Turke, 1997). In essence, the grandmother gene hypothesis suggests that early menopause has been shaped by natural selection to enhance the survival rate of a woman's children's children.

Sear, Mace, and McGregor (2000) studied tribal life in rural Gambia where families live at the level of subsistence and depend upon one another for basic survival. Their lifestyle is likely similar to the social and environmental context of most of our evolutionary history. The results of their research show that nutritional status, height, and the probability of survival of their young were significantly correlated with the presence of postmenopausal maternal grandmothers. On the other hand, the presence of fathers, paternal grandmothers, or other male kin had a negligible impact on either the nutritional status or survival rates of offspring. Similar findings have been obtained in studies of hunter-gatherer populations of Tanzania, premodern Japan, Canada, and Finland, and contemporary urban populations in the United States (Hawkes, O'Connell, & Jones, 1997; Lahdenperä et al., 2004; Pope et al., 1993).

Besides the timing of menopause, is it possible that women live longer because they are traditionally involved in caring for their young? That is, is there a health benefit involved in taking care of children because of the neurobiological processes it stimulates in our brains and bodies? Some interesting evidence that may support a connection between child care and longevity comes from looking at parenting responsibilities across different species of primates. A longevity advantage for females does exist in gorillas, orangutans, and humans, in which they are the primary caretakers. On the other hand, in species such as the owl and titi monkey, where the male is the primary caretaker of infants, males tend to survive longer. In Goeldi monkeys, where caretaking is shared, the longevity for both genders is equivalent (see Table 12.4).

TABLE 12.4
Child Care and Longevity Across Primate Species

| Primate | Female/Male Survival Ratio | Male Care |
|---------|---------------------------|-----------|
| Chimpanzee | 1.418 | Rare |
| Spider monkey | 1.272 | Rare |
| Orangutan | 1.203 | None |
| Gorilla | 1.199 | Pair-living, little direct role |
| Gibbon | 1.125 | Protects and plays with offspring |
| Human | 1.052–1.082 | Supports economically, some care |
| Goeldi monkey | 0.974 | Both parents carry infant |
| Siamang | 0.915 | Carries infant in second year |
| Owl monkey | 0.869 | Carries infant from birth |
| Titi monkey | 0.828 | Carries infant from birth |

*Adapted from Allman, Rosin, Kumar, & Hasenstaub, 1998.*

Given the amount of data supporting the beneficial effects of secure attachment, caretaking, human touch, and social support, it is plausible that nurturing, emotional attunement, and physical contact have salubrious effects that may provide primary caretakers with a survival advantage. It is possible that attachment bonds, caretaking experiences, and the neurochemicals and epigenetic phenomena they impact may well enhance our health and survival. Perhaps caring for our children and grandchildren may be more supportive of health and longevity than cholesterol medication and treadmills.

Interestingly, women who give birth after the age of 40 are almost four times more likely to live to be 100 years old (Perls, Alpert, & Fretts, 1997). While this is usually explained in terms of the protective nature of birth-related hormones, their enhanced longevity may be part of broader biological and psychological processes involved in intense caretaking (King & Elder, 1997). It is a good bet that taking care of a child tells the brain and body to trigger epigenetic and biochemical processes that enhance health and slow down aging.

# The Human Social Brain

*It is good to rub and polish our brains against those of others.*
                                                    —Montaigne

We have seen a great deal of evidence of the impact of early nurturance on the shaping of the social brain and its emotional circuitry. So when our early relationships are frightening, abusive, or nonexistent, our brains dutifully adapt to the realities of our unfortunate situations. However, there is reason to believe that these circuits retain experience-dependent plasticity throughout life, especially in close relationships (Bowlby, 1988; Davidson, 2000). Experience-dependent plasticity has been found in many areas of the brain, including the prefrontal cortex and hippocampus (Kolb & Gibb, 2002; Maletic-Savatic, Malinow, & Svoboda, 1999). These structures, central to learning and memory, are also key in shaping attachment schema. Further, research is emerging that in the transition from dating to marriage, there is a broad tendency to move from insecure and disorganized attachment schema to increasingly secure patterns (Crowell, Treboux, & Waters, 2002). On the other hand, social stress inhibits cell proliferation and neural plasticity, while social support, compassion, and kindness support positive neural growth (Czéh et al., 2007; Davidson, Jackson, & Kalin, 2000).

While rats possess the basic mechanisms of bonding and maternal behavior, our brains have more elaborate and sophisticated mechanisms for attachment. In fact, the human brain is criss-crossed with neural networks dedicated to receiving, processing, and communicating messages across the social synapse. The difference in humans is that the environmental programming of these experience-dependent circuits is far more lengthy and complex. Networks of our complex social brains include brain regions, neural systems, and regulatory networks listed in Table 12.5. These are the same circuits that therapists attempt to influence in reshaping the brain in ways which lead to more positive adaptation later in life. The idea that psychotherapy is a kind of reparenting may be more than a metaphor; it may be precisely what we are attempting to accomplish at the level of the epigenome. This research establishes attention, care, and nurturance as a way to influence the very structure of our brain and places psychotherapy at the heart of biological interventions. It is odd to think that Carl Rogers may someday find a place next to Crick and Watson in the pantheon of biologists.

Now let's shift our attention to the structures of the human brain that organize attachment, affect regulation, and the modulation of stress. For a more in-depth exploration of the social brain, see *The Neuroscience of Human Relationships* (Cozolino, 2006). Keep in mind that, just as in rats, these systems are also built by the attachments they come to control. Thus, our learning history comes to be reflected in the architecture of our neural systems.

TABLE 12.5
Structures and Systems of the Social Brain

**Cortical and Subcortical Structures**
Orbital and medial prefrontal cortices (ompfc)
Cingulate cortex and spindle (Von Economo) cells
Insula cortex
Somatosensory cortex
Amygdala, hippocampus
Hypothalamus

**Sensory, Motor, and Affective Systems**
Face recognition and expression reading
Imitation, mirroring, and resonance systems

**Regulatory Systems**
Attachment, stress and fear regulation (orbital medial
prefrontal cortex–amygdala balance)
Social engagement (the vagal system of autonomic regulation)
Social motivation (reward representation and reinforcement)

## Cortical and Subcortical Structures

*The prehistorical and primitive period represents the true infancy of the mind.*

—James Baldwin

The ompfc, insula, and cingulate cortices—the most evolutionarily primitive areas of the cortex—lie buried beneath and within the folds of the later evolving cortex. In fact, some neuroanatomists see these contiguous structures as comprising a functional system called the *basal forebrain* (Critchley, 2005; Heimer & Van Hoesen, 2006). The ompfc sits at the apex of the limbic system. As a convergence zone for polysensory, somatic, and emotional information, it is in the perfect position to synthesize information from both our internal and external worlds. In its position at the apex of the limbic system, the ompfc's inhibitory role in autonomic functioning highlights its contribution to the organization of behavior and affect regulation.

The ompfc allows us to translate the punishment and reward values of complex social information such as facial expressions, gestures, and eye contact into meaningful information, associate it with our own emotions, and thus organize attachment schema (O'Doherty et al., 2001; Tremblay & Schultz, 1999; Zald & Kim, 2001). The ompfc also mediates emotional responses and coordinates the activation and balance of the sympathetic and parasympathetic branches of the autonomic nervous system (Hariri et al., 2000; Price, Carmichael & Drevets, 1996).

The cingulate cortex is a primitive association area of visceral, motor, tactile, autonomic, and emotional information that begins to participate in brain activity during the second month of life (Kennard, 1955). It first appeared during evolution in animals exhibiting maternal behavior, play, and nursing, and when making sounds became involved with communication between predator and prey, potential mates, and mother and child (MacLean, 1985). The caretaking and resonance behaviors made possible by the cingulate also provide an important component of the neural infrastructure for social cooperation and empathy (Rilling et al., 2002; Vogt, 2005). Destruction of the anterior cingulate in mammals results in mutism, a loss of maternal responses, infant death due to neglect, and emotional and autonomic instability (Bush, Luu, & Posner, 2000; Bush et al., 2002; Paus, Petrides, Evans, & Meyer, 1993).

The anterior cingulate contains spindle-shaped neurons that appear to have evolved in humans and great apes to connect and regulate divergent streams of information (Nimchinsky et al., 1995, 1999). These cells may provide the neural connectivity necessary both for the development of self-control and the ability to engage in sustained attention to difficult problems (Allman et al., 2001, 2005). Spindle cells are especially fascinating because they emerge after birth and are experience-dependent. Early neglect, stress, and trauma may negatively impact the development and organization of the anterior cingulate and spindle cells, resulting in lifelong cognitive deficits, and emotional functioning may be based on the construction and health of these structures (Cohen et al., 2006; Ovtscharoff, Helmeke, & Braun, 2006).

The insula begins life on the lateral surfaces of the brain, only to become hidden by the rapid expansion of the frontal and temporal lobes.

The insula is sometimes described as the "limbic integration cortex" because of its massive connections to all limbic structures, and its feed-forward links with the frontal, parietal, and temporal lobes (Augustine, 1996). It provides the brain with a means to connect primitive bodily states with the experience and expression of bodily awareness, emotion, and behavior (Carr et al., 2003; Phan et al., 2002). In tandem with the anterior cingulate, the insula allows us to be aware of what is happening inside of our bodies and reflect on our emotional experiences (Bechara & Naqvi, 2004; Critchley et al., 2004; Gundel, Lopez-Sala, Ceballos-Baumann, 2004). Damage to the right insula can result in anosognosia, a condition where a patient seems unaware of and unfazed by severe paralysis on the left side of the body (Garavan, Ross, & Stein, 1999). Recent research suggests that the insula is involved with mediating the entire range of emotions from disgust to love (Bartels & Zeki, 2000; Calder et al., 2003).

The somatosensory cortex, located along the front of the parietal lobes, processes information about bodily experiences. It lies just behind the central gyrus and wraps deep within the Sylvian fissure that divides the parietal from the frontal lobes. Along with the insula and anterior cingulate cortices, it contains multiple representations of the body that process and organize our experience of touch, temperature, pain, joint position, and our visceral state. These different processing streams combine to create our experience of our physical selves. It also participates in what we call intuition or gut feelings by activating implicit memories related to our experiences and helping us to make decisions guided by feelings (Damasio, 1994). The experience of our own bodies becomes the model for our understanding and empathy with others (Damasio et al., 2000).

Working in concert with the ompfc, the subcortical amygdala is another core component of the social brain. The amygdala achieves a high degree of maturity by the eighth month of gestation, allowing it to associate a fear response to a stimulus prior to birth (LaBar et al., 1995; Ulfig, Setzer, & Bohl, 2003). As a primitive organ of appraisal, the amygdala closely monitors signals of safety and danger and mediates the fight-or-flight response via the autonomic nervous system (Davis, 1997; Ono, Nishijo, & Uwano, 1995; Phelps & Anderson, 1997). The ompfc can inhibit the amygdala based on conscious awareness and feedback from the environment (Beer et al., 2003). By the same token, when we are frightened and our amygdala is activated, it inhibits the ompfc and we have a difficult time being rational, logical, and in control of our thoughts. The amygdala also appears to contribute to our conscious experience of both emotional and physical pain (Mitra & Sapolsky, 2008; Neugebauer, Li, Bird, & Han, 2004). Since the networks connecting the ompfc and the amygdala are shaped by experience, our learning history of what is safe and dangerous, including our attachment schema, is thought to be encoded within this system.

The hippocampus is situated at the junction between the cortex and limbic system on both sides of the brain. In lower mammals like the rat, the hippocampus is a specialized spatial map of foraging territory. In humans, the parietal lobes evolved from the hippocampus and assist it in complex visual-spatial processing. The human hippocampus, along with its adjacent structures (parahippocampal gyrus, dentate gyrus), have come to be specialized in the organization of spatial, sequential, and emotional learning and memory (Edelman, 1989; McGaugh et al., 1993; Sherry et al., 1992; Zola-Morgan & Squire, 1990). In contrast to the amygdala, the hippocampus is a late bloomer, continuing to mature into early adulthood along with the dlpfc connections upon which it relies (Benes, 1989). Our lack of conscious memory for early childhood, known as childhood amnesia, is likely due to the slow developmental course of the hippocampus (Fuster, 1996; Jacobs et al., 2000; McCarthy, 1995).

The hypothalamus is a small and ancient structure that sits at the center of the brain below the thalamus and halfway between the cortex and the brainstem. It has extensive connections with the structures of the social brain within the frontal lobes, limbic system, and brainstem. I include the hypothalamus as part of the social brain because it is centrally involved with the translation of conscious experience into bodily processes and thus, the transduction of early experience into the building of the brain and body. Its various nuclei organize many bodily functions such as temperature regulation, hunger, thirst, and activity level. The hypothalamus is also involved in the regulation of sexual behavior and aggression. As the head of the HPA axis, it translates brain processes into hormonal secretions from the anterior pituitary. Among the hormones produced by the pituitary, follicle-stimulating hormone and prolactin are involved in reproduction and nursing. Adrenocorticotropic hormone, which is sent to the adrenal glands via the blood stream, stimulates the production of cortisol, which we will be discussing in depth later as it relates to caretaking and early stress.

## Sensory, Motor, and Affective Systems

*Common Sense is that which judges the things given to it by other senses.*
—Leonardo da Vinci

It is in the temporal lobes that our senses are integrated, organized, and combined with primitive drives and emotional significance in a "vertical" linkup across all three levels of the triune brain (Adams, Victor, & Ropper, 1997). For example, the recognition of faces and reading their expressions occurs in the top-down networks. Cells involved in both reading and identifying facial expressions are located in adjacent areas of the temporal lobes (Desimone, 1991; Hasselmo, Rolls, & Baylis, 1989). When we see faces, the areas of the brain that become activated lie in a processing stream dedicated to the identification of visual stimuli (Lu et al., 1991). The association region of the occipital lobe dedicated to the identification of faces is the fusiform face area (Gauthier et al., 2000; Halgren et al., 1999). These areas, in turn, are interconnected with other clusters of cells that are responsible for eye gaze, body posture, and facial expression as the brain constructs complex perceptions and social judgments from basic building blocks of visual information (Jellema, Baker, Wicker, & Perrett, 2000).

Regions in the anterior (front) portions of the superior temporal sulcus (STS) integrate information about various aspects of the same person (form, location, and motion), allowing us to identify others from different angles, in various places, and while they are in motion (Jellema, Maassen, & Perrett, 2004; Pelphrey et al., 2003; Vaina et al., 2001). The STS also contains mirror neurons, which activate either when we witness others engaging in behaviors or when we ourselves subsequently engage in these actions. By bridging neural networks dedicated to perception and movement, mirror neurons connect the observed and the observer by linking visual and motor experience. Resonance behaviors (based on mirror systems) are the reflexive imitation responses we make when interacting with others. It is hypothesized that mirror systems and resonance behaviors provide us with a visceral-emotional experience of what the other is experiencing, allowing us to know others from the inside out.

## Regulatory Systems

*We gain our ends only with the laws of nature; we control her only*
*by understanding her laws.*
                                                    —Jacob Bronowski

The body's regulatory systems are involved in the maintenance of internal homeostatic processes, balancing approach and avoidance, excitation and inhibition, and fight and flight responses. They also control metabolism, arousal, and our immunological functioning. It is through these systems that we regulate each other's biological and emotional states.

## The Stress, Fear, and Attachment System

*I'm not afraid of storms, for I'm learning how to sail my ship.*
                                                    —Louisa May Alcott

The HPA system regulates the secretion of hormones involved with the body's response to stress and threat. The immediate reaction to stress is vital for short-term survival, while the rapid return to normalization after the threat has passed is essential for long-term survival. Prolonged stress results in system damage and breakdown. The long-term effects of negative parenting experiences, failures of attachment, and early trauma are mediated via the HPA system. In terms of fear, we turn again to the amygdala, as it alerts a variety of brain centers that a fight-flight response is required. In turn, the activation of the sympathetic branch of the autonomic nervous system results in symptoms of anxiety, agitation, and panic. The prime directive of the amygdala is to protect us by pairing a stimulus with a fear response, and it works so fast that this pairing can be created far ahead of our conscious perception of threat. Throughout our lives, but especially during childhood, relationships with others regulate our stress and fear. A secure attachment indicates that we have learned to successfully utilize our relationships with others to quell our fears and modulate our arousal.

## The Social Engagement System

*Communication leads to community, that is, to understanding,*
*intimacy and mutual valuing.*
                                                    —Rollo May

The tenth cranial nerve, also called the vagus, is actually a complex communication system between the brain and multiple points within the body including the heart, lungs, throat, and digestive system. Its *afferent* (sensory) and *efferent* (motor) fibers allow for rapid continuous feedback between brain and body to promote homeostatic regulation and the optimal maintenance of physical health and emotional well-being (Porges, Doussard-Roosevelt, & Maiti, 1994). The vagal system is a central component of the autonomic nervous system. In the absence of external challenge, the vagus works to enhance digestion, growth, and social communication. When a challenge does arise, a decrease in vagal activation facilitates sympathetic arousal, high energy output, and the fight-flight response. Between rest and all-out activation, the vagus allows us to maintain continued engagement by modulating arousal during emotional interpersonal exchanges. The vagal system accomplishes this by modulating and fine-tuning sympathetic arousal.

Like the attachment system described earlier, the development of this engagement system and the fine-tuning of the vagal brake to regulate affect appear to depend on the quality of attachment relationships in early childhood. This allows us to internalize what we learn from experience with caretakers into moment-to-moment somatic regulation. The vagal system also controls the primary facial, mouth, and throat muscles involved in communication, and links them with an awareness and control of internal states, coordinating the cognitive and emotional processing necessary for relationships.

The "tone" of the vagus refers to the vagal system's dexterity in regulating the heart and other target organs (Porges et al., 1996). Inadequate development of this experience-dependent vagal tone can impact all levels of psychosocial and cognitive development (Porges et al., 1994). Children with poor vagal tone have difficulty in suppressing emotions in situations demanding their attention, making it difficult for them to engage with their parents, sustain a shared focus with playmates, and maintain attention on important material in the classroom (see Table 12.6 for more details).

Vagal regulation allows us to become upset, anxious, or angry with a loved one without withdrawing or becoming physically aggressive. We can hypothesize that many who engage in domestic violence, child abuse, and other forms of aggressive behavior may not have had the kinds of early attachment relationships required to build an adequate vagal system. Thus, good parenting not only teaches appropriate responses in challenging interpersonal situations, but it also builds vagal circuitry required to stay engaged.

TABLE 12.6
Correlates of Vagal Tone

| Higher Vagal Tone Correlates With | Lower Vagal Tone Correlates With |
|---|---|
| The ability to self-regulateIrritability | Irritability |
| Self-soothing capacity by 3 months of age | Behavioral problems at 3 years of age |
| The range and control of emotional states | Emotional dysregulation |
| More reliable autonomic responses | Distractibility |
| Suppression of heart rate variability | Hyper-reactivity to environmental and visceral stimulii |
| Enhanced attentional capacity and the ability to take in information | |
| Positive social engagement | Withdrawal |
| Increased behavioral organization | Impulsivity/acting out |
| Consistent caretaking/secure attachment | Insecure attachment |

## The Social Motivation System

> Interdependence is and ought to be as much the ideal of man as self-sufficiency. Man is a social being.
> —Mohandas Gandhi

Nelson and Panksepp (1998) postulated the existence of a *social motivation system* modulated by oxytocin, vasopressin, endogenous endorphins, and other neurochemicals related to reward, decreased physical pain, and feelings of well-being. While conserved from more primitive approach-avoidance and pain regulation circuitry, the social motivation system extends into the amygdala, anterior cingulate, and orbital medial prefrontal cortex. These circuits and neurochemicals are thought to regulate attachment, pair bonding, empathy, and altruistic behavior (Decety & Lamm, 2006; Seitz, Nickel, & Azari, 2006). In other words, as Fisher (1998) suggested, the social motivation system can be divided into three categories: those involved in bonding and attachment (regulated by peptides, vasopressin, and oxytocin), attraction (regulated by dopamine and other catecholamines), and sex drive (regulated by androgens and estrogens). The production of these various biochemical elements, as well as the creation of their receptors, are all subject to the influences of experience early in life.

In addition, the dopamine reward system of the subcortical area known as the ventral striatum is involved with more complex analysis of reward and social motivation. The ventral striatum becomes activated with an expectation of a social reward, such as when we anticipate being given candy or positive attention (Kampe et al., 2001; Pagnoni, Zink, Montague, & Berns, 2002; Schultz et al., 1992). For example, once the cortex has determined that we find someone attractive, the ventral striatum becomes activated when they look our way, giving the signal that the possibility for being rewarded with a desirable outcome has increased (Elliott, Friston, & Dolan, 2000; Schultz, Dayan, & Montague, 1997; Schultz, 1998). The activation of the ventral striatum translates the anticipation of reward into a physical impulse to approach. In this way, those whom we find attractive actually exert what feels like a gravitational pull on us.

## Summary

Recent research has provided us with new ways of understanding how early experience builds the brain. Maternal attention has been linked to the neurobiology of systems related to learning and memory, stress regulation, and attachment behavior. Although the human brain is far more complex than those of the animals upon whom this research has been conducted, findings in human research across a broad array of disciplines demonstrate consistent results in the areas of learning, resilience, and attachment. The neural hubs and regulatory networks described here are all built in an experience-dependent manner. That is, early relationships shape the building of neural circuitry, which guides how we are able to learn, react to stress, and attach to others in ways that parallel those seen in the animal research discussed earlier. As we learn more about the complexities of the human brain, we will understand how relationships build the brain, and how love becomes flesh.

Part V.

# The Disorganization of Experience

Chapter 13

# The Anxious and Fearful Brain

*Fear is the oldest and strongest emotion of mankind.*
—H. P. Lovecraft

All animals have been shaped by evolution to approach what is life sustaining and avoid what is dangerous. The success of rapid and accurate approach-avoidance decisions determines if an organism lives to reproduce and carry its genes forward to the next generation. Because vigilance for danger is a central mechanism of the process of natural selection, evolution may well favor an anxious gene (Beck et al., 1979). Some anxieties appear to be hard wired, specific to primates, and linked to both our present and past survival needs. Fear of spiders, snakes, heights, and open and closed spaces all harken back to the survival of our forest-dwelling ancestors. From an evolutionary perspective, our complex neural systems have all been sculpted to better serve the prime directive of survival.

The neural circuitry involved in fear and anxiety, although biased toward the right hemisphere, involves both hemispheres and all levels of the triune brain. The most primitive subcortical fight-or-flight circuitry, shared with our reptilian ancestors, interacts with the most highly evolved regions of the cortex. This results in the capacity to experience anxiety about everything from an unexpected tap on the shoulder to an existential crisis. The connection between every kind of anxiety and the core biological mechanisms of physical survival supports the philosophical notion that all anxiety, at its core, may be the fear of death (Tillich, 1974).

Anxiety and fear are the conscious emotional aspects of the body's ongoing appraisal of threat, telling us to be prepared to take action. Anxiety can be triggered by countless conscious or unconscious cues and has the power to shape our behaviors, thoughts, and feelings. At its most adaptive, anxiety encourages us to step back from the edge of a cliff, or to check to see if we signed our tax forms before sealing the envelope. At its least adaptive, anxiety steers us away from taking important and appropriate risks, pushing ourselves to reach personal goals, or engaging in new and potentially beneficial behaviors.

The response to stress, or *general adaptation syndrome* (Selye, 1979), results in a range of physiological changes designed to prepare the body for fight or flight. Energy is mobilized through increased cardiovascular and muscular tone, whereas digestion, growth, and immune responses are inhibited. As part of the stress response, a cascade of biochemical changes occur in the hypothalamus, pituitary, and adrenal glands (the HPA axis), as well as in the sympathetic nervous system. These biochemicals mediate the physical and psychological changes experienced during stress. Increased levels of glucocorticoids, epinephrine, and endogenous opioids are particularly relevant to a discussion of the psychological impact of stress and trauma, in that they alter attention, cognition, and memory. We experience the effects of the general adaptation syndrome in situations such as automobile accidents, at crucial moments during sporting events, or when engaging in public speaking. The dangers can be real, imagined, or experienced vicariously as we watch others in stressful or dangerous situations.

With the expansion of the cerebral cortex and the emergence of imagination, we have become capable of being anxious about situations we will never experience. We can now worry about monsters living under our beds and the incineration of the earth resulting from the sun's expansion. Because our imaginal capabilities have allowed for the construction of the self, we can also become anxious about potential threats to our psychological survival. Psychotherapists deal with a wide variety of anxiety disorders based in the fear of a social death. The expectation of rejection by another can result in social withdrawal; the fear of forgetting one's lines in a play can result in stage fright. Systems of physical survival have been conserved in the evolution of consciousness and the ego, to be triggered when threats to these abstract constructions are activated.

Consciously experienced anxiety provides the opportunity to face and work through one's fears. The common wisdom of getting back on the horse that threw you is advice clearly aimed at preventing the use of avoidance to control anxiety. In fact, the reduction of anxiety through avoidance reinforces the behavior and makes the feared stimulus seem all the worse. Unfortunately, anxiety can be paired with all kinds of automatic and internal sensations, emotions, and thoughts, which shape behavior outside of conscious awareness. Compounding the problem, the left hemisphere interpreter provides a rationale supporting and reinforcing avoidance: "It's inhuman to ride horses!" "Who needs planes?" "Why go out when it's so comfortable at home?" The avoidance of thoughts and feelings associated with feared stimuli both reflects and perpetuates a lack of integration among neural networks. Facing one's fears is a core component of all forms of psychotherapy.

We see this, for example, with adult women who were sexually or emotionally abused as children who sometimes come to therapy with chronic and severe weight problems. They do well on diets until they begin to be noticed by men, associated in implicit memory with the pain and shame of their childhood experiences. These negative emotional reactions lead them to return to behavioral patterns associated with an avoidance of such feelings, such as eating. The act of eating is doubly reinforcing because it provides nurturance, while gaining back the weight serves to protect against sexual advances.

Thus, what started out as a straightforward survival-based alarm system has also become a nuisance. This is another downside of the design compromises between speed and accuracy mentioned earlier (Mesulam, 1998). Evolution designed a brain that reacts quickly to a variety of subtle environmental cues. These same capabilities have negative consequences when applied to a complex and largely nonconscious psychological environment. An understanding of the neuroscience of anxiety and fear is helpful in both the conceptualization and treatment of most clinical disorders. In the following pages, we will look at the two loops of fear circuitry outlined by Joseph LeDoux, the role of the amygdala in the regulation of fear and anxiety proposed by Michael Davis, and Robert Sapolsky's work on the negative impact of long-term stress.

## Fast and Slow Fear Networks

*Fear is an emotion indispensible for survival.*
—Hannah Arendt

Through his research with animals, LeDoux (1994) demonstrated the existence of two separate yet interrelated neural circuits which regulate fear. The conservation of these systems during evolution allows us to apply these findings to human experience (Phelps, Delgado, Nearing, & LeDoux, 2004). The two systems (which we will call *fast* and *slow*) each play a somewhat different role in our reaction to danger. This model can be clinically useful for anxious and fearful clients by helping them understand the neurobiological mechanisms underlying their unsettling experiences.

The reflexive fast system acts immediately, sending information directly from the sense organs (eyes, ears, skin, nose, tongue) through the thalamus to the amygdala. And when I say fast, I mean fast: All of this processing can occur in one twelfth of a second. The amygdala evaluates the sensory input and translates it into bodily responses via its many connections with the autonomic nervous systems. The thalamus may aid in this rapid evaluation by maintaining crude representations of potentially dangerous things often encountered in the environment such as spiders, snakes, and dangerous predators (Brosch, Sander, & Scherer, 2007). These subcortical structures play an executive role in rapid appraisal because the increased time it would take to include the cortex might have too large a survival cost.

Simultaneously, the slow system sends sensory information on to the hippocampus and cortex for further evaluation. This system is slower because it contains more synaptic connections and involves conscious processing. Cortical circuits of memory and executive processing examine the information more carefully, compare it to memories of similar situations, and decide how to proceed. The slow circuit aids in fear processing by contextualizing the information in time and space. This slow system in humans—with its apex in the prefrontal cortex—has the additional task of making sense of the behavioral and visceral reaction already set into motion by the fast systems. In this way, our conscious executive functions discover the decisions that have already been made by our unconscious executives. We find ourselves already scared when we initially perceive what is frightening us; or ecstatic as our loved one comes into view. Figure 13.1 depicts the neural circuits of the fast and slow fear networks.

### FIGURE 13.1
### Fast and Slow Fear Circuits

*A depiction of the two pathways of information to the amygdala—one directly from the thalamus and the other through the cortex and hippocampus (adapted from LeDoux, J. Emotion, memory, and the brain. Copyright ©1994 by Scientific American, Inc. All rights reserved.)*

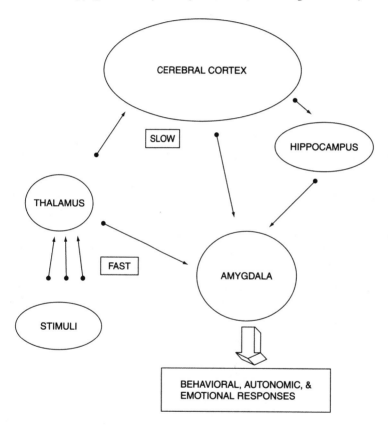

This dual circuitry helps us to understand why we often react to things before thinking and then have to apologize later on. In therapy, we often attempt to utilize the conscious linguistic structures of the slow circuit to modify or inhibit dysfunctional reflexes and emotional appraisals of the fast circuit. Coupled with relaxation techniques and enhanced awareness, exposure to a feared stimulus can serve to enhance the regulatory input of the slow cortical circuits by building new neural connections. Cognitive and behavioral interventions therefore increase the ability of the cortex to inhibit the amygdala.

There are many examples of these two systems in action. I walked into my garage one day to look for a tool when, out of the corner of my eye, I saw a small brown object near my foot. There are plenty of little critters in my neighborhood and they often crawl, burrow, or fly into my house. I immediately jumped back, my heart rate increased, my eyes widened, and I became tense, ready to act. Moving backward, I oriented toward the shape, saw that it looked more like a piece of wood than a rodent, and began to relax. After a few seconds, my heart rate and level of arousal were back to normal; the potential danger had passed.

Analyzing this experience in terms of the two systems, my peripheral vision saw the object and my amygdala appraised it in an overgeneralized fashion to be a threat. My amygdala activated a variety of sympathetic responses including startle, increased respiration, and avoidance. In the split second while my body was reacting, I reflexively oriented my head toward the shape, which brought it to the fovea of my retina, providing my hippocampus and cortex with more detailed visual information, allowing them to appraise it more accurately than my skittish amygdala. I suppose that a species-specific fear accounts for such a strong reaction to an animal weighing just a few ounces. This example, trivial as it may be, leads to a more serious application of LeDoux's theory to interpersonal relationships.

As the core of our social brain, the amygdala organizes the appraisals of what we have learned from our relationship history. In interpersonal situations, our amygdala reflexively and unconsciously appraises others in the context of our past experiences. From moment to moment, the reflexive activations of our fast systems (organized by past learning) shape the nature of our present experience (Bar et al., 2006). This is a powerful mechanism by which our early social learning influences our experience of the present. So, by the time we become conscious of others, our brain has already made decisions about them. In the case of prejudice, skin color triggers a set of assumptions upon which we evaluate other people (Olsson, Ebert, Banaji, & Phelps, 2005). At the opposite extreme, love at first sight is a sort of positive prejudice triggered by emotional memories projected onto another person.

# The Amygdala's Role in Anxiety and Fear

*No passion so effectually robs the mind of all its powers of acting and reasoning as fear.*

—Edmund Burke

The amygdala plays a central role in the activation of fear. It has been conserved and expanded during evolution in order to process increasingly complex cognitive, sensory, and emotional input. Its central role in appraisal and the triggering of the biochemical cascade of the fight-or-flight response makes it vital for processing memory, emotional regulation, bonding, and attachment. Electrical stimulation of the amygdala's central nucleus results in the experience of fear, whereas destruction of the amygdala will eliminate fear reactions altogether (Carvey, 1998). In fact, the destruction of the amygdala in animals results in an inability to acquire a conditioned fear response.

Although we are genetically programmed to become anxious about things like snakes or abandonment, fear can be learned by pairing any thought, feeling, or sensation with a noxious stimulus, such as a loud noise or an electric shock (Corcoran & Quirk, 2007). Learning to be anxious can occur at conscious and unconscious levels related to both internal and external stimuli. Like the hippocampus, the lateral areas of the amygdala are capable of long-term potentiation (LTP) involved in reinforcing connections among neurons. Remember that LTP is the process through which the association among neurons becomes strengthened and learning is established. The amygdala can learn, throughout life, to pair any stimulus (even physical affection or praise) with fear.

As we saw earlier in our discussion of memory, the hippocampus and amygdala organize interacting but dissociable systems of memory. Bechara and colleagues (1995) reported that a patient with bilateral (left and right) amygdala damage was unable to acquire a conditioned autonomic response to sensory stimuli. The patient was, however, able to consciously remember the conditioning situation because his hippocampi were still intact. Another patient with bilateral damage to the hippocampus showed no conscious memory for the conditioning situation but did acquire autonomic and behavioral conditioning. The authors concluded that the amygdala is "indispensable" for coupling emotional conditioning with sensory information while the hippocampus is required for conscious recollection (Bechara et al., 1995).

The neural projections from the amygdala to numerous anatomical targets cause the multiple physical expressions of anxiety, fear, and panic. Projections from the amygdala to the lateral hypothalamus result in sympathetic activation responsible for increased heart rate and blood pressure. The amygdala's stimulation of the trigeminal facial motor nerve even causes the facial expressions of fear (Davis, 1992). The amygdala is also essential in reading the fearful facial expressions of others (Baird et al., 1999). As you can see from Figure 13.2, the amygdala is well connected, making the fear response a powerful whole-body experience.

FIGURE 13.2
**Some Targets of the Amygdala in the Fear Response**

*Some of the many anatomical targets of the amygdala in the fear response,
and their biological and behavioral contribution.*

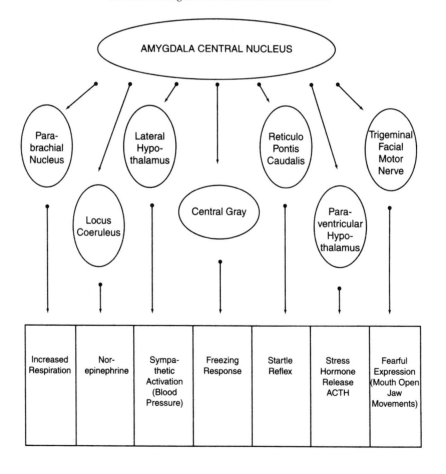

The triggering of the autonomic nervous system by the amygdala causes a racing heart, sweating, and other physiological symptoms as the body prepares for fight or flight. In the absence of real external danger, this is experience is called a *panic attack*. Sufferers often go to emergency rooms thinking they are having a heart attack. Individuals with panic disorder have increased neural activity in the amygdala (Reiman et al., 1989). Psychologically, victims report a sense of impending doom, feelings of unreality, and the thought that they are going crazy. Panic attacks are often triggered by stress or other conflicts in the sufferer's life, but he or she seldom makes the connection between these events and the panic attacks. Because the neural connections are contained within hidden neural layers, they are experienced as "coming out of the blue," leaving victims struggling to comprehend what is happening to them.

The amygdala's tendency toward generalization results in panic being triggered by an increasing number of internal and external cues (Douglas & Pribram, 1966). Because panic attacks are experienced as unpredictable and life threatening, they result in a limitation of activities. *Agoraphobia*, or fear of open spaces, develops as victims of panic attacks associate fear with a broader variety of situations. Hoping to avoid these attacks, sufferers restrict their activities to the point where they eventually become housebound. Simultaneously, the amygdala becomes conditioned to respond faster in people who become phobic, creating a vicious cycle of anxiety and fear (Larson et al., 2006). The behavior of these individuals becomes so shaped by fear that they come to avoid most of life. On the other hand, those of us with a slower and less active amygdala experience greater psychological well-being (van Reekum et al., 2007). One gift of aging is that the amygdala also appears to become less sensitive to fear as we grow older.

The development and connectivity of the amygdala have many implications for both early child development and psychotherapy. Without the inhibitory impact of the later-developing hippocampal-cortical networks, early fear experiences are unregulated, overwhelming full-body experiences. Because the amygdala is operational at birth, the experience of fear may be the strongest early emotion. Part of the power of early emotional learning may be the intensity of these unregulated negative affects in shaping early neural infrastructure. The infant is very dependent on caretakers to modulate these powerful experiences. Amygdala- and hippocampus-mediated memory systems are dissociable from one another, which means that early and traumatic memories can be stored without conscious awareness or cortical control. They will not be consciously remembered, but instead will emerge as sensory, motor, and emotional memories like traumatic flashbacks.

Another limbic structure closely connected to the amygdala is the bed nucleus of the stria terminalis (BNST). Like the amygdala, it is connected upward to the prefrontal cortex, as well as down into the autonomic nervous system. Unlike the amygdala, the BNST is sensitive to abstract cues and is capable of long-term activation, suggestive of both its later evolution and its role in anticipatory anxiety (Davis, 1998; Kalin et al., 2001). It appears that perhaps the amygdala specializes in fear while the BNST evolved to deal with the more complex triggers for anxiety that emerged as our brains became capable of imagining multiple potential outcomes. Interestingly, the BNST in rats is a structure that grows in response to maternal responsibilities. We have to wonder if, as the brain became specialized for caretaking, the scaffolding we need to create around our children pushed the evolution of a constant focus on potential dangers.

## The Locus Coeruleus and Norepinephrine

*Worry gives a small thing a big shadow.*
—Swedish proverb

One important descending projection from the amygdala and BNST connects them with the locus coeruleus (LC). The LC is a small structure with extensive projections throughout the brainstem, midbrain, and cerebral cortex. It is, in fact, connected with more parts of the brain than any other structure so far discovered (Aston-Jones, Valentino, VanBockstaele, & Meyerson, 1994). The LC is the brain's primary generator of norepinephrine (NE), which drives the activity of the sympathetic branch of the autonomic nervous system responsible for the fight-or-flight response. One effect of NE is to enhance the firing of neurons that are highly relevant to a present experience based on past learning (past fear responses), while inhibiting those involved in baseline activities.

This means that stimulation of the LC prepares us for danger by activating circuits dedicated to attention and preparation for action. NE activation makes us become vigilant, scan for danger, and maintain a posture of tense readiness. It also heightens our memory for danger, creating a sort of "print now" command for amygdala memory circuits (Livingston, 1967). The pathways containing these traumatic memories become hyperpotentiated, meaning that they are more easily triggered by less severe subsequent stressors. This allows us to be reminded in the future of similar dangers. During times of lowered hippocampal-cortical involvement (e.g., intoxication or near-sleep states), these stressful traumatic memories may become disinhibited as intrusive images and flashbacks. Translated into human and clinical terms, this means that surges of NE during periods of safety may result in past traumatic associations (anxiety, startle, visual images, etc.) being brought to awareness, which overshadow current experiences.

Stimulating the LC in animals results in a disruption of ongoing behavior and triggering of an orienting reflex, like the one I had to the small piece of wood. This is seen in patients with PTSD who respond to trauma-related cues decades after their traumatic experience. LC activity in primates results in a high degree of vigilance while interrupting sleep, grooming, and eating. Through a series of connections, the central nucleus of the amygdala stimulates the LC, which, in turn, is thought to be a major control area of the sympathetic nervous system (Aston-Jones et al., 1994). An understanding of the biochemistry and functioning of the LC is an important component of any theory of causes of anxiety disorders (Svensson, 1987).

## Stress and the Hippocampus

*Anxiety is a thin stream of fear trickling through the mind. If encouraged, it cuts a channel into which all other thoughts are drained.*
—Arthur Somers Roche

The human brain is well equipped to survive brief periods of stress without long-term damage. In an optimal state, stressful experiences can be quickly resolved with good coping skills and the help of caring others. However, people often come to psychotherapy with long histories of anxiety, which can have profound effects on the brain. Working with rats and vervet monkeys, Sapolsky and his colleagues demonstrated that sustained stress results in hippocampal atrophy and a variety of functional impairments (Sapolsky, 1990; Sapolsky, Uno, Rebert, & Finch, 1990). His research is particularly important because it may help explain some of the negative long-term effects of childhood trauma.

The biological link between prolonged stress and hippocampal atrophy appears to be mediated via the catabolic influence of stress hormones. Glucocorticoids (GC) such as cortisol are secreted by the adrenal gland to promote the breakdown of complex compounds so that they can be used for immediate energy. The first of these hormones was found to break down complex sugars, hence the name *gluco*corticoids. It was later found that they also block protein synthesis, inhibiting both new neural growth and the construction of proteins involved in immunological functioning. Overall, long-term learning and biological well-being are sacrificed for the sake of immediate survival. This makes great sense when stressors are short-lived. But when stress is chronic, high levels of cortisol put us at risk of physical illness, learning dysfunctions, and memory deficits. A number of roles of cortisol are seen in Table 13.1, along with its impact on the brain and its relationship to a variety of illnesses.

The focus on immediate survival supersedes all long-term maintenance, akin to burning the furniture to survive freezing in winter. Thus, these biological processes need to be reversed as soon as possible after the crisis has passed to allow the body to recover and return to functions of restoration and repair. It is apparent that this system was designed to cope with brief periods of stress in emergency situations; it was not designed to be maintained for weeks or years at a time. The complexities of cortical processing and anticipatory anxiety are poorly matched with these primitive stress systems.

Prolonged stress most affects two processes. First, it inhibits protein production in order to maintain higher levels of metabolism. Proteins are, of course, the building blocks of the immunological system (leukocytes, B-cells, T-cells, natural killer cells, etc.) and the suppression of protein synthesis also suppresses our body's ability to fight off infection and illness. This is one of the primary reasons for the high correlations found between prolonged stress and disease. Second, sustained higher levels of metabolism continue to pump sodium into neurons, eventually overwhelming the cell's ability to transport it out again. This results in destruction of the cell membrane and consequent cell death. This process

TABLE 13.1
Stress and the Hippocampus

**The Role of Cortisol**
Breaks down fats and proteins for immediate energy
Inhibits inflammatory processes
Inhibits protein syntheses within the immune system (leukocytes, B and T-cells, natural killer cells, etc.)
Suppresses gonadal hormones that support neural health, growth, and learning

**Chronic High Levels of Cortisol/Glucocorticoids Result In**
Decreased plasticity[1]
Dendritic degeneration[2]
Deficits of remyelination[3]
Cell death[4]
Inhibition of neurogenesis and neural growth[5]

**High Levels of Cortisol Correlate With:**
Impaired declarative memory and spatial reasoning[6]

**Compromised Hippocampi Result In**
Deficits of new learning[7]
Short- and long-term memory[8]

**Individuals With Smaller Hippocampi Include**
Adult victims of early trauma[9]
Post-traumatic stress disorder[10]
Temporal lobe epilepsy[11]
Schizophrenia[12]
Cushing's disease (hypercortisolism)[13]

has been found to be particularly damaging to the hippocampus, resulting in a variety of memory deficits and depression. Loss of volume in the hippocampus is related to cumulative GC exposure (Sapolsky et al., 1990). Sustained high levels of stress partly explain why early negative experiences in parenting and attachment have a lifelong impact on physical health, mental health, and learning.

The hippocampus, rich in GC receptors, plays a negative feedback role with the adrenal gland to inhibit GC production. If the hippocampus detects too many GCs together, it sends a message (via the hypothalamus or the pituitary) to the adrenal gland to slow down GC production (Sapolsky, Krey, & McEwen, 1984). The more receptors we have, the greater our feedback abilities to decrease cortisol production. Prolonged high levels of GCs increase the vulnerability of the hippocampus to a number of potential metabolic insults (Sapolsky, 1985; Woolley, Gould, & McEwen, 1990). At this point it is unclear if decreased volume reflects permanent damage to the hippocampus or a reversible inhibition of the growth of new neurons. In either case, less hippocampal mass means fewer GC receptors, which, in turn, means less negative feedback to the adrenal gland. Loss of volume in the hippocampus is related to cumulative GC exposure (Sapolsky et al., 1990).

Early trauma results in hippocampal impairment, which decreases our ability to inhibit the emotions triggered by amygdaloid memory systems. Further, deficits in reality testing and short-term memory will make the process of integrating traumatic experiences into conscious awareness more difficult. Longer periods of relationship building and pragmatic interventions focused on stress reduction and the development of coping skills may be necessary prerequisites for successful long-term therapy with victims of early stress and trauma. The hippocampus is also exquisitely sensitive to oxygen deprivation, so patients who have suffered metabolic disruptions, head trauma, or seizures may have hippocampal compromise, as well as mountain climbers, divers, or individuals with heart disease (Lombroso & Sapolsky, 1998; Regard, Oelz, Brugger, & Landis, 1989). High-dose cortisol administration for autoimmune diseases may also result in hippocampal damage (Sapolsky, 1996). All of these factors should be kept in mind when taking histories of patients with cognitive and neurological symptoms.

Impairment of the hippocampus from early chronic stress may make the therapeutic process more difficult for many clients. For example, Stein and his colleagues (Stein, Koverla, Hanna, Torchia, & McClarty, 1997) found that adult women who had experienced childhood abuse had significantly reduced left hippocampal volume. They also found that the amount of reduction was significantly correlated with increased dissociative symptoms. This relationship suggests that the left hippocampus may play a role in integrating memories into a cohesive narrative. The hippocampus is also thought to be involved in the flexible incorporation of new information into existing structures of memory (Eichenbaum, 1992). If this is the case, early abuse may result in damage to neural structures required to create new and more functional narratives.

Rats and humans differ in a number of ways besides whisker length. The increased size of the human brain and its additional processing capacity make it possible for us to worry about many more potential dangers, both real and imagined. In addition, our brains allow us to create complex situations such as traffic jams and overburdened schedules, generating ever-increasing levels of stress. Stressors such as these, which are experienced as inescapable, tend to have a greater sustained cortisol activation and negative impact on the brain. Although we like to think of childhood as a time of innocence and play, many children grow up in a state of constant distress. We saw this clearly in the attachment research where adults with anxious attachment patterns demonstrated a lack of recall for long periods of their childhoods. Parental physical or mental illness, community violence, poverty, and many other factors can contribute to this. Prolonged childhood stress can have lifelong effects on functioning related to hippocampal damage, immunological suppression, and other stress-related impairments.

## Learning Not to Fear

*Courage is acting in spite of fear.*
—Howard W. Hunter

It is an unfortunate twist of evolutionary fate that the amygdala is mature before birth while the systems that inhibit it take years to develop. This leaves us vulnerable to overwhelming fear with little to no ability to protect ourselves. On the other hand, evolution has also provided us with caretakers who allow us to link into their developed cortex until our own is ready. The way they protect us from fear and modulate our anxiety becomes a model upon which our own brain develops. Thus, we use proximity to our parents as our key method of fear regulation, just as cold-blooded animals use locomotion and change of location to regulate their internal temperature. Our attachment schemas come to reflect the success or failure of how we and our parents navigate this process. We have seen from the research with rats that maternal attention results in a brain that is better equipped to learn as well as to downregulate the immediate and long-term effects of stress. It turns out that in dealing with fear, the ability to learn as well as having a more resilient stress system are both important for facing life's challenges.

The hippocampus is constantly remodeled to keep abreast of current environmental changes. On the other hand, the amygdala's role is to remember a threat, generalize it to other possible threats, and carry it into the future. Because the amygdala exhibits persistent dendritic modeling, we are unable to completely forget painful and traumatic experiences (Rainnie et al., 2004; Vyas, Bernal, & Chattorji, 2003; Vyas, & Chattorji, 2004 ). The power of the amygdala and its stubbornness in the face of the hippocampus leads us to be biased toward anxiety and fear.

The phenomenon of *spontaneous recovery* of a phobia demonstrates how the fear we hoped was long gone was stored in our amygdala all along (Vansteenwegen et al., 2005). Getting past our fears and phobias does not entail forgetting to be afraid; rather, the extinction of fears represents new learning organized by our slow systems of the cortex and hippocampus. In other words, *extinction learning* represents the formation of new neural associations that somehow keep the memory stored in the amygdala from triggering the sympathetic nervous system (Milad & Quirk, 2002; Rau & Fanselow, 2007).

The ability of the prefrontal cortex in modulating amygdala activity is believed to occur through the development of descending inhibitory circuitry (Akirav & Maroun, 2007; Ochsner et al., 2004). Evidence for this includes the fact that this cortical-amygdala network exhibits a reciprocal activation pattern where more cortical activation results in less amygdala activation and vice versa. This may not only be why our problem-solving abilities can be shorted out by fear, but also why thinking about and being prepared for a situation lessens our fears. When we successfully use cognitive techniques to decrease anxiety, we are likely building these descending cortical networks to inhibit amygdala and autonomic activation (Schaefer et al., 2002).

Learning not to fear, just like secure attachment, appears to be a major contribution of the ompfc (Morgan, Romanski, & LeDoux, 1993; Phelps et al., 2004). Electrical stimulation of the homologous region in the cortex of rats results in both amygdala inhibition and a reduction of conditioned fear (Milad, Vidal-Gonzalez, & Quirk, 2004; Perez-Jaranay & Vives, 1991; Quirk, Likhtik, Pelletier, & Paré, 2003). Even the size of the ompfc in humans is positively correlated with our ability to inhibit a fearful response (Milad, Quinn, et al., 2005). Thus, it appears that top-down control of the amygdala allows us to learn to discontinue a fearful response to something that makes us afraid. In a study by Kim, those who were taught to interpret a surprised face as negative had greater amygdala activation while those who were guided to see it as positive had more ompfc activation (Kim et al., 2003). These studies support the notion that the ompfc modulates the activation of the amygdala based on contextual and motivational factors (Kim et al., 2005; Myers & Davis, 2007; Ochsner et al., 2002; Phan et al., 2005). In other words, the slow system regulates the fast system.

These top-down circuits organize, modulate, and direct attention in ways that shape experience and reinforce the existing emotional state (Bishop, 2007; Christakou , Robbins, & Everitt, 2004). Anxiety is associated with a reduced top-down control of threat cues just as there is a reduction of control over negative stimuli in depression (Bishop et al., 2004; Brewin & Smart, 2005). In other words, anxious people tend to find danger while depressed people discover the negative aspects of their environments. And while those of us with more attentional control will still have a bias to orient toward the threat, we will exert more top-down control as we become conscious of the stimulus (Derryberry & Reed, 2002). Once again, the slow system modulates the fast system.

Thus, the balance of activation among the prefrontal cortex and amygdala also guides visual attention based on relevance, emotion, and motivation (Gazzaley et al., 2007; Geday, Kupers, & Gjedde, 2007). This is one of the many networks that may become dysregulated in PTSD, resulting in disturbances of sensory processing and memory, and even causing visual hallucinations (Gilboa et al., 2004; Rauch, Shin, & Phelps, 2006). Dissociated PTSD patients have greater activation in neural networks involved in the representation of bodily states, suggesting a lack of adequate top-down modulation of these networks by frontal executive systems (Lanius et al., 2005). As one would expect, the severity of PTSD symptoms is positively associated with amygdala activation and negatively correlated with ompfc size and responsivity (Shin, Rauch, & Pitman, 2006; Williams et al., 2006).

As we saw in Figure 13.2, the central nucleus of the amygdala is an output region that projects to sites in the midbrain and hypothalamus responsible for generating different aspects of the fear response. The connections of the ompfc to the central nucleus of the amygdala are particularly strong, especially to GABAergic (inhibitory) neurons called *intercalated cells* (Freedman, Insel, & Smith, 2000; McDonald et al., 1999; Royer, Martina, & Paré, 1999). It is now believed that it is within the descending networks from the ompfc to the amygdala's central nucleus that extinction learning is remembered and carries out its inhibitory influences (Gottfried & Dolan, 2004; Quirk & Mueller, 2008). Because learning in this neural circuit conforms to what is known about the neurobiology of learning in general, the role of NMDA receptors, protein synthesis, cortisol, and other factors that modulate learning are likely involved in extinction learning (Elvander-Tottie et al., 2006; Santini et al., 2004).

Research shows that subjects involved in the cognitive appraisal of fearful faces show both a decrease in amygdala activation and an increase in prefrontal activation (Hariri et al., 2000, 2003). This same amygdala-prefrontal activity shift occurs during activation of a placebo effect (Wager et al., 2004) and recovery following the presentation of negative emotional material (Jackson et al., 2003). Individuals who manage to control their fear tend to have more activation in right frontal regions than those who do not (Johanson et al., 1998).

A deficit of extinction learning could be an alternative description of PTSD. Sufferers with PTSD show amygdala dysinhibition, making them vulnerable to the hallmark symptoms of intrusion and arousal (Akirav & Maroun, 2007). Patients with PTSD have also been shown to have smaller subregions within their ompfc in regions where intercalated cells are assumed to reside (Rauch et al., 2003). Also the thickness and activity levels of these prefrontal regions in patients with PTSD during extinction training correlates with their symptoms, supporting the association between their symptoms and deficits of cortically based extinction learning (Milad, Orr, et al., 2005; Phelps et al., 2004).

## The Recovery of Fears and Phobias Under Stress

> *Dangers bring fears, and fears more dangers bring.*
> —Richard Baxter

Jacobs and Nadel (1985) proposed the existence of two systems of learning and memory involved in fears and phobias. These two systems predicted and parallel LeDoux's model of fast and slow fear circuitry. The *taxon system* (fast system or amygdaloid system) is responsible for the acquisition of skills and rules, and the conditioning of stimulus-response connections. This system is context free, meaning that it contains no information about the time or location in which the learning took place. Taxon learning generalizes broadly and is primarily nonconscious. This is the system in which early learning of fear, safety, and attachment is organized and stored. The taxon system is represented in what cognitive psychologists call implicit and procedural memory.

The *locale system*—with the hippocampus and the cortex at its core—is responsible for cognitive maps necessary for external context, mental representations, and the pairing of memories with the situations in which they were learned. The development of the locale memory system parallels that of hippocampal-cortical circuits. Thus, although there is a great deal of learning during infancy (especially in the networks of the fearful and social brains), there is no source attribution or autobiographical narrative.

For example, a mother's fearful look when strangers approach may cause her child to develop a general wariness of the world, but not recognize the source of this apprehension in similar situations later in life. We enter middle childhood with neural networks programmed by early learning, experienced as basic emotional givens. In the absence of trauma, learning in adults involves a balanced integration of taxon and locale systems that connect sensory, motor, and emotional aspects of memory to its semantic and autobiographical components. For children and traumatized adults, the taxon system may function independently, resulting in an adaptive dissociation among various systems of memory and conscious awareness.

Jacobs and Nadel contended that stress both changes the inner biological environment activating the taxon system and suppresses the inhibitory effects of the locale system. These changes result in the emergence of earlier fears or frightening experiences that had been successfully inhibited. This theory certainly parallels the voluminous research demonstrating the contribution of stress to the emergence or worsening of psychiatric and physical disorders. They suggested that stress impairs or downgrades the functioning of the locale system, causing us to fall back on the more primitive organization of taxon (amygdaloid) systems. From a psychoanalytic perspective, this process may be understood as regression to more primitive self states and defense mechanisms. This process also parallels the return of neonatal reflexes (the cortical release signs previously discussed in patients with Alzheimer's disease or other forms of brain damage).

Despite the apparent extinction of a phobia or fear, the original memory is maintained and can become reactivated under stress. This neural explanation addresses the Freudian notion of *symptom substitution*, in which one fear or source of anxiety may be replaced by another after successful treatment of the first. In other words, a new trigger reactivates the still intact underlying neural circuitry, another way of saying what we covered earlier—that neurons within the amygdala exhibit persistent dendritic modeling (Vyas et al., 2003). Because of this, Jacobs and Nadel suggested that the therapist treating fears and phobias may need to generate stress as a part of treatment to activate and have access to these amygdala circuits. In addition, treatment may need to be continued well after behavioral manifestations are eliminated, as well as include stress management training. If the overall level of stress can be decreased, the likelihood of reactivating of primitive fear circuitry decreases.

Successful psychotherapy for anxiety, fears, and phobias has been shaped by the necessity of integrating fast and slow circuits, taxon and locale systems, and affect and cognition. Educating patients about panic leads to increased participation of the cortex during anxiety states. Cognitive therapy is all about utilizing the slow locale systems to inhibit and modulate fast taxon systems that have been shaped in maladaptive ways. *Stress inoculation*, or cognitive preparation for future stress, leads to an increasing opportunity for descending inhibition of the amygdaloid circuits by the hippocampal-cortical networks. Exposure, response prevention, and relaxation training result in the counterconditioning of unconscious associations stored in amygdaloid memory systems. This model of memory applies to all clinical situations, regardless of the presence of panic or anxiety disorders.

## Drowning in a Sea of Doom

> *There is no greater hell than to be a prisoner of fear.*
> —Ben Johnson

Tina's cardiologist suggested that she see a psychotherapist after a third visit to the emergency room. Each time, seemingly out of nowhere, Tina would become breathless and lightheaded; her heart would race until she felt as if it were going to burst from her chest. Convinced she was having a heart attack, Tina would call the paramedics. As she waited for the ambulance, Tina reported feeling like she was drowning in a "sea of doom." She would imagine her teenaged children growing up without her, and vividly recollect her own mother's death when she was a child. These feelings and images, together with the fear of death, would make her even more frightened. She told me that waiting for the ambulance felt like "an eternity."

Tina, who was actually in excellent health, was repeatedly told she was having panic attacks. It took three of these embarrassing episodes to convince her to seek therapy. She came to my office feeling defeated and very frightened, as if she was losing a lifelong battle to stay in control. During our first session, I learned that Tina had a difficult childhood, including abandonment by her father, prolonged financial difficulties, and the death of her mother when she was 15. Tina finished high school while living with an aunt, put herself through college, and became a successful real estate agent. A 4-year marriage had left her with two children, now in their teens, to raise on her own. Tina's identity was that of a survivor and hard worker who did not allow herself to depend on others. The panic attacks had shaken her self-confidence and created a fear of returning to the chaos, pain, and dependency of her childhood. She had hoped for a medical explanation to avoid revisiting her past.

I began treatment by educating Tina about her body's fear response and why it felt to her like she was having a heart attack. Her racing heart, lightheadedness, rapid breathing, and sense of danger were the result of the amygdala's multiple signals to prepare to fight or run. Gaining conscious regulation of her amygdala's alarm circuitry was the first order of business. We discussed strategies to ward off these attacks by slowing her breathing and employing relaxation techniques. During sessions, I would have Tina make herself anxious, and then assist her in calming down. This provided her with a sense of mastery in regulating amygdala activation. Understanding what was happening in her body and knowing that her life was not in danger relieved some of her fear.

The second phase of treatment focused on addressing the long-standing lifestyle issues that kept her in a chronic state of stress. We examined the heavy burden of responsibilities she carried and her lack of relaxation and recreation. Tina's financial fears led her to overbook her work schedule to the point of exhaustion. I learned that Tina constantly criss-crossed the Los Angeles freeway system, traveling between 30,000 and 40,000 miles each year. Between showing homes and shuttling her children from school to their various activities, we calculated that she was fighting traffic up to 6 hours a day, usually behind schedule. She began to understand the panic attacks as her body's way of telling her to make some changes to reduce her level of stress. Regular exercise, decreasing her sales territory, and making alternative arrangements for some of her children's transportation proved to be the most helpful solutions in these areas.

As these interventions became more routine, we explored the impact of her childhood experiences on both her self-image and lifestyle. Tina harbored the fear that she would die like her mother, leaving her children alone in the world. She tried to do everything she could for them, and save all the money they would need to go to college, all the time thinking that she would not be around much longer. Her financial planning was detailed and over the years she had followed through with it almost to the letter. The problem was that it had originally been created for two incomes; now she was doing it on her own. She came to see that her fear of death might become a self-fulfilling prophecy. Tina also came to realize that her heart was still broken over her mother's death, and that she had never allowed herself to grieve her loss, a luxury she had felt she could not afford. Opening herself to these feelings of loss was the beginning of her therapy.

## Summary

The fearful brain has two interconnected systems responsible for different aspects of fear processing. The fast or taxon system—with the amygdala at its core—makes rapid, reflexive, and unconscious decisions to provide for immediate survival. This system develops first and organizes learning related to attachment and affect regulation. It involves sensory, motor, and affective memories typical of early life and later traumatic memories. The slow or locale system, based in hippocampal-cortical networks, contextualizes and makes conscious what is being processed. The slow system's job is to regulate the activity of the amygdala by modulating its output based on a more complex appraisal of potentially dangerous situations. This system contextualizes experience in time and space, and supports conscious awareness via cortical connectivity.

These two systems, reflecting both top-down and left-right circuits, can become dissociated during prolonged periods of stress or trauma. In psychotherapy, we attempt to activate both fast and slow circuits, taxon and locale systems, and implicit and explicit forms of memory to inform and educate each about the other. When emotional taxon networks are inhibited, we use techniques to trigger them so that they can be activated and integrated with slow locale circuits. When these same networks are out of control, we recruit locale circuits to contextualize them in time and space and allow them to be tamed by the descending, inhibitory capabilities of cortical processes. The overall goal is the activation and integration of both systems.

Chapter 14

# Trauma and Neural Network Dissociation

*The beauty of the world has two edges, one of laughter, one of anguish, cutting the heart asunder.*

—Virginia Woolf

For each of us there is a point at which fear crosses the line into trauma, causing severe disturbances in the integration of cognitive, sensory, and emotional processing. The psychological and neurobiological reactions to traumatic experiences lie on a continuum of severity. As a general rule, the earlier, more severe, and more prolonged the trauma, the more negative and far reaching its effects (De Bellis, Baum, et al., 1999; De Bellis, Keshavan, et al., 1999). Unresolved trauma may result in symptoms of post-traumatic stress disorder (PTSD), which reflect the physiological dysregulation and dissociation of multiple neural networks.

## The Symptoms of Post-traumatic Stress Disorder

*The best way out is always through.*

—Robert Frost

Traumatic experiences result in a variety of well-understood physiological and psychological reactions to threat, which cause a number of predictable symptoms to emerge. These symptoms tend to gradually diminish after the resolution of the traumatic situation, as we gather support from others, and repeatedly talk through the experience. These conditions allow us to regain both neurobiological homeostasis and a sense of emotional control.

Talking through the trauma with supportive others creates the neurobiological conditions for the reestablishment of neural coherence. Put another way, constructing narratives in an emotionally supportive environment supports the psychological and neurobiological integration required to avoid dissociative reactions. Narratives drive the integration of cognition, affect, sensation, and behaviors, which can remain dissociated especially when early trauma, such as child sexual abuse, is never allowed to be discussed. The suffering of Holocaust survivors and combat veterans is often exacerbated by the political and social dynamics that encourage them to remain silent about their horrifying experiences.

When trauma is severe or chronic the victim can develop PTSD. PTSD is caused by the loss of the regulation of the neurobiological processes responsible for appraising and responding to threat. When this system becomes dysregulated, the body reacts as if the past trauma is continuing to occur. The three main symptom clusters of PTSD—hyperarousal, intrusion, and avoidance—reflect the loss of integration among neural networks controlling cognition, sensation, affect, and behavior.

*Hyperarousal* reflects a stress-induced dysregulation of the amygdala and autonomic nervous system, resulting in an exaggerated startle reflex, agitation, anxiety, and irritability. That jumpy feeling we get when we drink too much caffeine gives us a taste of this experience. Chronic hyperarousal leads one to experience the world as a more dangerous and hostile place. Constant agitation and wariness make us less desirable companions and can cut us off from the healthful effects of relationships.

*Intrusions* occur when traumatic experiences break into conscious awareness and are experienced as if they are happening in the present. There is no sense of distance from the trauma in time or place, because the corticohippocampal networks have not been able to contextualize the somatic, sensory, and emotional memories within networks of autobiographical memory. Intrusions may manifest as flashbacks, resulting in a veteran hitting the ground in response to a car backfiring, or a rape victim having a panic attack while making love to her husband. These are activations of subcortical systems cued by stimuli reminiscent of the trauma. You may remember from the chapters on memory and fear that the amygdala both controls this activation and tends to generalize from the initial stimuli to a wide variety of cues.

*Avoidance* is the attempt to defend against dangers by limiting contact with the world, withdrawing from others, and narrowing the range of thoughts and feelings. Avoidance can take the form of denial and repression, and, in more extreme instances, dissociation and amnesia. The power of avoidance was highlighted by the research of Williams (1994), who found that 38% of adult women who had suffered documented sexual abuse as children had no memory of the event. Compulsive activities can also aid in avoiding negative affect, as can alcohol and drug abuse, both so common in victims of trauma. Avoidance enables short-term anxiety reduction while maintaining the lack of neural network integration which perpetuates the illness.

When experienced in combination, these symptoms result in a cycle of activation and numbing, reflecting the body's memory for, and continued victimization by, the trauma (van der Kolk, 1994). Instead of serving to mobilize the body to deal with new external threats, traumatic memories trigger continuing frightening emotional responses. Someone suffering from PTSD is in a continual loop of unconscious self-traumatization, coping, and exhaustion. When these symptoms are experienced on a chronic basis, they can devastate every aspect of the victim's life, from physical well-being to the quality of relationships to the victim's experience of the world.

We have all heard the sayings "What doesn't kill you makes you stronger" and "Time heals all wounds." These bits of common wisdom conjure up pictures of difficult and traumatic experiences that, once overcome, result in greater levels of physical and emotional well-being. Although trials and tribulations can certainly be important learning experiences, they can also create permanent biological, neurological, and psychological compromise. Trauma produces widespread homeostatic dysregulations that interfere with all realms of personal and interpersonal functioning (Perry et al., 1995).

Support for the negative impact of trauma comes from research showing that cumulative lifetime trauma increases the likelihood of developing PTSD (Yehuda et al., 1995). A history of previous assaults increases the chances of developing PTSD following rape (Resnick, Yehuda, Pitman, & Foy, 1995). Likewise, childhood abuse victims are more likely to develop PTSD after adult combat exposure (Bremner, Southwick, et al., 1993). It has also been found that severe stress reactions during combat make subsequent negative reactions to mild and moderate stress more probable (Solomon, 1990).

## The Neurochemistry of PTSD

*Gulf War Syndrome is not one cause, not one illness. It is many causes, many illnesses.*

—Christopher Shays

States of acute stress result in predictable patterns of biochemical changes including increases in norepinephrine, dopamine, endorphins, and glucocorticoids, and a decrease in serotonin. These changes are part of the body's mobilization to confront threat. When stress is prolonged or becomes chronic, changes continue to occur in the baseline production, availability, and homeostatic regulation of these neurochemicals, resulting in long-term behavioral and psychological alterations. Each of these substances has its own role in the stress response and contributes in different ways to the long-term impact of PTSD.

As we have seen, increased levels of norepinephrine (NE) prepare us for fight-or-flight readiness and reinforce the biological encoding of traumatic memory. Higher long-term levels of NE result in an increase in arousal, anxiety, irritability, and a heightened or unmodulated startle response (Butler et al., 1990; Ornitz & Pynoos, 1989). Besides being stronger, the startle response is also more resistant to habituation in response to subsequent milder and novel stressors (Nisenbaum, Zigmond, Sved, & Abercrombie, 1991; Petty, Chae, Kramer, Jordan, & Wilson, 1994; van der Kolk, 1994). Being consistently startled increases the victim's experience of the world as an unsettling and dangerous place, a good example of a feedback loop between physiological and psychological processes. In fact, drugs that block the impact of NE are being used experimentally to determine if they may help victims of PTSD decrease their physiological response to reminders of their trauma (Brunet et al., 2008).

High levels of dopamine correlate with hypervigilance, paranoia, and perceptual distortions when under stress. Symptoms of social withdrawal and the avoidance of new and unfamiliar situations (neophobia) are shaped by these biochemical changes. Lower levels of serotonin have been found in traumatized humans and animals after being subjected to inescapable shock (Anisman, Zaharia, Meaney, & Merali, 1998; Usdin, Kvetnansky, & Kopin, 1976). Chronically low levels of serotonin are correlated with higher levels of irritability, depression, suicide, arousal, and violence (Canli & Lesch, 2007; Coccaro, Siever, Klar, & Maurer, 1989).

Elevated levels of endogenous opioids, which serve as analgesics to relieve pain in fight-or-flight situations, can have a profoundly negative impact on cognition, memory, and reality testing. Higher opioid levels also support emotional blunting, dissociation, depersonalization, and derealization, all of which provide a sense of distance from the traumatized body (Shilony & Grossman, 1993). However, when they become harmfully used as defenses, they disrupt our ability to stay engaged in day-to-day life.

As we have seen, high levels of glucocorticoids have a catabolic effect on the nervous system and are thought to be responsible for decreased hippocampal volume and related memory deficits (Bremner, Scott, et al., 1993; Nelson & Carver, 1998; Watanabe, Gould, & McEwen, 1992). The hippocampi of patients with PTSD related to childhood physical and sexual abuse have been shown to be 12% smaller than those of comparison subjects (Bremner et al., 1997). Another study showed that right hippocampi were 8% smaller in patients with combat-related PTSD (Bremner et al., 1995). Glucocorticoids sacrifice long-term conservation and homeostasis for short-term survival. Chronically high levels have negative effects on brain structures and the immune system, resulting in higher rates of learning disabilities and physical illness, which enhances victims' experience of being fragile and vulnerable individuals.

These biochemical and neuroanatomical changes are paralleled by such symptomatology as emotional dyscontrol, social withdrawal, and lower levels of adaptive functioning. Together, these and other negative effects of trauma result in compromised functioning in many areas of life. The impact of trauma depends on a complex interaction of the physical and psychological stages of development during which it occurs, the length and degree of the trauma, and the presence of vulnerabilities or past traumas. The impact of chronic trauma becomes woven into the structure of personality and is hidden behind other symptoms, making it difficult to identify, diagnose, and treat.

# Expanding the Definition of Trauma

*To the child . . . traumas are not experienced as events in life,
but as life defining.*

—Christopher Bollas

Trauma is not limited to surviving life-threatening experiences, as the standard diagnostic manual appears to suggest (American Psychiatric Association, 2000). For a young child, trauma may be experienced in the form of separation from parents, looking into the eyes of a depressed mother, or living in a highly stressful household (Cogill, Caplan, Alexandra, Robson, & Kumar, 1986). For an adolescent, trauma may come in the form of incessant teasing by peers or caring for an alcoholic parent. For an adult, chronic loneliness or the loss of a pet may be traumatic.

There is increasing evidence that stress is possible even before birth; an unborn child may become stressed as a result of the shared biological environment with its mother. Studies suggest that maternal stress is associated with lower birth weight, increased irritability, hyperactivity, and learning disabilities in children (Gunnar, 1992, 1998; Zuckerman, Bauchner, Parker, & Cabral, 1990). Rats born to stressed mothers show more clinging to the mother and decreased locomotion and environmental exploration (Schneider, 1992). Prenatal stress may also result in permanent alterations in dopamine activity and cerebral lateralization, making offspring more susceptible to anxiety and impairing their functioning as adults (Field et al., 1988). Children of Holocaust survivors have an increased prevalence of PTSD despite similar rates of exposure to traumatic events as children of non-Holocaust survivors. This suggests that they experienced a transferred vulnerability through interactions with their traumatized parents (Yehuda, 1999).

Maternal depression may serve as a highly stressful or traumatic experience for infants and children. Tiffany Field and her colleagues found that infants of depressed mothers show neurophysiological and behavioral signs of depression and stress, including greater right frontal lobe activation, higher levels of NE, lower vagal tone, and higher heart rates and cortisol levels (Field & Diego, 2008b; Field, Diego, & Hernandez-Reif, 2006). Just like their depressed mothers, these infants engage in less interactive behaviors (e.g., orienting toward and gazing at others) vital for healthy development. Infants of depressed mothers behave in this way even with other adults, making it difficult for them to success-fully interact with nondepressed others (Field et al., 1988).

In another study, it was found that depressed mothers were angry at their infants more often, disengaged from them more often, were more likely to poke them, and spent less time in matching emotional states (Field, Healy, Goldstein, & Guthertz, 1990). These results suggest that infants are modeling their mother's behavior, resonating with their depressed moods, and reacting to the negative behaviors directed toward them. Although we would not consider these infants traumatized in the traditional sense, the loss of maternal presence, engagement, and vitality may all be experienced as life threatening. Fortunately, it has been shown that interventions with depressed mothers and their infants have positive results. For example, remission of maternal depression and teaching mothers to massage their infants on a regular basis improves the infants' symptoms and the mothers' mood (Field, 1997).

The effects of early and severe trauma are extremely widespread, dev-astating, and difficult to treat. Because of the importance of a context of safety and bonding in the early construction of the brain, childhood trauma compromises core neural networks. It stands to reason that the most devastating types of trauma are those that occur at the hands of caretakers. Physical and sexual abuse by parents not only traumatizes children, but also deprives them of healing interactions and a safe haven. The wide range of effects involved in the adaptation to early unresolved trauma results in *complex post-traumatic stress disorder*.

## Complex Post-traumatic Stress Disorder

*The other day I heard someone knocking on my window. I'd rather be dead than hear that.*

—A 10-year-old kidnapping victim

Complex PTSD occurs in the context of early, prolonged, and inescapable trauma. It is called complex because of its extensive effects on all areas of physiology, development, and functioning (Herman, 1992; Navalta et al., 2004). The enduring personality traits and coping strate-gies that emerge in these situations tend to decrease positive adaptation and increase an individual's vulnerability to future trauma. This can manifest through engagement in abusive relationships, poor judgment, or a lack of adequate self-protection. Long-term PTSD has been shown to correlate with the presence of *neurological soft signs*, which suggest subtle neurological impairments (Gurvits et al., 2000), and may reflect a vulnerability to, or the impact of, the effects of trauma (Green, 1981).

For an adult under normal circumstances, a threat triggers a fight-or-flight response. The threat is dealt with and the flight-fight response soon subsides. Children are not well equipped to cope with threat in this way. Fighting and fleeing may actually be maladaptive because their survival depends on relying on those around them. When a child experiences trauma inflicted by a caretaker, or cries for help but no help arrives, he or she may shift from fear and hyperarousal to psychological and neurological dissociation (Perry et al., 1995). This may also be true for those women who are unable to outrun or outfight male attackers. The symptoms of agitation shown by traumatized children are often misdiagnosed as attention deficit disorder, while the numbing response in infants can be misinterpreted as a lack of awareness or sensitivity to pain.

Until recently, surgery was performed on infants without anesthesia because their gradual lack of protest was mistakenly interpreted as an insensitivity to pain rather than a lapsing into a state of shock (Zeltzer, Anderson, & Schecter, 1990). Survey research suggests that less than 25% of physicians performing circumcision on newborns use any form of analgesia (Wellington & Rieder, 1993), despite physiological indications that neonates are experiencing stress and pain during and after the procedure (Hoyle et al., 1983). These practices appear to be a holdover of beliefs that newborns either don't experience or don't remember pain (Marshall, Stratton, Moore, & Boxerman, 1980). Thus, our lack of appreciation for the possibility for traumatic reactions in neonates and children likely leads us to miss many PTSD reactions in the young.

Research with rats has demonstrated that exposure to inescapable shock sensitizes their hippocampi to subsequent releases of NE under stress (Petty et al., 1994). This suggests that prolonged stress and trauma may cause us to react more strongly to subsequent milder stress. This may help to explain the coping difficulties seen in victims of PTSD when confronted with mild to moderate stress (Petty et al., 1994). Think back to Sheldon, who still suffered from anxiety 60 years after his childhood experiences during World War II.

Dissociation allows the traumatized individual to escape the trauma via a number of biological and psychological processes. Increased levels of endogenous opioids create a sense of well-being and a decrease in explicit processing of overwhelming traumatic situations. Derealization and depersonalization reactions allow the victim to avoid the reality of his or her situation, or watch it as a detached observer. These processes can create an experience of leaving the body, traveling to other worlds, or immersing oneself into other objects in the environment. Many victims of violence and sexual abuse report watching themselves being attacked from a distance. Hyperarousal and dissociation in childhood create an inner biopsychological environment primed to establish boundaries between different emotional states and experiences. If it is too painful to experience the world from inside one's body, even one's self-identity can become organized outside the physical self.

Early traumatic experiences organize neuroanatomical networking, thus impacting experience and adaptation throughout development. The tendency to dissociate and disconnect various tracks of processing creates a bias toward unintegrated information processing across conscious awareness, sensation, affect, and behavior. General dissociative defenses resulting in an aberrant organization of networks of memory, fear, and the social brain contribute to deficits of affect regulation, attachment, and executive functioning (van der Kolk et al., 1996). The malformation of these interdependent systems results in many disorders that spring from extreme early stress. Compulsive disorders related to eating or gambling, somatization disorders in which emotions are converted into physical symptoms, and borderline personality disorder all reflect complex adaptations to early trauma (Saxe et al., 1994; van der Kolk et al., 1996).

## I Am Not Crazy!

*Demoralize the enemy from within by surprise, terror, sabotage, assassination.*

—Adolf Hitler

Jesse was referred to me by her neurologist after months of extensive medical and neurodiagnostic testing. Her team of doctors could find no physical cause for the debilitating pain she experienced in her head and upper body. She had tried alternative forms of treatment, such as chiropractics and acupuncture, without much relief. Jesse came to see me at the insistence of her husband, and she was not the least bit happy about it. She sat down with her arms crossed and her jaw set, glared at me, and said, "I am not crazy!"

For many years, life had been going well for Jesse. She had a solid marriage and a happy and healthy 4-year-old daughter. She found her work as an executive in a small information technology firm interesting. She liked her colleagues, and was a valued member of the team. About a year before, she had started experiencing pain in her head, hands, and back and began a fruitless search for a cure. The pain became the center of her attention as her interest and ability in being an executive, friend, wife, and mother gradually diminished. By the time she came for therapy, she was spending most of her days taking medication, sneaking away for naps, and withdrawing to her room whenever she could find an excuse. There was no longer any fun or relaxation in her life, and her husband had become seriously concerned.

Given her resistance to therapy and fear of being seen as crazy, developing a therapeutic relationship with Jesse was slow going. She reluctantly began to share about her very troubled childhood. Jesse felt she had obviously overcome her traumatic past based on her later success at work and in her marriage. Unfortunately, a common occurrence in her childhood was to be locked in her room by her father as a prelude to him beating her mother. She would lie in bed, frozen by both of their screams, her mother's cries for her, and the long ominous silences that followed. As she told me of her mother's physical abuse at the hands of her father, she remained confident that there was no connection between her present physical pain and the emotional pain of her youth.

Jesse would eventually begin to pound on the door and yell for her mother. As she grew older, however, she gave up her outward protests and instead lay in bed crying and clutching her face and head. This clutching eventually turned to self-abuse, which included driving her nails into her head and shoulders, drawing blood, and eventually scarring herself. She showed me some of her scars with a combination of shame and pride. As she described these experiences, I began to suspect that her pain symptoms might well be implicit somatic memories of her traumatic past. The stresses in her present life, including the fact that her own daughter was reaching the age she had been when she first became aware of the beatings, could all serve as triggers for these memories. From a psychological perspective, her physiological suffering could be seen as a form of loyalty and continued connection to her mother.

I decided not to share these interpretations because of Jesse's resistance to the possible psychological origins of her pain. Instead, I continued to encourage her to talk about her childhood in as much detail as she could tolerate. She went on to tell me about her teenage years, when she nursed her mother through the final months of a prolonged battle with cancer. Throughout my work with Jesse, I avoided any talk of her physical pain and continued to refocus her on sharing childhood experiences with me.

In the process of repeatedly sharing stories from her childhood, her memories became increasingly detailed. Her emotions too, became more available, and better matched to the situations she described. Jesse expressed her rage at her father for his violent behavior, and realized that she was also angry at her mother for not leaving him when Jesse was young. As she worked through these memories and put them into the perspective of her current life, Jesse gradually came to an understanding that instead of remaining loyal to her mother through physical suffering, she could identify with her by being a good parent to her own daughter.

As therapy progressed, we both came to notice that the intensity of her pain and the time she spent focusing on it gradually diminished. Without making a direct interpretation, the connections in Jesse's brain between her physical and emotional pain were forged. Toward the end of our last session, she thanked me for helping her, although she didn't understand how it happened. Jesse winked at me and said, "You are a tricky fellow."

## Traumatic Memory

*Memories are nothing but the lash with which yesterday flogs tomorrow.*
—Philip Moeller

It has long been recognized that high levels of stress impair learning of new information (Yerkes & Dodson, 1908). This is because the biochemical and hormonal changes triggered by stress impair protein synthesis and other neuroplastic processes required for memory encoding. Trauma can also impair integration across the domains of memory, and is capable of dissociating the usually integrated tracks of sensation, emotion, behavior, and conscious awareness.

When NE is administered to rats after an aversive event, low doses enhance memory retention whereas high doses impair it (Introini-Collison & McGaugh, 1987); this supports Yerkes and Dodson's theory that moderate levels of arousal enhance memory whereas high levels impair it. In a study by Cahill and his colleagues (Cahill, Prins, Weber, & McGaugh, 1994), subjects were read emotionally evocative and neutral stories and shown related slides. Half of the subjects were given propranolol (a drug that decreases the effects of NE), and the others were not. Results demonstrated that subjects who received propranolol had significantly impaired memory for emotion-arousing but not for neutral stories.

Activation of the amygdala and related physiological and biological changes are at the heart of modulating traumatic memory (Cahill & McGaugh, 1998). The release of norepinephrine during the stress response serves to heighten the activation of the amygdala, thus reinforcing and intensifying traumatic memories (McGaugh, 1990). Individuals with PTSD have had their amygdaloid memory systems imprinted with trauma at such an extreme level that their memories are resistant to cortical integration (van der Kolk et al., 1996). This results in decreased attention to and processing of external stimuli, giving the traumatic memories more power (Lanius et al., 2001). When we think of trauma overwhelming the defenses, we can also think in terms of an intense activation of subcortical networks serving to inhibit the participation of the hippocampus and cortex in the memory process.

Traumatic experience can disrupt the storage (encoding) of information and the integration of the various systems of attention and memory (Vasterling, Brailey, Constans, & Sutker, 1998; Yehuda et al., 1995; Zeitlin & McNally, 1991). Memory encoding for conscious explicit memory can be disrupted when the hippocampus is blocked or damaged by glucocorticoids, or is inhibited by heightened amygdala activation. This could lead to a lack of conscious memory for traumatic and highly emotional events (Adamec, 1991; Schacter, 1986; Squire & Zola-Morgan, 1991). *Memory integration* can be impaired by disruption of the corticohippocampal tracks dedicated to the integration of new memories into existing memory networks. Remember that these systems also provide contextualization in time and space, and integration of sensory, affective, and behavioral memory with conscious awareness.

Thus, although we may have very accurate physiological and emotional memories for a traumatic event, the factual information may be quite inaccurate given the inhibition of corticohippocampal involvement during the trauma. Add to this the tendency of the left hemisphere interpreter to confabulate a story in the absence of accurate information, and we may have what represents the underlying mechanisms responsible for what has unfortunately been referred to as false memory syndrome (Paz-Alonzo & Goodman, 2008).

## Traumatic Flashbacks and Speechless Terror

*Memories are contrary things; if you quit chasing them and turn your back, they often return on their own.*

—Stephen King

*Flashbacks* are frightening experiences commonly reported by traumatized individuals. They are described as full-body experiences of traumatic events, which include the physiological arousal, sensory stimulation, and emotional impact of the traumatic experience. In a sense, the victim of a flashback is transported back to the event, and as far as the brain is concerned, it is happening again. Flashbacks are so intense that they overwhelm the reality constraints of the present situation and send the victim into an all-too-familiar nightmare.

The power of traumatic flashbacks was driven home for me one day in a therapy session with a professional football player who was nearly twice my size. When recalling his early abuse, he began to cry softly as he spoke of one particularly painful experience from childhood. He described in agonizing detail his small body growing limp after repeated blows from his father's fists. Suddenly, he was standing over me, breathing heavily, his arms down at his sides. Despite my alarm, I managed to calmly ask him what he was feeling. While looking into my eyes he said in a child's voice, "Please don't hurt me anymore." His fear of me despite the difference in our sizes was a stark demonstration of the all-encompassing nature of flashbacks and their ability to override contemporary reality.

Traumatic flashbacks are memories of a different nature than are those of nontraumatic events. To begin with, they are stored in more primitive circuits with less cortical and left hemisphere involvement. Because of this, they are strongly somatic, sensory, and emotional, as well as inherently nonverbal (Krystal, Bremner, Southwick, & Charney, 1998). The lack of corticohippocampal involvement results in an absence of the localization of the memory in time, so that when it is triggered, it is experienced as occurring in the present. Flashbacks are also repetitive and stereotypic, often seeming to proceed at the pace at which the events originally occurred. This suggests that although the cortex may condense and abbreviate memories in narrative and symbolic form, these subcortical networks may store memories in more concrete, stimulus-response chains of sensations, behaviors, and emotions. In a sense they become procedural memories, similar to learning to play a piece of music note by note or a complex dance routine step by step.

In flashbacks, the amygdala-mediated fear networks biased toward the right hemisphere and subcortical systems become dominant. The amygdala's dense connectivity with the visual system most likely accounts for the presence of visual hallucinations as part of flashbacks. Bereaved individuals often report seeing their loved ones sitting in their favorite chair or walking across the room in a familiar way. Those who have been attacked will sometimes think they see their attacker out of the corner of their eye. This is in contrast to the hallucinations in schizophrenia that involve the temporal lobes and are usually auditory in nature.

Rauch and colleagues (1996) took eight patients suffering from PTSD and exposed them to two audiotapes: One was emotionally neutral and the other was a script of a traumatic experience. While they were listening to these tapes, patients' heart rates and regional cerebral blood flow (RCBF) were measured via PET scans. RCBF was greater during traumatic audiotapes in right-sided structures including the amygdala, orbitofrontal cortex, insular, anterior, and medial temporal lobe, and the anterior cingulate cortex. These are the areas thought to be involved with intense emotion.

An extremely interesting and potentially important clinical finding was a decrease in RCBF in and around Broca's area (an area of the left inferior frontal cortex that controls speech). These findings suggest an active inhibition of language centers during trauma. Based on these results, speechless terror—often reported by victims of trauma—may have neurobiological correlates consistent with what we know about brain architecture and brain–behavior relationships. This inhibitory effect on Broca's area may impair the encoding of conscious semantic memory for traumatic events. It will then naturally interfere with the development of narratives that serve to process the experience and lead to neural network integration and psychological healing. Activating

Broca's area and related left cortical networks of explicit memory may
be essential in psychotherapy with patients suffering from PTSD and
other anxiety-based disorders.

## Activating Broca's Area During a Flashback

*Hope will never be silent.*
                                            —Harvey Milk

Jan, seeing me for a one-time consultation, reported that she had suffered severe physical and sexual abuse throughout her early childhood
and into her late teens. She told me over the phone that her flashbacks
were increasing in frequency to three or four a day. Although her therapist had encouraged her to experience them and express her emotions as
much as possible, Jan felt like she was getting worse instead of better.
Expressing her feelings seemed to only trigger more frequent and intense
flashbacks. She reported becoming less and less functional, which made
her decide that she needed a different approach to therapy.

Jan arrived at my office with a stack of diaries and *The Wall Street
Journal* under her arm. It was hard to believe that this was the same person I had spoken to over the phone. My first thought was that dissociation is an amazing defense. Jan was a well-dressed woman in her mid-40s
who was obviously bright and had a good deal of self-insight. The childhood experiences she recounted in my office were horrendous, and I marveled at her very survival. Her intelligence and sheer will to live were
remarkable. It seemed obvious, however, that her repeated reexperiencing
of these memories was not helping. The nature of these memories was not
changing over time, nor were the emotions evoked by her memories
diminishing. In this case, each flashback seemed to retraumatize her anew.

She began by talking about her work, and then described the psychotherapy and other forms of treatment in which she had engaged.
Approximately 10 minutes into the session, as she was discussing the
family members who had abused her, she began to have a flashback. Jan
reported pain in various parts of her body and contorted as if what she
was describing was happening to her at that very moment. She began to
gag as the memory of the sexual abuse from decades earlier was evoked.
She was reexperiencing these painful episodes not only visually in her
mind, but as somatic memories throughout her body.

As she curled into a fetal position on the couch and gasped for breath, my mind raced trying to think of a way to help. Remembering the research done by Rauch and his colleagues, I decided to try to activate Broca's area. I began speaking to Jan in a firm but gentle voice, loud enough to reach her in the midst of her traumatic reenactment but not so loud as to frighten her and add to her trauma. I wondered if it mattered which ear I spoke into, and which ear has a more direct connection to the left hemisphere language centers. I moved closer to her (careful not to get too close) and repeated over and over, "This is a memory, it isn't happening now. You are remembering something that happened to you many years ago. It was a terrible experience but it is over. It is a memory. It is not happening now."

As I repeated these and similar statements, I was concerned that Jan would be unable to breathe or that my presence might cause her more fear. The words of one of my supervisors flashed through my mind: "Whatever you do, don't panic." I was also encouraged by the fact that she had survived this many times. After 10 minutes (which seemed to me like 10 hours), she calmed down and returned to the present. Jan reported that she heard me speaking as if I were far away, but focused on my voice and words as best she could. It was as if I were there in the past with her, calling to her from a safe future where she would be away from all these people who hurt her.

At the end of the session she thanked me and left; I didn't hear from her for a number of months. When she called one afternoon, she reported that since her visit with me, the nature of these flashbacks had changed. She said she had wanted to wait before she called me because she didn't expect that the change would last. Given her many years in a variety of unhelpful treatments, it was easy to be sympathetic to her negative expectations. Jan described that since our session, the flashbacks were less physically intense and less frequent. On a few occasions she had even been able to stop one that was coming on by thinking of my words during the session: "This is just a memory. You are safe now. No one can hurt you."

Perhaps most interesting was that she was now able to remember during her flashbacks that she was not a child, that she was not to blame, and it was those who were hurting her who were bad. Although her other therapists had told her this in the past, only recently could she process these thoughts during her flashbacks. I told her that I felt these were signs that the experiences were beginning to be connected to her conscious adult self, and that now she was able to fight and care for herself even in the face of her past. I encouraged her to keep talking throughout the flashback experiences and bring with her as much assertiveness, anger, and power as she could muster. After a few minutes, we ended our conversation and I sat back, struck at how neuroscience could indeed be applied to psychotherapy.

It is impossible for me to know with any certainty whether what I had done with Jan during our one meeting had anything to do with the changes she experienced during her flashbacks. If it did, perhaps the active ingredient was the simultaneous activation of the verbal areas of the left hemisphere along with the emotional centers of the right hemisphere and limbic structures that stored the flashbacks. Being simultaneously aware of inner and outer worlds may support a higher level of cortical functioning and increased network integration. In other words, this process results in a memory configuration that is no longer implicit only but instead becomes integrated with the contextualizing properties of explicit systems of memory in the cerebral cortex (Siegel, 1995).

Speechless terror, which has been recognized as part of posttraumatic reactions since ancient times, now has a neural correlate consistent with what is known about brain functions. Why does Broca's area become inhibited during trauma? Why would evolution select silence in times of crisis? Perhaps when one is threatened it is better to either run or fight or simply keep quiet and hope to stay undetected. In other words, evolution has taught the brain to "Shut up and do something!" when in danger. The freezing reaction of animals (being still and quiet when they sense a predator) allows them to be less visible (because a still and silent target is more difficult to detect). Spoken language is sound, which primitive fear circuitry is able to silence. Perhaps those early prehumans who hung around for conversation and negotiation with predators didn't fare well enough to pass down as many genes as did those who either kept quiet, fought, or ran away.

## The Addiction to Stress and Self-Harm

*Every form of addiction is bad, no matter whether the narcotic be alcohol or morphine or idealism.*

—C. G. Jung

Another clinical phenomenon with a possible biochemical mechanism is what appears to be an addiction to stress experienced by some patients with PTSD. While anxious and ill at ease in normal daily life, they report feeling calm and competent in risky or life-threatening situations. A so-called normal life leaves traumatized persons a blank screen onto which their dysregulated psyches can project fearful experiences, keeping them in a state of vigilance and fear (Fish-Murry, Koby, & van der Kolk, 1987). This may motivate the creation of stress, making a traumatized person vulnerable to creating new trauma. The new trauma would, in turn, stimulate the production of endogenous opioids that would lead to an increased sense of calm and well-being. Paradoxically, trauma would lead to a sense of competency and control.

Because these individuals are so physically worn down by this lifestyle, they often present in therapy with exhaustion, depression, and a variety of medical conditions. It is as if they have a drug addiction, except that it is completely unconscious and they are their own pharmacy. Initial work with these patients should focus on helping them reduce stress and learn to tolerate and understand the anxiety triggered by the absence of stress. This can usually be accomplished through a combination of stress-reduction techniques, medication, and psychotherapy.

The addiction to stress has a related but more severe variant: self-harm. Adults who engage in repeated self-harm commonly describe childhoods that included abuse, neglect, or a deep sense of shame. This correlation has led many theorists to explore the psychodynamic significance of self-harm as an ongoing negative attachment to destructive parents. Along these lines, suicide has been described as the final act of compliance with the parents' unconscious wish for the death of the child (Green, 1978). There appears to be a strong association between self-harm and attachment disorders because self-injurious behaviors are often a response to abandonment and loss.

Endogenous opioids may also play a role in some instances of self-harm and suicide (van der Kolk, 1988). This opioid system, originally used to cope with pain, was adapted by later-evolving networks of attachment to reinforce the positive effects of bonding (Pitman et al., 1990). Research has demonstrated that the frequency of self-harm decreases when patients are given a drug to block the effects of endogenous opioids (Pitman et al., 1990; van der Kolk, 1988). Abstracting from the animal model, this would suggest that the endorphins released during injury reverse the feelings of distress activated by abandonment. The analgesic effects of these morphinelike substances may account for the reports describing a sense of calm and relief after individuals cut, burn, or hurt themselves. Thus, self-injurious behaviors may be reinforced by both psychological factors and the endogenous opioid system.

Repeated suicide attempts are reinforced also by the rapid attention of health care professionals, family, and friends, which may boost endorphin levels triggered by the arrival of loved ones. When woven into coping strategies as a means of affect regulation, this attention-getting behavior results in a kind of characterological suicidality (Schwartz, 1979). This behavior parallels the distress calls of primates whose endorphin levels drop in the absence of the mother. The reappearance of the mother results in a raising of these endorphin levels and the infant discontinues its cry. Characterological suicidality can come to serve a similar biochemical regulatory purpose if this system was inadequately formed during childhood. Although there are many sound psychological explanations for the relationship of childhood abuse with self-harm and suicidality, a pharmacological intervention designed to block the impact of endogenous endorphins may also prove helpful.

## The Brain and Borderline Personality Disorder

*Life began with waking up and loving my mother's face.*
—George Eliot

According to Freud, participation in analysis requires sufficient ego strength to withstand the stress of therapy while simultaneously maintaining contact with reality. Based on this assumption, Freud did his best to make sure that his prospective clients were not psychotic. Psychotic individuals are characterized by severe distortions of reality, thought disorders, and decompensation under stress. They are also unable to differentiate their transference and other projective processes from external reality. Despite Freud's best efforts to screen out these clients from analysis, every so often he got a surprise. People who appeared to be neurotic would become psychotic during analysis. Freud referred to these people as having psychic structures on the borderline between neurotic and psychotic.

Over the years, the conception of a borderline psychic structure has evolved into what is now called *borderline personality disorder* (BPD). As we have already seen, BPD may represent one variant of complex PTSD, an idea supported by the frequent occurrence of early abuse, trauma, and the presence of dissociative symptoms in borderline individuals. Patients who carry this diagnosis are characterized by the following:

1. Hypersensitivity to real or imagined abandonment.
2. Disturbances of self-identity.
3. Intense and unstable relationships.
4. Alternating idealization and devaluation of themselves and others (black-and-white thinking).
5. Compulsive, risky, and sometimes self-destructive behaviors.

Although there are a number of theories concerning its cause, many feel that the etiology of BPD stems from early deficits in emotional regulation and problematic attachment relationships. Research also suggests that affective disorders in these patients and their parents occur above chance levels. This may lead to a combination of parental instability and biological difficulties of emotional regulation within the child. Overall, both their reported history and their symptoms suggest that early attachment was experienced as traumatic, emotionally dysregulating, and possibly life threatening.

I have come to feel that borderline individuals provide us with a window into the intense and chaotic experience of infancy. As we have seen (and this is where our neuroscientific knowledge comes in handy), the amygdala is highly functional at birth. Remember that the amygdala is at the center of neural networks involving both fear and attachment. The hippocampal and cortical networks that eventually organize and inhibit the amygdala grow gradually through childhood. Because of this developmental timetable and the prolonged dependence on others for survival, the experience of relationships must sometimes be as overwhelmingly frightening to infants as it is to patients with BPD.

The symptoms that emerge in this disorder cause patients to create problematic and chaotic relationships that can lead them through a lifetime of abandonments. It is even common for therapists to abandon these patients because of their intense criticism and hostility. I find that conceptualizing BPD patients essentially as frightened children helps me take their attacks less personally and maintain a therapeutic stance. I suspect that their primitive fear, rage, and shame are a form of early implicit memory activated by real or imagined criticism or abandonment. When these memory networks are triggered during treatment, they are so powerful that the patient is unable to maintain contact with reality. We see the same phenomena in PTSD flashbacks, most likely stored in the same implicit memory systems. This confused Freud because he believed everyone was either neurotic or psychotic. BPD was a horse of a different color.

Examining BPD in light of the neuroscience we have reviewed in previous chapters, here are a few of the neurobiological processes that may explain how these symptoms become encoded within neural networks:

1. Amygdaloid memory systems are primed during early traumatic attachment experiences to react to any indication of abandonment. A sympathetic fight-or-flight reaction is triggered, and baseline levels of stress hormones are raised.

2. Orbitofrontal systems are inadequately developed during attachment to engage in healthy self-soothing and the successful inhibition of the amygdala.

3. Orbitofrontal dissociation may result in disconnection between right- and left-hemisphere and top-down processing, partly accounting for rapid and dramatic shifts between positive and negative appraisals of relationships.

4. The networks of the social brain are unable to internalize images from early interactions with caretakers that could provide self-soothing and affect regulation.

5. Rapid fluctuations between sympathetic and parasympathetic states result in baseline irritability and a low threshold for sympathetic responses to real or imagined abandonment.

6. Chronic high levels of stress hormones compromise hippocampal functioning, decreasing the brain's ability to control amygdala functioning and exacerbating emotional dyscontrol.

7. Amygdaloid dyscontrol heightens the impact of early memory on adult functioning, increasing the contemporary impact of early bonding failures.

8. Hippocampal compromise decreases reality testing and memory functioning, hindering the maintenance of positive or soothing memories during states of high arousal.
9. Early bonding failures lead to lower levels of serotonin, resulting in greater risk of depression, irritability, and decreased positive reinforcement from interpersonal interactions.
10. Self-harm during dysregulated states results in endorphin release and a sense of calm, putting these individuals at risk for repeated self-abusive behavior.

These are just some of the factors that may be involved in the neurobiology of BPD. Because this diagnosis has so far been outside the purview of neurology, little brain research has been done with BPD patients. However, neuropsychological findings with these patients do suggest dysfunction in the frontal and temporal lobes (Paris, Zelkowitz, Guzder, Joseph, & Feldman, 1999; Swirsky-Sacchetti et al., 1993). Executive and memory functions within these brain networks do not provide adequate organization for these patients. We have learned that these functions are built and sculpted in the context of early relationships; it makes sense that they are impaired in BPD patients. The central concepts in the treatment are structure and limit setting, combined with flexibility and patience (just as it is with raising children). The therapist must provide an external scaffolding within which the client can rebuild these brain networks of memory, self-organization, and affect regulation. On another level, the therapist serves as an external neural circuit to aid in the integration of networks left disconnected during development.

## Neural Network Integration

*The patient discovers his true self little-by-little through experiencing his own feelings and needs, because the analyst is able to accept and respect them.*

—Alice Miller

Unresolved trauma disrupts integrated neural processing, so that conscious awareness is split from emotional and physiological experiences. In fact, dissociative symptoms immediately following a traumatic event are predictive of the later development of PTSD (Koopman et al., 1994;

McFarlane & Yehuda, 1996). Neurochemical changes and a lack of integration of right and left hemisphere functions may also impede interpersonal bonding and bodily regulation (Henry, Satz, & Saslow, 1984). Children victimized by psychological, physical, and sexual abuse have been shown to have a significantly greater probability of brainwave abnormalities in the left frontal and temporal regions (Ito et al., 1993). Brainwave dyscoherence may put individuals at higher risk for developing all forms of psychiatric disorders (Teicher et al., 1997).

The biochemical changes that occur secondary to trauma enhance primitive (subcortical) stimulus–response pairing of conditioned responses related to sensation, emotion, and behavior. These same changes undermine cortical systems dedicated to the integration of learning across systems of memory into a coherent and conscious narrative (Siegel, 1996). As we understand more about the neurobiological processes underlying PTSD, we will better learn how to treat and possibly prevent this debilitating yet curable mental illness. Therapies of all kinds, especially those within the cognitive schools, have proven successful in the reintegration of neural processing subsequent to trauma. Systematic desensitization, exposure, and response prevention can all enhance these integrative processes.

## Summary

The brain's reaction to trauma provides us with a window to the functions and effects of neural network dissociation. From the physiological symptoms of adult PTSD to the characterological adaptations of long-term adjustment to early trauma, we see the brain, body, and psyche attempting to survive in the face of overwhelming dysregulation.

The array of adaptations to stress and trauma are at the core of the work of the psychotherapist. The safe emergency of psychotherapy activates dissociated neural networks and attempts to reintegrate them in the service of decreased arousal and improved functioning. From the first moments of life, stress shapes our brains in ways that lead us to remember experiences most important for survival.

We need to expand our notion of trauma from the fields of combat and catastrophic events to the small and everyday interactions on which we depend for our survival. Most of our learning is not traumatic but rather subtle, nondramatic, and unconscious. The interactions between parent and child, the politics of the schoolyard, and experiences of small victories and defeats all contribute to shaping who we will become. We need to always keep in mind that as primates, attachment equals survival and abandonment equals death. This may help us appreciate the power of parental abuse and abandonment to shape children for the rest of their lives.

Chapter 15

# The Self in Exile: Narcissism and Pathological Caretaking

*Happiness is having a large, loving, caring, close-knit family in another city.*

—George Burns

Each of us is born twice: first from our mother's body over a few hours, and then again from our parents' psyche over a lifetime. As we have seen, the organization of the social brain is initially sculpted via parent–child interactions. These interactions shape the infrastructure of our moment-to-moment experience of other people and of the world. As the child's brain continues to form, self-awareness and self-identity gradually coalesce. Consciousness and identity are complex functions constructed from the contributions of multiple, primarily nonconscious, neural networks. Pathological states highlight the fact that the self is a fragile construction of the brain. Furthermore, there is considerable flexibility in the location, experience, and organization of the self within our imagination.

Victims of rape and torture frequently report out-of-body experiences during their ordeal. A young woman named Joanne described to me, in great detail, how she stood behind a closet door, watching herself being raped from across the room from where it was actually happening. Another client, Mark, who had been brutally attacked while getting into his car after work, told me that he watched himself from across the street as he was repeatedly stabbed. The perception of the self is also vulnerable to alteration and distortion. Anorectic clients, with their bones protruding through their skin and their health in serious jeopardy, insist they look fat. Patients with multiple personalities are perhaps the most complex example of the plasticity of self, because they generate many different subpersonalities associated with different experiences and emotional states.

Narcissism, a common form of self disturbance, is often related to a reversal of the mirroring process during childhood. Narcissistic children's social brains and sense of self are not shaped by their own emerging emotions and sensibilities; rather, they are determined by their parents' need for nurturance, attunement, and affect regulation. What emerges in the narcissist is what Winnicott called the false self, a pseudo-adult embedded in the networks of the left hemisphere interpreter, which filters out emotional input from the right hemisphere and the body. In this chapter, we explore the reversal of the mirroring process, and the adult conditions of pathological caretaking and codependency that emerge from these early suboptimal attachment experiences (Bachar et al., 2008).

## Silent Hammers

*I cannot give you the formula for success, but I can give you the formula for failure—which is . . . try to please everybody.*
—Herbert Swope

Jerry, a successful screenwriter, came to therapy complaining of depression and exhaustion. His long work hours and last-minute deadlines kept him in a constant state of stress. His minimal personal life centered on his girlfriend, Cara, whom he described as "high maintenance," likening their relationship to having a second job. Jerry experienced his life as a relentless struggle to please Cara, his boss, and everyone he knew. Despite his depression, Jerry felt guilty about coming to therapy, and expressed fear about wasting my time; he felt that he was the helper, not the one who received help. "After all," he said to me, "you could be spending your time seeing someone who really needs the help."

After a few sessions, it became clear to me that Jerry had spent the first half of his 39 years taking care of his immature and self-centered parents. All of his subsequent relationships appeared to fall into a similar pattern. Although he described his romantic relationships in positive terms, he also reported feeling deprived of attention and nurturance. He seemed to be attempting to please others in order to gain the love and attention he had always longed for from his parents. His efforts would invariably end in sadness, resentment, and withdrawal. Although he was exhausted from trying so hard and failing so completely, Jerry still maintained the hope that his efforts would someday pay off.

Working with Jerry was both fascinating and frustrating. He questioned nearly everything I said, revealing his distrust of anyone's ability to help him. On the other hand, his flair for the dramatic resulted in entertaining stories in almost every session. He had an uncanny ability to intuit my interests, and I would often lapse into being the audience for his one-man show. I soon realized that Jerry experienced me as another person to entertain and take care of while he waited to receive care in return. At the same time, he resisted my every attempt to help him.

Jerry was hesitant to discuss his childhood, saying that he remembered little of his life before he left for college. Our sessions consisted primarily of stories of his interactions with unappreciative others and his attempts to enlist my understanding and support for his side of the story. He was both comforted by my compassion and annoyed with my continued suggestions that he pay attention to his inner emotional world, especially when engaged with others. The intensity of his defenses reflected his emotional vulnerability and I needed to be careful not to move too quickly. On the other hand, if I went too slowly, he might become resentful and terminate therapy, as he had ended so many other relationships.

At some point, I suggested that he write a screenplay about himself. Jerry agreed and soon created a story about a little man named Hal who sat at a control panel in his head. Hal was a sort of ship's captain at the helm of the *U.S.S. Jerry*. When Jerry was alone, Hal would monitor the people in Jerry's life. A wall full of TV screens kept track of where they were, what they were doing, and whether they were thinking of Jerry. When he would come into contact with another ship, like his girlfriend Cara, Hal would select a holographic image of Jerry specifically for that person. Hal had a screen to monitor Jerry from the perspective of the other ship, to make sure that the hologram had the desired effect. Hal's purpose was best described by the show business adage: "Give the people what they want."

I was impressed by the clarity of the story of Hal. Jerry was telling me that his sense of self was organized around his theory of the minds of others. Nothing about Hal focused on Jerry's own thoughts, feelings, or needs. Jerry only knew he needed to understand the needs of others; for him, this was love; this was life. I realized Hal reflected the early sculpting of Jerry's social brain and how he survived childhood. The story of Hal was a reflection of implicit memory, symbolically representing the core emotional drama from his early life. Despite the obvious nature of this story, Jerry refused to entertain interpretations. He seemed to have great difficulty experiencing the world from his own point of view. In Jerry's conscious experience, he was Hal.

A few sessions later, Jerry used another metaphor to illustrate his inner world. He described himself as a house on a movie set with a perfectly detailed facade but no finished interior; there was no true place to live. If you looked behind the facade there were only exposed 2×4s and bare floors. He said, "A good director knows how to place his cameras to maintain the illusion of a real building." In a moment of receptivity and trust, he told me that his goal for therapy was to finish building and decorating the interior space so he could stop worrying about camera angles. Jerry was tired of feeling like a fraud in a world of real people. I could feel his inner world shifting as his emptiness surfaced into consciousness.

I told Jerry, "As we grow, the story of who we are is written in collaboration with those around us, especially our parents. They watch us, listen to us, and try to help us put into words what we struggle to express. This helps us to write our story. When parents didn't get this help as children, or are suffering with some problem, they may look to their children to help them find themselves."

I think this is what may have happened with Jerry's parents. He learned to be sensitive to them and attend to their needs when they should have been helping him write his story. In a sense, Jerry's story was written by default; in serving others he was hoping to find himself, and after all these years he was still searching. I suggested to Jerry that his choice of a writing career may have been an expression of his desire to write his story. Although there are many good and honorable aspects to serving others, I told him that it may be more important to write a new story where his own needs would be balanced with the needs of others.

Jerry asked, "Is this why, when people ask me how I am, the first thing I think about is how others in my life feel?" I nodded as I watched the muscles in his face relax. A new understanding of a familiar behavior was emerging, and his inner world was being reorganized. After a period of silence, he said softly, "I even do it with you, don't I? I pay you to take care of me, but I end up entertaining you and protecting you from my needs and negative feelings." The session was over and he walked silently out of the office. I wondered if he would be able to withstand the stress of these insights enough to return for our next session.

He did come back, and uncharacteristically touched my shoulder as he passed me on the way to his seat. "You're gonna think you're pretty smart when I tell you this one." I noticed his voice had changed: It was no longer the voice of an entertainer. Jerry was sharing this experience from a different place within himself. On the previous Friday, he had gone out with Cara and they didn't get back to her apartment until 3:00 A.M. The combination of alcohol and exhaustion made him fall asleep as soon as his head hit the pillow. After what seemed like only a few minutes, he was jarred awake by the banging of hammers outside the bedroom window. He picked up his throbbing head and saw on the clock that it was not even 7:00 in the morning. Jerry said, "I felt like my head was going to explode!"

Jerry's face became increasingly tense as he described the murderous fantasies passing through his mind. He imagined going outside and punching out the entire team of construction workers. Just as he was about to jump up and run outside, Cara looked up at him with an expression of exhausted rage and said, "I'm going to go out there and kill those guys." Apparently, they had been waking her up that way for most of the week.

Falling back on the couch in my office and letting out a sigh, Jerry began to describe how her words triggered something altogether familiar within him. "When I heard Cara's anger I became a different person. My exhaustion vanished. I felt energized and alive! I completely forgot about the construction workers. My total focus instantaneously shifted to making Cara feel better." He described jumping up as if well-rested and said, "A little breakfast will make you feel better." He became oblivious to the sound of the hammers and bounded into the kitchen as Cara pulled the pillows back over her head.

Ten minutes later, Jerry was at the stove brewing coffee, frying eggs, and about to call out "Breakfast is served," when he again noticed the hammers. He said, "I was amazed that I hadn't heard them since I had gotten out of bed." He realized that they hadn't stopped, but from the moment he saw the anger on Cara's face, he became completely involved in activities to cope with her feelings, utterly ignoring his own. He realized that attending to Cara's distress catapulted him out of his own.

As he stood, spatula in hand, these feelings triggered a long-forgotten memory. He remembered coming home from school to find his mother crying, head down in her arms on the kitchen table. Jerry remembered his terror as he went over and stood beside her. She didn't respond when he asked her what was wrong; she just continued sobbing. He didn't know what to do or who to call. His father had left them months before, and his mother had grown more silent and withdrawn with each passing week. He stood motionless, not knowing if she was even aware of his presence.

He tried to engage her in conversation, telling her about his day at school. He even told some inappropriate jokes in the hope of getting her angry enough to chase after him. She remained silent, crushed by the weight of her sadness. Jerry recalled growing increasingly desperate and afraid as time passed. He stood motionless as the afternoon light turned to dusk. He eventually came up with the idea to cook for her and went over to the stove to fry her some eggs, the only thing he knew how to make. After collecting what he needed, he pulled a chair over to the stove, stood on it, and started to cook. This seemed to get her attention. She came over and they cooked together in silence.

During our first few sessions, Jerry had mentioned his parents' divorce, his father's drinking, and his mother's depression. He characterized his home as "a vault of silence" with very little interaction or shared activities. The family took no meals or vacations together; most of their energy was used up in day-to-day survival. He spoke of these things in passing, with little emotion and an insistence that his childhood had no connection to his adult difficulties. He said he had coped with his family situation by burying himself in books and writing stories. This memory provided evidence for what I had suspected; Jerry had grown up with too much stress and too little parenting. He had lost himself in everyone else's stories but had not received the emotional support and mirroring he needed to write his own.

Jerry came away from the experience of the hammers and the memories they triggered with a new perspective. He could see, from this and other childhood memories that began to emerge, how he was constantly frightened by the emotional instability and distance of his parents. It was also clear that he, like Hal, was constantly monitoring the feelings and needs of others. I found it especially fascinating how his own anger, frustration, and exhaustion disappeared in the face of Cara's negative feelings. He later told me that he figured this was why he felt so uncomfortable and vulnerable when he wasn't in a relationship. Never having learned how to regulate his own feelings, it was safer to stay in the minds of others.

The power of these insights was unsettling for Jerry, and it took him many weeks to get back on track. As he regained his equilibrium, we began to apply this new knowledge to more aspects of his life. Thinking back on his romantic partners, he realized that they were never as good at anticipating or attending to his needs as he was to theirs. This imbalance led him to feel unloved and uncared for. At one point, he stood up abruptly and shouted, "I blamed them for not being as sick as I am." Jerry came to understand that feeling like an empty shell was connected to not knowing his own feelings. He said, "My feelings were never important when I was a kid. It's my feelings that are going to furnish those empty rooms inside of me and I have to have my own feelings to be whole."

These experiences were a turning point in Jerry's treatment. We created a common language and used it to explore Jerry's inner world. Hal gradually replaced some of the old monitors with new ones designed to track Jerry's own feelings. Eventually, Hal and his monitors became unnecessary. At times, Jerry feared he was being too selfish by considering his own needs. He did lose some friends who relied on his constant and unilateral attention. Cara and Jerry grew closer, however, and she admitted that she liked Jerry better when he didn't try to make her happy all the time. Jerry slowly recovered from his pathological caretaking and graduated to become a caring person.

Jerry's difficulties highlight a number of principles related to the development and organization of the brain that we examined in previous chapters. During childhood, Jerry's brain adapted to a demanding and nonnurturing emotional environment. From early in life, his survival depended on being highly aware of the feelings and needs of his parents. The neural systems of his social brain became hypersensitive to his parents' facial expressions, body language, and behaviors. This hypersensitivity helped Jerry monitor his parents' emotions and behave in ways that regulated their feelings and bonded them to him. Systems normally used to help children come to experience themselves were usurped to monitor other people in his life. This was how Hal was born. Jerry's mirroring skills continued to be utilized in adulthood with his friends, employers, and therapist through emotional caretaking and entertaining stories.

Because Jerry didn't have help processing and integrating his own emotions during childhood, they remained chaotic, frightening, and overwhelming long into his adult years. Caretaking was reinforced not only by those he attracted, but by the avoidance of his own disorganized emotions by attending to the feelings of others. Caretaking evolved into a form of affect regulation, as well as a way of connecting to others via a false self (Hal). This was demonstrated by the instantaneous inhibition of his feelings of anger at the construction workers when he realized Cara was awake and upset. From early in development, hidden layers of neural processing organized the inhibition of his own feelings and directed his social brain to focus on the internal state of others. This neural network organization was in place prior to Jerry's development of self-conscious awareness, making this way of experiencing the world completely unconscious and an a priori assumption in his life.

Jerry's evolving sense of self was shaped via these processes, through the eyes, minds, and hearts of others. Left-hemisphere processing networks, which inhibit affect and participate in the creation of stories about the self, allowed Jerry to become a functional adult with a successful writing career. His ability to describe himself symbolically, first as a monitoring robot and then as a director planning camera angles, reflected his subconscious awareness of his self-organization. Without assistance in connecting these insights to the organization of his conscious self, they remained correct but useless bits of information contained within dissociated neural networks.

Interpretations—such as the one Jerry made connecting his cooking eggs for Cara and taking care of his mother—triggered emotions of sadness and loss. Making his defenses conscious appeared to activate the emotional networks that the defenses had been inhibiting. The higher association areas involved in the organization of conscious awareness appear capable of the plasticity required for qualitative changes of experience. Implicit memories of early childhood—stored within networks of the social brain—were experienced emotionally and expressed in a variety of ways including Jerry's distrust of the ability of others to help him.

These were echoes of his disappointment in his parents' inability to assist him when he was young.

Jerry's insecure attachment resulted in a complex array of emotional and behavioral adaptations. His lack of conscious recall for much of his childhood was one example. Another was his unconscious expectation that the expression of his needs would be met by more emotional pain. All of Jerry's struggle to attain love and caring reflected his brain's adaptation to a childhood full of impingements and the absence of an integrated and integrating other. Jerry's parents did not assist him in creating a narrative identity grounded in his own experience. In therapy, I helped Jerry apply his considerable creative skills to write his own story.

## Interpretations and Neural Plasticity

*There's a world of difference between truth and facts. Facts can obscure the truth.*

—Maya Angelou

You may remember that interpretations are sometimes referred to as the therapist's scalpel. In making an interpretation, the therapist points out an unconscious aspect of the patient's experience, such as a defense he or she is using to avoid negative feelings. For a client who employs humor to avoid feelings of abandonment after a divorce, it might entail reminding him that he is experiencing many symptoms of depression or that his eyes are moist. For another who is enraged at a minor slight by a coworker, an interpretation might consist of connecting her present feelings to emotional memories of abuse from a previous relationship. In both of these instances, the therapist addresses what appears to be a disconnection among different tracks of cognitive, emotional, sensory, and behavioral processing.

When an interpretation is accurate and delivered in an appropriate and well-timed manner, a number of things occur. The client generally becomes quiet; there may be a change in facial expressions, posture, and tone of voice. Very often the client will begin to fully experience the emotions against which he or she was defending. There is a shift from fluent reflexive language to speaking in a slower and more self-reflective manner. Some clients report becoming confused or disoriented, whereas others describe physiological symptoms of panic or grief. Borderline clients can demonstrate extreme reactions to interpretations, including losing emotional control and functional decompensation. They may become extremely emotional, bolt from the consulting room, and engage in self-injurious behavior. Patients like these appear unable to cope with the emotions released when their defenses are made conscious.

What might be happening in the brain during and after an accurate and well-timed interpretation? Each interpretation that hits home is like the death of a small aspect of the false self. My suspicion is that it begins with seeing past the products of the left hemisphere interpreter, which disinhibits the activation of subcortical circuits containing negative memories. In the process of working through these new feelings, the client gradually regains emotional equilibrium, allowing for plasticity and new learning in prefrontal regions. The concurrent availability of negative subcortical memories and the enhanced ability of the cortex to create new connections allows neural networks containing various components of a particular memory to become integrated. Like breaking and resetting a bone that has healed badly, memories become unstable and can be reformed in a more positive way. This process allows painful implicit memories to be accessed by cortical networks for contextualization in time and space, and to be regulated and inhibited where no longer necessary.

Bringing a defense to consciousness activates both the cortical networks that organize the defense and the subcortical networks that contain the negative memories and associated affect. This disinhibition results in the emotional and physiological arousal seen in therapy as the amygdala becomes reactivated and alerts the body to the old danger. This may also be the mechanism for regression through the reactivation of old sensory-motor-affective memories stored in normally inhibited amygdaloid systems. There is most likely a shift in hemispheric bias from left to right, correlated with the breakthrough of negative emotions. This left-to-right shift may account for the cessation of reflexive social language of the left hemisphere interpreter and a shift to greater self-awareness.

Interpretations need to undergo a process called *working through*, meaning they need to be stated, restated, and applied to multiple situations and circumstances (parallel to relapse prevention in cognitive therapies). This process serves to connect new learning to multiple memory networks, and may need to reach a certain critical mass of connections throughout the brain to become reflexive. Working through reflects the expansion and stabilization of new associative matrices of memory. It is also reflected in the construction of a new narrative containing altered aspects of behaviors, feelings, and self-identity that serve as a way to retain and reinforce new learning.

## Pathological Caretaking

*By the time a man is 35, he knows that the images of the right man, the tough man, the true man which he received in high school do not work in life.*

—Robert Bly

Jerry's pathological caretaking is one possible expression of a disturbance of self referred to as *narcissism*. Narcissism is characterized by a two-sided existence: one reflecting an inflated sense of self-importance, the other mired in emptiness and despair. The origin of this formation of the self occurs when a child looking for love and attunement instead discovers the mother's own predicament (Miller, 1981). The child, robbed of the possibility of self-discovery, compensates by caring for the parent under a real or imagined threat of abandonment.

Bright and sensitive children attune to and regulate the parents' emotions and come to reflect what the parents want from them. These children will usually appear mature beyond their years and find comfort in their ability to regulate the feelings of the people around them. Because of their power to regulate the affect of one or both parents, these children are filled with a sense of inflated self-importance. Miller and Winnicott call pathological caretaking a particular manifestation of the false self, described by Jerry as both a theatrical facade and an inner robot monitoring others.

The other side of narcissism reflects aspects of the child's emotional world that have found no mirroring. This true self, or the part that is unique to the individual and searching for expression, is left undeveloped and eventually forgotten. This emotional core (or inner child) secretly and silently awaits parenting in each new relationship while dutifully taking care of the other. This aspect of the emotional self is the emptiness, loss, and shame of being abandoned, and how survival was contingent on taking care of others. This is the source of depression, the sense of being a fraud, and lack of an emotional connection with life.

The development of the social brain (and the subsequent formation of the sense of self) becomes dedicated to the prediction of, and attunement to, the moods and needs of the parent and others. This ability serves to ward off abandonment anxiety while truncating the development of an understanding, expression, and regulation of one's own feelings. Such children grow into self-awareness experiencing others' emotions as their own, and an overwhelming sense of responsibility, or even compulsion, to regulate the emotions of those around them. In Jerry's case, cooking breakfast for the upset women in his life helped him avoid his own poorly understood and dysregulated emotional world.

Thus, caretaking of others serves as a substitute for self-soothing abilities and inner emotional organization. Pathological caretakers come to therapy primarily because they are depressed and exhausted by their inability to create a boundary between themselves and the needs of others. Although being with others is hard work, being alone is even more difficult when they are not exhausted, because they need to regulate others to avoid their internal world. For these people, a battering or abusive relationship is far less frightening than solitude. Caretakers are difficult clients because they have learned during early attachment relationships that help is not forthcoming when they are in distress. Like Jerry, they have come to believe that it is best to put their inner needs out of mind and keep "giving the people what they want."

## Alice Miller: Archaeologist of Childhood Experience

*I was not out to paint beautiful pictures. . . . I wanted only to help the truth burst forth.*

—Alice Miller

The central importance of parental relationships in shaping the social brain is nowhere better articulated than in a series of elegantly simple works by the Viennese psychotherapist Alice Miller. Her work with what she called gifted children targeted adults, like Jerry, who were raised by parents whose emotional needs were greater than their ability to attune to their children. Taking a stand against her analytic colleagues, Miller reshaped the therapeutic role into one of being an advocate for the child within her adult patients. Reaching back through the years to reconnect with long-forgotten childhood experiences, she reinterpreted much of her clients' adult behaviors as a reflection of their adaptational histories. In observing the nonverbal reenactment of implicit memory, Miller formed hypotheses concerning what her clients had been exposed to, how their young brains had adapted, and what it would take to unearth the abandoned true self.

Miller's archaeological view of memory included the awareness that memory from different developmental stages reflects different modes of processing and understanding. In her role as advocate, she saw therapy as a process in which therapists help clients unearth their history, not from the point of view of the adult but from that of the child. Memories in these implicit subcortical networks do not change with time, but remain in their initial form as they were experienced at a very young age. Miller formulated this view from clinical experience rather than a knowledge of the multiple systems of explicit and implicit memory.

Miller used the term *double amnesia* to describe the process by which these children have had to first forget certain parts of themselves (e.g., feelings, thoughts, and fantasies) that could not be accepted or tolerated in their family. The second layer of forgetting is to forget that these feelings have been forgotten. These two layers of forgetting ensured that such children would not slip back into wanting what could not be had. Given our knowledge of the multiple systems of memory and their dissociability, Miller's double amnesia is most likely grounded in both the disconnection between systems of implicit and explicit memory, and constructing a self-narrative that excludes reference to personal needs.

The lack of assistance in the construction of a self-narrative, combined with the heightened anxiety and vigilance necessary for survival with narcissistic caretakers, leads to a deficit in the consolidation of autobiographical memory. The memories are not repressed; rather, they are unorganized by hippocampal cortical systems that would allow them to be accessible to conscious consideration. In this light, Miller's work is a reconstruction of the past, based on available conscious memory in combination with nonverbal expressions from implicit systems of memory. Such patients' present experiences are examined for emotional truths, then traced back through a hypothesized trajectory. The patients' considerable empathic ability can be utilized to their advantage by asking how they think some other child might feel in a situation similar to their own. This method, used a number of times, is often successful.

For Miller, gifted children are exquisitely sensitive to the cues of parents and have the innate ability to mold themselves to their parents' conscious and unconscious messages. These are the children who often come to be called codependent and are overrepresented in the service professions such as doctors, nurses, social workers, and therapists. In essence, their jobs are an attempt to parlay their defenses into a career. Jerry—with his sensitivity, intellect, and wit—fit well in this category.

Although the gifted children described by Miller may be quite functional, they often feel empty and devoid of vitality. Because their vitality and true self are not acceptable, these are inhibited and banished from awareness. This creates a vulnerability, not only to disturbances in personality but also to the unconscious transmission of "mirror reversal" to the next generation. Parents who have not been adequately parented themselves can look to their children for the nurturance and care they were unable to receive years before. Miller stated, "What these mothers had once failed to find in their own mothers they were able to find in their children, someone at their disposal who can be used as an echo, who can be controlled, is completely centered on them, will never desert them, and offers full attention and admiration" (1981, p. 35).

Children's instinct to bond with their parents drives them to do so regardless of the terms and conditions. When such children look into their mother's eyes and find no reflection but, rather, "the mother's own predicament," they will mold themselves (if able) to their mother's psychic needs. Compulsive compliance—initially adaptive in response to narcissistic or abusive caretakers—becomes maladaptive in relationships with others, and in the development of the self (Crittenden & DiLalla, 1988). Later in life, the gifted child's lack of rebellion becomes the problem. Unable to attend to their own emotional memories, and thus unable to construct the story of their lives, these children constantly search for someone who needs nurturance.

Because he or she was completely helpless in childhood to resist the coercion of the parents' unconscious, Miller felt that the child within the adult patient always needs an advocate. Our brains are designed to adapt to the environmental contingencies presented to us. Remember that the child's first reality is the parents' unconscious, transferred via right-hemisphere-to-right-hemisphere attunement well before self-awareness and self-identity. Because it is implanted in early implicit memory, it is never experienced as anything other than the self. Miller was quick to describe the tragedy for the parents who may be well aware of the pain from their own childhood and may have vowed to never make their children feel as they did. The intergenerational transmission continues because it is reflexive and unconscious, and because each generation, at some level, protects the image of the parents and guards against the pain of their own unfulfilled emotional needs.

Although patients do not generally have explicit memory for early relationships with their parents, Miller posits that these learning experiences are implicitly recorded in how the patients think of and treat themselves. The strictness and negativity in the patients' self-image and superego will expose their parents' negative or indifferent attitudes toward them years before (Miller, 1983). These implicit emotional and behavioral memories—in the form of attitudes, anxieties, and self-statements—contribute to the continued repression of real emotions and needs.

Because children equate punishment with guilt, abuse and neglect create a sense of innate badness. A teacher told Dr. Miller that after seeing a film about the Holocaust, several children in her class said, "But the Jews must have been guilty or they wouldn't have been punished like that" (Miller, 1983, p. 158). This assumption of guilt on the part of children both protects the parent and serves as the developmental core of a negative self-image. Because this self-image is organized and stored by implicit systems of affective memory, the child's later-developing identity forms around this a priori negative core. Caretaking and compulsive perfectionism reflect the ongoing attempt to compensate for the certainty of unworthiness and anticipation of abandonment.

## René Magritte and His Mother

*We must not fear daylight just because it almost always illuminates a miserable world.*

—René Magritte

A chilling example of the reversal of the mirroring process is demonstrated in a painting by the surrealist René Magritte, titled *The Spirit of Geometry* (see Figure 15.1). It depicts a mother holding a child but with a startling twist: Their heads and faces have been exchanged. Magritte was the eldest of three boys in a middle-class household in turn-of-the-

**FIGURE 15.1**
*The Spirit of Geometry*, René Magritte

*Magritte's image of a mother and her son may reflect an implicit
emotional memory of his relationship with his mother
(© 2002 C. Herscovici, Brussels/Artists Rights Society (ARS) New York).*

century Belgium. His mother suffered from depression throughout his
childhood, and made multiple suicide attempts. She was, in fact, locked
in her room each night for her own protection. As a young boy, René
was locked in with her to keep her company. One cold February morning, she managed to slip out of her room and drowned in the Sambre
river. René was obviously not successful in making his mother's life
worth living.

Based on his adult life, it is fair to assume that René was a bright and
sensitive child, and that he suffered from a lack of positive maternal
attention for most or all of his childhood. To lose his mother to suicide
at the age of 14 served as an additional blow to his sense of safety as a

child. This painting suggests that the young Magritte looked into his mother's eyes and found fatigue, depression, and emptiness. In her eyes he read, "You be the mommy, I'll be the baby," and he complied.

In retrospect, a biographer suggested that Magritte himself seemed at peace only when he was "tormented by problems" (Gablik, 1985). Much of the body of Magritte's surrealist work presents us with the message that the world is not what it appears to be. His respectable middle-class family had a dark and painful secret at its core, one that became a central aspect of the young boy's experience. Although as an adult, Magritte repeatedly stated that his early experiences had no bearing on his artistic work, it is difficult to imagine that the loss, betrayal, and abandonment of his childhood did not reverberate in his many works, warning us not to be fooled by the assumptions on which we depend.

## Summary

The separation between the true and false selves reflects the brain's ability to develop dissociated tracks of experience. Early trauma and stress in nonhealing environments can even result in the formation of multiple separate personalities, now referred to as *dissociative identity disorder* (DID). It is logical to assume that these different experiential states are encoded within different patterns of neural network activation. The existence of pathological caretaking, DID, and other disorders of the self demonstrate its fragility and its inclination to adapt to whatever social realities are presented to it.

The purpose of both the brain and the self is survival. For each of us, the organization of our own self—including our personality, defenses, coping styles, and the like—reflects the conditions to which we have had to adapt. Put another way, all aspects of the self are forms of implicit memory stored in neural networks that organize emotion, sensation, and behavior. These networks are sculpted in reaction to real or imagined threats as the brain strives to predict and control its physical and social environments.

Part VI.

# The Reorganization of Experience

# Chapter 16

# The Evolutionary Necessity of Psychotherapy

*The useless, the odd, the peculiar, the incongruous—are the signs of history.*

—S. J. Gould

The human brain is an amazing organ, capable of continual growth and lifelong adaptation to an ever-changing array of challenges. Our understanding of how the brain accomplishes this mandate increases with each new theoretical development and technological advance. At the same time, we are uncovering some of natural selection's more problematic choices. If necessity is the mother of invention, then evolution itself has created the necessity for psychotherapy by shaping a brain that is vulnerable to a wide array of difficulties.

Over the last century, psychotherapists have demonstrated that many of the brain's shortcomings can be counterbalanced by the application of skillfully applied techniques in the context of a caring relationship. Thus, in our ability to link, attune, and regulate each other's brains, evolution has also provided us a way to heal one another. Because we know that relationships are capable of building and rebuilding neural structures, psychotherapy can now be understood as a neurobiological intervention, with a deep cultural history. In psychotherapy, we are tapping the same principles and processes available in every relationship to connect to and heal another brain.

In this chapter we focus on the following eight problematic aspects of brain functioning that cause many people to come to psychotherapy:

1. The suppression of language and predictive capacity under stress
2. Divergent hemispheric processing
3. The bias toward early learning
4. The tenacity of fear
5. The damaging effects of stress hormones
6. The speed and amount of unconscious processing
7. The primacy of projection
8. Unconscious self-deception

This will serve as somewhat of a review in that it draws on many of the neuroscientific findings previously discussed. We will then apply some of these principles to a case of PTSD.

## The Suppression of Language and Predictive Capacity Under Stress

*When a man's knowledge is not in order, the more of it he has the greater will be his confusion.*

—Herbert Spencer

When animals hear a strange and potentially threatening sound, they freeze in their tracks, become silent, and scan the environment for danger. The logic behind this primitive reflex is quite clear—being still and silent make us less likely to be seen or heard as we prepare to respond to a potential threat. Research suggests that during these states of high arousal, Broca's area, responsible for speech production, becomes inhibited.

While this response may be a positive adaptation in animals without language, it is a high price for humans to pay for being frightened. Putting feelings into words and constructing narratives about our experiences are integral to emotional regulation, the interweaving of neural networks of emotion and cognition, and the experience of a coherent sense of self. Perhaps most important, a lack of language can separate us from the healing effects of positive connections with others. The loss of the ability to construct narratives is especially problematic in situations where individuals are forced into silence by their abusers, or after enduring the "unspeakable horrors" of torture, war, or the death of friends and family.

Losing the ability to verbalize feelings also interferes with building descending inhibitory cortical networks down to the amygdala. You may have had a traumatic experience like an auto accident or robbery where you felt compelled to tell the story over and over again in the following days and weeks. In time, the pressure to tell others diminishes as the emotions connected to the traumatic events slowly dissipate. I suspect that telling the story builds circuitry, which contributes to amygdala inhibition and the dissipation of fear.

Just as putting words together to form sentences requires sequencing and predicting what comes next, so does moment-to-moment sensorimotor functioning. So, besides its role in language, Broca's area also contributes to networks of prediction and anticipation. Thus, along with loss of language, traumatized individuals may also experience difficulties in the day-to-day navigation of life that the rest of us handle unconsciously and automatically. This inhibition of Broca's area is exacerbated by the amygdala's ability to inhibit prefrontal functioning during high states of arousal. This may be one of the reasons that traumatized individuals seem to experience more than their share of accidents, bad relationships, and misfortune. The combined loss of words and decreased predictive abilities enhance the long-term impact of the trauma by increasing the probability of ongoing stress and revictimization.

The "talking cure" stimulates language networks and encourages the creation of adaptive narratives about traumatic experience. The therapist's caring presence, availability, and skill promote a moderate state of arousal, which supports the neuroplastic processes necessary for building descending inhibitory fibers to limbic and brain stem centers. Putting feelings into words minimizes the active inhibition of Broca's area and supports the balance of right and left hemisphere processing. In therapy, we stimulate Broca's area, disinhibit language, restore predictive abilities, and support neuroplastic processes of adaptive learning.

## Divergent Hemispheric Processing

*The mind is the last to know.*

—Michael Gazzaniga

Over the course of primate and human evolution, the left and right cerebral cortices have become specialized to serve the formation of the conscious, linguistic self in the left and the somatic, emotional self in the right. It is likely that as the hemispheres differentiated, it became increasingly necessary for one to take executive control of conscious processing. There is considerable evidence that the left hemisphere took on this function, along with a lead role in maintaining moderate states of arousal and social connectedness. The right hemisphere constantly provides information to the left, but while we are awake, the left hemisphere may or may not allow this input into consciousness.

The disruption of a proper integration and balance between left and right hemisphere input can result in dominance of one hemisphere or the other. As we have seen, the overinhibition of the right hemisphere by the left can result in alexithymia, while an underinhibition can result in overemotionality, magical thinking, or auditory hallucinations. The proper integration and balance of the left and right prefrontal cortices are also necessary for the regulation of mood. When people are traumatized, there is an increased likelihood that the coordination between left and right functioning will be disrupted. The PTSD symptoms of intrusions are likely the clearest example of deficits of right hemisphere infiltration of the left.

When trauma occurs in early development, the hemispheres grow to be less coordinated and integrated, resulting in problems in affective regulation and positive social awareness. People with histories of childhood abuse and neglect have been shown to have a smaller corpus callosum and are more likely to suffer from symptoms of PTSD (De Bellis et al., 1999; Teicher et al., 2004). Their brains have fewer connecting fibers available to integrate right and left processes, and their development is characterized by a decreased lateral integration. As we have also seen, the left and right prefrontal cortices are biased toward positive and negative emotions, and a disturbance of the homeostatic balance of the two can result in extremes of depression and mania.

Therapists intuitively and intentionally seek to balance the expression of affect and cognition. We encourage overintellectualized and defended clients to be aware of and explore their feelings. On the other hand, we provide clients who are overwhelmed by anxiety, fear, or depression with tools to use the cognitive capabilities of their left hemispheres to counterbalance these emotions. The common imbalance between affect and cognition in many of our clients rests, in part, in the struggle between the hemispheres to integrate and learn a common language. The narratives we create in therapy strive to be inclusive of the conscious and unconscious realities of both hemispheres.

## The Bias Toward Early Learning

*In the practical use of our intellect, forgetting is as important
as remembering.*

—William James

At birth, the more primitive structures of our brains responsible for
social and emotional processing are highly developed, while the cortex
develops slowly through the first decades of life. Much of our most
important emotional and interpersonal learning occurs during our first
few years when our primitive brains are in control. We mature into self-
awareness having been programmed by early experience with sensory
and emotional assumptions that we accept as truth. As a result, a great
deal of extremely important learning takes place before we are consciously aware we are learning (Casey, Galvan, & Hare, 2005). For most
of us, the early interactions that shape our brains remain forever inaccessible to conscious memory, reflection, or modification. This artifact of
evolution, expressed in the sequential nature of our neural development,
turns the accidents of birth and the ups and downs of everyday life into
the beliefs and causes for which we suffer and die.

Early experiences shape structures in ways that have a lifelong impact
on three of our most vital areas of learning: attachment, emotional regulation, and self-esteem. These three spheres of learning establish our
abilities to connect with others, cope with stress, and feel we are love-
able and have value. Given how little control we have over our early
experience, and that anyone can have children regardless of their competence or sanity, an incredible amount of human brain building is left
to chance. In addition, we have seen that early experience shapes genetic
expression, which impacts our ability to learn, regulate our emotions,
and nurture our future children.

It is obvious that our dependency on early caretakers can influence us
in perfectly terrible ways. We see this in abused and neglected children
who often enter adolescence and adulthood with a variety of symptoms.
Explosive anger, eating disorders, drug and alcohol problems, and other
forms of acting out are common. They also have identity disturbances
and a poor self-image, exacerbated by angry feelings and antisocial
behaviors. Like a veteran with PTSD, the brains of these children
become shaped to survive the combat of their day-to-day lives, but are
ill-equipped to navigate peace.

In psychotherapy, we have tools that allow us to explore early experiences with the possibility of coming to understand our symptoms as forms of sensory, motor, and emotional memory. Projection, transference, self-esteem, and internal self-talk are all expressions of early implicit memories from which we can get a view of early unremembered interactions. Making the unconscious conscious is, in part, coming to an awareness and understanding of the impact of early experience. Once they can be consciously thought about and placed into a coherent narrative, we gain the ability to reintegrate dissociated neural networks of affect, cognition, abstract thinking, and bodily awareness. This process opens the door to decreasing shame and increasing self-compassion while creating the possibility for healing.

## The Tenacity of Fear

*It is the perpetual dread of fear, the fear of fear, that shapes the face of a brave man.*

—Georges Bernanos

At birth, the amygdala, the executive center of our brain, is fully developed. Its first job is to figure out who is safe and who is dangerous. Although the amygdala begrudgingly comes to share executive control with the prefrontal cortex, it remains capable of hijacking the brain in states of distress and fear. The amygdala's job is to remember any and all threats and to generalize these experiences to other signs of danger. In other words, the amygdala never forgets. Its tendency to generalize is why a panic attack outside the home can lead to agoraphobia or why getting scratched by a cat can soon morph into a fear of all furry animals. Evolution has shaped our brains to err on the side of caution and be afraid whenever it might be remotely useful. In contrast, the hippocampus is constantly remodeled in response to new information and can easily differentiate one furry animal from another.

Fear makes our thinking and behavior more rigid. We become afraid of taking risks and learning new things, which results in a tendency for those who are sick to remain sick. One recognized symptom of trauma is "neophobia" or the fear of anything new. Once our brains have been shaped by fear to perceive, think, and act in stereotyped ways, we tend to remain in rigid patterns that are reinforced by our very survival. Our internal logic is self-perpetuating, making it difficult for us to find answers that are different from the ones we already know. Our chance of learning then rests in getting input from other people. However, relationships with others are also difficult because fear may make us keep them at arm's length. When people are hurt or afraid, caring relationships are not easily entered into nor easy to benefit from. Openness and trust are fragile creatures, even with the people we love most.

The training of the therapist and the therapeutic context are designed to enhance support and trust, and provide consistent emotional availability. Within the consulting room, therapists attempt to be amygdala whisperers and work to reactivate networks of new learning in the hippocampus and prefrontal cortex. Warmth, empathic caring, and positive regard can create a state of mind that enhances neuroplastic processes and increases the likelihood of positive change. It now appears that therapists help people get over their fears, not by erasing traumatic memories but by building new connections to inhibit these memories from triggering autonomic arousal.

## The Damaging Effects of Stress Hormones

*Man is an over-complicated organism. If he is doomed to extinction he will die out for want of simplicity.*

—Ezra Pound

For our more primitive cousins with smaller cortices and simpler environments, danger is encountered and quickly resolved. They either escape or get eaten, win or lose. But when you add a huge cortex capable of building freeways and information superhighways, the brain has to adapt to a world of constant challenge where there is never any clear resolution. A large cortex also adds a memory for the future and endless possibilities for anticipatory anxiety. Beyond this we now have a vast imagination capable of creating frightening fantasies that our primitive brains are unable to distinguish from reality.

Stressful situations trigger the release of the stress hormone cortisol. Stress hormones are catabolic, which means they break down complex compounds for immediate energy. Cortisol's motto is "live for today, for tomorrow we may die." As one of the glucocorticoids, its job is to break down complex carbohydrates into usable energy for our muscles.

Another action of cortisol is to cut down on energy dedicated to protein synthesis. Because neural growth and our immune system depend on protein synthesis, prolonged high levels of stress hormones impair our ability both to learn and to remain healthy. The conservation of our primitive stress system, well adapted for a simple life and a small cortex, can leave our modern human brains bathed in high levels of stress hormones for long periods of time. This leads to compromises of brain maintenance, learning, and immunological functioning. Because chronic stress inhibits learning, successful psychotherapy depends on our ability to downregulate stress in our clients. From specific stress reduction techniques to the soothing effects of a supportive relationship, stress modulation and success in psychotherapy go hand in hand. Thus, stress reduction skills should not be limited only to specific diagnoses, because they are always necessary for psychotherapy to be successful.

## The Speed and Amount of Unconscious Processing

*Man is ready to die for an idea provided that idea is not quite clear to him.*

—Paul Eldridge

In order to survive, animals have to be tough or fast. The tortoise and the hare are good examples of these different, but equally viable survival strategies. While our elaborate cortices separate our brains from theirs, further down, all three are pretty similar. Our expanded cortex does allow us vast response flexibility over our more primitive cousins. Of course, thinking through options takes time and in some circumstances, a speedy reflex is far more adaptive. Because of this, we have retained many primitive reflexes and subcortical executive control of certain functions in the service of survival. Our harelike brains allow us to make rapid decisions and have knee-jerk responses.

While it takes approximately 500–600 milliseconds for an experience to register in conscious awareness, the amygdala can react to a potential threat in less than 50 milliseconds. This means that by the time we have become consciously aware of an experience, it has already been processed many times in our more primitive neural networks, activating memories and triggering implicit memories organized by past learning. This unconscious backdrop shapes the perception of what is being consciously attended to and constructs our experiences of the present moment. (Nomura et al., 2003; Wiens, 2006). When we finally become aware of the outcome of this process, we experience it as if we are living in the present, and act with free will based on conscious deliberation. There is extensive evidence that this is not really the case. We actually live about 500 milliseconds after the moment and our past learning severely limits our free will. The illusions of free will and control have obvious survival advantages, foremost of which is the ability to be assertive and confident in complex situations. The downside of this strategy is when we become so sure of our personal beliefs that we are unable to consider alternatives.

Ninety percent of the input to the cerebral cortex comes from internal neural processing. This makes sense for rapid appraisal and reflexive action based on past learning but also results in cognitive distortions that can keep us frightened, withdrawn, and confused. Think of the veteran years after combat, who ducks when he hears a car backfire or runs for cover as a news helicopter flies overhead. A person who experienced early abandonment may, as an adult, be perfectly capable of starting new relationships. At a certain point, however, intimacy may trigger implicit memories of insecure or disorganized attachment, leading him to become frightened and flee from a potentially healthy relationship (Koukkou & Lehmann, 2006). The impulse to run, driven by implicit memories embedded in primitive brain circuitry, can be overpowering and inescapable. The true reasons for this behavior are so accurately described by Christopher Bollas (1987) as the "unthought known."

Openness to questioning one's assumptions, especially when they are self-defeating and incorrect, is a key predictor of positive outcome in psychotherapy. Once clients begin to understand that what they assumed to be reality is actually a personal fabrication, they either flee or become fascinated. We attempt to get them to question their thoughts, beliefs, and assumptions and to "act in," that is, to come to sessions and talk about their impulses with the hope of integrating inhibitory cortical input with primitive memories, emotions, and urges. Attachment schemas, transference, and self-esteem are all examples of implicit memories that shape and distort conscious awareness. These very patterns of unconscious processing led Freud to develop psychoanalysis and to create a therapeutic context that supported an exploration of the unconscious. Psychotherapy encourages being skeptical of the perceived realities of our brains. Given how our brains work, this is a sound strategy, one we share with research scientists and Buddhist monks.

## The Primacy of Projection

*It is easy to spot an informed man—his opinions are just like your own.*
—Miguel De Unamuno

Human brains possess complex social networks which become activated as we observe and interact with those around us (Cozolino, 2006). Hours after birth, we begin to focus on and imitate the facial expressions of our caretakers. Mirror neurons begin to link observations and actions, allowing us to (a) learn from others by watching them, (b) anticipate and predict actions, and (c) activate emotional states supportive of emotional resonance and empathy. We also possess neural circuits that automatically analyze the actions and gestures of others, generating a theory of their mind—what they know, what their motivations may be, and what they might do next. As with mirror neurons, having an automatic theory of what is on the mind of another allows us to predict behavior to ensure our own individual safety while supporting group cohesion and the spread of culture.

The existence of these sophisticated social neural systems reflects the millions of years of natural selection that have been refining our brain's ability to read the emotions, thoughts, and intentions of others. All of this attention to others clearly shows us the importance of social information processing to our very survival. As a result, we are quick to think we know others because mind reading is instantaneous and obligatory. In biblical terms, it is a reflexive habit of the social brain to attend to the mote in our brother's eye and not to the beam in our own. Unfortunately, evolution has not seen fit to invest much neural circuitry into self-awareness. Projection is automatic and lessens anxiety while self-awareness requires effort and generates anxiety—which do you think is going to be the norm?

Given that we use our internal expressions as implicit models for how we understand others, it could be that what Freud called the defense mechanism of projection is actually a simple byproduct of how our brains interweave our automatic theories of others' minds with understandings of ourselves. This may be why we often discover our own truths in what we think and feel about others. And since our individual identities emerge from dyads, perhaps the separation of self and other is always a dicey distinction, one that many cultures do not even bother with. This may also be why self-analysis is generally not successful because the logic of self-inquiry is so interwoven with our implicit assumptions. The most naive observer can see many things about us that we cannot see in ourselves. In close relationships, we provide each other with another set of eyes outside of our bodies that can reflect our lives to us in ways that are impossible to perceive on our own.

In therapy, we teach our clients to ask themselves if the pot is calling the kettle black: that is, are their thoughts and feelings about others autobiographical? While in couples therapy, we encourage our clients to stop mind reading and learn to actually ask their partners what is on their minds. We engage in a parallel process whenever we explore how much of our reaction to a client is countertransferential. In our training as therapists, we learn to question our judgment and assumptions in light of our own personal histories. We also learn to use mirror neurons and theory of mind to enhance our attunement with our clients and explore their inner worlds. Taking back our projections and working with transference and countertransference in therapy allows us to use our thoughts about others as potential sources of personal information.

## Unconscious Self-Deception

*Men use thoughts to justify their wrongdoings, and speech only to conceal their thoughts.*

—Voltaire

Based both on neural architecture and everyday experience, self-insight does not appear to have exerted a strong pressure on natural selection. In fact, it may have been selected against because real self-knowledge creates the risk of doubt, hesitation, and demoralization. Defenses that distort our reality can help us by decreasing anxiety, shame, and depression. At the same time they can enhance social coherence by putting a positive spin on the behavior of those closest to us. This is most clearly seen in a mother's love. A wise judge once said that everyone he sends to prison has "a mother with an innocent child." Self-deception not only decreases anxiety, it also increases the likelihood of successfully deceiving others. If we believe our own confabulations, we are less likely to give away our real thoughts and intentions via nonverbal signs and behaviors. Reaction formation, or behaviors and feelings that are opposite of our true desires, is also quite effective. Freud's defense mechanisms and the attributional biases of social psychology document an array of these distortions.

Secure attachment and ego strength are correlated with our ability to hear feedback, accept our own limitations, and use less reality-distorting defenses—humor instead of repression and sublimation instead of denial. In psychodynamic psychotherapy, we provide our clients not only with interpretations, clarifications, and reflections but also with an alternative perspective (our own) that they can utilize to help discover themselves. Both client and therapist need to engage in reality testing, although the definition of reality can be slippery. This is why our own personal therapy is so important to our clients. In today's large social groups, self-awareness has become increasingly important for survival of the species, perhaps as important as self-deception is to the survival of the individual. Distorting reality to reduce one's anxiety may allow the rich to get richer and the righteous to feel justified, but in the long term there are consequences to the environment and social systems that have negative impacts on us all.

These ways in which the brain and mind have evolved have created a wide variety of threats to our emotional and physical well-being. I suspect that you have recognized many of your clients' problems in these discussions, and perhaps some of your own. These legacies of evolution make both clients and therapists vulnerable to dissociation and distress and lead us to a common search for solutions. Let's take a look at a case study where we can examine how these vulnerabilities can play out in life and in therapy.

## Patrick

*Man is born broken. He lives by mending.*
> —Eugene O'Neill

Patrick, a man in his mid-30s, came to therapy with the complaint that his life was "unraveling." Talkative and obviously bright, Patrick was the kind of person who could quickly launch into animated conversation. I felt immediately drawn into his stories and found our sessions interesting and enjoyable. I soon learned that he had grown up on the Connecticut coast, that his father was a fisherman with a "drinking problem," and that both his parents had died a few years earlier. A recent physical altercation during a relationship breakup triggered him to take stock of his life. "That's just not me," he said. "Something's very wrong." Over our first few sessions, two things stood out to me; he lived under a great deal of emotional pressure and alcohol was a pervasive presence in his current life.

Patrick's initial interest was to understand what had happened in his last relationship and during the breakup. Although he had the sense that some broader issues lay beneath the surface, he was unable to articulate what they might be. "That's your job," he told me with a smile. It was clear from our discussions that alcohol had been a part of Patrick's life from the beginning. His father's alcoholism had many negative effects on him and everyone in his family. Both Patrick and his ex-girlfriend drank heavily and alcohol was always present during their disputes. It became very clear that both Patrick and his father used alcohol to cope with anxiety, sadness, and loss.

What turned out to be my first important intervention was a matter-of-fact question about whether he felt he had a drinking problem. Given his father's addiction and all he had told me about his lifelong relationship with drinking, I expected to hear a "Duh!" and some sympathy for being so slow witted. Instead, Patrick was surprised and taken aback by my question. It seemed that he had never given any serious thought to being an alcoholic himself. At first, I was surprised by his surprise, and impressed by his brain's ability to compartmentalize different aspects of awareness. The power and persuasiveness of his early learning to normalize alcohol and deny emotions created a dissociation enabling him to be unaware of the proverbial elephant in the room.

Instead of being defensive, he began discussing his relationship with alcohol like an investigator looking for clues to a crime. He spontaneously shared that many difficulties in his relationships seemed to occur while drinking. Patrick could see that he used alcohol to deaden his emotions and that it caused him difficulties in school, at work, and in all of his relationships. As he listened to the unfolding of his own narrative, he gradually became aware of the fact that he shared his father's addiction. By the expressions on his face, it was clear that he was learning about himself by listening to his story—a story he had lived but never thought about. The role of alcohol in his father's life was clear but it never occurred to him to apply these insights to himself. Patrick was in the process of using language to integrate networks of emotion and thought, and reevaluating past experiences from a perspective of expanded self-awareness.

Once the reality of his own alcoholism was firmly established in conscious thought, he asked me what I thought he should do. Again expecting a "Duh!" I said, "Well, you could stop drinking, join Alcoholics Anonymous, and try working the steps." And again, Patrick reacted as if this were a novel idea that he might try out. Based on past experience, my expectation was that we would be working through his resistance for quite a while before he would give AA a try. But, true to his word, he stopped drinking, got involved in AA, found a sponsor, and worked the steps. (Note to beginning therapists—this sort of thing almost never happens.) The openness, enthusiasm, and rapidity with which Patrick gained awareness, explored, and tackled the issue made me wonder what his life would have been like with even a modicum of insightful parental guidance. His obvious intelligence and drive could have been applied to all kinds of challenges had he only been taught a language for his feelings, learned to be self-aware, or applied his problem-solving skills to his own life. His early chronic stress, combined with the family silence and shame, led him to inhibit language and conscious awareness.

Like many children of alcoholics, Patrick was great at giving advice to others while remaining a complete mystery to himself. His father's drinking, financial difficulties in the family, and problems with his siblings always took precedence over his personal needs. There was almost no time spent during his childhood on helping him learn how to cope with negative emotions—a learned and not innate ability. Like so many, he grew up alone, surrounded by friends and family, with only the ability to act out his inner emotional turmoil. His chaotic inner emotional world as well as his coping strategies and defensive styles were set early in life and held on into adulthood. The fear of both his internal chaos and of confronting it kept him drinking and running for decades.

Once sober, the emotions and defenses behind his addiction began to emerge. With the help of AA he learned about the typical struggles and pitfalls of alcoholism. These meetings eventually led him to explore the principles of Adult Children of Alcoholics (ACA), which proved to be of even more importance to him than the impact of his own drinking. Over the following months, his impulsivity and impatience, pathological care-taking of others, and inability to navigate negative emotions became the focus of therapy. Situation by situation, we deconstructed his assumptions and searched for new ways of thinking, feeling, and behaving. In essence, we were doing the work that should occur in childhood during countless interactions with parents. The tenacity of fear is impressive, causing many of us to spend a lifetime avoiding the pain and confusion of childhood.

During our sessions, Patrick mentioned his work in the New York financial district during 2001. For some reason, I had never thought to ask him how the terrorist attacks of 9/11 impacted him and, similarly, he never brought it up. When I asked if and how he was affected, he offhandedly mentioned that he lost many friends but didn't think he had suffered any ill effects. His tone of voice sounded hauntingly similar to when he described his early family life so I asked him to tell me about his experience and in response he told me the following story:

> I was living in New Jersey at the time and commuted to Wall Street via ferry across the Hudson. I overslept that morning, so instead of being at work at 8:30, I was still crossing the river at 9. Halfway across, some of us noticed smoke rising from downtown. People began gathering at the front of the ship to see what looked like a fire near the Trade Center. Minutes later, a southbound plane tracking the Hudson passed low overhead. We all watched as it passed over the Statue of Liberty, banked hard left, and headed back toward Manhattan.
>
> As the second plane hit we were close enough to the docks to see people running through the park. The concussion shock from the explosion made everyone move forward and back in a surreal way, like blades of grass in the wind. When the plane hit the second tower, we knew we were under attack. I was enraged and anxious to reach the dock to see what I could do to help. I remembered my father talking about Pearl Harbor and how he and his friends stood in line at the recruiting office the next morning.
>
> As we approached the dock, the crowds rushed forward to escape the carnage and chaos behind them. But just before we reached the dock, the ferry slowed and reversed direction to avoid being swamped by the massive crowd. As we headed back to New

Jersey, I began thinking about the people I knew who worked in the Trade Center and imagined what it would be like to be in those buildings as they burned. I remember feeling numb as I stared at the huge plume of smoke rising above the city. When we got back to Jersey we all stood in the terminal watching the television as the buildings collapsed, first one and then the other. Some of the women cried and even some men; we stood there in shock, leaning against one another for support.

The phones were down and there was nothing I could do but imagine where my friends were and if they had survived. Once I arrived back home, I couldn't take my eyes off the television. From time to time I would see someone I knew, dazed and covered with dust, staggering past the camera. I eventually noticed that it had grown dark and I was hungry. I was able to connect with my girlfriend later that night, and the next day we drove south in a sort of waking coma. Eventually we found a hotel room and got drunk for a few days.

Both Patrick's reaction to the impact of 9/11 and his own alcoholism were processed in a disassociated manner. This defense paralleled how he dealt with his experiences and feelings from childhood. Early in life he learned to stay away from his emotions through denial, hypomanic activity, and combative sports. Drinking, working, and socializing had all become compulsive ways of avoiding or inhibiting his feelings. His intellect allowed him to succeed in the workplace and rationalize his unhealthy behaviors. But upon awakening each day, he discovered the same sad, frightening, and lonely world.

The many negative effects of having an alcoholic parent are well known. The fear and uncertainty created by the alternating presence and absence of the alcoholic combined with an increased probability of extreme emotional reactions can have a devastating impact on all aspects of development. These children often learn not to be needy as they develop a false self to take care of the parent and maintain the artifice of a happy home. Unfortunately, they never receive the help they need to articulate their experiences and develop a comforting inner world. Their early terror persists in networks of implicit memory but they lack mechanisms for expression or social connection that could heal them. Thus, they recreate the chaos from which they are so desperately trying to escape by acting out their emotions while establishing relationships with abusive or empty others.

At first it was difficult for Patrick to focus on his own feelings and personal issues. His initial attention kept returning to the problems, shortcomings, and limitations of his girlfriend. It was only after he became less agitated and more self-reflective that he could see that he and his girlfriend shared many of the same problems. Like most of us, he found it easier to focus on her problems rather than his own. His gradual improvement required that he reorient his focus onto his own behaviors and feelings. Next Patrick had to develop a language with which to describe and share his inner world. And finally, over and over again, he had to experience his life from the inside out, and learn to connect with others as another human being rather than a caretaker or raging alcoholic.

## Summary

The sophistication of the human brain reflects millions of years of evolutionary adaptation where old structures were conserved and modified while new structures emerged and expanded. Countless interactive networks and design compromises created fertile ground for the disruption of smooth integration of neural systems. The very complexity of the development and functioning of the brain is also what makes it such a fragile structure. Assuming that the trillions of components arrive in their proper places and work according to their genetic templates, there are a host of other challenges to integrated psychological functioning. The discontinuity of conscious and unconscious processes, multiple memory systems, differences between the hemispheres, hidden processing layers, and multiple executive structures are all potential sources of dissociation and dysregulation. Disruption in the coordination and homeostatic balance of these neural systems is the neurobiological substrate of psychological distress and mental illness.

Evolution is driven by the physical survival of the species and thus, much of the brain's functioning is centered around automatic fight-or-flight mechanisms as opposed to conscious and compassionate decision making. Because of this, the conscious and unconscious management of fear and anxiety is a core component of our personalities, attachment relationships, and identities. The considerable degree of postnatal brain development and the disproportionate emphasis on early childhood experiences in the sculpting of the brain add to our vulnerability to psychological distress.

Psychotherapists are trained to use their social brains as a tool to connect to and modify the brains of their clients. Through interpersonal neurobiological processes, therapists serve as an external regulatory circuit to help reestablish the optimal flow of energy and information. This is done for the circuits within and among the cerebral hemispheres, and through all levels of the neuraxis from the primitive lower regions to the most recently evolved components of the neocortex. It is through this increased integration that more optimal mental processing is established and symptoms are replaced with functional behavior.

# Chapter 17

# Teaching Old Dogs New Tricks: Stimulating Neural Plasticity

*It is not the strongest of the species that survive, not the most intelligent, but the one most responsive to change.*
—Charles Darwin

Psychotherapy has survived for more than 100 years in the absence of an accepted brain-based model of change. The old view of the brain as a predetermined and static entity necessitated that the development of psychotherapy be independent from the biological sciences of even 20 years ago. Fortunately, current neuroscientific findings do not support neurological fatalism but find a brain capable of constantly adapting to new challenges. In fact, therapists have learned to utilize attachment, emotional attunement, and narratives as tools to modify the brain.

Therapists often lament the fact that parents don't do a better job during their children's early development, when relationships have such a powerful impact on their brains. But if we approach the brain from the perspective of ongoing plasticity, what are we capable of in our consulting rooms? How plastic is the brain? Can plasticity be enhanced, and how much of an effect can the therapeutic relationship have on the brain? These questions are central to psychotherapy, because we rely on the brain's ability to change well after traditional sensitive periods have passed.

Research on imprinting of parental figures in geese (Lorenz, 1991) and the importance of periods of visual exposure in the development of the occipital lobes in cats (Hubel & Wiesel, 1962) have been standard fare in undergraduate education and popular science for half a century. Unfortunately, these studies have created the impression that the timing of brain growth is entirely predetermined by template genetics (DNA) and that early experiences become indelibly etched into our neural architecture (Rutter & Rutter, 1993). Extracting the concepts of imprinting and critical periods from ethology and applying them to human development turns out to be quite misleading (Michel & Moore, 1995). We now know that genetic expression is controlled by experiences throughout life, and that changes in the environment, both good and bad, continue to have positive and negative effects on us. Also, our brains are more complex and expanded in regions that maintain more neuroplastic properties. Thus, learning in humans is far more complex and flexible than the original conceptions of imprinting and critical periods led scientists to believe (Hensch, 2004).

Recall that sensitive periods are times of exuberant growth in neural networks, corresponding with the rapid development of the skills and abilities to which they are dedicated (Chugani, 1998; Fischer, 1987). Although there is no doubt that these periods exist, what is in question is the indelibility of learning during these times, as well as the possibilities of modifying when they occur during development. As neuroscience finds more examples of neurogenesis and neuroplasticity, and epigenetic programming taking place in mature brains, there is an increasing recognition that we retain different kinds of neural plasticity throughout life (Bornstein, 1989).

The research on neural plasticity has historically focused on the brain's ability to adapt after early brain injury (Goldman, 1971; Goldman & Galkin, 1978; Henry et al., 1984). Today, plasticity is understood to be a basic principle of healthy brains at any age. Rather than lacking plasticity, the adult brain is now seen as having an increased tendency toward neural stabilization while retaining the ability for new learning. There also appears to be a shift in how information is processed in a manner more appropriate to different stages of life, which is another aspect of its plastic reorganization (Cozolino, 2008; Stiles, 2000). This vital shift in perspective has led to a rapid expansion of interest in and exploration of the neurobiological mechanisms of lifetime learning and change (Rosenzweig, 2001).

## Use-Dependent Plasticity

*Education is not a preparation for life; education is life itself.*
—John Dewey

You will remember that changes in synaptic strength in response to an inner or outer stimulus are believed to be the basis for learning. The process of long-term potentiation (LTP) prolongs excitation of cell assemblies that are synchronized and interconnected in their firing patterns (Hebb, 1949). This is only a small piece of a vastly complex set of mechanisms and interactions shaping the connection, timing, and organization of the firing between the billions of individual neurons woven into neural networks.

Plasticity reflects the ability of neurons to change the way they relate to one another as they adapt to changing environmental demands (Buonomano & Merzenich, 1998). This can occur in the modulation of signal transmission across synapses, changes in the organization of local neural circuits, and in the relationship between different functional neural networks (Trojan & Pokorny, 1999). It has been demonstrated that portions of the cortex involved in sensory and motor functions reorganize in response to changing uses, after injury, and during skill learning (Braun et al., 2000; Elbert et al., 1994; Karni et al., 1995). Violinists have larger cortical representations in areas dedicated to the fingers of the left hand than do non-string players (Elbert et al., 1995), Braille readers demonstrate similar patterns of cortical plasticity in sensory regions (Sterr et al., 1998a, 1998b); and cab drivers have larger hippocampi incorporating more visual-spatial knowledge (Maguire et al., 2006).

These and other studies have demonstrated *use-dependent plasticity* in both cortical and subcortical regions. Because of their early maturation and organization, sensory-motor areas have been thought to have the earliest sensitive periods and the most permanent neural organization. The extensive plasticity discovered in these regions suggests that executive and association areas of the frontal cortex (which are characterized by their adaptation to change) should demonstrate even more synaptogenesis, altered synaptic connections, and potentially neurogenesis (Beatty, 2001; Dalla, Bangasser, Edgecomb, & Shors, 2007; Gould, Reeves, Graziano, et al., 1999; Hodge & Boakye, 2001; Mateer & Kerns, 2000). In fact, research has found a continual increase in white matter volume in the frontal and temporal lobes of males well into the fifth decade of life (Bartzokis et al., 2001).

The activation and organization of the cortex appears capable of continual change, with expansion and contraction of cortical representation alternating with varying amounts of stimulation and deprivation (Polley, Chen-Bee, & Frostig, 1999). In other words, the brain is capable of more and faster functional reorganization than previously thought (Ramachandran, Rogers-Ramachandran, & Stewart, 1992). Our ability to learn new skills and information throughout life is clear evidence for ongoing neural plasticity. The study of the speed, degree, and nature of neural plasticity is a vast new scientific frontier, and the potential to enhance plasticity has profound implications for neurosurgery, education, neurorehabilitation, and psychotherapy (Classen, Liepert, Wise, Hallett, & Cohen, 1998; Johansson, 2000).

## Enhancing Plasticity

*Life is growth. If we stop growing, technically and spiritually, we are as good as dead.*

—Morihei Ueshiba

As we learn more about the biological mechanisms of sensitive periods, the possibility of controlling them begins to emerge (Moriceau & Sullivan, 2004). What if neuroscientists could learn how to reinstate sensitive periods in adults during psychotherapy? Huang and his colleagues (1999) found that the sensitive period of the visual cortex was accelerated in certain genetically altered mice. It turns out that a genetic variation in these mice results in the earlier secretion of brain-derived neurotrophic factor (BDNF), a neural growth hormone. Could BDNF reestablish sensitive periods and be used to stimulate more exuberant learning at any time during life?

Kang and Schuman (1995) found that BDNF and NT-3 (another neurotrophic factor) enhanced LTP activity when introduced to the hippocampus of an adult rat. In a related study, it was found that a strain of mice with higher levels of N-methyl-D-aspartate (NMDA) receptors had enhanced performance in learning and memory tasks (Tang et al., 1999). NMDA, a neurotransmitter involved in the formation of associations among neurons, is necessary for cortical reorganization, and has the ability to specify certain transcriptional processes related to neural plasticity (Jablonska et al., 1999; Rao & Finkbeiner, 2007; Wanisch, Tang, Mederer, & Wotjak, 2005). NMDA receptors have also been shown to be necessary for the initiation of LTP in monkeys (Myers et al., 2000).

This work has led to the suggestion that the use of D-cycloserine, which enhances the activation of NMDA receptors, may boost the effect of some forms of psychotherapy. One study showed an improved effect of exposure therapy with phobic individuals after using D-cycloserine (Ressler et al., 2004). The effects of cholinergic stimulation suggest it also plays a role in neural plasticity by activating neural growth hormones (Cowan & Kandel, 2001; Zhu & Waite, 1998). Future research with these biological subcomponents of learning and memory may lead to pharmacological interventions that could enhance the brain's ability to learn while taking piano lessons, preparing for the GREs, or during certain critical phases of psychotherapy (Davis, Myers, Chhatwal, & Ressler, 2006).

Just a few years ago, the conventional wisdom in neuroscience was that we were born with all the neurons we would ever have. More recent research has found an increasing number of areas within the brain where new neurons are generated. *Stem cells*, the basic structure for many types of cells that are capable of renewing themselves indefinitely, have so far been found in the olfactory bulb and a portion of the hippocampus called the *dentate gyrus* (Jacobs et al., 2000). When the biological processes that stimulate stem cells are understood, neurosurgeons may be able to trigger the growth of new tissue in damaged areas (Hodge & Boakye, 2001).

The underlying biochemistry of the processes of neuronal growth is also being investigated and may someday be utilized to enhance and support plasticity (Akaneya, Tsumoto, Kinoshita, & Hatanaka, 1997; Barde, 1989) and treat neurodegenerative disorders such as Alzheimer's and Parkinson's diseases (Carswell, 1993). The acceleration or reestablishment of sensitive periods, the enhancement of learning and memory via biochemical adjustments, and the cultivation of new cells all suggest the future possibility of intentional and strategic enhancement of neural plasticity. While these potential biological interventions are causes for hope, we are currently capable of enhancing plasticity through our day-to-day behaviors and interactions.

## Enriched Environments and Stimulating Lives

*Intellectual growth should commence at birth and cease only at death.*
—Albert Einstein

It has been known for decades that enriched and stimulating early environments can have a positive and long-term impact on both neural architecture and neurochemistry. Research has demonstrated that when rats are raised in complex and challenging environments, they show advances in many aspects of brain building (see Table 17.1). An enriching environment enables mammals to build larger, more complex, and more resilient brains.

TABLE 17.1
**The Impact of Enriched Environments in Experimental Animals**

| Increases In | |
| --- | --- |
| Weight and thickness of cortex[1] | Levels of neurotransmitters[7] |
| Weight and thickness of hippocampi[2] | Level of vascular activity[8] |
| Length of neuronal dendrites[3] | Level of metabolism[9] |
| Synapses among neurons[4] | Amount of gene expression[10] |
| Activity of glial cells[5] | Levels of nerve growth factor[11] |
| Levels of neural growth hormones[6] | |

The effects of the environment in stimulating brain growth are so robust that it occurs even in situations of malnutrition. If rats are malnourished but placed in enriched environments, they will have heavier brains than well-fed but less-stimulated rats. These findings exist despite the fact that the malnourished rats weigh significantly less (Bhide & Bedi, 1982). Although nutritional and environmental deprivation often go hand in hand, some deficits may be reversed in adulthood. Placing adult rats in enriched environments enhances synaptic plasticity and ameliorates the effects of earlier nervous system damage and genetically based learning deficits (Altman, Wallace, Anderson, & Das, 1968; Kolb

& Gibb, 1991; Maccari et al., 1995; Morley-Fletcher, Rea, Maccari, & Laviola, 2003; Schrott et al., 1992; Schrott, 1997).

Although controlled studies of nutritional and environmental deprivation are not possible with humans, some naturally occurring situations offer similar insights into the power of environmental enrichment. A study of Korean children adopted by families in the United States found that environmental enrichment counteracted their early malnutrition and deprivation. On measures of height and weight, these children eventually surpassed Korean averages, while their IQ scores reached or exceeded averages for American children (Winick, Katchadurian, & Harris, 1975). In a different study of postmortem brain samples of older adults, a consistent relationship was found between the length of dendrites in Wernicke's area and the subjects' level of education (Jacobs et al., 1993). It has also been suggested that an enriched environment may improve poststroke recovery in humans (Ulrich, 1984).

The theory of *cognitive reserve*, which arose from these observations, has triggered research comparing the brains and cognitive functioning in later life of people with varying levels of challenge and stimulation. The cognitive reserve hypothesis suggests that stimulating lives build more neural material, and the more you build, the more you can afford to lose and still function in a competent manner later in life (Richards & Deary, 2005; Stern, Alexander, Prohovnik, & Mayeux, 1992). A number of these studies support the idea that those who have had more education and challenging occupations tend to have brains that age better and resist the onset and progression of dementia.

It is believed that the cognitive declines associated with normal aging are related to the gradual degeneration of dendrites, neurons, and the biochemical mechanisms that support neural health and plasticity (Jacobs, Driscoll, & Schall, 1997; Morrison & Hof, 2003). People with more cognitive reserve typically have had better diets, higher quality educations, and more intellectually challenging jobs than those with lower reserve (Stern et al., 2005; Whalley, Deary, Appleton, & Starr, 2004). Factors like larger brain size, early learning, and greater occupational attainment are associated with greater cognitive reserve and seem to mitigate the effects of Alzheimer's disease, traumatic injury, and the general impact of brain aging (Compton, Bachman, Brand, & Avet, 2000; Kessler et al., 2003; Scarmeas et al., 2004; Schmand et al., 1997; Staff, Murray, Deary, & Whalley, 2004; Stern et al., 1995).

Skills most dependent upon frontal functions—such as verbal fluency, controlled processing, and the abstract thinking demanded by high-complexity occupations—appear to contribute most to cognitive reserve (Ardila, Ostrosky-Solis, Rosselli, & Gomez, 2000; Le Carret et al., 2003). So, while being a college professor does not protect against cognitive decline, fortunately for me, it may slow down some of its manifestations (Christensen, Henderson, Griffiths, & Levings, 1997). About 25% of older individuals showing no symptoms of Alzheimer's disease while alive show significant Alzheimer's-related brain pathology upon autopsy (Ince, 2001; Katzman et al., 1989). Those with more education had a significantly greater amount of plaques and tangles yet functioned as well as others with less advanced disease (Alexander et al., 1997). This suggests that individuals with more education can sustain a greater amount of neural damage, and still maintain the same level of cognitive functioning as those with less education.

Studies have also found that expected age-related intellectual decline can be halted or reversed in many older adults by increasing environmental and social stimulation (Schaie & Willis, 1986). The most probable explanation would be that these experiences correlate with biological processes that enhance plasticity, creating more elaborate, complex, and flexible brains. Given that psychotherapy is an enriched environment for social-emotional learning, we can assume that the challenges we provide our clients build more complex and resilient brains. Research has yet to explore the possibilities of enhanced longevity and brain health in those who engage in psychotherapy.

## Moderate States of Arousal

*I am always doing that which I cannot do, in order that I may learn how to do it.*

—Pablo Picasso

Something we do in all forms of psychotherapy that enhances neural plasticity is pay attention to creating moderate states of arousal in our clients. Regulating subjective units of distress in systematic desensitization, balancing confrontation and empathic attunement in psychoanalysis, or crafting the "safe emergency" of Gestalt therapy all reflect an appreciation for the delicate balance between challenge and support. We intuitively understand that people need to be motivated and aroused to learn, while simultaneously free from the autonomic activation that shuts down cortical plasticity. Knowing how to find and keep clients in learning's sweet spot is a vital element of the art of psychotherapy.

The nontechnical story goes something like this: When all is well and we are in a state of calm, there is no reason to learn anything new. When our needs for food, companionship, and safety are satisfied, the brain has done its job and there is no reason to invest energy in learning. At the other extreme, states of high arousal and danger are no time for new cortical learning but a call for immediate limbic action. A state of mind somewhere between the two appears optimal for new learning and problem solving (Anderson, 1976). An attitude best described as interest, enthusiasm, or curiosity is thought to stimulate positive arousal. In secure attachment, the child is able to use the parent as a safe haven and avoid experiencing autonomic activation in response to stress. A similar process is likely to take place in a secure therapeutic alliance, allowing clients to verbalize their experience rather than defending themselves or fleeing from the situation.

The formalization of this notion in experimental psychology, described in a classic paper by Robert Yerkes and John Dodson (1908), came to be known as the inverted-U learning curve. Contrary to expectation, they found that mice learned to avoid a moderate shock faster than one of high or low intensity. They charted their finding on a graph with arousal on the x-axis and learning (performance) on the y-axis (see Figure 17.1). Over the years this same phenomenon was found across species in a variety of learning tasks (Broadhurst, 1957; Stennet, 1957). While this research took place before we knew anything about the neurochemistry of learning, it makes sense that this same inverted-U pattern will be reflected in the underlying neurobiological processes of learning (Baldi & Bucherelli, 2005).

We now know that learning depends on building new dendritic structures, and on the ability of these structures to interconnect. Building dendrites is dependent on the synthesis of proteins guided by genetic transcription, while neuronal firing shapes the architecture of these dendrites to encode new learning. Not surprisingly, the hormones secreted by the HPA axis in response to stress (cortisol, norepinephrine, and endorphins), as well as other learning mechanisms (NMDA receptors, BDNF secretion, etc.), modulate learning on the same inverted U-shaped

FIGURE 17.1
The Inverted-U Learning Curve

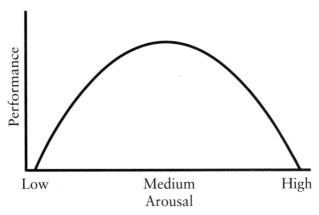

curve (Hardingham & Bading, 2003; Parsons, Stöffler, & Danysz, 2007). At moderate states of arousal, amygdala activation opens windows of modulated stimulation where top-down plasticity is facilitated (Popescu, Saghyan, & Paré, 2007). At moderate levels of arousal, these and many more systems enhance learning, while at high and low levels they inhibit new learning, in this same inverted-U pattern.

Hippocampal neurons require low levels of cortisol for structural maintenance, while higher levels of cortisol inhibit their neuroplastic properties (Gould, Woolley, & McEwen, 1990). Cortisol impacts learning and plasticity by regulating the protein synthesis required for dendritic growth and patterns of neural connectivity such as LTP, LTD, and primed burst potentiation (a low-threshold version of LTP) in this same pattern (Diamond, Bennett, Fleshner, & Rose, 1992; Domes et al., 2005; Lupien & McEwen, 1997; Roozendaal, 2000). High levels of stress also trigger endorphin release, which impedes both protein synthesis and the consolidation of explicit memory (Introini-Collison & McGaugh, 1987). See Table 17.2 for a sample of findings supporting this pattern of the biochemistry of arousal and its effects on learning.

Overall, the various neural systems dedicated to learning and arousal are tightly interwoven. They work together to activate plasticity and learning when it is needed to adapt to challenge, and turn it off in the absence of challenge or when the body needs to be mobilized for immediate survival. The inverted-U learning curve reflects both the underlying neurobiological processes and the many overt manifestations of learning seen in the laboratory, classroom, and consulting office. By understanding these principles, we can use them to optimize neural plasticity in the service of positive brain change.

**TABLE 17.2**
**The Inverted-U Curve of Learning and Arousal**

*mRNA expression*[1]

*Cortisol levels*
  Verbal memory[2]
  Social memory[3]
  Spatial memory[4]
  Hip prime burst potentials[5]
  Long-term potentiation[6]

*Norepinephrine levels*
  Olfactory plasticity[7]

*Endorphin levels*
  Protein synthesis and memory consolidation[8]

## Attachment Plasticity

> *Organic matter, especially nervous tissue, seems endowed with a very extraordinary degree of plasticity.*
>
> —William James

Attachment in infancy is usually conceptualized as relationship specific, while attachment in adulthood is thought of as a general aspect of character. Early attachment patterns may become generalized and self-perpetuating because of their impact on our neurobiology, our ability to regulate our emotions, and the expectations we have of ourselves, others, and the world. The sensory, emotional, and behavioral systems influenced by early attachment experiences can shape our brains in ways that make the past a model for creating the future.

We have learned a great deal from attachment research: how our primitive bonding instincts regulate anxiety, how categories of attachment reflect a parent's behavior and a child's reaction to stress, and how attachment schemas are carried into adulthood, affecting our choice of partners, the nature of our relationships, and the way we parent our own children. The enthusiasm we have about the power of attachment categories to explain emotional development often fails to acknowledge the considerable fluctuation of attachment styles over time. In our search for a straightforward explanation of intimate human relationships, it is easy to overlook the instability of attachment.

In an attempt to support the predictive power of attachment schemas, fluctuation and change are attributed to measurement problems or uncontrolled external variables such as positive and negative life events or changing relationships. But we seldom consider that an attachment schema should change because we think of it as a personality trait. As we saw in the animal research, maternal attention to rat pups was mediated by the environment in ways that made the pups a better fit to the environment to which the mother was responding. Perhaps because our brains are so much more complex, it takes greater effort and time for us to change, but the role of attachment may be essentially the same in humans.

In human subjects, we see that a decrease in security or the maintenance of insecurity during adolescence is more likely to occur in the presence of psychological, familial, or environmental stressors. Adolescents who see their mothers as supportive are more likely to gain security, while maternal depression correlates with a shift from secure to insecure attachment (Allen et al., 2004; Hamilton, 2000; Weinfield, Sroufe, & Egeland, 2000). Overall secure attachment, while not impervious, appears more resistant to change than insecure attachment, while negative life events operate to maintain insecure attachment (Hamilton, 2000; Kirkpatrick & Davis, 1994; Thompson, 1982). These findings certainly parallel the animal literature. The major implication for psychotherapy from all of these findings is that insecure attachment is subject to change as a result of positive social input (Pilowsky et al., 2008). As shown in Table 17.3, the consistency of attachment ratings, primarily secure versus insecure, is 24–64% depending on the study. This may be bad news for those interested in attachment as a stable trait, but good news for those of us in the business of change.

As a psychotherapist who is very interested in positive change, the messiness of the attachment construct and the variability of the data come as good news. I want attachment schemas to be a malleable form of implicit memory, so relationships with clients can alter them in a salubrious manner. In this way, psychotherapy becomes a guided attachment relationship for the purposes of assisted homeostasis (moderate states of arousal) and eventual repair of insecure attachment schemas (Amini et al., 1996; Cappas, Andres-Hyman, & Davidson, 2005; Corrigan, 2004; Siegel, 1999).

**TABLE 17.3**
**Attachment Plasticity**

| Time Span | Percentage of Subjects with Same Attachment Classification | Source |
|---|---|---|
| 6 months during infancy | 62  (N=100) | Vaughn et al., 1979 |
| 7 months during infancy | 53  (N=43) | Thompson, Lamb & Estes, 1982 |
| 2 years during infancy | 60  (N=189) | Egeland & Farber, 1984 |
| 3.5 years during childhood | 24  (N=223) | Vondra et al., 2001 |
| Childhood to adolescence | 63  (N=30) | Hamilton, 2000 |
| Childhood to adolescence | 42  (N=84) | Lewis, Feiring, & Rosenthal, 2000 |
| Childhood to adolescence | 39  (N=57) | Weinfield et al., 2000 |
| Childhood to adulthood | 64  (N=50) | Waters et al., 2000 |
| 17 weeks during adulthood | 55  (N=33) | Lawson et al., 2006 |
| 20 sessions of adult therapy | 34  (N=29) | Travis et al., 2001 |

*These studies reflect an array of ages, target populations, and methods of assessing attachment.*

Although there is evidence of organized attachment schemas by our first birthday, they do not appear to be set in neural stone. These naturally occurring changes and the fact that we attach and reattach with many people throughout our lives suggests that the underlying neural systems maintain their plasticity. If you doubt this, ask grandparents whether they feel attached to their grandchildren. In support of the neuroplasticity of attachment networks, research suggests that adults can create secure attachment for their children despite negative experiences in their own childhood. Earned autonomy, through the subconscious integration of early negative experiences, results in the ability to serve as a safe haven for one's own children.

Thus, the powerful shaping experiences of childhood can be modified through personal relationships, psychotherapy, and increased self-awareness. The ability to consciously process stressful and traumatic life events appears to correlate with more secure attachment, flexible affect regulation, and an increased availability of narrative memory. The integration of neural circuitry across cognitive, behavioral, sensory, and emotional domains is the likely neuroanatomical substrate of this earned autonomy. A healing relationship with a secure partner or with a good-enough therapist, in which past pain can be processed and resolved, supports earned autonomy and neural integration.

## The Power of a Healing Relationship

*Being deeply loved by someone gives you strength, while loving someone deeply gives you courage.*

—Lao Tzu

Because our brains are social organs interwoven with the brains of those around us, relationships have a direct impact on the biology of the brain. Psychotherapy is successful in large part because of the therapist's empathic abilities and the client's belief in the therapist's humanity and skill. Through the instillation of optimism and hope, a therapist (or any healer) uses powerful mechanisms of mind to shape the functioning of the brain. The mind's impact on the brain has been studied in a variety of fields from social neuroscience to psychoneuroimmunology, and referred to as the effects of expectancy, placebo, or self-fulfilling prophecy. These are all examples of the mind leading the brain via the power of relationships.

The term *placebo*, Latin for "I shall please," reflects the ancient idea that response to an inactive treatment results from the patient's desire to live up to the doctor's expectations. The placebo effect has been expanded to include sugar pills and other nonactive treatments, in contrast to what are considered to be active chemical compounds. More generally, the placebo effect is the expectation for illness outcome based on what the patient is led to believe by the doctor. Moerman and Jonas (2002) suggested renaming it "the meaning response," reflective of the fact that the placebo effect is mediated via the meaning assigned to it by the patient. Until modern times, medicine men and women, shamans, and witch doctors understood and utilized this phenomenon in their role as tribal healers (Frank, 1963). Similarly, the expectancy effect is likely at play in the fact that ill Chinese Americans born during inauspicious years have significantly shorter life spans. The size of this effect is proportional to how strongly they hold on to traditional cultural beliefs (Phillips, Ruth, & Wagner, 1993). Placebo effects are seen as a nuisance in Western science, and the patients benefiting from them are pathologized as weak minded, impressionable, or malingering.

Modern technological medicine has led to a decline in the use of the meaning response as the role of the doctor has shifted from healer to technician. This is especially ironic given that placebo control groups are a staple of the research upon which their clinical decision making should be based. Don't the time, money, and effort expended in this standard of research methodology support the power of patient expectancy to impact symptom expression? Perhaps doctors have become far too impressed with their technology while neglecting the power of their humanity.

In a similar manner, expectancy and placebo effects are usually relegated to the category of nonspecific effects in psychotherapy outcome research. I would argue that these effects are in fact specific—that is, we know exactly what social and psychological factors lead to healing. Carl Rogers outlined them well during the 1960s as warmth, acceptance, caring, and unconditional positive regard. Epidemiologists call them social support, network connectivity, and shared spiritual beliefs. We will someday be able to specify and measure the neuroanatomical and biochemical mechanisms of positive human interactions.

Different activation patterns in the brain during successful placebo response reflect the multiple neural pathways involved in mind–brain regulation. In neuroscience terms, the placebo effect is an example of top-down cortical modulation of mood, emotion, and immune activity (Beauregard, 2007; Ocshner et al., 2004). The placebo effect relies heavily upon the prefrontal lobes to integrate social experiences with positive affect and an optimistic state of mind. In the same way that a mother can shape a child's brain by stroking his hair and telling him that things will get better, a doctor can influence a client's immune system by presenting an optimistic prognosis and projecting confidence about the proposed treatment.

The placebo effect is a social phenomenon that likely activates the same reward systems (dopamine-serotonin-endorphin) triggered by loving touch and the anticipation of positive connections and feelings (Esch & Stefano, 2005; Fricchione & Stefano, 2005). The amygdala, which regulates our experience of fear and pain, is inhibited by positive emotions and activated by negative emotions (Neugebauer et al., 2004). We know, for example, that placebo and opioid analgesia share a common neural pathway, which strongly suggests we are capable of opioid self-administration (Pariente et al., 2005).

There are many examples of the social, top-down regulation of emotion. When a woman holds her husband's hand in the face of threat, fear activation is attenuated. Not surprisingly, the better she feels about the relationship, the greater the soothing effect of his hand will be (Coan, Schaefer, & Davidson, 2006). Soothing touch is obviously powerful, but so too is a soothing facial expression or a kind word communicated in an attuned emotional state. Some evidence for this has been found when levels of arousal (as measured by skin conductance) were monitored simultaneously in clients and therapists during sessions. During states of matched arousal, there were significantly more positive social and emotional interactions between client and therapist than when they were out of sync (Marci, Ham, Moran, & Orr, 2007).

Even in Parkinson's disease, it is believed that the anticipation of positive reward (a frontal-cortical process) stimulates the release of dopamine from the nucleus accumbens (a subcortical region called the ventral striatum). Because dopamine depletion is the central cause of Parkinsonian symptoms, this release of dopamine results in symptomatic improvement. See Table 17.4 for an outline of studies that have demonstrated changes in neural activation related to the placebo effect.

### TABLE 17.4
### The Impact of Positive Expectancy (Placebo) on Brain Activation

**Major Depression**

Increased activity in prefrontal, anterior cingulate, premotor, parietal, posterior insula, and posterior cingulate[1]

Decreased activity in subgenual cingulate, parahippocampus, and thalamus[2]

**Pain Disorders**

Increased activity in lateral and orbital PFC, anterior cinglate, cerebellum, right fusiform gyrus, parahippocampus, and pons[3]

Increased activity in the right dorsolateral cortex, anterior cingular cortex, and midbrain[4]

Increased bilateral orbitofrontal activity and anterior cingulate cortex contralateral to pain stimulus[5]

Reduced activity in anterior cingulate cortex, anterior insula, and thalamus[6]

Increased activity in the prefrontal cortex[7]

Activated endogenous opioids in dlpfc, anterior insula, and nucleus accumbens[8]

**Parkinson's Disease**

Reduced activity in subthalamic nuclei[9]

Increase in striatal dopamine[10]

When physicians encourage their peers to use the placebo effect to enhance illness outcome, the suggestions are very similar to the basic principles of client-centered therapy. For example, an article in the *Journal of Family Practice* suggested a "sustained partnership" with patients characterized by an interest in the whole person, knowing the patient over time, caring, sensitivity and empathy, being viewed as reliable and trustworthy, adapting medical goals to the needs of the patient, and encouraging full participation by the patient (Brody, 2000). Another physician in a piece from the *British Medical Journal* asked, "For a thousand years the action of the placebo has made vast numbers of patients feel better. Have we today provided a consultation in which the placebo does not act?" (Thomas, 1987, p. 1202). These are the aspects of traditional healing still employed by psychotherapy that appear to have been lost in modern technical medicine.

The implications of the power of the placebo effect to change the brain are profound. Our awe of technical medicine leads us to underestimate the importance of the doctor's role as healer, and patients' abilities to contribute to their own healing through the modulation of their endogenous biochemistry. There are many ways in which the power of the placebo effect could be harnessed and used to increase the effectiveness of medical treatment including increasing visits, encouraging and supportive interactions, and shaping patients' experiences by telling them what positive outcomes they should expect (Walach & Jonas, 2004; see Table 17.5 for a list of their suggestions). Ironically, we are only required to tell clients of the many risks and negative side effects, which likely guide their response to treatment in the opposite direction.

### TABLE 17.5
#### Leveraging the Placebo Effect in Medical Treatment

Increase frequency of contact

Determine what treatments your patient believes in

Align beliefs among patient, doctor, family, and culture

Be sure you believe in the treatment you are administering

Inform patients about what they can expect

Deliver treatment in a warm and caring way

Listen and provide empathy and understanding

Touch the patient

*Findings from the medical research supporting the power of specific doctor-patient interactions. Adapted from Walach and Jonas (2004).*

All of the "givens" of classical healing and psychotherapy have been squeezed out of modern Western medicine. Perhaps these nonspecific ingredients of a healing relationship will someday be interwoven with the technical aspects of modern medicine.

## Summary

The power of psychotherapy to change the brain rests in our ability to recognize and alter unintegrated or dysregulated neural networks. As knowledge of neural plasticity and neurogenesis increases, so will our ability to impact and alter the brain. The possibility exists that sensitive periods can be reinstated in the context of psychotherapy, and that stress can be utilized in a controlled manner to "edit and re-edit" emotional memories (Post et al., 1998). Although the practical application of these principles to humans remains on the distant horizon, the possibilities of the involvement of psychotherapy in brain sculpting are evident. It is certain that psychotherapists are already enhancing plasticity without the help of genetic manipulation or chemical interventions.

Therapy is a safe emergency because of the supportive structure in which difficult emotional learning takes place. A client's sense of safety is enhanced by the therapist's skill, knowledge, and confidence, which support emotional regulation and maintaining moderate states of arousal. It is quite possible that the caring, encouragement, and enthusiasm of the therapist also reinforce learning, neural growth, and plasticity through the enhanced production of dopamine, serotonin, and other neurochemicals (Barad, 2000; Kilgard & Merzenich, 1998; Kirkwood, Rozas, Kirkwood, Perez, & Bear, 1999). Successful therapeutic techniques may be successful because of their very ability to change brain chemistry in a manner that enhances neural plasticity.

In the recent shift to neural optimism, critical periods of neural development are being reconsidered as important but, perhaps, not the final word on neural structure. The impact of enriched environments has demonstrated the brain-building capacity of positive experiences throughout the life span. More recent research in neural plasticity (e.g., use-dependent plasticity, neurotransmitter alteration, stem cell implantation) suggests that new experiences, and future potential biological interventions, may be capable of providing us with many tools with which to rebuild the brain. Psychotherapy is on the verge of an exploding new paradigm: the psychotherapist as neuroscientist.

Chapter 18

# The Psychotherapist as Neuroscientist

*In this field we are merely at the foothills of an enormous mountain range . . . unlike other areas of science, it is still possible for an individual or small group to make important contributions.*
—Eric Kandel

Psychotherapists are applied neuroscientists who create individually tailored enriched learning environments designed to enhance brain functioning and mental health. We are skilled at teaching clients to become aware of unconscious processing, take ownership of their projections, and risk anxiety in the service of emotional maturation (Holtforth et al., 2005). In our work, illusions, distortions, and defenses are exposed, explored, and tested or modified with understandings closer to reality. Implicit memory—in the form of attachment schemas, transference, and superego—are made conscious and explained as expressions of early experiences. We use a combination of empathy, affect, stories, and behavioral experiments to promote neural network growth and integration.

Through all of this work, subcortical networks that store memories of fears, phobias, and traumas are activated and made accessible for integration with cortical inhibitory circuitry. This essential integration allows for linkage among explicit and implicit circuits, conscious awareness, and the control of negative memories, sensations, and emotions. Regardless of the client's particular problem, psychotherapy teaches a method to help us better understand and use our brains. And as the dialogue between psychotherapy and neuroscience continues to evolve, an increasing number of scientific findings will be applied to both theory and clinical practice.

Important factors in the therapeutic process have been identified as an empathic and supportive relationship, maintenance of moderate states of arousal, activation of both cognition and emotion, and co-construction of narratives. A safe and empathic relationship establishes an emotional and neurobiological context conducive to neural plasticity. It also serves as a scaffold within which a client can better tolerate the stress required for neural reorganization. We have already seen that birds are able to learn their songs after sensitive periods when exposed to other birds singing, but are unable to learn the same songs heard from a tape recorder (Baptista & Petrinovich, 1986). Under certain conditions, birds require positive social interactions and nurturance in order to learn (Eales, 1985). And the stronger the relationship between human trainers and their birds, the greater the learning will be for both (Pepperberg, 2008). These studies, combined with what we know about changes in biochemistry during interpersonal interactions, suggest that a positive and attuned relationship enhances neural plasticity and learning. The nearly insatiable drive of adolescents to be in constant contact with one another may reflect the underlying drive for neural stimulation during this crucial developmental period. Emotional expression and modulation have been incorporated into psychotherapy because of their impact on these underlying biological processes.

The importance of the activation of both emotion and cognition is recognized by most psychotherapists. Releasing emotions associated with painful memories, facing a feared situation, or experimenting with new interpersonal relationships all involve some sort of stress, anxiety, or fear. Although this way of thinking has been accepted clinically, we now have considerable evidence to support the idea that moderate levels of arousal optimize the production of neurotransmitters and neural growth hormones that enhance LTP, learning, and cortical reorganization (Cowan & Kandel, 2001; Zhu & Waite, 1998).

Trauma undoubtedly changes us in many ways, from our startle response to our attachments and self-identity. Dissociation in reaction to trauma represents a breakdown of neural integration and plasticity. In therapy, we use moderate levels of arousal to access cortical mechanisms of plasticity in controlled ways with specific goals. The safe emergency of therapy provides both the psychological support and the biological stimulation necessary for rebuilding the brain. Much of neural integration and reorganization takes place in the association areas of the frontal, temporal, and parietal lobes serving to coordinate, regulate, and direct multiple neural circuits of memory and emotion.

The importance of the co-construction of narratives is grounded in the coevolution of the cerebral cortex and language, reflecting the evolution of our brains as social organs. Language within significant relationships has shaped the brain during evolution and continues to do so throughout our lives. Because of this, narratives embedded within an emotionally meaningful relationship (like psychotherapy) are capable of resculpting neural networks throughout life. Through the use of autobiographical memory, we can create narratives that bridge processing from various neural networks into a cohesive story of the self. Narratives allow us to combine—in conscious memory—our knowledge, sensations, feelings, and behaviors supporting underlying neural network integration.

The co-construction of narratives with parents serves as a medium of transfer of the internal world of the parent to the child, from generation to generation. These narratives reflect the implicit values, problem-solving strategies, and worldviews of the parents. They also serve to define us to ourselves and others, and guide us through our complex social world. The more inclusive our narratives are in terms of blending sensation, emotion, and cognition, the greater our ongoing ability to integrate multiple neural networks. Research in attachment has demonstrated that the coherence and inclusiveness of narratives correlate with both attachment security and self-reflective capacity (Main, 1993; Fonagy, Gergely, Jurist, & Target, 2002).

In the process of evolution, different levels of language have emerged that appear to parallel different layers of consciousness:

1. A reflexive social language (of the left hemisphere interpreter) serves the purpose of creating a logically cohesive and positive presentation to others. This language evolved from grooming and hand gestures with the primary goal of group affiliation and coordination.
2. An internal language, also reflexive, allows us to have private thoughts, plan and guide behavior, and deceive others. There is an

aspect of internal language that preserves early learning expressed through critical voices in our heads, reflecting early shame experiences.

3. A third language, one of self-reflection, appears to be far less reflexive and arises in states of openness, low defensiveness, and safety.

Although the first two levels of language occur spontaneously, self-reflective language requires higher levels of neural network integration, affect regulation, and cognitive processing. Reflexive language keeps us in the present moment, while reflective language demonstrates our ability to escape from the present moment, gain perspective on our thoughts and feelings, and make decisions about what we would like to change and how to change it. Attaining and utilizing this level of language is one goal of psychodynamic psychotherapy.

Three levels of language sharing a common lexicon can result in a great deal of confusion. Many people report feeling crazy because of the simultaneous and contradictory beliefs they struggle with on a day-to-day basis. Psychotherapy often involves sorting out these audio tracks in order to provide us with a clearer idea of just what is going on in there. The co-construction of narratives, in the context of a healing relationship, which sort out these inner contradictions may well be the optimal context for significant plasticity in socioemotional neural networks.

## Diagnosis and Treatment

*The principal activities of brains are making changes in themselves.*
—Marvin L. Minsky

Functional brain imaging has opened a window to the living human brain in the acts of motor tasks, imagining a feared situation, being empathic, or telling a lie. An examination of areas activated during these and many other behaviors has enhanced our understanding of which neural networks participate in various human functions. Although the application of scanning technology to psychopathology is still in its infancy, there have already been many important and provocative findings. As scanning techniques become more precise and the hardware more affordable, they will no doubt become incorporated into the practice of psychotherapy.

Neuroimaging has the potential to aid in diagnosis, treatment selection, and the prediction of treatment outcome (Etkin et al., 2005; Linden, 2006). As part of an initial assessment, it could help therapists pinpoint areas of neural activation and inhibition. Treatment planning will eventually come to include specific psychotherapeutic and pharmacological interventions to enhance the growth and integration of affected networks. Regular scans during the course of therapy may someday be a useful adjunct to psychological tests, as ways of fine-tuning the therapeutic process and measuring treatment success.

Associations between psychiatric symptoms and changes in the relative metabolism of different areas of the brain are in the process of being uncovered. We have already seen lower levels of metabolism in the left prefrontal cortices of depressed patients (Baxter et al., 1985, 1989) and increased metabolism in the right prefrontal and limbic region of patients with PTSD (Rauch et al., 1996). The importance of the right frontal region in PTSD is supported by clinical evidence such as the onset of PTSD after injury to the right frontal area (Berthier, Posada, & Puentes, 2001) and a "cure" of PTSD symptoms after a right frontal lobe stroke (Freeman & Kimbrell, 2001). The inhibition of Broca's area during intense fear states is already a focus of cognitive-behavioral therapies, and a reactivation of the language centers may become a standard measure of success in the treatment of PTSD and other anxiety-related disorders. All of these findings support the existence of specific circuitry involved in the recognition, reaction, and regulation of anxiety and fear in the aftermath of traumatic experiences.

The focus of this new work, however, is somewhat different than the old localization theories that attributed disorders of behavior to specific areas of the brain. We now understand that each region of the brain participates in multiple neural systems with highly complex interactions and homeostatic functions. Thus, it is actually the relationship between clinical symptoms and relative activity levels of specific neural networks that are salient. The neurobiology of obsessive-compulsive disorder (OCD) has been of particular interest in this regard. A neural circuit thought to mediate OCD includes the ompfc and subcortical structures called the *caudate nucleus, globus pallidus*, and *thalamus*. This cortical-subcortical circuit, involved with the primitive recognition of and reaction to contamination and danger, becomes locked into an activation loop in patients with OCD (Baxter et al., 1992). It is hypothesized that the ompfc, or some other component of the OCD circuit, activates the circuit with a worry signal, decreasing inhibition of the thalamus, which in turn excites the ompfc and caudate (Baxter et al., 1992). The result is a feedback loop that is highly resistant to inhibition or shutting down.

## Network Homeostasis and Treatment Outcome

*The constant conditions which are maintained in the body might be termed* equilibria.

—Walter Cannon

Considerable evidence supports the idea that the reregulation of neural networks parallels some of the symptomatic changes we witness in psychotherapy. In general, decreases in fear and anxiety correlate with activation reductions in bottom and right hemisphere regions. In OCD, there is a reduction in activation in a region dedicated to the control and inhibition of impulses (ompfc). In the successful treatment of social and spider phobias, there is a decrease in activation in limbic and primitive cortical areas and in right hemisphere processing, paralleling the decreased fear activation that goes along with symptom reduction. In situations where there is a deficit in cognitive processing such as in schizophrenia and brain injury, we see symptom reduction correlated with increased frontal activation. Keep in mind that the correlations do not prove causal relationships; changes in brain activation patterns could also be secondary to symptomatic changes, or both could be due to some third unknown factor.

Patterns of brain activation in both panic disorder and PTSD are a bit more complex. In both of these disorders, sensory and memory networks are hijacked by the amygdala and become internal sources of fear. While studies have not yet focused on changes in brain activation related to positive treatment outcome, we can speculate that positive treatment response would correlate with decreased activation in the amygdala, sensory motor areas, and the cerebellum (Bryant et al., 2008; Pissiota et al., 2002), along with increased ompfc activation (Phan et al., 2006; Williams et al., 2006). There would also be a decreased activation in regions dedicated to autobiographical memory, and an increase in the processing of information from the current external environment (Sakamoto et al., 2005).

Psychotherapy outcome research with a number of disorders has found changes in brain activation paralleling symptomatic improvement. In each case, treatment seems to have reestablished a homeostatic balance between interactive neural networks that were previously out of balance. Table 18.1 outlines the studies that have been performed to measure the neural correlates of successful therapy across a variety of patient populations.

TABLE 18.1
Successful Psychotherapy and Changes in Neural Activation

| Diagnosis and Treatment | Result |
| --- | --- |
| *OCD* | |
| BT vs. fluoxetine | Both: Decreased metabolism in right caudate[1] |
| BT vs. fluoxetine | BT: Left ompfc activation correlated with positive response |
| | Fluoxetine: changes in the opposite direction[2] |
| BT vs. controls | Decreased CBF in right caudate[3] |
| CBT | Decreased metabolism in right caudate |
| CBT and fluoxeitine | Increased bilateral grey matter[4] |
| | Increased right parietal white matter[5] |
| *Social phobia* | |
| CBT vs. citalopram | Both: decreased amygdala, hippocampal, and adjacent cortex activation |
| | CBT: decreased periaqueductal gray activation |
| | Citalopram: decreased thalamic activation[6] |
| *Spider phobia* | |
| CBT | Decreased activation in parahippocampal gyrus and dlpfc[7] |
| CBT | Decreased PFC activation biased toward right hemisphere[8] |
| CBT | Decreased activation in the insula and anterior cingulate[9] |
| *Post-traumatic stress disorder* | |
| EMDR (case study) | Increased activation in anterior cingulate and left frontal lobe[10] |
| *Panic disorder* | |
| CBT vs. Antidepressants | CBT: RH decreases in inferior temporal and frontal regions |
| | LH increases in inferior frontal, medial temporal, and insula |
| | Antidepressants: RH decreases in frontal and temporal lobes |
| | LH increases in frontal and temporal lobes[11] |

*continued on next page*

TABLE 18.1 continued

| | |
|---|---|
| CBT | Decreased activation in right hippo campus, left ACC, left cerebellum and pons |
| | Increased activation in medial prefrontal cortex[12] |
| *Major depressive disorder* | |
| CBT vs. paroxetine | CBT: decreased frontal activation / increased limbic |
| | Paroxetine: changes in the opposite direction[13] |
| CBT vs. venlafaxine | Both: decreased bilateral opfc and left mpfc activation and increased activation in right occipital-temporal cortex[14] |
| IPT vs. venlafaxine | IPT: increased activation in right posterior cingulate and right basal ganglia |
| | Venlafaxine: increased activation in right posterior temporal and right basal ganglia[15] |
| IPT vs. paroxetine | Both: decreased activation in prefrontal cortex |
| | Both: increased activation in inferior temporal and insula[16] |
| IPT vs. paroxetine | Both: symptom reduction with decreased frontal activation |
| | Both: positive correlation with cognitive symptoms[17] |
| *Schizophrenia* | |
| Cognitive rehab | Increased frontal activation with improved performance[18] |
| Cognitive rehab | Increased activation in right inferior frontal cortex and occipital lobe[19] |
| *Traumatic brain injury* | |
| Cognitive rehab | Global activation increase in 3 of 5 patients[20] |

*The results shown in this table should be considered preliminary because of small sample sizes and variations in methodology.*

*BT, behavior therapy; CBT, cognitive-behavioral therapy; IPT, interpersonal therapy; EMDR, eye movement desensitization and reprocessing. Adapted and expanded from Roffman et al. (2005).*

Functional scan studies have demonstrated that improvement of OCD symptoms is correlated with decreased activation of the ompfc and caudate nucleus (Rauch et al., 1994). Especially interesting to psychotherapists is the fact that these changes in brain metabolism are the same whether patients are successfully treated with psychotherapy or medication (Baxter et al., 1992; Schwartz et al., 1996). Although psychotherapy and medication are the first choices for treatment, they are not always successful. Scan-guided psychosurgery for patients who do not respond to any other forms of treatment can disrupt runaway feedback by severing neural links within the OCD circuit (Biver et al., 1995; Irle, Exner, Thielen, Weniger, & Ruther, 1998; Rubino et al., 2000).

Because symptoms can have multiple underlying causes, diagnoses aided by neural network activity could improve diagnostic accuracy. Increased specificity will naturally lead to increasingly specific psychotherapeutic and pharmacological interventions. Tourette's syndrome—a disorder characterized by involuntary vocalizations and motor tics—often occurs in individuals who also suffer with OCD, enuresis, or ADHD. This is not a coincidence, because these disorders share underlying neural circuitry and neurotransmitters (Cummings & Frankel, 1985). They all stem from problems with the inhibition of subcortical impulses by the frontal cortical areas. Thus, structural, biochemical, and regulatory abnormalities in these interrelated top-down networks can result in all four conditions. When this circuit is more fully understood, symptoms of OCD, ADHD, enuresis, and Tourette's syndrome may all become subsets of some future diagnosis referred to by the neural networks responsible for these functions.

In anxiety and depression, some studies show that therapy achieves results through increased cortical versus subcortical activation, while others show changes in the activation patterns within the frontal lobes (Porto et al., 2009). And while psychotherapy and medication can both lead to symptom reduction, there is only partial neuroanatomical overlap in how they achieve their results (Roffman et al., 2005). In other words, the same results can be achieved by different treatment strategies and through changes in the balance among different neural networks. This is in no way bad news for psychotherapy. Cognitive therapy by experienced therapists is equally efficacious as medication in moderate to severe depression (DeRubeis et al., 2005). For depressed patients with a history of child abuse, psychotherapy has been shown to be more effective, with the addition of medication showing small benefits (Nemeroff et al., 2003).

## The Centrality of Stress

*It's not stress that kills us, it is our reaction to it.*
        —Hans Selye

Although some stress is a normal part of life, early, prolonged, or severe stress can result in significant and long-term impairments in learning, attachment, and physiological regulation (Glaser, 2000; O'Brien, 1997;

Sapolsky, 1996). Stress plays a role in the expression and severity of most, if not all, psychiatric and medical disorders. Therefore, assessing and targeting stress as a focus of psychotherapeutic intervention should always be an aspect of healing relationships. Since therapists are trained to think in terms of diagnostic categories and treatment modalities, stress often flies under our diagnostic radar. Understanding and working to regulate our clients' stress is central to psychotherapeutic success because of its impact on neuroplastic processes.

An emerging concept in treatment involves buffering victims of stress from neural compromise by altering their neurochemistry. One way of accomplishing this is to block the secretion or uptake of norepinephrine and glucocorticoids soon after a traumatic experience (Brunet et al., 2008; Liu et al., 1997; Meaney et al., 1989; Watanabe, Gould, Daniels, Cameron, & McEwen, 1992). It has also been found that the neurotransmitter neuropeptide-Y is found in higher concentrations in the amygdalas of individuals who respond more favorably to high levels of stress (Morgan et al., 2000). Artificially increasing levels of neuropeptide-Y may buffer the nervous system from some of the damaging effects of stress.

Chemical blockade or disruption of particular amygdala circuits may decrease some of the symptoms of PTSD such as the startle and freeze responses (Goldstein, Rasmusson, Bunney, & Roth, 1996; Lee & Davis, 1997). It has even been suggested that stimulation of the amygdala could lead to the extinction of conditioned fear (Li, Weiss, Chaung, Post, & Rogawski, 1998). Understanding the role of LTP and other forms of plasticity in the amygdala, as well as its role in fear conditioning, may provide another avenue for future interventions in psychosis and PTSD (LaBar, Gatenby, Gore, LeDoux, & Phelps, 1998; Rogan & LeDoux, 1996; Rogan, Staubli, & LeDoux, 1997).

We have seen that higher levels of maternal attention in rats decrease the pups' subsequent HPA activation in response to stress (Liu et al., 1997). Although I doubt that encouraging human mothers to lick their children will be of much help, human infants demonstrate the same pattern in response to maternal massage (Field et al., 1996), and within securely attached relationships (Spangler & Grossman, 1993). Maternal depression, separation, and deprivation are severe stressors for infants, resulting in a variety of negative biological, emotional, and social consequences (Gunnar, 1992). Aggressive treatment of depression in new mothers, along with teaching them how to massage and better interact with their infants, may counteract some of the negative impact of maternal depression. Therapy focused on resolving a mother's attachment difficulties or past trauma prior to giving birth may also be helpful in reducing stress in their infants, children, and adolescents (Trapolini, Ungerer, & McMahon, 2008).

An increased appreciation of the effects of maternal separation may guide us as to the advisability of optional infant–mother separation. Where separation is unavoidable in cases of illness and death, the ability to lessen the impact of stress hormones via interpersonal and chemical interventions may prevent problems later in life. Given the amount of exposure in our society to stressful events such as abuse, neglect, abandonment, and community violence, the impact of severe stress on mothers and the developing brains of their children should be a serious public health concern (Bremner & Narayan, 1998).

Research findings suggest that early stress leads to a vulnerability to depression later in life (Widom, DuMont, & Czaja, 2007). This, in part, is mediated by deficient organization of frontal circuitry, and the establishment of lower levels of excitatory neurotransmitters and growth hormones during sensitive developmental periods. Early childhood experiences leading to a bias toward right hemisphere activation may also play a role in the long-term development of depression. As we discussed in the chapter on laterality, magnetic stimulation of the left hemisphere of depressed patients and the right hemisphere of patients with mania has shown promising results and may serve as a future alternative to electroconvulsive therapy (Grisaru et al., 1998; Klein et al., 1999; Teneback et al., 1999; Pascual-Leone et al., 1996).

In line with these findings, activation of the left hemisphere through sensory stimulation results in a higher degree of self-serving attributions and positive affect (Drake & Seligman, 1989). Relative left frontal activation appears linked to a state of mind of "self-enhancement," which may decrease the risk for psychopathology and be manipulated by changes in attitude or practices such as mindfulness meditation (Tomarken & Davidson, 1994). The more we understand the relationship between laterality and affect, the more we may be able to incorporate techniques of selective activation of right and left hemispheres into multimodal treatments for mood disorders and other psychiatric difficulties.

PTSD is primarily mediated and maintained by neurobiological processes outside conscious control. The activation of Broca's area in the face of high levels of affect appears to be an important mechanism of action in most interventions with patients suffering from PTSD and other anxiety disorders. We know that the ompfc modulates and inhibits amygdala activity, the very circuit we are activating when we help clients to employ cognition to inhibit their fears.

Despite new theories connecting neural communication and psychopathology, no major form of psychotherapy has emerged with the stated goal of neural network integration. This being said, techniques such as the caloric test and the eye movements used in EMDR seem to involve left-right and top-down integration as an active element. Previously, we discussed the phenomenon of sensory neglect, which occurs when there is damage to the right parietal lobe (assumed to be responsible for the integration of sensory and motor information from both sides of the brain). In the caloric test, stimulation with cold water to the left ear results in rapid side-to-side eye movements while activating regions of the right temporal lobe (Friberg et al., 1985). Although there has been one report of permanent remission of sensory neglect with this treatment, for most the cure is only temporary (Rubens, 1985). The bilateral activation of attentional centers in reaction to the caloric test results in increased integration of previously dissociated attention and information-processing systems (Bisiach et al., 1991).

In the treatment of PTSD with EMDR, past traumatic events are recalled and subjected to a protocol that involves focusing attention on ideas, self-beliefs, emotions, and bodily sensations. In addition, EMDR uses periodic stimulation through watching the therapist's hand going back and forth or having the legs touched alternately (Shapiro, 1995). This bilateral and alternating (side-to-side) stimulation may serve to activate attention centers in both temporal lobes in a manner similar to the caloric test. Alternating activation may, in fact, enhance neural network connectivity and the integration of traumatic memories into normal information processing.

Techniques such as EMDR may thwart or reverse the brain's tendency toward neural network dissociation secondary to trauma. Bilateral stimulation may enhance the reconsolidation of traumatic memories with cortical-hippocampal circuits providing contextualization in time and place. Activation of these same circuits creates the possibility of building descending inhibitory links to subcortical sensory-affective memory circuits (Siegel, 1995). Thus, the right-left stimulation of attention may simultaneously trigger integration of affect with cognition, sensation, and behavior throughout the brain.

Once the relationships among neural circuits are more fully understood, psychotherapists may employ these and other noninvasive techniques to stimulate the brain in ways that enhance neural network integration. Could activation of right hemisphere emotional regions during therapy with alexithymic patients aid in the integration of emotional processes with left hemisphere linguistic circuitry? Could activation of the left hemisphere during emotional dyscontrol in borderline patients enhance their ability to gain cognitive perspective and emotional regulation?

For conditions involving too much emotional inhibition, new learning may be stimulated by creating moderate levels of affect in therapy; this learning, in turn, may create a biochemical environment more conducive to the integration of emotional circuitry into consciousness (Bishof, 1983; Chambers et al., 1999). This may be the underlying neurobiology of Freud's belief that the presence of affect is necessary for change. Simultaneous activation of neural networks of emotion and cognition may result in a binding of the two in a way that allows for the conscious awareness and integration of emotion.

## Treatment Rationales and Combinations

*Sometimes I lie awake at night, and ask, "Where have I gone wrong?"*
*Then a voice says to me, "This is going to take more than one night."*
—Charles Schulz

The fundamental premise put forth in this book is that any form of psychotherapy is successful to the degree to which it positively impacts the underlying neural network growth and integration. I expect future research to continue supporting this basic hypothesis. Furthermore, evolving technologies will provide us with increasingly accurate ways of measuring activity within the brain and a greater understanding of exactly what it is we are measuring. My hope is that including neural network activity in our case conceptualization may help to establish a common language for us to select, combine, and evaluate the treatments we provide. It will, one hopes, help us to move past debates between competing schools of thought to a more inclusive approach to psychotherapy.

One long and hard-fought debate about treatment continues between supporters of psychopharmacology and psychotherapy despite empirical support for both approaches, individually and in combination. Brain functioning offers us a way to look more deeply into the effects of both talk and medication in regulating the brain and stimulating neuroplasticity. Patients who come to see me for psychotherapy are often adamant in their refusal to consider medication. Some feel frightened or shamed if I suggest the use of drugs as an adjunct to psychotherapy. At the same time I know that many discount talk therapy and will only seek help from therapists who will prescribe medication. All clients could benefit from education about brain functioning and the potential (even synergistic) power of both interventions. On the one hand, the therapeutic alliance supports positive expectancy, medication compliance, and psychological well-being. On the other, medication can help to achieve a state of body and mind that allows clients to benefit from psychotherapy.

Many patients who suffer brain damage resulting from accidents participate in multimodal rehabilitation programs that include physical, cognitive, and psychosocial interventions. The general approach to rehabilitation after brain injury is to first assess which systems have been damaged and which have been spared. The next step is to develop a program that plays to the patients' strengths and attempts to compensate for their weaknesses. Traffic and industrial accidents often result in damage to the frontal cortex, making disorders of attention, concentration, memory, executive functioning, and emotional regulation common in neurological rehabilitation. These same difficulties are common in many forms of psychological distress and psychiatric illness.

The traditional split between mind and brain has resulted in the separate development of the fields of psychotherapy, neuropsychology, and rehabilitation. When psychological difficulties are conceptualized in the context of a brain–behavior relationship, applying techniques from cognitive rehabilitation in psychotherapy becomes an interesting possibility. For example, abnormalities of frontal lobe functioning have been found in OCD, depression, and ADHD. Because these disorders share many symptoms afflicting patients with brain injury, psychotherapy patients with these and other psychiatric diagnoses may benefit from the strategies of cognitive rehabilitation (Parente & Herrmann, 1996).

An example of this was given in an earlier chapter, when I discussed how the simple memory strategies I used to assist my patient Sophia in remembering her appointments helped us to establish a solid alliance. My working assumption was that a combination of decreased hippocampal volume due to chronic stress and hypometabolism in the temporal lobes related to depression created real, brain-related memory dysfunctions (Bremner, Scott, et al., 1993; Brody et al., 2001). The success of cognitive-behavioral treatments with depressed and anxious patients underlines the importance of focusing on basic issues of reality testing, focused attention, and emotional regulation in order to support prefrontal functioning (Schwartz, 1996).

Findings with borderline clients of damage or dysfunction of the frontal and temporal lobes support the use of cognitive rehabilitation techniques with this population (Paris et al., 1999; Swirsky-Sacchetti et al., 1993). This may help explain why borderline patients require increased levels of structure to scaffold their erratic executive control and emotional instability. Manipulation and organization of the physical environment, sensory stimulation, and the type and amount of activity all impact brain functioning. Psychoeducation and enlisting family and friends in the therapeutic process (as utilized extensively in rehabilitation after brain damage) are also potential mechanisms of change. A good example of this is dialectical behavioral therapy (Linehan, 1993), which combines exposure, cognitive modification, skills development, and problem-solving skills to support prefrontal functioning.

Diagnostic and treatment approaches focused on cognitive deficits serve to decrease shame and help to create a stronger treatment alliance. Highly structured skill-building techniques, in the context of support and understanding, may provide disorganized patients the opportunity for early and clearly measurable success experiences. As our understanding of neural networks related to memory, affect, and behavior expands, prosthetic aids to these systems will be created and applied in the psychotherapy context. Increasing interdisciplinary coordination of this kind will require more comprehensive training for psychotherapists, not only in neuroscience but also in cognition, memory, and rehabilitation science. Removing the traditional barriers between psychotherapy and rehabilitation may lead to a higher quality of care and greater treatment success.

## Why Neuroscience Matters to Psychotherapists

*In science the important thing is to modify and change one's ideas
as science advances.*

—Herbert Spencer

The psychotherapist as healer exists within a long tradition of rabbis, priests, medicine women, and shamans. At the same time, findings in social neuroscience make it clear that we are also in the current scientific mainstream. In contrast to technological medicine, we understand our profound personal role in the healing relationship while simultaneously respecting the subjective experience of our clients. In the absence of a brain-based model of change, the leaders of our fields have learned to stimulate and guide neuroplastic processes to help build, integrate, and regulate our clients' brains. But why does an academic understanding of neuroscience make any difference to our work? Here are a few thoughts.

On a practical level, adding a neuroscientific perspective to our clinical thinking allows us to talk with clients about the shortcomings of our brains instead of the problems with theirs. The truth appears to be that many human struggles, from phobias to obesity, are consequences of brain evolution and not deficiencies of character. Identifying problems that we hold in common and developing methods to circumvent or correct them is a solid foundation upon which to base a therapeutic alliance.

As we come to better understand the neural correlates of mental health and emotional well-being, we may be able to use this knowledge to aid us in diagnosis and treatment. Neuroscience may also someday provide us with a rationale for an informed eclecticism as well as additional means of evaluating outcome. We will be able to see which combination of treatments impacts targeted neural networks and how changes in the activation of these circuits correspond with symptom expression. Neuroscience can also provide a common language to communicate with physicians, pharmacologists, and neurologists who may also be treating our clients. Finally, if you are anything like me, you might find a neuroscientific perspective to be an exciting addition to many case conceptualizations.

Some therapists bristle at the integration of neuroscience and psychotherapy, calling it irrelevant or reductionistic. I think I understand their perspective and concerns—if you have a model of therapy that works, why bother with the brain? Would Rogers, Kohut, or Beck have been better therapists if they had been trained as neuroscientists? Probably not. On the other hand, it is hard for me to grasp how the brain could be irrelevant to changing the mind. And while I dislike reductionism as much as the next person, doesn't a tendency toward reductionism say more about the thinker than the nature of natural phenomena? Our knowledge of neuroscience highlights the fact that we primates have complex and imperfect brains and should remain skeptical about what we think we know. In other words, primates would be wise to doubt their beliefs and remain open to new ideas.

It is humbling and more than a little frightening to realize that we rely on what may be the most complex structure in the universe with little knowledge of how it works. But even though we are only at the dawn of understanding the brain, an appreciation of its evolutionary history, developmental sculpting, and peculiarities of design can surely encourage us to begin to use it more wisely. Practical things—like understanding the neural damage resulting from drugs, stress, and early deprivation—should influence everything from personal decision making to public policy. The neural network dissociation that often results from exposure to combat should make us pay closer attention to those whom we put in harm's way. Even our tendencies to distort reality in the direction of personal experience and egocentric needs should lead us to examine our beliefs and opinions more carefully.

We now know that mind and brain are indivisible and that disorders traditionally thought of as psychological need to be reconceptualized to include their neurobiological mechanisms. And if brain dysfunction is central to a client's difficulties, the "most illuminating interpretation" may not be as valuable as a little accurate neurobiological knowledge (Yovell, 2000).

Self-awareness is a relatively new phenomenon in evolutionary history. Psychotherapy increases neural integration through challenges that expand our experience of and perspective on ourselves and the world. The challenge of expanding consciousness is to move beyond reflex, fear, and prejudice to a mindfulness and compassion for ourselves and others. Understanding the promise and limitations of our brains is but one essential step in the evolution of human consciousness.

In conclusion, our brains are inescapably social, their structures and functioning deeply embedded in the family, tribe, and society. And while the brain has many shortcomings and vulnerabilities, our ability to link with, attune to, and regulate each other's brains provides us with a way of healing. This is why the power of human relationships is at the heart of psychotherapy. From my perspective, the value of neuroscience for psychotherapists is not to explain away the mind or generate new forms of therapy, but to help us grasp the neurobiological substrates of the talking cure in an optimistic and enthusiastic continuation of Freud's *Project for a Scientific Psychology*.

# Credits

**Table 6.1:** [1] Davidson and Fox, 1982 [2] Canli et al.,1998 [3] Wheeler, Davidson, & Tomarken, 1993 [4] Davidson & Fox, 1982; Harmon-Jones & Allen, 1998 [5] Tomarken, Davidson, Wheeler, & Dass, 1992 [6] Coan, Allen, & Harmon-Jones, 2001; Davidson et al., 1990; Ekman & Davidson, 1993; [7] Urry et al., 2004 [8] Fox & Davidson, 1988 [9] Harmon-Jones & Allen, 1998 [10] Harmon-Jones & Sigelman, 2001 [11] Harmon-Jones & Sigelman, 2001 [12] Davidson et al., 1990 [13] Fox & Davidson, 1986 [14] Canli et al., 1998 [15] Davidson & Fox, 1982 [16] Wheeler et al., 1993 [17] Kalin, Shelton, Davidson, & Kelley, 2001 [18] Fox & Davidson, 1988 [19] Davidson & Fox, 1989

**Table 7.1:** [1] Minagawa-Kawai et al., 2008; Nitschke et al., 2004 [2] Berthoz et al., 2002; Mitchell, Banaji, & Macrae, 2005 [3] Mitchell, Macrae, & Banaji, 2006 [4] Gusnard et al., 2002 [5] Goel & Dolan, 2001 [6] Frey & Petrides, 2000; Nobre et al., 1999 [7] Ongur & Price, 2000 [8] Bechara et al., 1998; Gallagher et al., 1999; Gehring & Willoughby, 2002; Kringelbach, 2005; Krueger et al., 2006; O'Doherty, 2004 [9] Bechara et al., 1994; O'Doherty et al., 2002 [10] Matsumoto & Tanaka, 2004 [11] McGuire et al., 1996 [12] Dias, Robbins, & Roberts, 1996; Simpson, Drevets, et al., 2001; Simpson, Snyder, et al., 2001; Quirk & Beer, 2006 [13] Malloy et al., 1993; Teasdale et al., 1999; Beer et al., 2006 [14] Koechlin, Ody, & Kouneiher, 2003; [15] Dias et al., 1996; Fuster, 1997; Nagahama et al., 2001 [16] Knight & Grabowecky, 1995 [17] Rezai et al., 1993; Petrides, Alivisatos, & Frey, 2002 [18] Henson, Shallice, & Dolan, 1999 [19] Levesque, Eugène, Joanette, Paquette, et al., 2003 [20] Pascual-Leone et al., 1996 [21] Kroger et al., 2002; Malloy et al., 1993; Teasdale et al., 1999 [22] Mitchell et al., 2006 [23] Gray, Braver, & Raichle, 2002

**Table 7.3:** [1] Tamm, Menon, & Reiss, 2006 [2] Bush et al., 1999; Tamm, Menon, Ringel, & Reiss, 2004 [3] Tamm et al., 2004 [4] Rubia et al., 1999 [5] Yu-Feng et al., 2007 [6] Tamm et al., 2004 [7] Zang et al., 2005 [8] Yu-Feng et al., 2007 [9] Lou, Henriksen, & Bruhn, 1984 [10] Lee et al., 2005 [11] Castellanos et al., 2002 [12] Casey, Castellanos, & Giedd, 1997 [13] Li et al., 2007 [14] Markis et al., 2007 [15] Mackie et al., 2007 [16] Ashtari et al., 2005

**Table 8.1:** [1] Dehaene, Molko, Cohen, & Wilson, 2004 [2] Victor & Roper, 2001 [3] Sirigu et al., 1996 [4] Colby, 1998; Driver & Mattingley, 1998 [5] Newman et al., 2003 [6] Rorden, Mattingley, Karnath, & Driver, 1997; Snyder & Chatterjee, 2004 [7] Karnath, 1997; Ungerleider & Haxby, 1994 [8] Schwartz et al., 2005 [9] Battelli et al., 2001; Claeys et al., 2003 [10] Griffiths et al., 1998 [11] Snyder & Chatterjee, 2004 [12] Anderson & Mountcastle, 1983 [13] Pia et al., 2004

**Table 8.2:** [1] Griffiths et al., 1998 [2] Chochon et al., 1999 [3] Newman et al., 2003 [4] Uddin et al., 2005 [5] Dehaene et al., 2003 [6] Molko et al., 2003 [7] Chochon et al., 1999 [8] Molko et al., 2003; Rushworth, Krams, & Passingham, 2001 [9] Newman et al., 2003 [10] Newman et al., 2003 [11] Antal et al., 2008 [12] Grefkes & Fink, 2005; Wolpert, Goodbody, & Husain, 1998 [13] Wolpert et al., 1998 [14] Jonides et al., 1998 [15] Wagner et al., 2005 [16] Marshuetz et al., 2000; Van Opstal, Verguts, & Fias, 2008 [17] Husain & Nachev, 2007 [18] Astafiev et al., 2003 [19] Mountcastle, 1995 [20] Orban et al., 1999 [21] Castelli, Glaser, & Butterworth, 2006; Fias et al., 2003; Lemer et al., 2003 [22] Fias et al., 2007 [23] Ruby & Decety, 2001 [24] Iacoboni et al., 2004; Jackson & Decety 2004 [25] Vogeley et al., 2004

**Table 12.1:** [1] Bredy et al., 2003; Champagne et al., 2008 [2] Weaver, Grant, & Meaney, 2002; Weaver, Meaney, & Szyf, 2006 [3] Garoflos et al., 2008; Menard, Champagne, & Meaney, 2004 [4] Liu et al., 2000 [5] Zhang et al., 2005 [6] Menard et al., 2004 [7] Weaver et al., 2004 [8] Caldji, Diorio, & Meaney, 2003 [9] Caldji, Diorio, Anisman, & Meaney, 2004; Caldji et al., 1998 [10] Braun & Poeggel, 2001 [11] Champagne et al., 2003 [12] Champagne et al., 2001, 2003, 2006 [13] Cameron, Fish, & Meaney, 2008

**Table 12.2:** [1] Zhang at al., 2002 [2] Marais et al., 2008 [3] Leventopoulos et al., 2007 [4] Caldji et al., 2000; Hsu et al., 2003; [5] Rees, Steiner, & Fleming, 2006 [6] Blaise et al., 2007 [7] Brake et al., 2004 [8] Kuhn & Schanberg, 1998 [9] Kalinichev et al., 2002 [10] Coutinho et al., 2002 [11] Weaver et al., 2006 [12] Ovscharoff & Braun, 2001 [13] Akbari et al., 2007

**Table 12.3:** [1] McCormick et al., 2000; Meaney et al., 1988, 1991; O'Donnell et al., 1994; Smythe, Rowe, & Meaney, 1994 [2] Sarrieau, Sharma, & Meaney, 1988 [3] Plotsky & Meaney, 1993 [4] Kosten, Lee, & Kim, 2007 [5] Siviy & Harrison, 2008 [6] Garoflos et al., 2007 [7] Vallée et al., 1997 [8] Vallée et al., 1999 [9] Costela et al., 1995; Tejedor-Real et al., 1998 [10] Weaver et al., 2000 [11] Collette et al., 2000

**Table 13.1:** [1] Krugers et al., 2006 2. Wantanabe, Gould, & McEwen, 1992 [3] Alonso, 2000 [4] Sapolsky, 1990 [5] Dranovsky & Hen, 2006; Kelly, Mullany, & Lynch, 2000; Pham et al., 2003; Prickaerts et al., 2004 [6] Kuhlmann, Piel, & Wolf, 2005; Kirschbaum et al., 1996; Newcomer et al., 1994, 1999 [7] West, 1993; Lupien et al., 1998 [8] Bremner, Scott, et al., 1993 [9] Bremner, Southwick, et al., 1993; Vythilingam et al., 2002 [10] Bremner et al., 1995; 1997; Bremner, 2006; de Lanerolle et al., 1989 [11] Villarreal et al., 2002 [12] Falkai & Bogerts, 1986; Nelson et al., 1998 [13] Bourdeau et al., 2002; Condren & Thakore, 2001

**Table 17.1:** [1] Bennett, Diamond, Krech, & Rosenzweig, 1964; Diamond et al., 1964 [2] Kempermann et al., 1998; Walsh, Budtz-Olsen, Penny, & Cummins, 1969 [3] Kolb & Whishaw, 1998 [4] Kolb & Whishaw, 1998 [5] Kolb & Whishaw, 1998 [6] Ickes et al., 2000 [7] Nilsson et al., 1993 [8] Sirevaag & Greenough, 1988 [9] Sirevaag & Greenough, 1988 [10] Guzowski, Setlown, Wagner, & McGaugh, 2001 [11] Torasdotter et al., 1998

**Table 17.2:** [1] Fujikawa et al., 2000 [2] Abercrombie et al., 2003; Andreano & Cahill, 2006; Domes et al., 2005 [3] Takahashi et al., 2004 [4] Conrad, Lupien, & McEwen, 1999; Kerr, Huggett, & Abraham, 1994; Park et al., 2006; Yau et al., 1995 [5] Diamond et al., 1992 [6] Pavlides et al., 1995 [7] Sullivan, Wilson, & Leon, 1989 [8] Introini-Collison & McGaugh, 1987

**Table 17.4:** [1] Mayberg et al., 2002 [2] Mayberg et al., 2002 [3] Kong et al., 2006 [4] Pariente et al., 2005 [5] Petrovic et al., 2002 [6] Wager et al., 2004 [7] Wager et al., 2004 [8] Zubieta et al., 2005 [9] Benedetti et al., 2004 [10] Fuente-Fernandez et al., 2001

**Table 18.1:** [1] Baxter et al., 1992 [2] Brody et al., 1998 [3] Nakatani et al., 2003 [4] Schwartz et al., 1996 [5] Lazaro et al., 2009 [6] Furmark et al., 2002 [7] Paquette et al., 2003 [8] Johanson et al., 2006 [9] Straube et al., 2006 [10] Levin, Lazrove, & Van der Kolk, 1999 [11] Prasko et al., 2004 [12] Sakai et al., 2006 [13] Goldapple et al., 2004 [14] Kennedy et al., 2007 [15] Martin et al., 2001 [16] Brody, Saxena, Stoessel, et al., 2001 [17] Brody, Saxena, Schwartz, et al., 2001 [18] Penades et al., 2002 [19] Wykes et al., 2002 [20] Laatsch et al., 1999

# References

Abercrombie, H. C., Kalin, N. H., Thurow, M. E., Rosenkranz, M. A., & Davidson, R. J. (2003). Cortisol variation in humans affects memory for emotionally laden and neutral information. *Behavioral Neuroscience, 117,* 505–516.

Adamec, R. E. (1991). Partial kindling of the ventral hippocampus: Identification of changes in limbic physiology which accompany changes in feline aggression and defense. *Physiology and Behavior, 49,* 443–454.

Adams, R. D., Victor, M., & Ropper, A. H. (1997). *Principles of neurology.* New York: McGraw-Hill.

Ahern, G. L., Schomer, D. L., Kleefield, J., Blume, H., Rees-Cosgrove, G., Weintraub, S., et al. (1991). Right hemisphere advantage for evaluating emotional facial expressions. *Cortex, 27,* 193–202.

Ainsworth, M. D. S., Blehar, M. C., Waters, E., & Wall, S. (1978). *Patterns of attachment: A psychological study of the strange situation.* Hillsdale, NJ: Erlbaum.

Akaneya, Y., Tsumoto, T., Kinoshita, S., & Hatanaka, H. (1997). Brain-derived neurotrophic factor enhances long-term potentiation in rat visual cortex. *Journal of Neuroscience, 17,* 6707–6716.

Akbari, E., Chatterjee, D., Levy, F., & Fleming, A. (2007). Experience-dependent cell survival in the maternal rat brain. *Behavioral Neuroscience, 121,* 1001–1011.

Akirav, I., & Maroun, M. (2007). The role of the medial prefrontal cortex-amygdala circuit in stress effects on the extinction of fear. *Neural Plasticity,* doi:10.1155/2007/30873.

Alberini, C. M. (2005). Mechanisms of memory stabilization: Are consolidation and reconsolidation similar or distinct processes? *Trends in Neuroscience, 28*(1), 51–56.

Alexander, G. E., DeLong, M. R., & Strick, P. L. (1986). Parallel organization of functionally segregated circuits linking basal ganglia and cortex. *Annual Review of Neuroscience, 9,* 357–381.

Alexander, G. E., Furey, M. L., Grady, C. L., Pietrini, P., Brady, D. R., Mentis, M. J., et al. (1997). Association of premorbid intellectual function with cerebral metabolism in Alzheimer's disease: Implications for the cognitive reserve hypothesis. *American Journal of Psychiatry, 154,* 165–172.

Alexander, M. P., Stuss, D. T., & Benson, D. F. (1979). Capgras syndrome: A reduplicative phenomenon. *Neurology, 29,* 334–339.

Allen, J. P., McElhaney, K. B., Kuperminc, G. P., & Jodl, K. M. (2004). Stability and change in attachment security across adolescence. *Child Development, 75,* 1792–1805.

Allen, J. S., Bruss, J., & Damasio, H. (2005). The aging brain: The cognitive reserve hypothesis and hominid evolution. *American Journal of Human Biology, 17,* 673–689.

Allen, J. S., Damasio, H., & Grabowski, T. J. (2002). Normal neuroanatomical variation in the human brain: An MRI-volumetric study. *American Journal of Physical Anthropology, 118,* 341–358.

Allen, N. J., & Barres, B. A. (2005). Signaling between glia and neurons: Focus on synaptic plasticity. *Current Opinion in Neurobiology, 15,* 542–548.

Allman, J., Rosin, A., Kumar, R., & Hasenstaub, A. (1998). Parenting and survival in anthropoid primates: Caretakers live longer. *Proceedings of the National Academy of Sciences, USA, 95,* 6866–6869.

Allman, J. M., Hakeem, A., Erwin, J. M., Nimchinsky, E., & Hof, P. (2001). The anterior cingulate cortex: The evolution of an interface between emotion and cognition. *Annals of the New York Academy of Sciences, 935,* 107–117.

Allman, J. M., Watson, K. K., Tetreault, N. A., & Hakeem, A. Y. (2005). Intuition and autism: A possible role for Von Economo neurons. *Trends in Cognitive Sciences, 9,* 367–373.

Al-Mousawi, A. H., Evans, N., Ebmeier, K. P., Roeda, D., Chaloner, F., & Ashcroft, G. W. (1996). Limbic dysfunction in schizophrenia and mania. A study using 18F-labeled fluorodeoxyglucose and positron emission tomography. *British Journal of Psychiatry, 169,* 509–516.

Alonso, G. (2000). Prolonged corticosterone treatment of adult rats inhibits the proliferation of oligodendrocyte progenitors present throughout white and gray matter regions of the brain. *Glia, 31,* 219–231.

Alonso, M., Vianna, M. R. M., Depino, A. M., de Souza, T. M., Pereira, P., Szapiro, G., et al. (2002). BDNF-triggered events in the rat hippocampus are required for both short- and long-term memory. *Hippocampus, 12,* 551–560.

Altman, J., Wallace, R. B., Anderson, W. J., & Das, G. D. (1968). Behaviorally induced changes in length of cerebrum in rats. *Developmental Psychobiology, 1,* 112–117.

American Psychiatric Association. (2000). *Diagnostic and statistical manual of mental disorders* (4th ed., text revision). Washington, DC: American Psychiatric Association.

Amini, F., Lewis, T., Lannon, R., Louie, A., Baumbacher, G., McGuinness, T., et al. (1996). Affect, attachment, memory: Contributions toward psychobiologic integration. *Psychiatry, 59*(3), 213–239.

Andersen, R. A., & Mountcastle, V. B. (1983). The influence of the angle of gaze upon the excitability of the light-sensitive neurons of the posterior parietal cortex. *Journal of Neuroscience, 3*(3), 532–548.

Andersen, R. A., Snyder, L. H., Bradley, D. C., & Xing, J. (1997). Multimodal representation of space in the posterior parietal cortex and its use in planning movements. *Annual Review of Neuroscience, 20*, 303–330.

Anderson, A. K., Wais, P. E., & Gabrieli, J. D. E. (2006). Emotion enhances remembrance of neutral events past. *Proceedings of the National Academy of Sciences, USA, 103*, 1599–1604.

Anderson, C. M., Polcari, A., Lowen, S. B., Renshaw, P. F., & Teicher, M. H. (2002). Effects of methyphenidate on functional magnetic resonance relaxometry of the cerebellar vermis in boys with ADHD. *American Journal of Psychiatry, 159*, 1322–1328.

Anderson, C. R. (1976). Coping behaviors as intervening mechanisms in the inverted-U stress-performance relationship. *Journal of Applied Psychology, 61*(1), 30–34.

Anderson, M. C., & Green, C. (2001). Suppressing unwanted memories by executive control. *Nature, 410*, 366–369.

Andreano, J. M., & Cahill, L. (2006). Glucocorticoid release and memory consolidation in men and women. *Psychological Science, 17*, 466–470.

Andreasen, N. C. (2001). *Brave new brain: Conquering mental illness in the era of the genome.* New York: Oxford University Press.

Anisman, H., Zaharia, M. D., Meaney, M. J., & Merali, Z. (1998). Do early-life events permanently alter behavioral and hormonal responses to stressors? *International Journal of Developmental Neuroscience, 16*, 149–164.

Ansorge, M. S., Zhou, M., Lira, A., Hen, R., & Gingrich, J. A. (2004). Early-life blockade of the 5-HT transporter alters emotional behavior in adult mice. *Science, 306*, 879–881.

Antal, A., Baudewig, J., Paulus, W., & Dechent, P. (2008). The posterior cingulated cortex and planum temporale/parietal operculum are activated by coherent visual motion. *Visual Neuroscience, 25*, 17–26.

Ardila, A., Ostrosky-Solis, F., Rosselli, M., & Gomez, C. (2000). Age-related cognitive decline during normal aging: The complex effect of education. *Archives of Clinical Neuropsychology, 15*, 495–513.

Arnsten, A. F. T. (2000). Genetics of childhood disorders: XVIII. ADHD, Part 2: Norepinephrine has a critical modulatory influence on prefrontal cortical function. *Journal of the American Academy of Child and Adolescent Psychiatry, 39*, 374–383.

Arnsten, A. F. T., & Goldman-Rakic, P. S. (1998). Noise stress impairs prefrontal cortical cognitive function in monkeys: Evidence for a hyperdopaminergic mechanism. *Archives of General Psychiatry, 55*, 362–368.

Arnsten, A. F. T., & Li, B. (2005). Neurobiology of executive functions: Catecholamine influences on prefrontal cortical functions. *Biological Psychiatry, 57*, 1377–1384.

Ashtari, M., Kumra, S., Bhaskar, S., Clarke, T., Thaden, E., Cervellione, K. L., et al. (2005). Attention-deficit/hyperactivity disorder: A preliminary diffusion tensor imaging study. *Biological Psychiatry, 57*, 448–455.

Astafiev, S., Shulman, G., Stanley, C., Snyder, A., Van Essen, D., & Corbetta, M. (2003). Functional organization of human intraparietal and frontal cortex for attending, looking and pointing. *Journal of Neuroscience, 23*, 4689–4699.

Aston-Jones, G., Valentino, R. J., VanBockstaele, E. J., & Meyerson, A. T. (1994). Locus coeruleus, stress, and PTSD: Neurobiology and clinical parallels. In M. M. Murburg (Ed.), *Catecholamine function in posttraumatic stress disorder: Emerging concepts* (pp. 17–62). Washington, DC: American Psychiatric Press.

Augustine, J. R. (1996). Circuitry and functional aspects of the insular lobe in primates including humans. *Brain Research Reviews, 22*, 229–244.

Baars, B. J. (2002). The conscious access hypothesis: Origins and recent evidence. *Trends in Cognitive Sciences, 6*(1), 47–52.

Bachar, E., Kanyas, K., Latzer, Y., Canetti, L., Bonne, O., & Lerer, B. (2008). Depressive tendencies and lower levels of self-sacrifice in mothers, and selflessness in their anorexic daughters. *European Eating Disorders Review, 16*, 184–190.

Bagby, R. M., & Taylor, G. J. (1997). Affect dysregulation and alexithymia. In G. J. Taylor, R. M. Bagby, & J. D. A. Parker (Eds.), *Disorders of affect regulation: Alexithymia in medical and psychiatric illness* (pp. 26–45). Cambridge: Cambridge University Press.

Baird, A. A., Gruber, S. A., Fein, D. A., Maas, L. C., Steingard, R. J., Renshaw, P. F., et al. (1999). Functional magnetic resonance imaging of facial affect recognition in children and adolescents. *Journal of the American Academy of Child and Adolescent Psychiatry, 38*, 195–199.

Baldi, E., & Bucherelli, C. (2005). The inverted "U-shaped" dose-effect relationships in learning and memory: Modulation of arousal and consolidation. *Nonlinearity in Biology, Toxicology, and Medicine, 3*, 9–21.

Baptista, L. F., & Petrinovich, L. (1986). Song development in the white-crowned sparrow: Social factors and sex differences. *Animal Behavior, 34*, 1359–1371.

Bar, M., Kassam, K. S., Ghuman, A. S., Boshyan, J., Schmidt, A. M., Dale, A. M., et al. (2006). Top-down facilitation of visual recognition. *Proceedings of the National Academy of Sciences, USA, 103*, 449–454.

Barad, M. (2000). *A biological analysis of transference.* Paper presented at the UCLA Annual Review of Neuropsychiatry, February 2, Indian Wells, California.

Barbas, H. (1995). Anatomic basis of cognitive-emotional interactions in the primate prefrontal cortex. *Neuroscience and Biobehavioral Reviews, 19*, 499–510.

Barde, Y. A. (1989). Trophic factors and neuronal survival. *Neuron, 2*, 1525–1534.

Bargh, J. A., & Chartrand, T. L. (1999). The unbearable automaticity of being. *American Psychologist, 54,* 462–479.

Barry, R. J., Clarke, A. R., McCarthy, R., Selikowitz, M., Johnstone, S. J., & Rushby, J. A. (2004). Age and gender effects in EEG coherence: I. Developmental trends in normal children. *Clinical Neurophysiology, 115,* 2252–2258.

Bartels, A., & Zeki, S. (2000). The neural basis of romantic love. *NeuroReport, 11,* 3829–3834.

Bartzokis, G., Beckson, M., Lu, P. H., Nuechterlein, K. H., Edwards, N., & Mintz, J. (2001). Age-related changes in frontal and temporal lobe volumes in men. *Archives of General Psychiatry, 58,* 461–465.

Bateson, G. (1972). Steps to an ecology of mind. New York: Ballantine Books.

Battelli, L., Cavanagh, P., Intrilligator, J., Tramo, M. J., Henaff, M., Michel, F., et al. (2001). Unilateral right parietal damage leads to bilateral deficit for high-level motion. *Neuron, 32,* 985–995.

Baxter, L. R., Phelps, M. E., Mazziotta, J. C., Schwartz, J. M., Gerner, R. H., Selin, C. E., et al. (1985). Cerebral metabolic rates for glucose metabolism in mood disorders. *Archives of General Psychiatry, 42,* 441–447.

Baxter, L. R., Schwartz, J. M., Bergman, K. S., Szuba, M. P., Guze, B. H., Mazziotta, J. C., et al. (1992). Caudate glucose metabolic rate changes with both drug and behavior therapy for obsessive-compulsive disorder. *Archives of General Psychiatry, 40,* 681–689.

Baxter, L. R., Schwartz, J. M., Phelps, M. E., Mazziotta, J. C., Guze, B. H., Selin, C. E., et al. (1989). Reduction of prefrontal cortex glucose metabolism common to three types of depression. *Archives of General Psychiatry, 46,* 243–250.

Beatty, J. (2001). *The human brain: Essentials of behavioral neuroscience.* Thousand Oaks, CA: Sage.

Beauregard, M. (2007). Mind does really matter: Evidence from neuroimaging studies of emotional self-regulation, psychotherapy, and placebo effect. *Progress in Neurobiology, 81*(4), 218–236.

Beauregard, M., Lévesque, J., & Bourgouin, P. (2001). Neural correlates of conscious self-regulation of emotion. *Journal of Neuroscience, 21,* RC165, 1–6.

Bechara, A., Damasio, A. R., Damasio, H., & Anderson, S. W. (1994). Insensitivity to future consequences following damage to human prefrontal cortex. *Cognition, 50,* 7–15.

Bechara, A., Damasio, H., Tranel, D., & Anderson, S. W. (1998). Dissociation of working memory from decision making within the human prefrontal cortex. *Journal of Neuroscience, 18,* 428–437.

Bechara, A., Damasio, H., Tranel, D., & Damasio, A. (1997). Deciding advantageously before knowing the advantageous strategy. *Science, 275,* 1293–1295.

Bechara, A., & Naqvi, N. (2004). Listening to your heart: Interoceptive awareness as a gateway to feeling. *Nature Neuroscience, 7,* 102–103.

Bechara, A., Tranel, D., Damasio, H., Adolphs, R., Rockland, C., & Damasio, A. R. (1995). Double dissociation of conditioning and declarative knowledge relative to the amygdala and hippocampus in humans. *Science, 269,* 1115–1118.

Beck, A. T. (1976). *Cognitive therapy and emotional disorders.* New York: International University Press.

Beck, A. T., Rush, A. J., Shaw, B. F., & Emery, G. (1979). *Cognitive therapy of depression.* New York: Guilford.

Beeghly, M., & Cicchetti, D., (1994). Child maltreatment, attachment, and the self-system: Emergence of an internal state lexicon in toddlers at high social risk. *Development and Psychopathology, 6,* 5–30.

Beer, J. S., Heerey, E. A., Keltner, D., Scabini, D., & Knight, R. T. (2003). The regulatory function of self-conscious emotion: Insights from patients with orbitofrontal damage. *Journal of Personality and Social Psychology, 85,* 594–604.

Beer, J. S., John, O. P., Scabini, D., & Knight, R. T. (2006). Orbitofrontal cortex and social behavior: Integrating self-monitoring and emotion-cognition interactions. *Journal of Cognitive Neuroscience, 18*(6), 871–879.

Bekinschtein, P., Cammarota, M., Katche, C., Slipczuk, L., Rossato, J. I., Goldin, A., et al. (2008). BDNF is essential to promote persistence of long-term memory storage. *Proceedings of the National Academy of Sciences, USA, 105,* 2711–2716.

Bell, M. A., & Fox, N. A. (1992). The relations between frontal brain electrical activity and cognitive development during infancy. *Child Development, 63,* 1142–1163.

Belmaker, R. H., & Grisaru, N. (1999). Anti-bipolar potential for transcranial magnetic stimulation. *Bipolar Disorders, 1*(2), 71–72.

Benedetti, F., Colloca, L., Torre, E., Lanotte, M., Melcarne, A., Pesare, M., et al. (2004). Placebo-responsive Parkinson patients show decreased activity in single neurons of subthalamic nucleus. *Nature Neuroscience, 7,* 587–588.

Benes, F. M. (1989). Myelination of cortical-hippocampal relays during late adolescence. *Schizophrenia Bulletin, 15,* 585–593.

Benes, F. M., Taylor, J. B., & Cunningham, M. C. (2000). Convergence and plasticity of monoaminergic systems in the medial prefrontal cortex during the postnatal period: Implications for the development of psychopathology. *Cerebral Cortex, 10,* 1014–1027.

Bennett, A. J., Lesch, K. P., Heils, A., Long, J. C., Lorenz, J. G., Shoaf, S. E., et al. (2002). Early experience and serotonin transporter gene variation interact to influence primate CNS function. *Molecular Psychiatry, 7,* 118–122.

Bennett, E. L., Diamond, M. C., Krech, D., & Rosenweig, M. R. (1964). Chemical and anatomical plasticity of brain. *Science, 146,* 610–619.

Benson, F. D. (1994). *The neurology of thinking.* New York: Oxford University Press.

Berntson, G. C., Bechara, A., Damasio, H., Tranel, D., & Cacioppo, J. T. (2007). Amygdala contribution to selective dimensions of emotion. *Social Cognitive and Affective Neuroscience, 2,* 123–129.

Berntson, G. G., & Cacioppo, J. T. (2008). The functional neuroarchitecture of evaluative processes. In A. J. Elliot (Ed.), *Handbook of approach and avoidance motivation* (pp. 305–316). New York: CRC Press.

Berthier, M. L., Posada, A., & Puentes, C. (2001). Dissociative flashbacks after right frontal injury in a Vietnam veteran with combat-related posttraumatic stress disorder. *Journal of Neuropsychiatry and Clinical Neurosciences, 13,* 101–105.

Berthoz, S., Armony, J. L., Blair, R. J. R., & Dolan, R. J. (2002). An fMRI study of intentional and unintentional (embarrassing) violations of social norms. *Brain, 125,* 1696–1708.

Berton, O., McClung, C. A., DiLeone, R. J., Krishnan, V., Renthal, W., Russo, S. J., et al.
(2006). Essential role of BDNF in the mesolimbic dopamine pathway in social defeat stress. *Science, 311,* 864–868.

Bhide, P. G., & Bedi, K. S. (1982). The effects of environmental diversity on well-fed and previously undernourished rats: I. Body and brain measurements. *Journal of Comparative Neurology, 207,* 403–409.

Birnbaum, S., Gobeske, K. T., Auerbach, J., Taylor, J. R., & Arnsten, A. F. T. (1999). A role for norepinephrine in stress-induced cognitive deficits: a-1-adrenoceptor mediation in the prefrontal cortex. *Biological Psychiatry, 46,* 1266–1274.

Bischoff-Grethe, A., Proper, S. M., Mao, H., Daniels, K. A., & Berns, G. S. (2000). Conscious and unconscious processing of nonverbal predictability in Wernicke's area. *Journal of Neuroscience, 20,* 1975–1981.

Bishof, H. (1983). Imprinting and cortical plasticity: A comparative review. *Neuroscience and Biobehavioral Reviews, 7,* 213–225.

Bishop, S. J. (2007). Neurocognitive mechanisms of anxiety: An integrative account. *Trends in Cognitive Sciences, 11*(7), 307–316.

Bishop, S., Duncan, J., Brett, M., & Lawrence, A. (2004). Prefrontal cortical function and anxiety: Controlling attention to threat-related stimuli. *Nature Neuroscience, 7*(2), 184–187.

Bishop, S., Duncan, J., & Lawrence, A. D. (2004). State anxiety of the amygdala response to unattended threat-related stimuli. *Journal of Neuroscience, 24,* 10364–10368.

Bisiach, E., & Luzzatti, C. (1978). Unilateral neglect of representational space. *Cortex, 14,* 129–133.

Bisiach, E., Rusconi, M. L., & Vallar, G. (1991). Remission of somatoparaphrenic delusions through vestibular stimulation. *Neuropsychologia, 29,* 1029–1031.

Biver, F., Goldman, S., Francois, A., De La Porte, C., Luxen, A., Gribomont, B., et al. (1995). Changes in metabolism of cerebral glucose after stereotactic leukotomy for refractory obsessive-compulsive disorder: A case report. *Journal of Neurology, Neurosurgery and Psychiatry, 58,* 502–505.

Black, J. E. (1998). How a child builds its brain: Some lessons from animal studies of neural plasticity. *Preventive Medicine, 27,* 168–171.

Blaise, J. H., Koranda, J. L., Chow, U., Haines, K. E., & Doward, E. C. (2007). Neonatal isolation stress alters bidirectional long-term synaptic plasticity in amygdalo-hippocampal synapses in freely behaving adult rats. *Brain Research, 1193*, 25–33.

Blanke, O., & Arzy, S. (2005). The out-of-body experience: Disturbed self-processing at the temporo-parietal junction. *Neuroscientist, 11*, 11–24.

Blass, R. B., & Carmeli, Z. (2007). The case against neuropsychoanalysis. On fallacies underlying psychoanalysis' latest scientific trend and its negative impact on psychoanalytic discourse. *International Journal of Psychoanalysis, 88*, 19–40.

Blonder, L. X., Bowers, D., & Heilman, K. M. (1991). The role of right hemisphere in emotional communication. *Brain, 114*, 1115–1127.

Blum, D. (2002). *Love at Goon Park.* Cambridge: Perseus.

Bollas, C. (1987). *The shadow of the object: Psychoanalytic of the unthought known.* New York: Columbia University Press.

Bonda, E., Petrides, M., Frey, S., & Evans, A. C. (1994). Frontal cortex involvement in organized sequences of hand movements: Evidence from a positron emission tomography study [abstract]. *Social Neuroscience Abstracts, 20*, 353.

Bonda, E., Petrides, M., Ostry, D., & Evans, A. (1996). Specific involvement of human parietal systems and the amygdala in the perception of biological motion. *Journal of Neuroscience, 16*, 3737–3744.

Bornstein, M. H. (1989). Sensitive periods in development: Structural characteristics and causal interpretations. *Psychological Bulletin, 105*, 179–197.

Borod, J. C., Cicero, B. A., Obler, L. K., Welkowitz, J., Erhan, H. M., Santschi, C., et al. (1998). Right hemisphere emotional perception: Evidence across multiple channels. *Neuropsychology, 12*, 446–458.

Bourdeau, I., Bard, C., Noel, B., Leclerc, I., Cordeau, M. P., Belair, M., et al. (2002). Loss of brain volume in endogenous Cushing's syndrome and its reversibility after correction hypercortisolism. *Journal of Clinical Endocrinology and Metabolism, 87*, 1949–1954.

Bowen, M. (1978). *Family therapy in clinical practice.* Northvale, NJ: Jason Aronson.

Bowlby, J. (1969). *Attachment.* New York: Basic Books.

Bowlby, J. (1988). *A secure base: Clinical applications of attachment theory.* London: Routledge.

Bradshaw, J. (1990). *Homecoming: Reclaiming and championing your inner child.* New York: Bantam Books.

Brake, W. G., Zhang, T. Y., Diorio, J., Meaney, M. J., & Gratton, A. (2004). Influence of early postnatal rearing conditions on mesocorticolimbic dopamine and behavioural responses to psychostimulants and stressors in adult rats. *European Journal of Neuroscience, 19*, 1863–1874.

Branchi, I., D'Andrea, I., Sietzema, J., Fiore, M., Di Fausto, V., Aloe, L., et al. (2006). Early social enrichment augments adult hippocampal BDNF levels and survival of BrdU-positive cells while increasing anxiety- and "depression"-like behavior. *Journal of Neuroscience Research, 83*, 965–973.

Branchi, I., Francia, N., & Alleva, E. (2004). Epigenetic control of neurobehavioral plasticity: The role of neurotrophins. *Behavioral Pharmacology, 15*(5–6), 353–362.

Braun, C., Scweizer, R., Elbert, T., Borbaumer, N., & Taub, E. (2000). Differential activation in somatosensory cortex for different discrimination tasks. *Journal of Neuroscience, 20,* 446–450.

Braun, K., & Poeggel, G. (2001). Recognition of mother's voice evokes metabolic activation in the medial prefrontal cortex and lateral thalamus of Octodon degus pups. *Neuroscience, 103,* 861–864.

Bredy, T. W., Grant, R. J., Champagne, D. L., & Meaney, M. J. (2003). Maternal care influences neuronal survival in the hippocampus of the rat. *European Journal of Neuroscience, 18,* 2903–2909.

Bredy, T., Zhang, T., Grant, R., Diorio, J., & Meaney, M. (2004). Peripubertal environmental enrichment reverses the effects of maternal care on hippocampal development and glutamate receptor subunit expression. *European Journal of Neuroscience, 20*(5), 1355–1362.

Bremner, J. (2006). Stress and brain atrophy. *CNS and Neurological Disorders—Drug Targets, 5,* 503–512.

Bremner, J. D., & Narayan, M. (1998). The effects of stress on memory and the hippocampus throughout the life cycle: Implications for childhood development and aging. *Development and Psychopathology, 10,* 871–885.

Bremner, J. D., Randall, P., Scott, T., & Bronen, R. (1995). MRI-based measurement of hippocampal volume in patients with combat-related posttraumatic stress disorder. *American Journal of Psychiatry, 152,* 973–983.

Bremner, J. D., Randall, P., Vermetten, E., Staib, L., Bronen, R. A., Mazure, C., et al. (1997). Magnetic resonance imaging-based measurement of hippocampal volume in posttraumatic stress disorder related to childhood physical and sexual abuse: A preliminary report. *Biological Psychiatry, 41,* 23–32.

Bremner, J. D., Scott, T. M., Delaney, R. C., Southwick, S. M., Mason, J. W., Johnson, D. R., et al. (1993). Deficits of short-term memory in posttraumatic stress disorder. *American Journal of Psychiatry, 150,* 1015–1019.

Bremner, J. D., Southwick, S. M., Johnson, D. R., Yehuda, R., & Charney, D. S. (1993). Childhood physical abuse and combat-related posttraumatic stress disorder in Vietnam veterans. *American Journal of Psychiatry, 150,* 235–239.

Brennan, K. A., & Shaver, P. R. (1995). Dimensions of adult attachment, affect regulation, and romantic relationship functioning. *Personality and Social Psychology Bulletin, 21,* 267–283.

Brennan, P. A., Pargas, R., Walker, E. F., Green, P., Newport, D. J. & Stowe, Z. (2008). Maternal depression and infant cortisol: Influences of timing, comorbidity and treatment. *Journal of Child Psychology and Psychiatry, 49,* 1099–1107.

Brewin, C. R., Dalgleish, T., & Joseph, S. (1996). A dual representation theory of post traumatic stress disorder. *Psychological Research, 103,* 670–686.

Brewin, C. R., & Smart, L. (2005). Working memory capacity and suppression of intrusive thoughts. *Journal of Behavior Therapy and Experimental Psychiatry, 36,* 61–68.

Broadhurst, P. L. (1957). Emotionality and the Yerkes-Dodson law. *Journal of Experimental Psychology, 54*(5), 345–352.

Brodal, P. (1992). *The central nervous system.* New York: Oxford University Press.

Brody, A. L., Mandelkern, M. A., Olmstead, R. E., Jou, J., Tiongson, E., Allen, V., et al. (2007). Neural substrates of resisting craving during cigarette cue exposure. *Biological Psychiatry, 62,* 642–651.

Brody, A. L., Saxena, S., Mandelkern, M. A., Fairbanks, L. A., Ho, M. L., & Baxter, L. R. (2001). Brain metabolic changes associated with symptom factor improvement in major depressive disorder. *Biological Psychiatry, 50,* 171–178.

Brody, A. L., Saxena, S., Schwartz, J. M., Stoessel, P. W., Maidment, K., Phelps, M. E., et al. (1998). FDG-PET predictors of response to behavioral therapy and pharmacotherapy in obsessive compulsive disorder. *Psychiatry Research: Neuroimaging, 84,* 1–6.

Brody, A. L., Saxena, S., Stoessel, P., Gillies, L. A., Fairbanks, L. A., Alborzian, S., et al. (2001). Regional brain metabolic changes in patients with major depression treated with either paroxetine or interpersonal therapy. *Archives of General Psychiatry, 58,* 631–640.

Brody, H. (2000). The placebo response: Recent research and implications for family medicine. *Journal of Family Practice, 49,* 649–654.

Brosch, T., Sander, D., & Scherer, K. R. (2007). That baby caught my eye . . . Attention capture by infant faces. *Emotion, 7*(3), 685–689.

Brothers, L. (1997). *Friday's footprint.* New York: Oxford University Press.

Brown, H. D., Kosslyn, S. M., Breiter, H. C., Baer, L., & Jenike, M. A. (1994). Can patients with obsessive-compulsive disorder discriminate between percepts and mental images? A signal detection analysis. *Journal of Abnormal Psychology, 103,* 445–454.

Brown, S. M., Henning, S., & Wellman, C. L. (2005). Mild, short-term stress alters dendritic morphology in rat medial prefrontal cortex. *Cerebral Cortex, 15,* 1714–1722.

Bruder, G. E., Stewart, J. W., Mercier, M. A., Agosti, V., Leite, P., Donovan, S., et al. (1997). Outcome of cognitive-behavioral therapy for depression: Relation to hemispheric dominance for verbal processing. *Journal of Abnormal Psychology, 106*(1), 138–144.

Bruner, J. S. (1990). *Acts of meaning.* Cambridge, MA: Harvard University Press.

Brunet, A., Orr, S. P., Tremblay, J., Robertson, K., Nader, K., & Pitman, R. K. (2008). Effects of post-retrieval propranolol on psychophysiologic responding during subsequent script-given traumatic imagery in post-traumatic stress disorder. *Journal of Psychiatric Research, 42,* 503–506.

Bryant, R. A., Kemp, A. H., Felmingham, K. L., Liddell, B., Oliveri, G., Peduto, A., et al. (2008). Enhanced amygdala and medial prefrontal activation during nonconscious processing of fear in posttraumatic stress disorder: An fMRI study. *Human Brain Mapping, 29,* 517–523.

Buchanan, T. W., Tranel, D., & Adolphs, R. (2006). Impaired memory retrieval correlates with individual differences in cortisol response but not autonomic response. *Learning and Memory, 13,* 382–387.

Buonomano, D. V., & Merzenich, M. M. (1998). Cortical plasticity: From synapses to maps. *Annual Review of Neuroscience, 21,* 149–186.

Bush, G., Frazier, J. A., Rauch, S. L., Seidman, L. J., Whalen, P. J., Jenike, M. A., et al. (1999). Anterior cingulate cortex dysfunction in attention deficit/hyperactivity disorder revealed by fMRI and the counting Stroop. *Biological Psychiatry, 45,* 1542–1552.

Bush, G., Luu, P., & Posner, M. I. (2000). Cognitive and emotional influences in anterior cingulate cortex. *Trends in Cognitive Sciences, 4,* 215–222.

Bush, G., Valera, E. M., & Seidman, L. J. (2005). Functional neuroimaging of attention deficit/hyperactivity disorder: A review and suggested future directions. *Biological Psychiatry, 57,* 1273–1284.

Bush, G., Vogt, B. A., Holmes, J., Dale, A. M., Greve, D., Jenike, M. A., et al. (2002). Dorsal anterior cingulate cortex: A role in reward-based decision making. *Proceedings of the National Academy of Sciences, USA, 99,* 507–512.

Butler, R. W., Braff, D. L., Rauch, J. L., Jenkins, M. A., Sprock, J., & Geyer, M. A. (1990). Physiological evidence of exaggerated startle response in a subgroup of Vietnam veterans with combat-related PTSD. *American Journal of Psychiatry, 147,* 1308–1312.

Cabeza, R., & St. Jacques, P. (2007). Functional neuroimaging of autobiographical memory. *Trends in Cognitive Sciences, 11*(5), 219–227.

Cacioppo, J. T., & Berntson, G. (Eds.). (2004). *Social neuroscience: Key readings in social psychology.* New York: Psychology Press.

Cahill, L., & McGaugh, J. L. (1998). Mechanisms of emotional arousal and lasting declarative memory. *Trends in Neurosciences, 21,* 294–299.

Cahill, L., Prins, B., Weber, M., & McGaugh, J. L. (1994). Beta-adrenergic activation and memory for emotional events. *Nature, 371,* 702–704.

Calder, A. J., Keane, J., Manly, T., Sprengelmeyer, R., Scott, S., Nimmo-Smith, S., et al. (2003). Facial expression recognition across the adult life span. *Neuropsychologia, 41,* 195–202.

Caldji, C., Diorio, J., Anisman, H., & Meaney, M. (2004). Maternal behavior regulated benzodiazepine/GABA receptor subunit expression in brain regions associated with fear in BALB/c and C67BL/6 mice. *Neuropsychopharmacology, 29,* 1344–1352.

Caldji, C., Diorio, J., & Meaney, M. J. (2003). Variations in maternal care alter GABA-sub(A) receptor subunit expression in brain regions associated with fear. *Neuropsychopharmacology, 28,* 1950–1959.

Caldji, C., Francis, D., Sharma, S., Plotsky, P. M., & Meaney, M. J. (2000). The effects of early rearing environment on the development of GABA-sub(A) and central benzodiazepine receptor levels and novelty-induced fearfulness in the rat. *Neuropsychopharmacology, 22,* 219–229.

Caldji, C., Tannenbaum, B., Sharma, S., Francis, D., Plotsky, P. M., & Meaney, M. J. (1998). Maternal care during infancy regulates the development of neural systems mediating the expression of fearfulness in the rat. *Proceedings of the National Academy of Sciences, USA, 95*, 5335–5340.

Cameron, N. M., Champagne, F. A., Parent, C., Fish, E. W., Ozaki-Kuroda, K., & Meaney, M. J. (2005). The programming of individual differences in defensive responses and reproductive strategies in the rat through variations in maternal care. *Neuroscience and Biobehavioral Reviews, 29*, 843–865.

Cameron, N., Fish, E., & Meaney, M. (2008). Maternal influences on the sexual behavior and reproductive success of the female rat. *Hormones and Behavior, 54*, 178–184.

Campbell, J. (1949). *The hero with a thousand faces*. Novato, CA: New World Library.

Canli, T., Desmond, J. E., Zhao, Z., Glover, G., & Gabrieli, J. D. E. (1998). Hemispheric asymmetry for emotional stimuli detected with fMRI. *NeuroReport, 9*, 3233–3239.

Canli, T., & Lesch, K. (2007). Long story short: The serotonin transporter in emotion regulation and social cognition. *Nature Neuroscience, 10*, 1103–1109.

Canli, T., Qiu, M., Omura, K., Congdon, E., Haas, B. W., Amin, Z., et al. (2006). Neural correlates of epigenesis. *Proceedings of the National Academy of Sciences, USA, 103*, 16033–16038.

Cappa, S., Sterzi, R., Vallar, G., & Bisiach, E. (1987). Remission of hemineglect and anosognosia during vestibular stimulation. *Neuropsychologia, 25*, 775–782.

Cappas, N. M., Andres-Hyman, R., & Davidson, L. (2005). What psychotherapists can begin to learn from neuroscience: Seven principles of a brain-based psychotherapy. *Psychotherapy: Theory, Research, Practice, Training, 42*(3), 374–383.

Carr, L., Iacoboni, M., Dubeau, M. C., Mazziotta, J. C., & Lenzi, G. L. (2003). Neural mechanisms of empathy in humans: A relay from neural systems for imitation to limbic areas. *Proceedings of the National Academy of Sciences, USA, 100*, 5497–5502.

Carswell, S. (1993). The potential for treating neurodegenerative disorders with NGF-inducing compounds. *Experimental Neurology, 124*, 36–42.

Carvey, P. M. (1998). *Drug action in the central nervous system*. New York: Oxford University Press.

Casey, B. J., Castellanos, F. X., & Giedd, J. N. (1997). Implications of right frontostriatal circuitry in response inhibition and attention-deficit/hyperactivity disorder. *Journal of the American Academy of Child and Adolescent Psychiatry, 36*, 374–383.

Casey, B. J., Galvan, A., & Hare, T. A. (2005). Changes in cerebral functional organization during cognitive development. *Current Opinion in Neurobiology, 15*, 239–244.

Castellanos, F. X., Lee, P., Sharp, W., Jeffries, N., Greenstein, D., Clasen, L., et al. (2002). Developmental trajectories of brain volume abnormalities in children and adolescents with attention-deficit/hyperactivity disorder. *American Medical Association Journal, 288,* 1740–1748.

Castelli, F., Glaser, D. E., & Butterworth, B. (2006). Discrete and analogue quantity processing in the parietal lobe: A functional MRI study. *Proceedings of the National Academy of Sciences, USA, 103,* 4693–4698.

Ceci, S., & Bruch, M. (1993). Suggestibility of the child witness: A historical review and synthesis. *Psychological Bulletin, 113,* 403–439.

Chambers, R. A., Bremner, J. D., Moghaddam, B., Southwick, S. M., Charney, D. S., & Krystal, J. H. (1999). Glutamate and posttraumatic stress disorder: Toward a psychobiology of dissociation. *Seminars in Clinical Neuropsychiatry, 4*(4), 274–281.

Chaminade, T., & Decety, J. (2002). Leader or follower? Involvement of the inferior parietal lobule in agency. *NeuroReport, 13,* 1975–1978.

Champagne, D., Bagot, R., Hasselt, F., Meaney, M., Kloet, E., Joels, M., et al. (2008). Maternal care and hippocampal plasticity: Evidence for experience-dependent structural plasticity, altered synaptic function, and differential responsiveness to glucocorticoids and stress. *Journal of Neuroscience, 28,* 6037–6045.

Champagne, F., Diorio, J., Sharma, S., & Meaney, M. J. (2001). Naturally occurring variations in maternal behavior in the rat are associated with differences in estrogen-inducible central oxytocin receptors. *Proceedings of the National Academy of Sciences, USA, 98,* 12736–12741.

Champagne, F. A., Francis, D. D., Mar, A., & Meaney, M. J. (2003). Variations in maternal care in the rat as a mediating influence for the effects of environment on development. *Physiology and Behavior, 79,* 359–371.

Champagne, F., Ian, C., Weaver, G., Diorio, J., Dymov, S., Szyf, M., et al. (2006). Maternal care associated with methylation of the estrogen receptor-a1b promoter and estrogen receptor-a expression in the medial preoptic area of female offspring. *Endocrinology, 147,* 2909–2915.

Chapman, L. F., Walter, R. D., Markham, C. H., Rand, R. W., & Crandall, P. H. (1967). Memory changes induced by stimulation of hippocampus or amygdala in epilepsy patients with implanted electrodes. *Transactions of the American Neurological Association, 92,* 50–56.

Charnov, E. L., & Berrigan, D. (1993). Why do female primates have such long lifespans and so few babies? Or life in the slow lane. *Evolutionary Anthropology, 1,* 191–194.

Chavez, C. M., McGaugh, J. L., & Weinberger, N. M. (2009). The basolateral amygdala modulates specific sensory memory representations in the cerebral cortex. *Neurobiology of Learning of Memory, 91,* 382–392.

Cheng, D. T., Knight, D. C., Smith, C. N., & Helmstetter, F. J. (2006). Human amygdala activity during the expression of fear responses. *Behavioral Neuroscience, 120,* 1187–1195.

Chiron, C., Jambaque, I., Nabbout, R., Lounes, R., Syrota, A., & Dulac, O. (1997). The right brain is dominant in human infants. *Brain, 120,* 1057–1065.

Chochon, F., Cohen, L., Demoortele, S., & Dehaene, S. (1999). Differential contributions of the left and right parietal lobules to number processing. *Journal of Cognitive Neuroscience, 11*(6), 617–630.

Christakou, A., Robbins, T. W., & Everitt, B. J. (2004). Prefrontal cortical-ventral striatal interactions involved in affective modulation of attentional performance: Implications for corticostriatal circuit function. *Journal of Neuroscience, 24*, 773–780.

Christensen, A. J., Edwards, D. L., Wiebe, J. S., Benotsch, E. G., McKelvey, L., Andrews, M., et al. (1996). Effect of verbal self-disclosure on natural killer cell activity: Moderating influence of cynical hostility. *Psychosomatic Medicine, 58*, 150–155.

Christensen, H., Henderson, A. S., Griffiths, K., & Levings, C. (1997). Does ageing inevitably lead to declines in cognitive performance? A longitudinal study of elite academics. *Personality and Individual Differences, 23*, 67–78.

Christman, S. D. (1994). The many sides of the two sides of the brain. *Brain and Cognition, 26*, 91–98.

Christodoulou, G. N., & Malliara-Loulakaki, S. (1981). Delusional misidentification syndromes and cerebral "dysrhythmia." *Psychiatrica Clinica, 14*, 245–251.

Chugani, H. T. (1998). A critical period of brain development: Studies of cerebral glucose utilization with PET. *Preventive Medicine, 27*, 184–188.

Chugani, H. T., & Phelps, M. E. (1991). Imaging human brain development with positron emission tomography. *Journal of Nuclear Medicine, 32*, 23–26.

Chugani, H. T., Phelps, M. E., & Mazziotta, J. C. (1987). Positron emission tomography study of human brain functional development. *Annals of Neurology, 22*, 487–497.

Claeys, K. G., Lindsey, D. T., De Schutter, E., & Orban, G. A. (2003). A higher order motion region in human inferior parietal lobule: Evidence from fMRI. *Neuron, 40*, 631–642.

Classen, J., Liepert, J., Wise, S. P., Hallett, M., & Cohen, L. G. (1998). Rapid plasticity of human cortical movements representation induced by practice. *Journal of Neurophysiology, 79*, 1117–1123.

Clovis, C., Pollock, J., Goodman, R., Impey, S., Dunn, J., Mandel, G., et al. (2005). Epigenetic mechanisms and gene networks in the nervous system. *Journal of Neuroscience, 25*, 10379–10389.

Coan, J. A., Allen, J. B., & Harmon-Jones, E. (2001). Voluntary facial expression and hemispheric asymmetry over the frontal cortex. *Psychophysiology, 38*, 912–925.

Coan, J. A., Schaefer, H. S., & Davidson, R. J. (2006). Lending a hand: Social regulation of the neural response to threat. *Psychological Science, 17*, 1032–1039.

Cobb, S. (1944). *Foundations of neuropsychiatry*. Baltimore: Williams and Wilkins.

Coccaro, E. F., Siever, L. J., Klar, H. M., & Maurer, G. (1989). Serotonergic studies in patients with affective and personality disorders. *Archives of General Psychiatry, 46*, 587–598.

Cogill, S. R., Caplan, H. L., Alexandra, H., Robson, K. M., & Kumar, R. (1986). Impact of maternal postnatal depression on cognitive development of young children. *British Medical Journal, 292,* 1165–1167.

Cohen, R. A., Grieve, S., Hoth, K. F., Paul, R. H., Sweet, L., Tate, D., et al. (2006). Early life stress and morphometry of the adult anterior cingulate cortex and caudate nuclei. *Biological Psychiatry, 59*(10), 975–982.

Colby, C. L. (1998). Action-oriented spatial reference frames in cortex. *Neuron, 20,* 15–24.

Colby, C. L., & Goldberg, M. E. (1999). Space and attention in parietal cortex. *Annual Review of Neuroscience, 22,* 319–349.

Collette, J., Millam, R., Klasing, K., & Wakenell, P. (2000). Neonatal handling of Amazon parrots alters the stress response and immune function. *Applied Animal Behavior Science, 66,* 335–349.

Compton, D. M., Bachman, L. D., Brand, D., & Avet, T. L. (2000). Age-associated changes in cognitive function in highly educated adults: Emerging myths and realities. *International Journal of Geriatric Psychiatry, 15,* 75–85.

Condren, R. M., & Thakore, J. H. (2001). Cushing's disease and melancholia. *Stress, 4,* 91–119.

Conrad, C. D., Lupien, S. J., & McEwen, B. S. (1999). Support for a bimodal role for type II adrenal steroid receptors in spatial memory. *Neurobiology of Learning and Memory, 72,* 39–46.

Coplan, J. D., & Lydiard, R. B. (1998). Brain circuits in panic disorder. *Biological Psychiatry, 44,* 1264–1276.

Corbetta, M., & Shulman, G. (2002). Control of goal-directed and stimulus-driven attention in the brain. *Nature Reviews Neuroscience, 3,* 201–215.

Corcoran, K. A., & Quirk, G. J. (2007). Activity in prelimbic cortex is necessary for the expression of learned, but not innate, fears. *Journal of Neuroscience, 27,* 840–844.

Coren, S., & Porac, C. (1977). Fifty centuries of right-handedness: The historical record. *Science, 198,* 631–632.

Corina, D. P., Vaid, J., & Bellugi, U. (1992). The linguistic basis of left hemisphere specialization. *Science, 255,* 1258–1260.

Cornette, L., Dupont, P., Salmon, E., & Orban, G. (2001). The neural substrate of orientation working memory. *Journal of Cognitive Neuroscience, 13,* 813–828.

Corrigan, F. (2004). Psychothrapy as assisted homeostasis: Activation of emotional processing mediated by the anterior cingulate cortex. *Medical Hypothesis, 63,* 968–973.

Costela, C., Tejedor-Real, P., & Gibert-Rahola, A. (1995). Effects of neonatal handling on learned helplessness model of depression. *Physiology and Behavior, 57*(2), 407–410.

Coutinho, S. V., Plotsky, P. M., Sablad, M., Miller, J. C., Zhou, H., Bayati, A. I., et al. (2002). Neonatal maternal separation alters stress-induced responses to viscerosomatic nociceptive stimuli in rat. *American Journal of Physiology Gastrointestinal and Liver Physiology, 282,* G307–G316.

Cowan, W. M., & Kandel, E. R. (2001). A brief history of synapses and synaptic transmission. In W. M. Cowan, T. C. Sudhof, & C. F. Stevens (Eds.), *Synapses* (pp. 1–88). Baltimore: Johns Hopkins University Press.

Cozolino, L. J. (1997). The intrusion of early implicit memory into adult consciousness. *Dissociation, 10,* 44–53.

Cozolino, L. J. (2006). *The neuroscience of human relationships: Attachment and the developing social brain.* New York: Norton.

Cozolino, L. J. (2008). *The healthy aging brain: Sustaining attachment, attaining wisdom.* New York: Norton.

Crick, F. (1994). *The astonishing hypothesis: The scientific search for the soul.* New York: Charles Scribner's Sons.

Critchley, H. (2005). Neural mechanism of autonomic, affective, and cognitive integration. *Journal of Comparative Neurology, 493,* 154–166.

Critchley, H., Daly, E., Phillips, M., Brammer, M., Bullmore, E., Williams, S., et al. (2000). Explicit and implicit mechanisms for processing of social information from facial expressions: A functional magnetic resonance imaging study. *Human Brain Mapping, 9,* 93–105.

Critchley, H. D., Melmed, R. N., Featherstone, E., Mathias, C. J., & Dolan, R. J. (2002). Volitional control of autonomic arousal: A functional magnetic resonance study. *NeuroImage, 16,* 909–919.

Critchley, H. D., Wiens, S., Rotshtein, P., Öhman, A., & Solan, R. J. (2004). Neural systems supporting interoceptive awareness. *Nature Neuroscience, 7,* 189–195.

Crittenden, P. M., & DiLalla, D. L. (1988). Compulsive compliance: The development of an inhibitory coping strategy in infancy. *Journal of Abnormal Child Psychology, 16,* 585–599.

Crowell, J. A., Treboux, D., & Waters, E. (2002). Stability of attachment representations: The transition to marriage. *Developmental Psychology, 38,* 467–479.

Culham, J. C., & Kanwisher, N. G. (2001). Neuroimaging of cognitive functions in human parietal cortex. *Current Opinion in Neurobiology, 11,* 157–163.

Cummings, J. L. (1993). Frontal-subcortical circuits and human behavior. *Archives of Neurology, 50,* 873–880.

Cummings, J. L., & Frankel, M. (1985). Gilles de la Tourette syndrome and the neurological basis of obsessions and compulsions. *Biological Psychiatry, 20,* 117–126.

Cutting, J. (1992). The role of the right hemisphere in psychiatric disorders. *British Journal of Psychiatry, 160,* 583–588.

Czéh, B., Müller-Keuker, J. I. H., Rygula, R., Abumaria, N., Hiemke, C., Domenici, E., et al. (2007). Chronic social stress inhibits cell proliferation in the adult medial prefrontal cortex: Hemispheric asymmetry and reversal by fluoxetine treatment. *Neuropsychopharmacology, 32,* 1490–1503.

Dalla, C., Bangasser, D. A., Edgecomb, C., & Shors, T. J. (2007). Neurogenesis and learning: Acquiring and asymptotic performance predict how many cells survive in the hippocampus. *Neurobiology of Learning and Memory, 88,* 143–148.

Damasio, A. R. (1994). *Descartes' error.* New York: Putnam and Sons.

Damasio, A. R., Grabowski, T. J., Bechara, A., Damasio, H., Ponto, L. L. B., Parvizi, J., et al. (2000). Subcortical and cortical brain activity during the feeling of self-generated emotions. *Nature Neuroscience, 3,* 1049–1056.

Daskalakis, Z. J., Christensen, B. K., Fitzgerald, P. B., & Chen, R. (2002). Transcranial magnetic stimulation: A new investigational and treatment tool in psychiatry. *Journal of Neuropsychiatry Clinical Neuroscience, 14,* 406–415.

Davidson, R. J. (1999). The neurobiology of personality and personality disorders. In D. S. Charney, E. J. Nestler, & B. S. Bunney (Eds.), *Neurobiology of mental illness* (pp. 841–854). New York: Oxford University Press.

Davidson, R. J. (2000). Affective style, psychopathology, and resilience: Brain mechanisms and plasticity. *American Psychologist, 55,* 1196–1214.

Davidson, R. J. (2002). Anxiety and affective style: Role of prefrontal cortex and amygdala. *Biological Psychiatry, 51,* 68–80.

Davidson, R. J. (2004). Well-being and affective style: Neural substrates and biobehavioural correlates. *Philosophical Transactions of the Royal Society: Biological Sciences, 359,* 1395–1411.

Davidson, R. J., Ekman, P., Saron, C. D., Senulis, J. A., & Friesen, W. V. (1990). Approach-withdrawal and cerebral asymmetry: Emotional expression and brain physiology I. *Journal of Personality and Social Psychology, 58,* 330–341.

Davidson, R. J., & Fox, N. A. (1982). Asymmetrical brain activity discriminates between positive and negative affective stimuli in human infants. *Science, 218,* 1235–1237.

Davidson, R. J., & Fox, N. A. (1989). Frontal brain asymmetry predicts infants' response to maternal separation. *Journal of Abnormal Psychology, 98,* 127–131.

Davidson, R. J., Irwin, W., Anderle, M. J., & Kalin, N. H. (2003). The neural substrates of affective processing in depressed patients treated with venlafaxine. *American Journal of Psychiatry, 160,* 64–75.

Davidson, R. J., Jackson, D. C., & Kalin, N. H. (2000). Emotion, plasticity, context, regulation: Perspectives from affective neuroscience. *Psychological Bulletin, 126,* 890–909.

Davidson, R. J., Kabat-Zinn, J., Schumacher, J., Rosenkranz, M., Muller, D., Santorelli, S. F., et al. (2003). Alterations in brain and immune function produced by mindfulness meditation. *Psychosomatic Medicine, 65,* 564–570.

Davis, M. (1992). The role of the amygdala in fear and anxiety. *Annual Review of Neuroscience, 15,* 353–375.

Davis, M. (1997). Neurobiology of fear responses: The role of the amygdala. *Journal of Neuropsychiatry and Clinical Neurosciences, 9,* 382–402.

Davis, M. (1998). Are different parts of the extended amygdala involved in fear versus anxiety? *Biological Psychiatry, 44,* 1239–1247.

Davis, M., Myers, K. M., Chhatwal, J., & Ressler, K. J. (2006). Pharmacological treatments that facilitate extinction of fear: Relevance to psychotherapy. *Journal of the American Society for Experimental NeuroTherapeutics, 3,* 82–96.

De Bellis, M. D., Baum, A. S., Birmaher, B., Keshavan, M. S., Eccard, C. H., Boring, A. M., et al. (1999). Developmental traumatology part I: Biological stress systems. *Biological Psychiatry, 45*, 1259–1270.

De Bellis, M. D., Keshavan, M. S., Clark, D. B., Casey, B. J., Giedd, J. N., Boring, A. M., et al. (1999). Developmental traumatology part II: Brain development. *Biological Psychiatry, 45*, 1271–1284.

de Casper, A. J., & Fifer, W. P. (1980). Of human bonding: Newborns prefer their mother's voices. *Science, 208*, 1174–1176.

Decety, J. (1994). Mapping motor representations with positron emission tomography. *Nature, 371*, 600–602.

Decety, J., Chaminade, T., Grèzes, J., & Meltzoff, A. N. (2002). A PET exploration of the neural mechanisms involved in reciprocal imitation. *NeuroImage, 15*, 265–272.

Decety, J.. & Lamm, C. (2006). Human empathy through the lens of social neuroscience. *Scientific World Journal, 6*, 1146–1163.

Dehaene, S., Molko, N., Cohen, L., & Wilson, A. J. (2004). Arithmetic and the brain. *Current Opinion in Neurobiology, 14*, 218–224.

Dehaene, S., Piazza, M., Pinel, P., & Cohen, L. (2003). Three parietal circuits for number processing. *Cognitive Neuropsychology, 20*(3), 487–506.

de Lanerolle, N. C., Kim, J. H., Robbins, R. J., & Spencer, D. D. (1989). Hippocampal interneuron loss and plasticity in human temporal lobe epilepsy. *Brain Research, 495*, 387–395.

Dennett, D. C. (1991). *Consciousness explained.* Boston: Little, Brown.

Derryberry, D., & Reed, M. A. (2002). Anxiety-related attentional biases and their regulation by attentional control. *Journal of Abnormal Psychology, 111*(2), 225–236.

DeRubeis, R. J., Hollon, S. D., Amsterdam, J. D., Shelton, R. C., Young, P. R., Salomon, R. M., et al. (2005). Cognitive therapy vs. medications in the treatment of moderate to severe depression. *Archives of General Psychiatry, 62*, 409–416.

Desimone, R. (1991). Face-selective cells in the temporal cortex of monkeys. *Journal of Cognitive Neuroscience, 3*, 1–8.

Devinsky, O. (2000). Right cerebral hemisphere dominance for a sense of corporeal and emotional self. *Epilepsy and Behavior, 1*, 60–73.

Devinsky, O., Morrell, M. J., & Vogt, B. A. (1995). Contributions of anterior cingulate cortex to behavior. *Brain, 118*, 279–306.

De Waal, F. (1989). *Peacemaking among primates.* New York: Penguin Books.

Diamond, D. M., Bennett, M. C., Fleshner, M., & Rose, G. M. (1992). Inverted-U relationships between the level of peripheral corticosterone and the magnitude of hippocampal primed burst potentiation. *Hippocampus, 2*(4), 421–430.

Diamond, M. C., Krech, D., & Rosenweig, M. R. (1964). The effects of enriched environment on the histology of the rat cerebral cortex. *Journal of Comparative Neurology, 123*, 111–119.

Diamond, M. C., Law, F., Rhodes, H., Lindner, B., Rosenweig, M. R., Krech, D., et al. (1966). Increases of cortical depth and glia numbers in rats subjected to enriched environments. *Journal of Comparative Neurology, 128,* 117–126.

Diamond, M. C., Scheibel, A. B., Murphy, G. M., & Harvey, T. (1985). On the brain of a scientist: Albert Einstein. *Experimental Neurology, 88,* 198–204.

Dias, R., Robbins, T. W., & Roberts, A. C. (1996). Dissociation in prefrontal cortex of affective and attentional shifts. *Nature, 380,* 69–72.

Dimond, S. J., & Farrington, L. (1977). Emotional response to films shown to the right or left hemisphere of the brain measured by heart rate. *Acta Psychologica, 41,* 255–260.

Diorio, J., & Meaney, M. (2007). Maternal programming of defensive responses through sustained effects on gene expression. *Journal of Psychiatry and Neuroscience, 32*(4), 275–285.

Dolan, R. J. (1999). On the neurology of morals. *Nature Neuroscience, 2,* 927–929.

Dolan, R. (2007). Keynote address: Revaluing the orbital prefrontal cortex. *Annals of the New York Academy of Sciences, 1121,* 1–9.

Dolcos, F., & McCarthy, G. (2006). Brain systems mediating cognitive interference by emotional distraction. *Journal of Neuroscience. 26,* 2072–2079.

Domes, G., Rothfischer, J., Reichwald, U., & Hautzinger, M. (2005). Inverted-U function between salivary cortisol and retrieval of verbal memory after hydrocortisone treatment. *Behavioral Neuroscience, 119*(2), 512–517.

Dougherty, D. D., Rauch, S. L., Deckerbach, T., Marci, C., Loh, R., Shin, L. M., et al. (2004). Ventromedial prefrontal cortex and amygdala dysfunction during an anger induction positron emission tomography study in patients with major depressive disorder with anger attacks. *Archives of General Psychology, 61,* 795–804.

Dougherty, R. F., Ben-Shachar, M., Deutsch, G. K., Hernandez, A., Fox, G. R., & Wandell, B. A. (2007). Temporal-callosal pathway diffusivity predicts phonological skills in children. *Proceedings of the National Academy of Sciences, USA, 104,* 8556–8561.

Douglas, R. J. (1967). The hippocampus and behavior. *Psychological Bulletin, 67,* 416–442.

Douglas, R. J., & Pribram, K. H. (1966). Learning and limbic lesions. *Neuropsychologia, 4,* 197–220.

Drake, R. A. (1984). Lateral asymmetry of personal optimism. *Journal of Research in Personality, 18,* 497–507.

Drake, R. A., & Seligman, M. E. P. (1989). Self-serving biases in causal attributions as a function of altered activation asymmetry. *International Journal of Neuroscience, 45,* 199–204.

Dranovsky, A., & Hen, R. (2006). Hippocampal neurogenesis: Regulation by stress and antidepressants. *Biological Psychiatry, 59,* 1136–1143.

Drevets, W. C. (1998). Functional neuroimaging studies of depression: The anatomy of melancholia. *Annual Review of Medicine, 49,* 341–361.

Drevets, W. C., & Raichle, M. E. (1998). Reciprocal suppression of regional cerebral blood during emotional versus higher cognitive processes: Implications for interactions between emotion and cognition. *Cognition and Emotion, 12*(3), 353–385.

Driver, J., & Mattingley, J. B. (1998). Parietal neglect and visual awareness. *Nature Neuroscience, 1*(1), 17–22.

Dudai, Y. (2006). Reconsolidation: The advantage of being refocused. *Current Opinion in Neurobiology, 16*, 174–178.

Dunbar, R. I. (1996). *Grooming, gossip, and the evolution of language.* Cambridge: Harvard University Press.

Durston, S., Tottenham, N. T., Thomas, K. M., Davidson, M. C., Eigsti, I., Yang, Y., et al. (2003). Differential patterns of striatal activation in young children with and without ADHD. *Biological Psychiatry, 53*, 871–878.

Dwivedi, Y., Rizavi, H. S., Conley, R. R., Roberts, R. C., Tamminga, C. A., & Pandey, G. N. (2003). Altered gene expression of brain-derived neurotrophic factor and receptor tyrosine kinase B in postmortem brain of suicide subjects. *Archives of General Psychiatry, 60*, 804–815.

Eales, L. A. (1985). Song learning in zebra finches: Some effects of song model availability on what is learnt and when. *Animal Behavior, 37*, 507–508.

Edelman, G. M. (1987). *Neural Darwinism.* New York: Basic Books.

Edelman, G. M. (1989). *The remembered present: A biological theory of consciousness.* New York: Basic Books.

Edin, F., Macoveanu, J., Olesen, P., Tegner, J., & Klingberg, T. (2007). Stronger synaptic connectivity as a mechanism behind development of working memory-related brain activity during childhood. *Journal of Cognitive Neuroscience, 19*(5), 750–760.

Egeland, B., & Farber, E. A. (1984). Infant-mother attachment: Factors related to its development and changes over time. *Child Development, 55*, 753–771.

Eichenbaum, H. (1992). The hippocampal system and declarative memory in animals. *Journal of Cognitive Neuroscience, 4*, 217–231.

Eisenberg, L. (1995). The social construction of the human brain. *American Journal of Psychiatry, 152*, 1563–1575.

Ekman, P., & Davidson, R. J. (1993). Voluntary smiling changes regional brain activity. *Psychological Science, 4*, 342–347.

Elbert, T., Flor, H., Birbaumer, N., Knecht, S., Hampson, S., Larbig, W., et al. (1994). Extensive reorganization of the somatosensory cortex in adult humans after nervous system injury. *NeuroReport, 5*, 2593–2597.

Elbert, T., Pantev, C., Wienbruch, C., Rockstroh, B., & Taub, E. (1995). Increased cortical representation of the fingers of the left hand in string players. *Science, 270*, 305–307.

Eliot, L. (1999). *What's going on in there? How the brain and mind develop in the first five years of life.* New York: Bantam Books.

Ellenberger, H. F. (1970). *The discovery of the unconscious.* New York: Basic Books.

Elliott, R., Agnew, Z., & Deakin, J. (2008). Medial orbitofrontal cortex codes relative rather than absolute value of financial rewards in humans. *European Journal of Neuroscience, 77,* 2213–2218.

Elliott, R., Friston, K. J., & Dolan, R. J. (2000). Dissociable neural responses in human reward systems. *Journal of Neuroscience, 20,* 6159–6165.

Ellis, A. (1962). *Reason and emotion in psychotherapy.* Secaucus, NJ: Lyle Stuart.

Elvander-Tottie, E., Eriksson, T. M., Sandin, J., & Ögren, S. O. (2006) N-methyl-d-aspartate receptors in the medial septal area have a role in spatial and emotional learning in the rat. *Neuroscience, 142*(4), 963–978.

Encinas, J. M., Vaahtokari, A., & Enikolopov, G. (2006). Fluoxetine targets early progenitor cells in the adult brain. *Proceedings of the National Academy of Sciences, USA, 103,* 8233–8238.

Eriksson, P. S., Perfileva, E., Bjork-Eriksson, T., Alborn, A. M., Nordborg, C., Peterson, D. A., et al. (1998). Neurogenesis in the adult human hippocampus. *Nature Medicine, 4,* 1313–1317.

Esch, T., & Stefano, G. B. (2005). The neurobiology of love. *Neuroendocrinology Letters, 26*(3), 175–192.

Eslinger, P. J. (1998). Neurological and neuropsychological bases of empathy. *European Neurology, 39,* 193–199.

Etchison, M., & Kleist, D. (2000). Review of narrative therapy: Research and utility. *The Family Journal, 8*(1), 61–66.

Etkin, A., Phil, M., Pittenger, C., Polan, H. J., & Kandel, E. R. (2005). Toward a neurobiology of psychotherapy: Basic science and clinical applications. *Journal of Neuropsychiatry Clinical Neuroscience, 17,* 145–158.

Falkai, P., & Bogerts, B. (1986). Cell loss in the hippocampus of schizophrenics. *European Archives of Psychiatry and Neurological Sciences, 236,* 154–161.

Federspiel, A., Volpe, U., Horn, H., Dierks, T., Franck, A., Vannini, P., et al. (2005). Motion standstill leads to activation of inferior parietal lobe. *Human Brain Mapping, 27,* 340–349.

Feinberg, T. E., & Shapiro, R. M. (1989). Misidentification-reduplication and the right hemisphere. *Neuropsychiatry, Neuropsychology, and Behavioral Neurology, 2,* 39–48.

Feldman, R., Greenbaum, C. W., & Yirimiya, N. (1999). Mother-infant affect synchrony as an antecedent of the emergence of self-control. *Developmental Psychology, 35,* 223–231.

Fellin, T., Pascual, O., & Haydon, P. G. (2006). Astrocytes coordinate synaptic networks: Balanced excitation and inhibition. *Physiology, 21,* 208–215.

Fernandes, C. C., Pinto-Duarte, A., Ribeiro, J. A., & Sebastião, A. M. (2008). Postsynaptic action of brain-derived neurotrophic factor attenuates α7 nicotinic acetylcholine receptor-mediated responses in hippocampal internerons. *Journal of Neuroscience, 28,* 5611–5618.

Fias, W., Lammertyn, J., Caessens, B., & Orban, G. (2007). Processing of abstract knowledge in the horizontal segment of the intraparietal sulcus. *Journal of Neuroscience, 27,* 8952–8957.

Fias, W., Lammertyn, J., Reynvoet, B., Dupont, P., & Orban, G. (2003). Parietal representation of symbolic and nonsymbolic magnitude. *Journal of Cognitive Neuroscience, 15*(1), 47–56.

Field, T. M. (1997). The treatment of depressed mothers and their infants. In L. Murry & P. J. Cooper (Eds.), *Postpartum depression and child development* (pp. 221–236). New York: Guilford.

Field, T., & Diego, M. (2008a). Cortisol: The culprit prenatal stress variable. *International Journal of Neuroscience, 118*, 1181–1205.

Field, T., & Diego, M. (2008b). Maternal depression effects on infant frontal EEG asymmetry. *International Journal of Neuroscience, 118*, 1081–1108.

Field, T., Diego, M., & Hernandez-Reif, M. (2006). Prenatal depression effects on the fetus and newborn: A review. *Infant Behavior and Development, 29*, 445–455.

Field, T. M., Gizzle, N., Scafidi, F., Abrams, S., Richardson, S., Kuhn, C., et al. (1996). Massage therapy for infants of depressed mothers. *Infant Behavior and Development, 19*, 107–112.

Field, T. M., Healy, B., Goldstein, S., & Guthertz, M. (1990). Behavior-state matching and synchrony in mother-infant interactions of nondepressed versus depressed dyads. *Developmental Psychology, 26*, 7–14.

Field, T. M., Healy, B., Goldstein, S., Perry, S., & Bendell, D. (1988). Infants of depressed mothers show "depressed" behavior even with nondepressed adults. *Child Development, 59*, 1569–1579.

Field, T. M., Woodson, R., Greenberg, R., & Cohen, D. (1982). Discrimination and imitation of facial expressions by neonates. *Science, 218*, 179–181.

Figiel, G. S., Epstein, C., McDonald, W. M., Amazon-Leece, J., Figiel, L., Saldivia, A., et al. (1998). The use of rapid-rate transcranial magnetic stimulation (rTMS) in refractory depression. *Journal of Clinical Neuropsychiatry and Clinical Neurosciences, 10*, 20–25.

Fine, M. L. (1989). Embryonic, larval and adult development of the sonic neuromuscular system in the oyster toadfish. *Brain, Behavior and Evolutions, 34*, 13–24.

Fischer, K. W. (1987). Relations between brain and cognitive development. *Child Development, 58*, 623–632.

Fischer, K. W., Shaver, P. R., & Carnochan, P. (1990). How emotions develop and how they organize development. *Cognition and Emotion, 4*, 81–127.

Fish, E. W., Shahrokh, D., Bagot, R., Caldji, C., Bredy, T., Szyf, M., et al. (2004). Epigenetic programming of stress responses through variations in maternal care. *Annals of the New York Academy of Sciences, 1036*, 167–180.

Fisher, H. E. (1998). Lust, attraction, and attachment in mammalian reproduction. *Human Nature, 9*, 23–52.

Fisher, H. E. (2004). *Why we love: The nature and chemistry of romantic love*. New York: Holt Paperbacks.

Fisher, P. M., Meltzer, C. C., Ziolko, S. K., Price, J. C., Moses-Kolko, E. L., Berga, S. L., et al. (2006). Capacity for 5-HT1A—mediated autoregulation predicts amygdala reactivity. *Nature Neuroscience, 9*(11), 1362–1363.

Fish-Murry, C. C., Koby, E. V., & van der Kolk, B. A. (1987). Evolving ideas: The effects of abuse on children's thought. In B. A. van der Kolk (Ed.), *Psychological trauma* (pp. 89–110). Washington, DC: American Psychiatric Press.

Fleming, A. S., & Korsmit, M. (1996). Plasticity in the maternal circuit: Effects of maternal experience on Fos-lir in hypothalamic, limbic, and cortical structures in the postpartum rat. *Behavioral Neuroscience, 110*, 567–582.

Fonagy, P., Gergely, G., Jurist, E., & Target, M. (2002). *Affect regulation, mentalization, and the development of self*. New York: Other Press.

Fonagy, P., Steele, H., & Steele, M. (1991). Maternal representations of attachment during pregnancy predict the organization of infant-mother attachment at one year of age. *Child Development, 62*, 891–905.

Fonagy, P., Steele, M., Steele, H., Moran, G. S., & Higgitt, A. C. (1991). The capacity to understand mental states: The reflective self in parent and child and its significance for security of attachment. *Infant Mental Health Journal, 12*, 201–218.

Forbes, E. E., Shaw, D. S., Silk, J. S., Feng, X., Cohn, J. F., Fox, N. A., et al. (2008). Children's affect expression and frontal EEG asymmetry: Transactional associations with mothers' depressive symptoms. *Journal of Abnormal Child Psychology, 36*, 207–221.

Fowler, C. D., Liu, Y., Ouimet, C., & Wang, Z. (2002). The effects of social environment on adult neurogenesis in the female prairie vole. *Journal of Neurobiology, 51*, 115–128.

Fox, M. D., Snyder, A. Z., Vincent, J. L., Corbetta, M., Van Essen, D. C., & Raichle, M. E. (2005). The human brain is intrinsically organized into dynamic, anticorrelated functional networks. *Proceedings of the National Academy of Sciences, USA, 102*, 9673–9678.

Fox, N. A. (1991). If it's not left it's right: Electroencephalograph asymmetry and the development of emotion. *American Psychologist, 46*, 863–872.

Fox, N. A., & Davidson, R. J. (1986). Taste-elicited changes in facial signs of emotion and the assymetry of brain electrical activity in human newborns. *Neuropsychologia, 24*, 417–422.

Fox, N. A., & Davidson, R. J. (1988). Patterns of brain electrical activity during facial signs of emotion in 10-month-old infants. *Developmental Psychology, 24*, 230–236.

Francis, D., Diorio, J., Plotsky, P., & Meaney, M. (2002). Environmental enrichment reverses the effects of maternal separation on stress reactivity. *Journal of Neuroscience, 22*, 7840–7843.

Frank, J. (1963). *Persuasion and healing*. New York: Schoken Books.

Freedman, L. J., Insel, T. R., & Smith, Y. (2000). Subcortical projections of area 25 (subgenual cortex) of the macaque monkey. *Journal of Comparative Neurology, 421*(2), 172–188.

Freeman, T. W., & Kimbrell, T. (2001). A "cure" for chronic combat-related posttraumatic stress disorder secondary to a right frontal lobe infarct: A case report. *Journal of Neuropsychiatry and Clinical Neurosciences, 13*, 106–109.

Freud, S. (1968). Project for a scientific psychology. In J. Strachey (Ed.), *New introductory lectures on psychoanalysis: Standard edition of the complete psychological works of Sigmund Freud* (Vol. 22), pp. 3–182). London: Hogarth Press. (Original work published in 1895).

Freud, S. (1975). The dynamics of transference. In J. Strachey (Ed.), *The standard edition of the complete psychological works of Sigmund Freud* (Vol. 12, pp. 99–108). London: Hogarth Press. (Original work publlished in 1912).

Frey, S., & Petrides, M. (2000). Orbitofrontal cortex: A key prefrontal region for encoding information. *Proceedings of the National Academy of Sciences, USA, 97*(15), 8723–8727

Freyd, J. J. (1987). Dynamic mental representations. *Psychological Reviews, 94,* 427–438.

Friberg, L., Olsen, T. S., Roland, P. E., Paulsen, O. B., & Lassen, N. A. (1985). Focal increase of blood flow in the cerebral cortex of man during vestibular stimulation. *Brain, 108,* 609–623.

Fricchione, G., & Stefano, G. B. (2005). Placebo neural systems: Nitric oxide, morphine and the dopamine brain reward and motivation circuitries. *Medical Science Monitor, 11*(5), MS54–65.

Frick, R. B. (1982). The ego and the vestibulocerebellar system: Some theoretical perspectives. *Psychoanalytic Quarterly, 51,* 93–122.

Fuente-Fernández, R., Ruth, T. J., Sossi, V., Schulzer, M., Calne, D. B., & Stoessl, A. J. (2001). Expectation and dopamine release: Mechanism of the placebo effect in Parkinson's disease. *Science, 293,* 1164–1166.

Fujikawa, T., Soya, H., Fukuoka, H., Alam, K. S. M., Yoshizato, H., McEwan, B. S., et al. (2000). A biphasic regulation of receptor mRNA expressions for growth hormone, glucocorticoid and mineralocorticoid in the rat dentate gyrus during acute stress. *Brain Research, 874,* 186–193.

Furmark, T., Tillfors, M., Marteinsdottir, I., Fischer, H., Pissiota, A., Långström, B., et al. (2002). Common changes in cerebral blood flow in patients with social phobia treated with citalopram or cognitive-behavioral therapy. *Archives of General Psychiatry, 59,* 425–433.

Fuster, J. M. (1996). Frontal lobe and the cognitive foundation of behavioral action. In A. R. Damasio, H. Damasio, & Y. Christen (Eds.), *Neurobiology of decision-making* (pp. 47–61). Berlin: Springer-Verlag.

Fuster, J. M. (1997). *The prefrontal cortex.* Philadelphia: Lippincott-Raven.

Fuster, J. M. (2004). Upper processing stages of the perception-action cycle. *Trends in Cognitive Science, 8*(4), 143–145.

Fuster, J. M., Bonder, M., & Kroger, J. K. (2000). Cross-modal and cross-temporal association in neurons of frontal cortex. *Nature, 405,* 347–351.

Gablik, S. (1985). *Magritte.* New York: Thames and Hudson.

Gainotti, G. (1972). Emotional behavior and hemispheric side of the lesion. *Cortex, 8,* 41–55.

Galin, D. (1974). Implications for psychiatry of left and right cerebral specialization: A neurophysiological context for unconscious processes. *Archives of General Psychiatry, 31,* 572–583.

Galin, D., Johnstone, J., Nakell, L., & Herron, J. (1979). Development for the capacity for tactile information transfer between hemispheres in normal children. *Science, 204,* 1330–1331.

Gallagher, M., McMahon, R. W., & Schoenbaum, G. (1999). Orbitofrontal cortex and representation of incentive value in associative learning. *Journal of Neuroschince, 19,* 6610–6614.

Gallese, V., Fadiga, L., Fogassi, L., & Rizzolatti, G. (1996). Action recognition in the premotor cortex. *Brain, 119,* 593–609.

Galynker, I. I., Cai, J., Ongseng, F., Fineston, H., Dutta, E., & Serseni, D. (1998). Hypofrontality and negative symptoms in major depressive disorder. *Journal of Nuclear Medicine, 39,* 608–612.

Ganis, G., Kosslyn, S. M., Stose, S., Thompson, W. L., & Yurgelun-Todd, D. A. (2003). Neural correlates of different types of deception: An fMRI investigation. *Cerebral Cortex, 13,* 830–836.

Garavan, H., Ross, T. J., & Stein, E. A. (1999). Right hemisphere dominance of inhibitory control: An event-related functional MRI study. *Proceedings of the National Academy of Sciences, USA, 96,* 8301–8306.

Garoflos, E., Stamatakis, A., Pondiki, S., Apostolou, A., Philippidis, H., & Sylianopoulou, F. (2007). Cellular mechanism underlying the effect of a single exposure to neonatal handling on neurotrophin-3 in the brain of 1-day-old rats. *Neuroscience, 148,* 349–358.

Garoflos, E., Stamatakis, A., Rafrogianni, A., Pondiki, S., & Sylianopoulou, F. (2008). Neonatal handling on the first postnatal day leads to increased maternal behavior and fos levels in the brain of the newborn rat. *Developmental Psychobiology, 50*(7), 704–713.

Gartside, S. E., Leitch, M. M., McQuade, R., & Swarbrick, D. J. (2003). Flattening the glucocorticoid rhythm causes changes in hippocampal expression of messenger RNAs coding structural and functional proteins: Implications for aging and depression. *Neuropsychopharmacology, 28,* 821–829.

Gauthier, I., Tarr, M. J., Moylan, J., Skudlarski, P., Gore, J. C., & Anderson, A. W. (2000). The fusiform "face area" is part of a network that processes faces at the individual level. *Journal of Cognitive Neuroscience, 12,* 495–504.

Gazzaley, A., Rissman, J., Cooney, J., Aaron, R., Seibert, T., Clapp, W., et al. (2007). Functional interactions between prefrontal and visual association cortex contribute to top-down modulation of visual processing. *Cerebral Cortex, 17,* i125–i135.

Gazzaniga, M.S. (1989). Organization of the human brain. *Science, 245,* 947–952.

Gazzaniga, M. S. (1995). Consciousness and the cerebral hemispheres. In M. S. Gazzaniga (Ed.), *The cognitive neuroscience* (pp.1391–1400). Cambridge, MA: MIT Press.

Gazzaniga, M. S., LeDoux, J. E., & Wilson, D. H. (1977). Language, praxis, and the right hemisphere: Clues to some mechanisms of consciousness. *Neurology, 27,* 1144–1147.

Geday, J., Kupers, R., & Gjedde, A. (2007). As time goes by: Temporal constraints on emotional activation of inferior medial prefrontal cortex. *Cerebral Cortex, 17,* 2753–2759.

Gedo, J. E. (1991). *The biology of clinical encounters: Psychoanalysis as a science of mind.* Hillsdale, NJ: Analytic Press.

Gehring, W. J., & Willoughby, A. R. (2002). The medial frontal cortex and the rapid processing of monetary gains and losses. *Science, 295,* 2279–2282.

George, M. D., Wasserman, M. D., Kimbrell, J. T., Little, M. D., Williams, W. E., Danielson, A. L., et al. (1997). Mood improvement following daily left prefrontal repetitive transcranial magnetic stimulation in patients with depression: A placebo-controlled crossover trial. *American Journal of Psychiatry, 154,* 1752–1756.

Geschwind, N., & Galaburda, A. M. (1985). Cerebral lateralization: Biological mechanisms, associations and pathology: I. A hypothesis and a program for research. *Archives of Neurology, 42,* 428–459.

Geuze, E., Vermetten, E., & Bremner, J. D. (2005). MR-based in vivo hippocampal volumetrics: 2. Findings in neuropsychiatric disorders. *Molecular Psychiatry, 10,* 160–184.

Ghashghaei, H. T., & Barbas, H. (2002). Pathways for emotion: Interactions of prefrontal and anterior temporal pathways in the amygdala of the rhesus monkey. *Neuroscience, 115,* 1261–1279.

Ghashghaei, H. T., Hilgetag, C. C., & Barbas, H. (2007). Sequence of information processing for emotions based on the anatomic dialogue between prefrontal cortex and amygdala. *NeuroImage, 34,* 905–923.

Gibson, J. J. (1966). *The senses considered as perceptual systems.* Boston: Houghton Mifflin.

Gilbertson, M. W., Shenon, M. E., Ciszewski, A., Kasai, K., Lasko, N. B., Orr, S. P., et al. (2002). Smaller hippocampal volume predicts pathologic vulnerability to psychological trauma. *Nature Neuroscience, 5,* 1242–1247.

Gilboa, A., Shalev, A., Laor, L., Lester, H., Louzoun, Y., Chisin, R., et al. (2004). Functional connectivity of the prefrontal cortex and the amygdala in posttraumatic stress disorder. *Biological Psychiatry, 55,* 263–272.

Gilliland, B. E., & James, R. K. (1998). *Theories and strategies in counseling and psychotherapy.* Boston: Allyn and Bacon.

Gitlin, M. J. (2007). *The psychotherapist's guide to psychopharmacology.* New York: Free Press.

Glaser, D. (2000). Child abuse and neglect and the brain—A review. *Journal of Child Psychiatry and Allied Disciplines, 41,* 97–116.

Gloor, P. (1978). Inputs and outputs of the amygdala: What the amygdala is trying to tell the rest of the brain. In K. E. Livingston & O. Hornykiewicz (Eds.), *Limbic mechanisms: The continuing evolution of the limbic system concept* (pp. 189–209). New York: Plenum Press.

Goel, V., & Dolan, R. J. (2003). Reciprocal neural response within lateral and ventral medial prefrontal cortex during hot and cold reasoning. *NeuroImage, 20,* 2314–2321.

Goel, V., Grafman, J., Sadato, N., & Hallett, M. (1995). Modeling other minds. *NeuroReport, 6,* 1741–1746.

Goldapple, K., Segal, Z., Garson, C., Lau, M., Bieling, P., Kennedy, S., et al. (2004). Modulation of cortical-limbic pathways in major depression. *Archives of General Psychiatry, 61,* 34–41.

Goldberg, E., & Costa, L. D. (1981). Hemispheric differences in the acquisition and use of descriptive systems. *Brain and Language, 14,* 144–173.

Goldman, P. S. (1971). Functional development of the prefrontal cortex in early life and the problem of neural plasticity. *Experimental Neurology, 32,* 366–387.

Goldman, P. S., & Galkin, T. W. (1978). Prenatal removal of frontal association cortex in the fetal rhesus monkey: Anatomical and functional consequences in postnatal life. *Brain Research, 152,* 451–485.

Goldstein, K. (1939). *The organism: A holistic approach to biology derived from pathological data in man.* New York: American Books.

Goldstein, L. E., Rasmusson, A. M., Bunney, B. S., & Roth, R. H. (1996). Role of the amygdala in the coordination of behavioral, neuroendocrine, and prefrontal cortical monoamine responses to psychological stress in the rat. *Journal of Neuroscience, 16,* 4787–4798.

Goleman, D. (2006). *Emotional Intelligence* (10th ed.). New York: Bantam Books.

Golomb, J., de Leon, M. J., Kluger, A., George, A. E., Tarshish, C., & Ferris, S. H. (1993). Hippocampal atrophy in normal aging: An association with recent memory impairment. *Archives of Neurology, 50,* 967–973.

Goodman, R. R., Snyder, S. H., Kuhar, M. J., & Young, W. S., III. (1980). Differential of delta and mu opiate receptor localizations by light microscope autoradiography. *Proceedings of the National Academy of Sciences, USA, 77,* 2167–2174.

Gottfried, J. A., & Dolan, R. J. (2004). Human orbitofrontal cortex mediates extinction learning while accessing conditioned representations of value. *Nature Neuroscience, 7,* 1145–1153.

Gottfried, J. A., O'Doherty, J., & Dolan, R. J. (2003). Encoding predictive reward value in human amygdala and orbitofrontal cortex. *Science, 301,* 1104–1107.

Gould, E. (2007). How widespread is adult neurogenesis in mammals? *Nature Reviews Neuroscience, 8,* 481–488.

Gould, E., McEwen, B. S., Tanapat, P., Galea, L. A. M., & Fuchs, E. (1997). Neurogenesis in the dentate gyrus of the adult tree shrew is regulated by psychosocial stress and NMDA receptor activation. *Journal of Neuroscience, 17,* 2492–2498.

Gould, E., Reeves, A. J., Fallah, M., Tanapat, P., Gross, C. G., & Fuchs, E. (1999). Hippocampal neurogenesis in adult old world primates. *Proceedings of the National Academy of Sciences, USA, 96,* 5263–5267.

Gould, E., Reeves, A. J., Graziano, M. S. A., & Gross, C. G. (1999). Neurogenesis in the neocortex of adult primates. *Science, 628,* 548–552.

Gould, E., Tanapat, P., Hastings, N. B., & Shors, T. J. (1999). Neurogenesis in adulthood: A possible role in learning. *Trends in Cognitive Sciences, 3,* 186–191.

Gould, E., Woolley, C., & McEwan, B. (1990). Short-term glucocorticoid manipulations affect neuronal morphology and survival in the adult dentate gyrus. *Neuroscience, 37,* 367–375.

Gould, S. J. (1977). *Ontogeny and phylogeny.* Cambridge, MA: Belknap Press.

Grafton, S. T., Arbib, M. A., Fadiga, L., & Rizzolatti, G. (1996). Localization of grasp representations in humans by positron emission tomography. 2: Observation compared with imagination. *Experimental Brain Research, 112,* 103–111.

Gray, J. R., Braver, T. S., & Raichle, M. E. (2002). Integration of emotion and cognition in the lateral prefrontal cortex. *Proceedings of the National Academy of Sciences, USA, 99,* 4115–4120.

Green, A. (1978). Self-destructive behavior in battered children. *American Journal of Psychiatry, 135,* 579–582.

Green, A. (1981). Neurological impairments in maltreated children. *Child Abuse and Neglect, 5,* 129–134.

Greenough, W. T. (1987). Experience effects on the developing and mature brain: Dendritic branching and synaptogenesis. In N. A. Krasnegor, E. M. Blass, M. A. Hofer, & W. P. Smotherman (Eds.), *Perinatal development: A psychobiological perspective* (pp. 195–221). Orlando: Academic Press.

Grefkes, C., & Fink, G. R. (2005). The functional organization of the intraparietal sulcus in humans and monkeys. *Journal of Anatomy, 207,* 3–17.

Griffiths, T. D., Rees, G., Rees, A., Green, G., Witton, C., Rowe, D., et al. (1998). Right parietal cortex is involved in the perception of sound movement in humans. *Nature Neuroscience, 1,* 74–79.

Grisaru, N., Chudakov, B., Yaroslavsky, Y., & Belmaker, R. H. (1998). Transcranial magnetic stimulation in mania: A controlled study. *American Journal of Psychiatry, 155,* 1608–1610.

Gross, C. G. (2000). Neurogenesis in the adult brain: Death of a dogma. *Nature Review of Neuroscience, 1,* 67–73.

Güemes, I., Guillen, V., & Ballesteros, J. (2008). Psychotherapy versus drug therapy in depression in outpatient care. *Actas Esp Psiquiatr, 36*(5), 299–306.

Gundel, H., Lopez-Sala, A., & Ceballos-Baumann, A. O. (2004). Alexithymia correlates with the size of the right anterior cingulate. *Psychosomatic Medicine, 66,* 132–140.

Gunnar, M. R. (1992). Reactivity of the hypothalamic-pituitary-adrenocortical system to stressors in normal infants and children. *Pediatrics, 90*(Suppl. 3), 491–479.

Gunnar, M. R. (1998). Quality of care and buffering of neuroendocrine stress reactions: Potential effects on the developing human brain. *Preventive Medicine, 27,* 208–211.

Gunnar, M. R., & Stone, C. (1984). The effects of positive maternal affect on infant responses to pleasant, ambiguous, and fear-provoking toys. *Child Development, 55*, 1231–1236.

Gurvits, T. V., Gilbertson, M. W., Lasko, N. B., Tarhan, A. S., Simeon, D., Maclin, M. L., et al. (2000). Neurological soft signs in chronic posttraumatic stress disorder. *Archives of General Psychiatry, 57*, 181–183.

Gusnard, D. A., Akbudak, E., Shulman, G. L., & Raichle, M. E. (2002). Medial prefrontal cortex and self-referential mental activity: Relation to a default mode of brain function. *Proceedings of the National Academy of Sciences, USA, 98*, 4259–4264.

Guzowski, J. F., Setlow, B., Wagner, E. K., & McGaugh, J. L. (2001). Experience-dependent gene expression in the rat hippocampus after spatial learning: A comparison of the immediate-early genes Arc, c-fos, and zif268. *Journal of Neuroscience, 21*, 5089–5098.

Halassa, M. M., Fellin, T., & Haydon, P. G. (2007). The tripartite synapse: Roles for gliotransmission in health and disease. *Trends in Molecular Medicine, 13*(2), 54–63.

Halgren, E., Dale, A. M., Sereno, M. I., Tootell, R. B. H., Marinkovic, K., & Rosen, B. R. (1999). Location of human face-selective cortex with respect to retinotopic areas. *Human Brain Mapping, 7*, 29–37.

Halgren, E., Walter, R. D., Cherlow, D. G., & Crandall, P. H. (1978). Mental phenomena evoked by electrical stimulation of the human hippocampal formation and amygdala. *Brain, 101*, 83–117.

Hamilton, C. E. (2000). Continuity and discontinuity of attachment from infancy through adolescence. *Child Development, 71*, 690–694.

Hampden-Turner, C. (1981). Maps of the mind. New York: Macmillan.

Hane, A., & Fox, N. (2006). Ordinary variations in maternal caregiving influence human infants' stress reactivity. *Psychological Science, 17*, 550–556.

Hardingham, G. E., & Bading, H. (2003). The yin and yang of NMDA receptor signaling. *Trends in Neurosciences, 26*(2), 81–89.

Hariri, A. R., Bookheimer, S. Y., & Mazziotta, J. C. (2000). Modulating emotional responses: Effects of a neocortical network on the limbic system. *NeuroReport, 11*(1), 43–48.

Hariri, A. R., Drabant, E. M., & Weinberger, D. R. (2006). Imaging genetics: Perspectives from studies of genetically driven variation in serotonin function and corticolimbic affective processing. *Biological Psychiatry, 59*, 888–897.

Hariri, A. R., Mattay, V. S., Tessitore, A., Fera, F., & Weinberger, D. R. (2003). Neocortical modulation of the amygdala response to fearful stimuli. *Biological Psychiatry, 53*, 494–501.

Harlow, J. (1868). Recovery from the passage of an iron bar through the head. *Publication of the Massachusetts Medical Society, 2*, 329–346.

Harlow, H. F., & Suomi, S. J. (1971). Social recovery by isolation-reared monkeys. *Proceedings of the National Academy of Sciences, USA, 68*, 1534–1538.

Harmon-Jones, E., & Allen, J. J. B. (1998). Anger and frontal brain activity: EEG asymmetry consistent with approach motivation despite negative affective valence. *Journal of Personality and Social Psychology, 74,* 1310–1316.

Harmon-Jones, E., & Sigelman, J. (2001). State anger and prefrontal brain activity: Evidence that insult-related relative left-prefrontal activation is associated with experienced anger and aggression. *Journal of Personality and Social Psychology, 80*(5), 797–803.

Hasselmo, M. E., Rolls, E. T., & Baylis, G. C. (1989). The role of expression and identity in the face-selective responses of neurons in the temporal visual cortex of the monkey. *Behavior Brain Research, 32,* 203–218.

Hawkes, K., O'Connell, J. F., & Jones, N. G. B. (1997). Hadza women's time allocation, offspring provisioning, and the evolution of long postmenopausal life spans. *Current Anthropology, 38,* 551–577.

Hazan, C., & Shaver, P. R. (1990). Love and work: An attachment-theoretical perspective. Journal of Personality and Social Psychology, 59, 270–280.

Hebb, D. O. (1949). *The organization of behavior: A neuropsychological theory.* New York: Wiley.

Heider, F. (1958). *The psychology of interpersonal relations.* New York: Wiley.

Heimer, L., & Van Hoesen, G. W. (2006). The limbic lobe and its output channels: Implications for emotional functions and adaptive behavior. *Neuroscience and Biobehavioral Reviews, 30,* 126–147.

Heimer, L., Van Hoesen, G. W., Trimble, M., & Zahm, D. S. (2008). *Anatomy of neuropsychiatry: The new anatomy of the basal forebrain and its implications for neuropsychiatric illness.* Amsterdam: Academic Press.

Heinz, A., Braus, D. F., Smolka, M. N., Wrase, J., Puls, I., Hermann, D., et al. (2005). Amygdala-prefrontal coupling depends on a genetic variation of the serotonin transporter. *Nature Neuroscience, 8*(1), 20–21.

Henry, R. R., Satz, P., & Saslow, E. (1984). Early brain damage and the ontogenesis of functional asymmetry. *Early Brain Damage, 1,* 253–275.

Hensch, T. K. (2004). Critical period regulation. *Annual Review of Neuroscience, 27,* 549–579.

Henson, R. N. A., Shallice, T., & Dolan, R. J. (1999). Right prefrontal cortex and episodic memory retrieval: A functional MRI test of the monitoring hypothesis. *Brain, 122,* 1367–1381.

Herman, B. A., & Panksepp, J. (1978). Effects of morphine and naloxone on separation distress and approach attachment: Evidence for opiate mediation of social effect. *Pharmacology, Biochemistry and Behavior, 9,* 213–220.

Herman, J. L. (1992). Complex PTSD: A syndrome in survivors of prolonged and repeated trauma. *Journal of Traumatic Stress, 5,* 377–391.

Herschkowitz, N., Kegan, J., & Zilles, K. (1997). Neurobiological basis of behavioral development in the first year. *Neuropediatrics, 28,* 296–306.

Hesse, E. (1999). The adult attachment interview: Historical and current perspectives. In J. Cassidy & P. R. Shaver (Eds.), *Handbook of attachment: Theory, research, and clinical applications* (pp. 395–433). New York: Guilford.

Hirsten, W. & Ramachandran, V. S. (1997). Capgras syndrome: A novel probe for understanding the neural representation of the identity and familiarity of persons. *Proceedings of the Royal Society of London: Biological Sciences, 264,* 437–444.

Hodge, C. J., & Boakye, M. (2001). Biological plasticity: The future of science in neurosurgery. *Neurosurgery, 48,* 2–16.

Holtforth, M. G., Grawe, K., Egger, O., & Berking, M. (2005). Reducing the dreaded: Change of avoidance motivation in psychotherapy. *Psychotherapy Research, 15,* 261–271.

Holthoff, V. A., Beuthien-Baumann, B., Zündorf, G., Triemer, A., Lüdecke, S., Winiecki, P., et al. (2004). Changes in brain metabolism associated with remission in unipolar major depression. *Acta Psychiatrica Scandinavica, 110,* 184–194.

Hood, K. E., Dreschel, N. A., & Granger, D. A. (2003). Maternal behavior changes after immune challenge of neonates with developmental effects on adult social behavior. *Developmental Psychobiology, 42,* 17–34.

Hoppe, K. D. (1977). Split-brains and psychoanalysis. *Psychoanalytic Quarterly, 46,* 220–244.

Hoppe, K. D., & Bogen, J. E. (1977). Alexithymia in twelve commissurotomized patients. *Psychotherapy and Psychosomatics, 28,* 148–155.

Hoshaw, B. A., Malberg, J. E., & Lucki, I. (2005). Central administration of IGF-I and BDNF leads to long-lasing antidepressant-like effects. *Brain Research, 1037,* 204–208.

Hoyle, R. L., Bromberger, B., Groversman, H. D., Klauber, M. R., Dixon, S. D., & Snyder, J. M. (1983). Regional anesthesia during newborn circumcision: Effect on infant pain response. *Clinical Pediatrics (Philadelphia), 22,* 813–818.

Hsu, F., Zhang, G., Raol, Y., Valentino, R., Coulter, D., & Brooks-Kayal, A. (2003). Repeated neonatal handling with maternal separation permanently alters hippocampal GABA receptors and behavioral stress responses. *Proceedings of the National Academy of Sciences, USA, 100,* 12213–12218.

Huang, Z. J., Kirkwood, A., Pizzarusso, T., Porciatti, V., Morales, B., Bear, M. F., et al. (1999). BDNF regulates the maturation of inhibition and the critical period of plasticity in mouse visual cortex. *Cell, 98,* 739–755.

Hubel, D. H., & Wiesel, T. N. (1962). Receptive field binocular interaction and functional architecture in the cat's visual cortex. *Journal of Physiology, 160,* 106–154.

Hurley, R. A., Taber, K. H., Zhang, J., & Hayman, L. A. (1999). Neuropsychiatric presentation of multiple sclerosis. *Journal of Neuropsychiatry and Clinical Neurosciences, 11,* 5–7.

Husain, M., & Nachev, P. (2007). Space and the parietal cortex. *Trends in Cognitive Sciences, 11*(1), 30–36.

Huttenlocher, P. R. (1994). Synaptogenesis in human cerebral cortex. In G. Dawson & K. W. Fischer (Eds.), *Human behavior and the developing brain* (pp. 137–152). New York: Guilford.

Iacoboni, M. (2008). *Mirroring people.* New York: Farrar, Straus and Giroux.

Iacoboni, M., Lieberman, M., Knowlton, I., Moritz, M., Throop, C., & Fiske, A. (2004). Watching social interactions produces dorsomedial prefrontal and medial parietal BOLD fMRI signal increases compared to a resting baseline. *NeuroImage, 21*, 1167–1173.

Ickes, B. R., Pham, T. M., Sanders, L. A., Albeck, D.S., Mohammed, A. H., & Grandholm, A. C. (2000). Long-term environmental enrichment leads to regional increases in neurotrophin levels in rat brains. *Experimental Neurology, 164*, 45–52.

Ince, P. G. (2001). Pathological correlates of late-onset dementia in a multi-centre, community-based population in England and Wales. *The Lancet, 357*, 169–175.

Ingvar, D. H. (1985). "Memory for the future": An essay on the temporal organization of conscious awareness. *Human Neurobiology, 4*, 127–136.

Introini-Collison, I., & McGaugh, J. L. (1987). Naloxone and beta-endorphin alter the effects of post-training epinephrine on retention of an inhibitory avoidance response. *Psychopharmacology, 92*, 229–235.

Irle, E., Exner, C., Thielen, K., Weniger, G., & Ruther, E. (1998). Obsessive-compulsive disorder and ventromedial frontal lesions: Clinical and neuropsychological findings. *American Journal of Psychiatry, 155*, 255–263.

Ito, Y., Teicher, M. H., Glod, C. A., Harper, D., Magnus, E., & Gelbard, H. A. (1993). Increased prevalence of electrophysiological abnormalities in children with psychological, physical, and sexual abuse. *Journal of Neuropsychiatry, 5*, 401–408.

Izard, C. E., Porges, S. W., Simons, R. F., Haynes, O. M., Hyde, C., Parisi, M., et al. (1991). Infant cardiac activity: Developmental changes and relations with attachment. *Developmental Psychology, 27*, 432–439.

Jablonska, B., Gierdalski, M., Kossut, M., & Skangiel-Kramska, J. (1999). Partial blocking of NMDA receptors reduces plastic changes induced by short-lasting classical conditioning in the SL barrel cortex of adult mice. *Cerebral Cortex, 9*, 222–231.

Jackson, D. C., Mueller, C. J., Dolski, I., Dalton, K. M., Nitschke, J. B., Urry, H. L., et al. (2003). Now you feel it, now you don't: Frontal brain electrical asymmetry and individual differences in emotion regulation. *Psychological Science, 14*, 612–617.

Jackson, P. L., & Decety, J. (2004). Motor cognition: A new paradigm to study self-other interactions. *Current Opinion in Neurobiology, 14*, 259–263.

Jacobs, B., Driscoll, L., & Schall, M. (1997). Life-span dendritic and spine changes in areas 10 and 18 of human cortex: A quantitative Golgi study. *Journal of Comparative Neurology, 386*, 661–680.

Jacobs, B., Schall, M., & Scheibel, A. B. (1993). A quantitative dendritic analysis of Wernicke's area in humans: II. Gender, hemispheric, and environmental factors. *Journal of Comparative Neurology, 327*, 97–111.

Jacobs, B., & Scheibel, A. B. (1993). A quantitative dendritic analysis of Wernicke's area in humans: I. Lifespan changes. *Journal of Comparative Neurology, 327*, 83–96.

Jacobs, B. L., van Praag, H., & Gage, F. H. (2000). Depression and the birth and death of brain cells. *American Scientist, 88,* 340–345.

Jacobs, W. J., & Nadel, L. (1985). Stress-induced recovery of fears and phobias. *Psychological Review, 92,* 512–531.

Janoff-Bulman, R. (1992). *Shattered assumptions: Towards a new psychology of trauma.* New York: Free Press.

Jason, G., & Pajurkova, E. (1992). Failure of metacontrol: Breakdown in behavioral unity after lesions of the corpus callosum and inferomedial frontal lobes. *Cortex, 28,* 241–260.

Jaynes, J. (1976). *The origin of consciousness in the breakdown of the bicameral mind.* Boston: Houghton Mifflin.

Jeannerod, M., Arbib, M. A., Rizzolatti, G., & Sakata, H. (1995). Grasping objects: The cortical mechanism of visuomotor transformation. *Trends in Neurosciences, 18,* 314–320.

Jellema, T., Baker, C. I., Wicker, B., & Perrett, D. I. (2000). Neural representation for the perception of the intentionality of actions. *Brain and Cognition, 44,* 280–302.

Jellema, T., Maassen, F., & Perrett, D. I. (2004). Single cell integration of animate form, motion and location in the superior temporal cortex of the macaque monkey. *Cerebral Cortex, 14,* 781–790.

Ji, J., & Maren, S. (2007). Hippocampal involvement in contextual modulation of fear extinction. *Hippocampus, 17,* 749–758.

Johanson, A., Gustafson, L., Passant, U., Risberg, J., Smith, G., Warkentin, S., et al. (1998). Brain function in spider phobia. *Psychiatry Research: Neuroimaging Section, 84,* 101–111.

Johanson, A., Risberg, J., Tucker, D. M., & Gustafson, L. (2006). Changes in frontal lobe activity with cognitive therapy for spider phobia. *Applied Neuropsychology, 13*(1), 34–41.

Johansson, B. B. (2000). Brain plasticity and stroke rehabilitation: The Willis lecture. *Stroke, 31,* 223–230.

Johnson, M. (1987). *The body in the mind.* Chicago: University of Chicago Press.

Johnstone, T., van Reekum, C. M., Urry, H. L., Kalin, N. H., & Davidson, R. J. (2007). Failure to regulate: Counterproductive recruitment of top-down prefrontal-subcortical circuitry in major depression. *Journal of Neuroscience, 27,* 8877–8884.

Jonides, J., Schumacher, E. H., Smith, E. E., Koeppe, R. A., Awh, E., Reuter-Lorenz, P. A., et al. (1998). The role of parietal cortex in verbal working memory. *Journal of Neuroscience, 18,* 5026–5034.

Joseph, R. (1996). *Neuropsychiatry, neuropsychology, and clinical neuroscience.* Baltimore: Williams and Wilkins.

Kalia, M. (2005). Neurobiological basis of depression: An update. *Metabolism, 54*(5), 24–27.

Kalin, N. H., Larson, C., Shelton, S. E., & Davidson, R. J. (1998). Asymmetric frontal brain activity, cortisol, and behavior associated with fearful temperament in rhesus monkeys. *Behavioral Neuroscience, 112,* 286–292.

Kalin, N. H., Shelton, S. E., Davidson, R. J., & Kelley, A. E. (2001). The primate amygdala mediates acute fear but not the behavioral and physiological components of anxious temperament. *Journal of Neuroscience, 21,* 2067–2074.

Kalin, N. H., Shelton, S. E., & Lynn, D. E. (1995). Opiate systems in mother and infant primates coordinate intimate contact during reunion. *Psychoneuroendocrinology, 20,* 735–742.

Kalin, N. H., Shelton, S. E., & Snowdon, C. T. (1993). Social factors regulating security and fear in infant rhesus monkeys. *Depression, 1,* 137–142.

Kalinichev, M., Easterlin, K., Plotsky, P., & Holtzman, S. (2002). Long-lasting changes in stress-induced corticosteron response and anxiety-like behaviors as a consequence of neonatal maternal separation in Long-Evans rats. *Pharmacology, Biochemistry and Behavior, 73,* 131–141.

Kalisch, R., Korenfeld, E., Stephan, K. E., Weiskopf, N., Seymour, B., & Dolan, R. J. (2006). Context-dependent human extinction memory is mediated by a ventromedial prefrontal and hippocampal network. *Journal of Neuroscience, 26,* 9503–9511.

Kampe, K. K. W., Frith, C. D., Dolan, R. J., & Frith, U. (2001). Reward value of attractiveness and gaze. *Nature, 413,* 589–590.

Kandel, E. R. (1998). A new intellectual framework for psychiatry. *American Journal of Psychiatry, 155,* 457–469.

Kang, H., & Schuman, E. (1995). Long-lasting neurotrophin-induced enhancement of synaptic transmission in the adult hippocampus. *Science, 267,* 1658–1662.

Kaplan, H. S., & Robson, A. J. (2002). The emergence of humans: The coevolution of intelligence and longevity with intergenerational transfers. *Proceedings of the National Academy of Sciences, USA, 99,* 10221–10226.

Karmiloff-Smith, A., Klima, E., Bellugi, U., Grant, J., & Baron-Cohen, S. (1995). Is there a social module? Language, face processing, and theory of mind in individuals with Williams syndrome. *Journal of Cognitive Neuroscience, 7,* 196–208.

Karnath, H. O. (1997). Spatial orientation and the representation of space with parietal lobe lesions. *Philosophical Transactions of the Royal Society, Biological Sciences, 352,* 1411–1419.

Karni, A., Meyer, G., Jezzard, P., Adams, M. M., Turner, R., & Ungerleider, L. G. (1995). Functional MRI evidence for adult cortex plasticity during motor skill learning. *Nature, 377,* 155–158.

Karten, Y. J. G., Olariu, A., & Cameron, H. A. (2005). Stress in early life inhibits neurogenesis in adulthood. *Trends in Neurosciences, 28*(4), 171–172.

Katz, L. C., & Shatz, C. J. (1996). Synaptic activity and the construction of cortical circuits. *Science, 274,* 1133–1138.

Katzman, R., Aronson, M., Fuld, P., Kawas, C., Brown, T., Morgenstern, H., et al. (1989). Development of dementing illness in an 80-year-old volunteer cohort. *Annals of Neurology, 25*, 317–324.

Keenan, J. P., McCutcheon, B., Freund, S., Gallup, G. G., Sanders, G., & Pascual-Leone, A. (1999). Left hand advantage in a self-face recognition task. *Neuropsychologia, 37*, 1421–1425.

Kehoe, P., & Blass, E. M. (1989). Conditioned opioid release in ten-day-old rats: Reversal of stress with maternal stimuli. *Developmental Psychobiology, 19*, 385–398.

Kelly, A., Mullany, P. M., & Lynch, M. A. (2000). Protein synthesis in entorhinal cortex and long-term potentiation in dentate gyrus. *Hippocampus, 10*, 431–437.

Kempermann, G., Kuhn, H. G., & Gage, F. H. (1997). More hippocampal neurons in adult mice living in an enriched environment. *Nature, 386*, 493–495.

Kempermann, G., Kuhn, H. G., & Gage, F. H. (1998). Experience-induced neurogenesis in the senescent dentate gyrus. *Journal of Neuroscience, 18*, 3206–3212.

Kennard, M. A. (1955). The cingulate gyrus in relation to consciousness. *Journal of Nervous and Mental Disease, 121*, 34–39.

Kennedy, S. H., Evans, K. R., Kruger, S., Mayberg, H. S., Meyer, J. H., McCann, S., et al. (2001). Changes in regional brain glucose metabolism measured with positron emission tomography after paroxetine treatment of major depression. *American Journal of Psychiatry, 158*, 899–905.

Kennedy, S. H., Konarski, J. Z., Segal, Z. V., Lau, M. A., Bieling, P. J., McIntyre, R. S., et al. (2007). Differences in brain glucose metabolism between responders to CBT and venlafaxine in a 16-week randomized controlled trial. *American Journal of Psychiatry, 164*, 778–788.

Kern, S., Oakes, T., Stone, C., McAuliff, E., Kirschbaum, C., & Davidson, R. (2008). Glucose metabolic changes in the prefrontal cortex are associated with HPA axis response to psychosocial stressor. *Psychoneuroendocrinology, 33*, 517–529.

Kerr, D. S., Huggett, A. M., & Abraham, W. C. (1994). Modulation of hippocampal long-term potentiation and long-term depression by corticosteroid receptor activation. *Psychobiology, 22*(2), 123–133.

Kessler, R. C., Berglund, P., Demler, O., Jin, R., Koretz, D., Merikangas, K. R., et al. (2003). The epidemiology of major depressive disorder: Results from the National Comorbidity Survey Replication (NCS-R). *Journal of the American Medical Association, 289*, 3095–3105.

Keverne, E. B., Martens, N. D., & Tuite, B. (1989). Beta-endorphin concentrations in cerebrospinal fluid of monkeys are influenced by grooming relationships. *Psychoneuroendocrinology, 18*, 307–321.

Kilgard, M. P., & Merzenich, M. M. (1998). Cortical map reorganization enabled by nucleus basalis activity. *Science, 279*, 1714–1718.

Kim, H., Somerville, L. H., Johnstone, T., Alexander, A. L., & Whalen, P. J. (2003). Inverse amygdala and medial prefrontal cortex responses to surprised faces. *NeuroReport, 14,* 2317–2322.

Kim, J. J., & Diamond, D. M. (2002). The stressed hippocampus, synaptic plasticity and lost memories. *Nature Reviews Neuroscience, 3,* 453–462.

Kim, J. J., Koo, J. W., Lee, H. J., & Han, J. S. (2005). Amygdalar inactivation blocks stress-induced impairments in hippocampal long-term potentiation and spatial memory. *Journal of Neuroscience, 25,* 1532–1539.

Kim, J. J., Lee, H. J., Han, J., & Packard, M. G. (2001). Amygdala is critical for stress-induced modulation of hippocampal long-term potentiation and learning. *Journal of Neuroscience, 21,* 5222–5228.

Kimble, D. P. (1968). Hippocampus and internal inhibition. *Psychological Bulletin, 70,* 285–295.

King, V., & Elder, G. H., Jr. (1997). The legacy of grandparenting: Childhood experiences with grandparents and current involvement with grandchildren. *Journal of Marriage and the Family, 59,* 848–859.

Kinsley, C. H., Trainer, R., Stafisso-Sandoz, G., Quadros, P., Keyser Marcus, L., Hearon, C., et al. (2006). Motherhood and the hormones of pregnancy modify concentrations of hippocampal neuronal dendritic spines. *Hormones and Behaviour, 49,* 131–142.

Kirkpatrick, L. A., & Davis, K. E. (1994). Attachment style, gender, and relationship stability: A longitudinal analysis. *Journal of Personality and Social Psychology, 66*(3), 502–512.

Kirkwood, A., Rozas, C., Kirkwood, J., Perez, F., & Bear, M. F. (1999). Modulation of long-term synaptic depression in visual cortex by acetylcholine and norepinephrine. *Journal of Neuroscience, 19,* 1599–1609.

Kirschbaum, C., Wolf, O. T., May, M., Wippich, W., & Hellhammer, D. H. (1996). Stress- and treatment-induced elevations of cortisol levels associated with impaired declarative memory in healthy adults. *Life Sciences, 58*(17), 1475–1483.

Klein, E., Kreinin, I., Chistyakov, A., Koren, D., Mecz, L., Marmur, S., et al. (1999). Therapeutic efficacy of right prefrontal slow repetitive transcranial magnetic stimulation in major depression. *Archives of General Psychiatry, 56,* 315–320.

Kling, A., & Steklis, H. D. (1976). A neural substrate for affiliative behavior in nonhuman primates. *Brain Behaviors, 13,* 216–238.

Klingberg, T., Forssberg, H., & Westerberg, H. (2002). Increased brain activity in frontal and parietal cortex underlies the development of visuospatial working memory capacity during childhood. *Journal of Cognitive Neuroscience, 14*(1), 1–10.

Knight, R. T., & Grabowecky, M. (1995). Escape from linear time: Prefrontal cortex and conscious experience. In M. S. Gazzaniga (Ed.), *The cognitive neurosciences* (pp. 1357–1372). Cambridge, MA: MIT Press.

Knight, R. T., Staines, R. W., Swick, D., & Chao, L. L. (1999). Prefrontal cortex inhibition and excitation in distributed neural networks. *Acta Psychologica, 101*(2–3), 159–178.

Knowles, P. A., Conner, R. L., & Panksepp, J. (1989). Opiate effects on social behavior of juvenile dogs as a function of social deprivation. *Pharmacology, Biochemistry and Behavior, 33*, 533–537.

Knutson, K. M., Mah, L., Manly, C. F., & Grafman, J. (2007). Neural correlates of automatic beliefs about gender and race. *Human Brain Mapping, 28*, 915–930.

Koechlin, E., Ody, C., & Kouneiher, F. (2003). The architecture of cognitive control in the human prefrontal cortex. *Science, 302*, 1181–1185.

Kohut, H. (1984). *How does analysis cure?* Chicago: University of Chicago Press.

Kolb, B., & Gibb, R. (1991). Environmental enrichment and cortical injury: Behavioral and anatomical consequences of frontal cortex lesions. *Cerebral Cortex, 1*, 189–198.

Kolb, B., & Gibb, R. (2002). Frontal lobe plasticity and behavior. In T. Donald & T. Robert (Eds.), *Principles of frontal lobe function* (pp. 541–556). New York: Oxford University Press.

Kolb, B., & Whishaw, I. Q. (1998). Brain plasticity and behavior. *Annual Review of Psychology, 49*, 43–64.

Kong, J., Gollub, R. L., Rosman, I. S., Webb, J. M., Vangel, M. J., Kirsch, I., et al. (2006). Brain activity associated with expectancy-enhanced placebo analgesia as measured by functional magnetic resonance imaging. *Journal of Neuroscience, 26*, 381–388.

Konig, P., & Engel, A. K. (1995). Correlated firing in sensory-motor systems. *Current Opinions in Neurobiology, 5*, 511–519.

Koopman, C., Classen, C., & Spiegel, D. (1994). Predictors of posttraumatic stress symptoms among survivors of the Oakland/Berkeley, Calif. firestorm. *American Journal of Psychiatry, 151*, 888–894.

Kosten, T., Lee, H., & Kim, J. (2007). Neonatal handling alters learning in adult male and female rats in a task-specific manner. *Brain Research, 1154*, 144–153.

Koukkou, M., & Lehmann, D. (2006). Experience-dependent brain plasticity: A key concept for studying nonconscious decisions. *International Congress Series, 1286*, 45–52.

Kringelbach, M. L. (2005). The human orbitofrontal cortex: Linking reward to hedonic experience. *Nature Reviews Neuroscience, 6*, 691–702.

Kroger, J. K., Sabb, F. W., Fales, C. L., Bookeimer, S. Y., Cohen, M. S., & Holyoak, K. J. (2002). Recruitment of anterior dorsolateral prefrontal cortex in human reasoning: A parametric study of relational complexity. *Cerebral Cortex, 12*, 477–485.

Krueger, F., Moll, J., Zahn, R., Heinecke, A., & Grafman, J. (2006). Event frequency modulates the processing of daily life activities in human medial prefrontal cortex. *Cerebral Cortex.* doi:10.1093/cercor/bhl143

Krugers, H. J., Goltstein, P. M., van der Linden, S., & Joels, M. (2006). Blockade of glucocorticoid receptors rapidly restores hippocampal CA1 synaptic plasticity after exposure to chronic stress. *European Journal of Neuroscience, 23,* 3051–3055.

Krystal, J. H., Bremner, J. D., Southwick, S. M., & Charney, D. S. (1998). The emerging neurobiology of dissociation: Implication for treatment of posttraumatic stress disorder. In J. D. Bremner & C. R. Marmar (Eds.), *Trauma, memory, and dissociation* (pp. 321–364). Washington, DC: American Psychiatric Press.

Kuhlmann, S., Piel, M., & Wolf, O. T. (2005). Imparied memory retrieval after psychosocial stress in healthy young men. *Journal of Neuroscience, 25,* 2977–2982.

Kuhn, C. M., & Schanberg, S. M. (1998). Responses to maternal separation: Mechanisms and mediators. *International Journal of Developmental Neuroscience, 16,* 261–270.

Kukolja, J., Schlapfer, T., Keysers, C., Klingmuller, D., Maier, W., Fink, G., et al. (2008). Modeling a negative response bias in the human amygdala by noradregenic-glucocorticoid interactions. *Progress in Brain Research, 167,* 35–51.

Laatsch, L., Pavel, D., Jobe, T., Lin, Q., & Quintana, J. C. (1999). Incorporation of SPECT imaging in a longitudinal cognitive rehabilitation therapy programme. *Brain Injury, 13,* 555–570.

LaBar, K. S., Gatenby, J. C., Gore, J. C., LeDoux, J. E., & Phelps, A. E. (1998). Human amygdala activation during conditioned fear acquisition and extinction: A mixed-trial FMRI study. *Neuron, 20,* 937–945.

LaBar, K. S., LeDoux, J. E., Spencer, D. D., & Phelps, E. A. (1995). Impaired fear conditioning following unilateral temporal lobectomy in humans. *Journal of Neuroscience, 15,* 6846–6855.

Lachmann, F. M., & Beebe B. A. (1996). Three principles of salience in the organization of the patient-analyst interaction. *Psychoanalytic Psychology, 13,* 1–22.

Ladd, C., Thrivikraman, K., Hout, R., & Plotsky, P. (2005). Differential neuroendocrine responses to chronic variable stress in adult Long Evans rats exposed to handling-maternal separation as neonates. *Psychoneuroendocrinology, 30,* 520–533.

Lahdenperä, M., Lummaa, V., Helle, S., Tremblay, M., & Russell, A. F. (2004). Fitness benefits of prolonged post-reproductive lifespan in women. *Nature, 428,* 178–181.

Langer, E. J. (1978). Rethinking the role of thought in social interaction. In J. H. Harvey, W. Ickes, & R .F. Kidd (Eds.), *New directions in attribution research* (Vol. 2, pp. 35–58). Hillsdale, NJ: Erlbaum.

Lanius, R. A., Williamson, P. C., Bluhm, R. L., Densmore, M., Boksman, K., Neufeld, R. W. J., et al. (2005). Functional connectivity of dissociative responses in posttraumatic stress disorder: A functional magnetic resonance imaging investigation. *Biological Psychiatry, 57,* 873–884.

Lanius, R. A., Williamson, P. C., Densmore, M., Boksman, K., Gupta, M. A., Neufeld, R. W., et al. (2001). Neural correlation of traumatic memories in posttraumatic stress disorder: A functional MRI investigation. *American Journal of Psychiatry, 158*, 1920–1922.

Larson, C., Schaefer, H., Siegle, G., Jackson, C., Anderle, M., & Davidson, R. (2006). Fear is fast in phobic individuals: Amygdala activation in response to fear-relevant stimuli. *Biological Psychiatry, 60*, 410–417.

Lawson, D. M., Barnes, A. D., Madkins, J. P., & Francios-Lamonte, B. M. (2006). Changes in male partner abuser attachment styles in group treatment. *Psychotherapy: Theory, Research, Practice, Training, 43*(2), 232–237.

Lázaro, L., Bargalló, N., Castro-Fornieles, J., Falcón, C., Andrés, S., Calvo, R., et al. (2009). Brain changes in children and adolescents with obsessive-compulsive disorder before and after treatment: A voxel-based morphometric MRI study. *Psychiatry Research: Neuroimaging, 172*(2), 140–146.

Le Carret, N., Lafont, S., Letenneur, L., Dartigues, J. F., Mayo, W., & Fabrigoule, C. (2003). The effect of education on cognitive performances and its implication for the constitution of the cognitive reserve. *Developmental Neuropsychology, 23*, 317–337.

LeDoux, J. E. (1986). Sensory systems and emotion: A model of affective processing. *Integrative Psychiatry, 4*, 237–243.

LeDoux, J. E. (1994). Emotion, memory and the brain. *Scientific American, 270*(6), 32–39.

LeDoux, J. E. (1996). *The emotional brain*. New York: Simon and Schuster.

LeDoux, J. E., Romanski, L. M., & Xagoraris, A. E. (1989). Indelibility of subcortical emotional memories. *Journal of Cognitive Neuroscience, 1*, 238–243.

LeDoux, J. E., Wilson, D. H., & Gazzaniga, M. S. (1977). A divided mind: Observations on the conscious properties of the separated hemispheres. *Annals of Neurology, 2*, 417–421.

Lee, R. D. (2003). Rethinking the evolutionary theory of aging: Transfers, not births, shape senescence in social species. *Proceedings of the National Academy of Sciences, USA, 100*, 9637–9642.

Lee, T. M. C., Liu, H. L., Chan, C. C. H., Fang, S. Y., & Gao, J. H. (2005). Neural activities associated with emotion recognition observed in men and women. *Molecular Psychiatry, 10*, 450–455.

Lee, Y., & Davis, M. (1997). Role of the hippocampus, the bed nucleus of the stria terminalis and the amygdala in the excitatory effect of corticotropin-releasing hormone on the acoustic startle reflex. *Journal of Neuroscience, 17*, 6434–6446.

Lemer, C., Dehaene, S., Spelke, E., & Cohen, L. (2003). Approximate quantities and exact number words: Dissociable systems. *Neuropsychologica, 41*, 1942–1958.

Leonard, C. M., Rolls, E. T., Wilson, F. A. W., & Baylis, G. C. (1985). Neurons in the amygdala of the monkey with responses selective for faces. *Behavioral Brain Research, 15*, 159–176.

Leventopoulos, M., Rüedi-Bettschen, D., Knuesel, I., Feldon, J., Pryce, C. R., & Opacka-Juffry, J. (2007). Long-term effects of early life deprivation on brain glia in Fischer rats. *Brain Research, 1142,* 119–126.

Lévesque, J., Eugène, F., Joanette, Y., Mensour, B., Beaudoin, G., Leroux, J. M., et al. (2003). Neural correlates of sad feelings in healthy girls. *Neuroscience, 121,* 545–551.

Lévesque, J., Eugène, F., Joanette, Y., Paquette, V., Mensour, B., Beaudoin, G., et al. (2003). Neural circuitry underlying voluntary suppression of sadness. *Biological Psychiatry, 53,* 502–510.

Lévesque, J., Joanette, Y., Mensour, B., Beaudoin, G., Leroux, J. M., Bourgouin, P., et al. (2004). Neural basis of emotional self-regulation in childhood. *Neuroscience, 129,* 361–369.

Levin, P., Lazrove, S., & van der Kolk, B. (1999). What psychological testing and neuroimaging tell us about the treatment of posttraumatic stress disorder by eye movement desensitization and reprocessing. *Journal of Anxiety Disorders, 13,* 159–172.

Levy, D. A. (1997). *Tools of critical thinking.* Boston: Allyn & Bacon.

Levy, J., Trevarthen, C., & Sperry, R. W. (1972). Perception of bilateral chimeric figures following hemispheric disconnection. *Brain, 95,* 61–78.

Lewicki, P., Hill, T., & Czyzewska, M. (1992). Nonconscious acquisition of information. *American Psychologist, 47,* 796–801.

Lewis, M., Feiring, C., & Rosenthal, S. (2000). Attachment over time. *Child Development, 71,* 707–720.

Li, H., Weiss, S. R. B., Chaung, D. M., Post, R. M., & Rogawski, M. A. (1998). Bidirectional synaptic plasticity in the rat basolateral amygdala: Characterization of an activity-dependent switch sensitive to the presynaptic metabotropic glutamate receptor antagonist 2S-alpha-ethyglutamic acid. *Journal of Neuroscience, 18,* 1662–1670.

Li, X., Jiang, J., Zhu, W., Yu., C., Sui, M., Wang, Y., et al. (2007). Asymmetry of prefrontal cortical convolution complexity in males with attention-deficit/hyperactivity disorder using fractal information dimension. *Brain and Development, 29,* 649–655.

Lieberman, M. D., Eisenberger, N. I., Crockett, M. J., Tom, S. M., Pfeifer, J. H., & Way, B. M. (2007). Putting feelings into words: Affect labeling disrupts amygdala activity in response to affective stimuli. *Psychological Science, 18,* 421–428.

Linden, D. E. J. (2006). How psychotherapy changes the brain—the contribution of functional neuroimaging. *Molecular Psychiatry, 11,* 528–538.

Linehan, M. (1993). *Cognitive-behavioral treatment of borderline personality disorder.* New York: Guilford.

Liu, D., Diorio, J., Day, J. C., Francis, D. D., & Meaney, M. J. (2000). Maternal care, hippocampal synaptogenesis and cognitive development in rats. *Nature Neuroscience, 3,* 799–806.

Liu, D., Diorio, J., Tannenbaum, B., Caldji, C., Francis, D., Freedman, A., et al. (1997). Maternal care, hippocampal glucocorticoid receptors, and hypothalamic-pituitary-adrenal responses to stress. *Science, 277,* 1659–1662.

Liu, L., Wong, T. P., Pozza, M. F., Lingenhoehl, K., Wang, Y., Sheng, M., et al. (2004). Role of NMDA receptor subtypes in governing the direction of hippocampal synaptic plasticity. *Science, 304,* 1021–1024.

Livingston, R. B. (1967). Reinforcement. In G. C. Quarton, T. Melnick, & F. O. Schmitt (Eds.), *The neurosciences* (pp. 568–576). New York: Rockefeller University Press

Loftus, E. (1988). *Memory.* New York: Ardsley House.

Loftus, E. F., Milo, E. M., & Paddock, J. R. (1995). The accidental executioner: Why psychotherapy must be informed by science. *Counseling Psychologist, 23,* 300–309.

Lombroso, P. J., & Sapolsky, R. (1998). Development of the cerebral cortex: Stress and brain development. *Journal of the Academy of Child and Adolescent Psychiatry, 37,* 1337–1339.

Lonstein, J. S., Simmons, D. A., Swann, J. M., & Stern, J. M. (1998). Forebrain expression of c-fos due to active maternal behaviour in lactating rats. *Neuroscience, 82,* 267–281.

Lorberbaum, J. P., Newman, J. D., Dubno, J. R., Horwitz, A. R., Nahas, Z., Teneback, C. C., et al. (1999). Feasability of using fMRI to study mothers responding to infant cries. *Depression and Anxiety, 10,* 99–104.

Lord, C. G., Ross, L., & Lepper, M. (1979). Biased assimilation and attitude polarization: The effects of prior theories on subsequently considered evidence. *Journal of Personality and Social Psychology, 37,* 1231–1247.

Lorenz, K. (1991). *Here am I—where are you: The behavior of the Greylag Goose.* New York: Brace Jovanovich.

Lou, H., Nowak, M., & Kajaer, T. W. (2005). The mental self. *Progress in Brain Resources, 150,* 197–204.

Lou, H. C., Henriksen, L., & Bruhn, P. (1984). Focal cerebral hypoperfusion in children with dysphasia and/or attention deficit disorder. *Archives of Neurology, 41,* 825–829.

Lou, H. C., Luber, B., Crupain, M., Keenan, J. P., Nowak, M., Kjaer, T. W., et al. (2004). Parietal cortex and representation of the mental self. *Proceedings of the National Academy of Sciences, USA, 101,* 6827–6832.

Lovell, J., & Kluger, J. (1994). *Lost moon: The perilous voyage of Apollo 13.* New York: Simon & Schuster.

Lu, S. T., Hamalainen, M. S., Hari, R., Ilmoniemi, R. J., Lounasmaa, O. V., Sams, M., et al. (1991). Seeing faces activates three separate areas outside the occipital visual cortex in man. *Neuroscience, 43,* 287–290.

Luna, B. (2004). Algebra and the adolescent brain. *Trends in Cognitive Sciences, 8,* 437–439.

Lupien, S., de Leon, M., de Santi, S., Convit, A., Tarshish, C., Nair, N., et al. (1998). Cortisol levels during human aging predict hippocampal atrophy and memory deficits. *Nature Neuroscience, 1,* 69–73.

Lupien, S. J., & McEwen, B. S. (1997). The acute effects of corticosteroids on cognition: Integration of animal and human model studies. *Brain Research Reviews, 24*(1), 1–27.

Maccari, S., Piazza, P. V., Kabbaj, M., Barbazanges, A., Simon, H., & Le Moal, M. (1995). Adoption reverses the long-term impairment in glucocorticoid feedback induced by prenatal stress. *Journal of Neuroscience, 15*(1), 110–116.

Mackie, S., Shaw, P., Lenroot, R., Pierson, R., Greenstein, D. K., Nugent, T. F., et al. (2007). Cerebellar development and clinical outcome in attention deficit hyperactivity disorder. *American Journal of Psychiatry, 164*, 647–655.

MacLean, P. D. (1985). Brain evolution relating to family, play, and the separation call. *Archives of General Psychiatry, 42*, 405–417.

MacLean, P. D. (1990). *The triune brain in evolution: Role of paleocerebral functions.* New York: Plenum Press.

Macrae, C. N., Moran, J. M., Heatherton, T. F., Banfield, J. F., & Kelley, W. M. (2004). Medial prefrontal activity predicts memory for self. *Cerebral Cortex, 14*, 647–654.

Maguire, E. A., Woollett, K., & Spiers, H. J. (2006). London taxi drivers and bus drivers: A structural MRI and neuropsychological analysis. *Hippocampus, 16*, 1091–1101.

Maher, B. A. (1974). Delusional thinking and perceptual disorder. *Journal of Individual Psychology, 30*, 98–113.

Maier, S. F., Amat, J., Baratta, M. V., Paul, E., & Watkins, L. R. (2006). Behavioral control, the medial prefrontal cortex, and resilience. *Dialogues in Clinical Neuroscience, 8*, 397–406.

Main, M., (1993). Discourse, prediction, and the recent studies in attachment: Implications for psychoanalysis. *Journal of the American Psychoanalytic Association, 41*, 209–244.

Main, M., & Goldwyn, R. (1998). *Adult attachment scoring and classification system.* Unpublished manuscript, University of California at Berkeley.

Main, M., Kaplan, N., & Cassidy, J. (1985). Security in infancy, childhood, and adulthood: A move to the level of representation. In I. Bretherton & E. Waters (Eds.), *Growing points of attachment theory and research. Monographs of the Society for Research in Child Development, 50*(1–2, Serial No. 209, pp. 66–104).

Malenka, R. C., & Siegelbaum, S. A. (2001). Synaptic plasticity: Diverse targets and mechanisms for regulating synaptic efficacy. In W. M. Cowan, T. C. Sudhof, & C. F. Stevens (Eds.), *Synapses* (pp. 393–453). Baltimore, MD: Johns Hopkins University Press.

Maletic-Savatic, M., Malinow, R., & Svoboda, K. (1999). Rapid dendritic morphogenesis in CA1 hippocampal dendrites induced by synaptic activity. *Science, 283*, 1923–1927.

Malloy, P., Bihrle, A., Duffy, J., & Cimino, C. (1993). The orbitomedial frontal syndrome. *Archives of Clinical Neuropsychology, 8*, 185–201.

Marais, L., van Rensburg, S. J., van Zyl, J. M., Stein, D. J., & Daniels, W. M. U. (2008). Maternal separation of rat pups increases the risk of developing depressive-like behavior after subsequent chronic stress by altering corticosterone and neurotrophin levels in the hippocampus. *Neuroscience Research, 61*(1), 106–112.

Marci, C. D., Ham, J., Moran, E., & Orr, S. P. (2007). Physiologic correlates of perceived therapist empathy and social-emotional process during psychotherapy. *Journal of Nervous and Mental Disease, 195*(2), 103–111.

Markis, N., Biederman, J., Vatera, E., Bush, G., Kaiser, J., Kennedy, D. N., et al. (2007). Cortical thinning of the attention and executive function networks in adults with attention-deficit/hyperactivity disorder. *Cerebral Cortex, 17*, 1364–1375.

Marr, D. (1971). A theory of archicortex. *Philosophical Transactions of the Royal Society, 262*, 23–81.

Marshall, R. E., Stratton, W. C., Moore, J., & Boxerman, S. B. (1980). Circumcision I: Effects upon newborn behavior. *Infant Behavioral Development, 3*, 1–14.

Marshuetz, C., Smith, E., Jonides, J., DeGutis, J., & Chenevert, T. (2000). Order information in working memory: fMRI evidence for parietal and prefrontal mechanisms. *Journal of Cognitive Neuroscience, 12*(2), 130–144.

Martin, A., Wiggs, C., Ungerleider, L., & Haxby, J. (1996). Neural correlates of category-specific knowledge. *Nature, 379*, 649–652.

Martin, S. D., Martin, E., Rai, S. S., Richardson, M. A., & Royall, R. (2001). Brain blood flow changes in depressed patients treated with interpersonal psychotherapy or venlafaxine hydrochloride. *Archives of General Psychiatry, 58*, 641–648.

Massey, P. V., Johnson, B. E., Moult, P. R., Auberson, Y. P., Brown, M. W., Molnar, E., et al. (2004). Differential roles of NR2A and NR2B-containing NMDA receptors in cortical long-term potentiation and long-term depression. *Journal of Neuroscience, 24*, 7821–7828.

Mateer, C. A., & Kerns, K. A. (2000). Capitalizing on neuroplasticity. *Brain and Cognition, 42*, 106–109.

Mathew, R. J., Meyer, J. S., Francis, D. J., Semchuk, K. M., & Claghorn, J. L. (1980). Cerebral blood flow in depression. *American Journal of Psychiatry, 137*, 1449–1450.

Matsumoto, K., & Tanaka, K. (2004). The role of the medial prefrontal cortex in achieving goals. *Current Opinion in Neurobiology, 14*, 178–185.

Mayberg, H. S. (1997). Limbic-cortical dysregulation: A proposed model of depression. *Journal of Neuropsychiatry, 9*, 471–481.

Mayberg, H. S., Liotti, M., Brannan, S. K., McGinnis, S., Mahurin, R. K., Jerabek, P. A., et al. (1999). Reciprocal limbic-cortical function and negative mood: Converging PET findings in depression and normal sadness. *American Journal of Psychiatry, 156*, 675–682.

Mayberg, H. S., Silva, J. A., Brannan, S. K., Tekell, J. L., Mahurin, R. K., McGinnis, S., et al. (2002). The functional neuroanatomy of the placebo effect. *American Journal of Psychiatry, 159,* 728–737.

McCarthy, G. (1995). Functional neuroimaging of memory. *The Neuroscientist, 1,* 155–163.

McCormick, J. A., Lyons, V., Jacobson, M. D., Noble, J., Diorio, J., Nyirenda, M., et al. (2000). 5'-Heterogeneity of glucocorticoid receptor messenger RNA is tissue specific: Differential regulation of variant transcripts by early-life events. *Molecular Endocrinology, 14,* 506–517.

McDonald, A. J., Shammah-Lagnado, S. J., Shi, C., & Davis, M. (1999). Cortical afferents to the extended amygdala. *Annals of the New York Academy of Sciences, 877,* 309–338.

McFarlane, A. C., & Yehuda, R. (1996). Resilience, vulnerability, and the course of posttraumatic reactions. In B. A. van der Kolk, A. C. McFarlane, & L. Weisaeth (Eds.), *Traumatic stress: The effects of overwhelming experience on mind, body, and society* (pp. 129–154). New York: Guilford.

McGaugh, J. L. (1990). Significance and remembrance: The role of neuromodulatory systems. *Psychological Science, 1,* 15–25.

McGaugh, J. L. (2004). The amygdala modulates the consolidation of memories of emotionally arousing experiences. *Annual Review of Neuroscience, 17,* 1–28.

McGaugh, J. L., Introini-Collison, I. B., Cahill, L. F., Castellano, C., Dalmaz, C., Parent, M. B., et al. (1993). Neuromodulatory systems and memory storage: Role of the amygdala. *Behavioral Brain Research, 58,* 81–90.

McGowan, P. O., Sasaki, A., D'Alessio, A. C., Dymov, S., Labonte, B., Szyf, M., et al. (2009). Epigenetic regulation of the glucocorticoid receptor in human brain associates with childhood abuse. *Nature Neuroscience, 12*(3), 342–348.

McGuire, P. K., Paulesu, E., Frackowiak, R. S. J., & Frith, C. D. (1996). Brain activity during stimulus independent thought. *NeuroReport, 7*(13), 2095–2099.

Meaney, M. J., Aitken, D. H., van Berkel, C., Bhatnagar, S., & Sapolsky, R. M. (1988). Effect of neonatal handling on age-related impairments associated with the hippocampus. *Science, 239,* 766–768.

Meaney, M. J., Aitken, D. H., Viau, V., Sharma, S., & Sarrieau, A. (1989). Neonatal handling alters adrenocortical negative feedback sensitivity and hippocampal type II glucocorticoid receptor binding in the rat. *Neuroendocrinology, 50,* 597–604.

Meaney, M. J., Mitchell, J. B., Aitken, D. H., Bhatnagar, S., Bodnoff, S. R., Iny, L. J., et al. (1991). The effects of neonatal handling on the development of the adrenocortical response to stress: Implications for neuropathology and cognitive deficits in later life. *Psychoneuroendocrinology, 16*(1–3), 85–103.

Meaney, M. J., & Szyf, M. (2005). Maternal care as a model for experience-dependent chromatin plasticity? *Trends in Neurosciences, 28,* 456–463.

Medendorp, W. P., Goltz, H. C., Crawford, D., & Vilis, T. (2005). Integration of target and effector information in human posterior parietal cortex for the planning of action. *Journal of Neurophysiology, 93,* 945–962.

Menard, J. L., Champagne, D. L., & Meaney, M. J. P. (2004). Variations of maternal care differentially influence "fear" reactivity and regional patterns of cFos immunoreactivity in response to the shock-probe burying test. *Neuroscience, 129*(2), 297–308.

Menkes, D. L., Bodnar, P., Ballesteros, R. A., & Swenson, M. R. (1999). Right frontal lobe slow frequency transcranial magnetic stimulation (SF-r-TMS) is an effective treatment for depression: A case-control pilot study of safety and efficacy. *Journal of Neurology, Neurosurgery, and Psychiatry, 67,* 113–115.

Merrin, E. L., & Silberfarb, P. M. (1979). The Capgras phenomenon. *Archives of General Psychiatry, 33,* 965–968.

Mesulam, M. M. (1981). A cortical network for directed attention and unilateral neglect. *Annals of Neurology, 10,* 309–325.

Mesulam, M. M. (1998). From sensation to cognition. *Brain, 121,* 1013–1052.

Meyers, C. A., Berman, S. A., Scheibel, R. S., & Hayman, A. (1992). Case report: Acquired antisocial personality disorder associated with unilateral left orbital frontal lobe damage. *Journal of Psychiatry and Neuroscience, 17,* 121–125.

Michael, N., & Erfurth, A. (2002). Treatment of bipolar mania with right prefrontal rapid transcranial magnetic stimulation. *Journal of Affective Disorders, 78,* 253–257.

Michel, G. F., & Moore, C. L. (1995). *Developmental psychobiology: An interdisciplinary science.* Cambridge, MA: MIT Press.

Milad, M. R., Orr, S. P., Pitman, R. K., & Rauch, S. L. (2005). Context modulation of memory for fear extinction in humans. *Pyschophysiology, 42,* 456–464.

Milad, M. R., Quinn, B. T., Pitman, R. K., Orr, S. P., Fischl, B., & Rauch, S. L. (2005). Thickness of ventromedial prefrontal cortex in humans is correlated with extinction in memory. *Proceedings of the National Academy of Sciences, USA, 102,* 10706–10711.

Milad, M. R., & Quirk, G. J. (2002). Neurons in medial prefrontal cortex signal memory for fear extinction. *Nature, 420,* 70–74.

Milad, M. R., Vidal-Gonzalez, I., & Quirk, G. J. (2004). Electrical stimulation of medial prefrontal cortex reduces conditioned fear in a temporally specific manner. *Behavioral Neuroscience, 118*(2), 389–394.

Miller, A. (1981). *Prisoners of childhood: The drama of the gifted child and the search for the true self.* New York: Basic Books.

Miller, A. (1983). *For your own good: Hidden cruelty in child-rearing and the roots of violence.* New York: Farrar, Straus, & Giroux.

Miller, H., Alvarez, V., & Miller (1990). *The psychopathology and psychoanalytic psychotherapy of compulsive caretaking.* Unpublished manuscript.

Minagawa-Kawai, Y., Matsuoka, S., Dan, I., Naoi, N., Nakamura, K., & Kojima, S. (2008). Prefrontal activation associated with social attachment: Facial emotion recognition in mothers and infants. *Cerebral Cortex, 19*(2), 284–292.

Mirescu, C., Peters, J. D., & Gould, E. (2004). Early life experience alters response of adult neurogenesis to stress. *Nature Neuroscience, 7,* 841–846.

Mitchell, J. P., Banaji, M. R., & Macrae, C. N. (2005). The link between social cognition and self-referential thought in the medial prefrontal cortex. *Journal of Cognitive Neuroscience, 17,* 1306–1315.

Mitchell, J. P., Macrae, C. N., & Banaji, M. R. (2006). Dissociable medial prefrontal contributions to judgments of similar and dissimilar others. *Neuron, 50,* 655–663.

Mitra, R., & Sapolsky, R. M. (2008). Acute corticosterone treatment is sufficient to induce anxiety and amygdaloid dendritic hypertrophy. *Proceedings of the National Academy of Sciences, USA, 105,* 5573–5578.

Modney, B. K., & Hatton, G. I. (1994). Maternal behaviors: Evidence that they feed back to alter brain morphology and function. *Acta Paediatrica Supplement, 397,* 29–32.

Modney, B., Yang, Q., & Hatton, G. (1990). Activation of excitatory amino acid inputs to supraoptic neurons. II. Increased dye-coupling in maternally behaving virgin rats. *Brain Research, 513,* 270–273.

Moerman, D. E., & Jonas, W. B. (2002). Deconstructing the placebo effect and finding the meaning response. *Annals of Internal Medicine, 136,* 471–476.

Molko, N., Cachia, A., Riviere, D., Mangin, J. F., Brauandet, M., Bihan, D. L., et al. (2003). Functional and structural alteration of the intrapietal sulcus in a developmental dyscalculia of genetic origin. *Neuron, 40,* 847–858.

Monfils, M., Cowansage, K. K., & LeDoux, J. E. (2007). Brain-derived neurotrophic factor: Linking fear learning to memory consolidation. *Molecular Pharmacology, 72,* 235–237.

Morgan, C. A., Wang, S., Southwick, S. M., Rasmusson, A., Hazlett, G., Hauger, R. L., et al. (2000). Plasma neuropeptide-Y concentrations in humans exposed to military survival training. *Biological Psychiatry, 47,* 902–909.

Morgan, M. A., Romanski, L. M., & Le Doux, J. E. (1993). Extinction of emotional learning: Contribution of medial prefrontal cortex. *Neuroscience Letters, 163,* 109–113.

Moriceau, S., & Sullivan, R. M. (2004). Corticosterone influences on mammalian neonatal sensitive-period learning. *Behavioral Neuroscience, 118*(2), 274–281.

Morley-Fletcher, S., Rea, M., Maccari, S., & Laviola, G. (2003). Environmental enrichment during adolescence reverses the effects of prenatal stress on play behaviour and HPA axis reactivity in rats. *European Journal of Neuroscience, 18,* 3367–3374.

Morrison, J. H., & Hof, P. R. (2003). Changes in cortical circuits during aging. *Clinical Neuroscience Research, 2,* 294–304.

Mountcastle, V. B. (1995). The parietal system and some higher brain functions. *Cerebral Cortex, 5,* 377–390.

Myers, J. J., & Sperry, R. W. (1985). Interhemispheric communication after section of the forebrain commissures. *Cortex, 21,* 249–260.

Myers, K. M., & Davis, M. (2007). Mechanisms of fear extinction. *Molecular Psychiatry, 12*, 120–150.

Myers, W. A., Churchill, J. D., Muja, N., & Garraghty, P. E. (2000). Role of NMDA receptors in adult primates cortical somatosensory plasticity. *Journal of Comparative Neurology, 418*, 373–382.

Nachmias, M., Gunnar, M. R., Mangelsdorf, S., Parritz, R. H., & Buss, K. (1996). Behavioral inhibition and stress reactivity: The moderating role of attachment security. *Child Development, 67*, 508–522.

Nagahama, Y., Okada, T., Katsumi, Y., Hayashi, T., Yamauchi, H., Oyanagi, C., et al. (2001). Dissociable mechanisms of attentional control within the human prefrontal cortex. *Cerebral Cortex, 11*, 85–92.

Nakatani, E., Nakgawa, A., Ohara, Y., Goto, S., Uozumi, N., Iwakiri, M., et al. (2003). Effects of behavior therapy on regional cerebral blood flow in obsessive-compulsive disorder. *Psychiatry Resources, 124*(2), 113–120.

Nasrallah, H. A. (1985). The unintegrated right cerebral hemispheric consciousness as alien intruder: A possible mechanism for Schneiderian delusions in schizophrenia. *Comprehensive Psychiatry, 20*, 273–282.

Nauta, W. J. H. (1971). The problem of the frontal lobe: A reinterpretation. *Journal of Psychiatric Research, 8*, 167–187.

Navalta, C. P., Polcari, A., Webster, D. M., Boghossian, A., & Teicher, M. H. (2004). Effects of childhood sexual abuse on neuropsychological cognitive function in college women. *Journal of Neuropsychiatry and Clinical Neuroscience, 18*(1), 45–53.

Nebes, R. D. (1971). Superiority of the minor hemisphere in commissurotomized man for the perception of part-whole relationships. *Cortex, 7*, 333–349.

Nedergaard, M., Ransom, B., & Goldman, S. A. (2003). New roles for astrocytes: Redefining the functional architecture of the brain. *Trends in Neurosciences, 26*, 523–530.

Nelson, C. A., & Carver, L. J. (1998). The effects of stress and trauma on brain and memory: A view from developmental cognitive neuroscience. *Development and Psychopathology, 10*, 793–809.

Nelson, E. E., & Panksepp, J. (1998). Brain substrates of infant-mother attachment: Contributions of opioids, oxytocin, and norepinephrine. *Neuroscience and Biobehavioral Reviews, 22*, 437–452.

Nelson, K. (1993). The psychological and social origins of autobiographical memory. *Psychological Science, 4*, 7–14.

Nelson, M. D., Saykin, A. J., Flashman, L. A., & Riordan, H. J. (1998). Hippocampal volume reduction in schizophrenia as assessed by magnetic resonance imaging: A meta-analytic study. *Archives of General Psychiatry, 55*, 433–440.

Nemeroff, C., Heim, C. M., Thase, M. E., Klein, D. N., Rush, A., & Schatzberg, A. (2003). Differential responses to psychotherapy versus pharmacotherapy in patients with chronic forms of major depression and childhood trauma. *Proceedings of the National Academy of Sciences, USA, 25*, 14293–14296.

Nesse, R. M., & Lloyd, A. T. (1992). The evolution of psychodynamic mechanisms. In J. H. Barkow, L. Cosmides, & J. Tooby (Eds.), *The adapted mind: Evolutionary psychology and the generation of culture* (pp. 601–626). New York: Oxford University Press.

Neugebauer, V., Li, W., Bird, G., & Han, J. (2004). The amygdala and persistent pain. *The Neuroscientist, 10*(3), 221–234.

Neumann, I. D. (2008). Brain oxytocin: A key regulator of emotional and social behaviors in both females and males. *Journal of Neuroendocrinology, 20,* 858–865.

Newberg, A., Alavi, A., Baime, M., Pourdehnad, M., Santanna, J., & Aquili, E. (2001). The measurement of cerebral blood flow during the complex cognitive task of meditation: A preliminary SPECT study. *Psychiatric Research: Neuroimaging Section, 106,* 113–122.

Newcomer, J. W., Craft, S., Hershey, T., Askins, K., & Bardgett, M. E. (1994). Glucocorticoid-induced impairment in declarative memory performance in adult humans. *Journal of Neuroscience, 14,* 2047–2053.

Newcomer, J. W., Selke, G., Melson, A. K., Hershey, T., Craft, S., Richards, K., et al. (1999). Decreased memory performance in healthy humans induced by stress-level cortisol treatment. *Archives of General Psychiatry, 56,* 527–533.

Newman, D. (1982). Perspective-taking versus context in understanding lies. *Quarterly Newsletter of the Laboratory of Comparative Human Cognition, 4,* 26–29.

Newman, S. D., Carpenter, P. A., Varma, S., & Just, M. A. (2003). Frontal and parietal participation in problem solving in the Tower of London: fMRI and computational modeling of planning and high-level perception. *Neuropsychologia, 41,* 1668–1682.

Nichols, K., & Champness, B. (1971). Eye gaze and the GRS. *Journal of Experimental Social Psychology, 7,* 623–626.

Nielson, K. A., Yee, D., & Erickson, K. I. (2005). Memory enhancement by a semantically unrelated emotional arousal source induced after learning. *Neurobiology of Learning and Memory, 84,* 49–56.

Nikolaenko, N. N., Egorov, A. Y., & Freiman, E. A. (1997). Representational activity of the right and left hemispheres of the brain. *Behavioral Neurology, 10,* 49–59.

Nilsson, L., Mohammed, A. K. H., Henriksson, B. G., Folkesson, R., Winblad, B., & Bergstrom, L. (1993). Environmental influence on somatostatin levels and gene expression in the rat brain. *Brain Research, 628,* 93–98.

Nimchinsky, E. A., Gilissen, E., Allman, J. M., Perl, D. P., Erwin, J. M., & Hof, P. R. (1999). A neuronal morphologic type unique to humans and great apes. *Proceedings of the National Academy of Sciences, USA, 96,* 5268–5273.

Nimchinsky, E. A., Vogt, B. A., Morrison, J. H., & Hof, P. R. (1995). Spindle neurons of the human anterior cingulate cortex. *Journal of Comparative Neurology, 355,* 27–37.

Nisenbaum, L. K., Zigmond, M. J., Sved, A. F., & Abercrombie, E. D. (1991). Prior exposure to chronic stress results in enhanced synthesis and release of hippocampal norepinephrine in response to novel stressors. *Journal of Neuroscience, 11*, 1478–1484.

Nishitani, N., & Hari, R. (2000). Temporal dynamics of cortical representation for action. *Proceedings of the National Academy of Sciences, USA, 97*, 913–918.

Nishitani, N., Schürmann, M., Amunts, K., & Hari, R. (2004). Broca's regions: From action to language. *Physiology, 20*, 60–69.

Nitschke, J. B., Nelson, E. E., Rusch, B. D., Fox, A. S., Oakes, T. R., & Davidson, R. J. (2004). Orbitofrontal cortex tracks positive mood in mothers viewing pictures of their newborn infants. *NeuroImage, 21*(2), 583–592.

Nobre, A. C., Coull, J. T., Frith, C. D., & Mesulam, M. M. (1999). Orbitofrontal cortex is activated during breaches of expectation in tasks of visual attention. *Nature Neuroscience, 2*, 11–12.

Nolte, J. (2008). *The human brain: An introduction to its functional anatomy* (6th ed.). St. Louis, MO: Mosby.

Nomura, M., Iidaka, T., Kakehi, K., Tsukiura, T., Hasegawa, T., Maeda, Y., et al. (2003). Frontal lobe networks for effective processing of ambiguously expressed emotions in humans. *Neuroscience Letters, 348*, 113–116.

Northoff, G., Heinzel, A., Bermpohl, F., Niese, R., Pfennig, A., Pascual-Leone, A., et al. (2004). Reciprocal modulation and attenuation in the prefrontal cortex: An fMRI study on emotional-cognitive interaction. *Human Brain Mapping, 21*, 202–212.

Nottebohm, F. (1981). A brain for all seasons: Cyclical anatomical changes in song-control nuclei of the canary brain. *Science, 214*, 1368–1370.

Oatley, K. (1992). Integrative action of narrative. In D. J. Stein & J. E. Young (Eds.), *Cognitive science and clinical disorders* (pp. 151–172). New York: Academic Press.

Oberheim, N. A., Wang, X., Goldman, S., & Nedergaard, M. (2006). Astrocytic complexity distinguishes the human brain. *Trends in Neurosciences, 29*, 547–553.

O'Brien, J. T. (1997). The "glucocorticoid cascade" hypothesis in man. *British Journal of Psychiatry, 170*, 199–201.

Ochs, E., & Capps, L. (2001). *Living narrative: Creating lives in everyday storytelling.* Cambridge, MA: Harvard University Press.

Ochsner, K. N., Beer, J. S., Robertson, E. R., Cooper, J. C., Gabrieli, J. D. E., Kihlstrom, J. F., et al. (2005). The neural correlates of direct and reflected self-knowledge. *NeuroImage, 28*, 797–814

Ochsner, K. N., Bunge, S. A., Gross, J. J., & Gabrieli, J. D. E. (2002). Rethinking feelings: An fMRI study of the cognitive regulation of emotion. *Journal of Cognitive Neuroscience, 14*, 1215–1229.

Ochsner, K. N., & Gross, J. J. (2008). Cognitive emotion regulation. Insights from social cognitive and affective neuroscience. *Current Directions in Psychological Science, 17*(2), 153–158.

Ochsner, K. N., Ray, R. D., Cooper, J. C., Robertson, E. R., Chopra, S., Gabrieli, J. D. E., et al. (2004). For better or for worse: Neural systems supporting the cognitive down- and up-regulation of negative emotion. *NeuroImage, 23*, 483–499.

O'Doherty, J. (2004). Reward representation and reward-related learning in the human brain: Insights from neuroimaging. *Current Opinion in Neurobiology, 14*, 769–776.

O'Doherty, J., Kringelbach, M. L., Rolls, E. T., Hornak, J., & Andrews, C. (2001). Abstract reward and punishment representations in the human orbitofrontal cortex. *Nature Neuroscience, 4*, 95–102.

O'Doherty, J. P., Deichmann, R., Critchley, H. D., & Dolan, R. J. (2002). Neural responses during anticipation of a primary taste reward. *Neuron, 33*, 815–826.

O'Donnell, D., Larocque, S., Seckl, J. R., & Meaney, M. J. (1994). Postnatal handling alters glucocorticoid, but not mineralocorticoid messenger RNA expression in the hippocampus of adult rats. Brain Research. *Molecular Brain Research, 26*(1–2), 242–248.

Ohman, A., Carlsson, K., Lundqvist, D., & Ingvar, M. (2007). On the unconscious subcortical origin of human fear. *Physiology and Behavior, 92*, 180–185.

O'Keefe, J., & Nadel, L. (1978). *The hippocampus as a cognitive map.* Oxford: Clarendon.

Olsson, A., Ebert, J. P., Banaji, M. R., & Phelps, E. A. (2005). The role of social groups in the persistence of learned fear. *Science, 309*, 785–787.

Olsson, A., & Phelps, E. A. (2007). Social learning of fear. *Nature Neuroscience, 10*, 1095–1102.

Öngür, D., & Price, J. L. (2000). The organization of networks within the orbital and medial prefrontal cotex of rats, monkeys, and humans. *Cerebral Cortex, 10*, 206–219.

Ono, T., Nishijo, H., & Uwano, T. (1995). Amygdala role in conditioned associative learning. *Progress in Neurobiology, 46*, 401–422.

Orban, G. A., Sunaert, S., Todd, J. T., Van Hecke, P., & Marchal, G. (1999). Human cortical regions involved in extracting depth from motion. *Neuron, 24*, 929–940.

Orban, G., Claeys, K., Nelissen, K., Smans, R., Sunaert, S., Todd, J., et al. (2006). Mapping the parietal cortex of human and non-human primates. *Neuropsychologia, 44*, 2647–2667.

Orlinsky, D. E., & Howard, K. J. (1986). Process and outcome in psychotherapy. In S. L. Garfield & A. E. Bergin (Eds.), *Handbook of psychotherapy and behavior change* (pp. 311–381). New York: John Wiley & Sons.

Ornitz, E. M., & Pynoos, R. S. (1989). Startle modulation in children with posttraumatic stress disorder. *American Journal of Psychiatry, 146*, 866–870.

Ouspensky, P. D. (1954). *The psychology of man's possible evolution.* New York: Alfred Knopf.

Ovtscharoff, W., Jr., & Braun, K. (2001). Maternal separation and social isolation modulate the postnatal development of synaptic composition in the infralimbic cortex of Octodon degus. *Neuroscience, 104,* 33–40.

Ovtscharoff, W., Helmeke, C., & Braun, K. (2006). Lack of paternal care affects synaptic development in the anterior cingulate cortex. *Brain Research, 1116,* 58–63.

Pagnoni, G., Zink, C. F., Montague, R., & Berns, G. S. (2002). Activity in human ventral striatum locked to errors of reward prediction. *Nature Neuroscience, 5,* 97–98.

Panksepp, J. (1998). *Affective neuroscience: The foundation of human and animal emotions.* New York: Oxford University Press.

Panksepp, J., Nelson, E., & Siviy, S. (1994). Brain opioids and mother-infant social motivation. *Acta Paediatrica, 83*(397), 40–46.

Paquette, V., Lévesque, J., Mensour, B., Leroux, J., Beaudoin, G., Bourgouin, P., et al. (2003). "Change the mind and you change the brain": Effects of cognitive-behavioral therapy on the neural correlates of spider phobia. *NeuroImage, 18,* 401–409.

Parente, R., & Herrmann, D. (1996). *Retraining cognition.* Gaithersburg, MD: Aspen Publications.

Pariente, J., White, P., Frackowiak, R. S. J., & Lewith, G. (2005). Expectancy and belief modulate the neuronal substrates of pain treated by acupuncture. *NeuroImage, 25,* 1161–1167.

Paris, J., Zelkowitz, P., Guzder, J., Joseph, S., & Feldman, R. (1999). Neuropsychological factors associated with borderline pathology in children. *Journal of the Academy of Child and Adolescent Psychiatry, 38,* 770–774.

Park, C. R., Campbell, A. M., Woodson, J. C., Smith, T. P., Fleshner, M., & Diamond, D. M. (2006). Permissive influence of stress in the expression of a u-shaped relationship between serum corticosterone levels and spatial memory errors in rats. *Dose-Response, 4,* 55–74.

Park, M. K., Hoang, T. A., Belluzzi, J. D., & Leslie, F. M. (2003). Gender specific effect of neonatal handling on stress reactivity of adolescent rats. *Journal of Neuroendocrinology, 15*(3), 289–295.

Parsons, C. G., Stöffler, A., & Danysz, W. (2007). Memantine: A NMDA receptor antagonist that improves memory by restoration of homeostasis in the glutamatergic system—too little activation is bad, too much is even worse. *Neuropharmacology, 53,* 699–723.

Pascual-Leone, A., Rubio, B., Pallardo, F., & Catala, M. D. (1996). Rapid-rate transcranial magnetic stimulation of left dorsolateral prefrontal cortex in drug-resistant depression. *Lancet, 348,* 233–237.

Paus, T., Petrides, M., Evans, A. C., & Meyer, E. (1993). Role of the human anterior cingulate cortex in the control of oculomotor, manual, and speech responses: A positron emission tomography study. *Journal of Neurophysiology, 70,* 453–469.

Pavlides, C., Watanabe, Y., Magarinos, A. M., & McEwen, B. S. (1995). Opposing roles of the type I and type II adrenal steroid receptors in hippocampal long-term potentiation. *Neuroscience, 68*(2), 387–394.

Pawluski, J., & Galea, L. (2006). Hippocampal morphology is differentially affected by reproductive experience in the mother. *Journal of Neurobiology, 66*(1), 71–81.

Paz-Alonso, P. M., & Goodman, G. S. (2008). Trauma and memory: Effects of post-event misinformation, retrieval order, and retention interval. *Memory, 16*(1), 58–75.

Peers, P. V., Ludwig, C. J. H., Rorden, C., Cusack, R., Bonfiglioli, C., Bundesen, C., et al. (2005). Attentional functions of parietal and frontal cortex. *Cerebral Cortex, 15*, 1469–1484.

Pelphrey, K. A., Singerman, J. D., Allison, T., & McCarthy, G. (2003). Brain activation evoked by perception of gaze shifts: The influence of context. *Neuropsychologia, 41*, 156–170.

Penades, R., Boget, T., Lomena, F., Mateos, J., Catalan, R., Gasto, C., et al. (2002). Could the hypofrontality pattern in schizophrenia be modified through neuropsychological rehabilitation? *Acta Psychiatrica Scandinavica, 105*, 202–208.

Pencea, V., Bingaman, K. D., Wiegland, S. J., & Luskin, M. B. (2001). Infusion of brain-derived neurotrophic factor into the lateral ventricle of the adult rat leads to new neurons in the parenchyma of the striatum, septum, thalamus, and hypothalamus. *Journal of Neuroscience, 21*, 6706–6717.

Penfield, W., & Perot, P. (1963). The brain's record of auditory and visual experience. *Brain, 86*, 595–696.

Pennebaker, J. W. (1997). Writing about emotional experiences as a therapeutic process. *Psychological Science, 8*(3), 162–166.

Pennebaker, J. W., & Beall, S. K. (1986). Confronting a traumatic event: Toward an understanding of inhibition and disease. *Journal of Abnormal Psychology, 95*(3), 274–281.

Pennebaker, J. W., Kiecolt-Glaser, J. K., & Glaser, R. (1988). Disclosure of traumas and immune function: Health implications for psychotherapy. *Journal of Consulting and Clinical Psychology, 56*, 239–245.

Pepperberg, I. M. (2008). *Alex and Me: How a scientist and a parrot uncovered a hidden world of animal intelligence—and formed a deep bond in the process*. New York: HarperCollins.

Pérez-Jaranay, J. M., & Vives, F. (1991). Electrophysiological study of the response of medial prefrontal cortex neurons to stimulation of the basolateral nucleus of the amygdala in the rat. *Brain Research, 564*, 97–101.

Perls, F., Hefferline, R., & Goodman, P. (1951). *Gestalt therapy: Excitement and growth in human personality*. New York: Dell.

Perls, T. T., Alpert, L., & Fretts, R. C. (1997). Middle-aged mothers live longer. *Nature, 389*, 133.

Perrett, D. I., Rolls, E. T., & Caan, W. (1982). Visual neurons responsive to faces in the monkey temporal cortex. *Experimental Brain Research, 47,* 329–342.

Perrett, D. I., Smith, A. J., Potter, D. D., Mistlin, A. J., Head, A. D., Milner, A. D., et al. (1984). Neurons responsive to faces in the temporal cortex: Studies of functional organization, sensitivity to identity and relation to perception. *Human Neurobiology, 3,* 197–208.

Perry, B. D., Pollard, R. A., Blakley, T. I., Baker, W. L., & Vigilante, D. (1995). Childhood trauma, the neurobiology of adaptation, and "use dependent" development of the brain: How "states" become "traits." *Infant Mental Health Journal, 16,* 271–291.

Persinger, M. A., & Makarec, K. (1991). Greater right hemisphericity is associated with lower self-esteem in adults. *Perceptual and Motor Skills, 73,* 1244–1246.

Pessoa, L. (2008). On the relationship between emotion and cognition. *Nature Reviews Neuroscience, 9,* 148–158.

Petrides, M., Alivisatos, B., & Frey, S. (2002). Differential activation of the human orbital, mid-ventrolateral, and mid-dorsolateral prefrontal cortex during the processing of visual stimuli. *Proceedings of the National Academy of Sciences, USA, 99,* 5649–5654.

Petrie, K. J., Booth, R. J., & Pennebaker, J. W. (1998). The immunological effects of thought suppression. *Journal of Pesonality and Social Psychology, 75,* 1264–1272.

Petrie, K. J., Booth, R. J., Pennebaker, J. W., Davison, K. P., & Thomas, M. G. (1995). Disclosure of trauma and immune response to a hepatitis B vaccination program. *Journal of Consulting and Clinical Psychology, 63,* 787–792.

Petrovic, P., Kelso, E., Petersson, K. M., & Ingvar, M. (2002). Placebo and opioid analgesia—Imaging a shared neuronal network. *Science, 295,* 1737–1740.

Petty, F., Chae, Y., Kramer, G., Jordan, S., & Wilson, L. (1994). Learned helplessness sensitizes hippocampal norepinephrine to mild stress. *Biological Psychiatry, 35,* 903–908.

Pezawas, L., Meyer-Lindenberg, A., Drabant, E. M., Verchinski, B. A., Munoz, K. E., Kolachana, B. S., et al. (2005). 5-HTTLPR polymorphism impacts human cingulate-amygdala interactions: A genetic susceptibility mechanism for depression. *Nature Neuroscience, 8,* 828–834.

Pfrieger, F. W., & Barres, B. A. (1996). New views on synapse-glia interactions. *Current Opinions in Neurobiology, 6,* 615–621.

Pham, K., Nacher, J., Hof, P. R., & McEwen, B. (2003). Repeated restraint stress suppresses neurogenesis and induces biphasic PSA-NCAM expression in the adult rat dentate gyrus. *European Journal of Neuroscience, 17,* 879–886.

Pham, T. M., Soderstrom, S., Henriksson, B. G., & Mohammed, A. H. (1997). Effects of neonatal stimulation on later cognitive function and hippocampal nerve growth factor. *Behavioral Brain Research, 86,* 113–120.

Phan, K. L., Britton, J. C., Taylor, S. F., Fig, L. M., & Liberzon, I. (2006). Corticolimbic blood flow during nontraumatic emotional processing in posttraumatic stress disorder. *Archives of General Psychiatry, 63,* 184–192.

Phan, K. L., Fitzegerald, D., Nathan, P., Moore, G., Uhde, T., & Tancer, M. (2005). Neural substrates for voluntary suppression of negative affect: A functional magnetic resonance imaging study. *Biological Psychiatry, 57,* 210–219.

Phan, K. L., Wager, T., Taylor, S. F., & Liberzon, I. (2002). Functional neuroanatomy of emotion: A meta-analysis of emotion activation studies in PET and fMRI. *NeuroImage, 16,* 331–348.

Phelps, E. A. (2006). Emotion and cognition: Insights from studies of the human amygdala. *Annual Review of Psychology, 57,* 27–53.

Phelps, E. A., & Anderson, A. K. (1997). Emotional memory: What does the amygdala do? *Current Biology, 7,* R311–R314.

Phelps, E. A., Delgado, M. R., Nearing, K. I., & LeDoux, J. E. (2004). Extinction learning in humans: Role of the amygdala and vmPFC. *Neuron, 43,* 897–905.

Phelps, E., Ling, S., & Carrasco, M. (2006). Emotion facilitates perception and potentiates the perceptual benefits of attention. *Psychological Science, 17*(4), 292–299.

Phillips, D. P., Ruth, T. E., & Wagner, L. M. (1993). Psychology and survival. *The Lancet, 342,* 1142–1145.

Pia, L., Neppi-Modona, M., Ricci, R., & Berti, A. (2004). Special issue: The anatomy of anosognosia for hemiplegia: A meta-analysis. *Cortex, 40,* 367–377.

Piazza, M., Izard, V., Pinel, P., Le Bihan, D., & Dehaene, S. (2004). Tuning curves for approximate numerosity in the human intraparietal sulcus. *Neuron, 44,* 547–555.

Pilowsky, D. J., Wickramaratne, P., Talati, A., Tang, M., Hughes, C. W., Garber, J., et al. (2008). Children of depressed mothers 1 year after the initiation of maternal treatment: Findings from the STAR*D-Child study. *American Journal of Psychiatry, 165,* 1136–1147.

Pissiota, A., Frans, O., Fernandez, M., von Knorring, L., Fischer, H., & Fredrikson, M. (2002). Neurofunctional correlates of posttraumatic stress disorder: A PET symptom provocation study. *European Archives of Psychiatry and Clinical Neuroscience, 252,* 68–75.

Pitman, R. K., Orr, S. P., van der Kolk, B. A., Greenberg, M. S., Meyerhoff, J. L., & Mougey, E. H. (1990). Analgesia: A new dependent variable for the biological study of posttraumatic stress disorder. In M. E. Wolf & A. D. Mosnaim (Eds.), *Posttraumatic stress disorder: Etiology, phenomenology, and treatment* (pp. 140–147). Washington, DC: American Psychiatric Press.

Pittenger, C., & Duman, R. S. (2008). Stress, depression, and neuroplasticity: A convergence of mechanisms. *Neuropsychopharmacology, 33,* 88–109.

Pizzagalli, D., Pascual-Marqui, R. D., Nitschke, J. B., Oakes, T. R., Larson, C. L., Abercrombie, H. C., et al. (2001). Anterior cingulate activity as a predictor of degree of treatment reponse in major depression: Evidence from brain electrical tomography analysis. *American Journal of Psychiatry, 158,* 405–415.

Platt, M. L., & Glimcher, P. W. (1999). Neural correlates of decision variables in parietal cortex. *Nature, 400,* 233–238.

Ploj, K., Roman, E., Bergstrom, L., & Nylander, I. (2001). Effects of neonatal handling on nociceptin/orphanin FQ and opioid peptide levels in female rats. *Pharmacology, Biochemistry and Behavior, 69,* 173–179.

Plotsky, P. M., & Meaney, M. J. (1993). Early, postnatal experience alters hypothalamic corticotropin-releasing factor (CRF) MRNA, median eminence CRF content and stress-induced release in adult rats. *Molecular Brain Research, 18,* 195–200.

Pochon, J. B., Levy, R., Fossati, P., Lehericy, S., Poline, J. B., Pillon, B., et al. (2002). The neural system that bridges reward and cognition in humans: An fMRI study. *Proceedings of the National Academy of Sciences, USA, 99*(8), 5669-5674.

Polley, D. B., Chen-Bee, C. H., & Frostig, R. D. (1999). Two directions of plasticity in the sensory-deprived adult cortex. *Neuron, 24,* 623–637.

Pope, S. K., Whiteside, L., Brooks-Gunn, J., Kelleher, K. J., Rickert, V. I., Bradley, R. H., et al. (1993). Low-birth-weight infants born to adolescent mothers. Effects of coresidency with grandmother on child development. *Journal of the American Medical Association, 269,* 1396–1400.

Popescu, A. T., Saghyan, A. A., & Paré, D. (2007). NMDA-dependent facilitation of corticostriatal plasticity by the amygdala. *Proceedings of the National Academy of Sciences, USA, 104*(1), 341–346.

Porges, S. W. (2007). The polyvagal perspective. *Biological Psychology, 74*(2), 116–143.

Porges, S. W., Doussard-Roosevelt, J. A., & Maiti, A. K. (1994). Vagal tone and the physiological regulation of emotion. In N. Fox (Ed.), Biological and behavioral foundations of emotion regulation. *Monographs of the Society for Research in Child Development, 59*(2–3, Serial No. 240, pp. 167–186).

Porges, S. W., Doussard-Roosevelt, J. A., Portales, A. L., & Greenspan, S. I. (1996). Infant regulation of the vagal "brake" predicts child behavior problems: A psychobiological model of social behavior. *Developmental Psychobiology, 29,* 697–712.

Porto, P. R., Oliveria, L., Mari, J., Volchan, E., Figueira, I., & Ventura, P. (2009). Does cognitive behavior therapy change the brain? A systematic review of neuroimaging in anxiety disorders. *Journal of Neuropsychiatry and Clinical Neuroscience, 21,* 114–125.

Post, R. M., & Weiss, S. R. B. (1997). Emergent properties of neural systems: How focal molecular neurobiological alterations can affect behavior. *Development and Psychopathology, 9,* 907–929.

Post, R. M., Weiss, S. R. B., Li, H., Smith, A., Zhang, L. X., Xing, G., et al. (1998). Neural plasticity and emotional memory. *Development and Psychopathology, 10,* 829–855.

Prasko, J., Horácek, J., Záleský, R., Kopecek, M., Novák, T., Pasková, B., et al. (2004). The change of regional brain metabolism (18FDG PET) in panic disorder during the treatment with cognitive behavioral therapy or anidepressants. *Neuroendocrinology Letters, 25,* 340–348.

Pribram, K. H. (1991). *Brain and perception: Holonomy and structure in figural processing.* Hillsdale, NJ: Erlbaum.

Pribram, K. H., & Gill, M. M. (1976). *Freud's "Project" re-assessed: Preface to contemporary cognitive theory and neuropsychology.* New York: Basic Books.

Price, B. H., Daffner, K. R., Stowe, R. M., & Mesulam, M. M. (1990). The comportmental learning disabilities of early frontal lobe damage. *Brain, 113,* 1383–1393.

Price, J. L., Carmichael, S. T., & Drevets, W. C. (1996). Networks related to the orbital and medial prefrontal cortex; a substrate for emotional behavior? *Progress in Brain Research, 107,* 523–536.

Prickaerts, J., Koopmans, G., Blokland, A., & Scheepens, A. (2004). Learning and adult neurogenesis: Survival with or without proliferation? *Neurobiology of Learning and Memory, 81,* 1–11.

Pruessner, J. C., Baldwin, M. W., Dedovic, K., Renwick, R., Mahani, N. K., Lord, C., et al. (2005). Self-esteem, locus of control, hippocampal volume, and cortisol regulation in young and old adulthood. *NeuroImage, 28,* 815–826.

Pulver, S. E. (2003). On the astonishing clinical irrelevance of neuroscience. *Journal of the American Psychoanalytic Association, 51,* 755–772.

Purves, D., & Lichtman, J. (1980). Elimination of synapses in the developing nervous system. *Science, 210,* 153–157.

Purves, D., & Voyvodic, J. T. (1987). Imaging mammalian nerve cells and their connections over time in living animals. *Trends in Neurosciences, 10,* 398–404.

Quintana, J., & Fuster, J. M. (1999). From perception to action: Temporal integrative functions of prefrontal and parietal neurons. *Cerebral Cortex, 9,* 213–221.

Quirk, G. J., & Beer, J. S. (2006). Prefrontal involvement in the regulation of emotion: Convergence of rat and human studies. *Current Opinion in Neurobiology, 16,* 723–727.

Quirk, G. J., Likhtik, E., Pelletier, J. G., & Pare, D. (2003). Stimulation of medial prefrontal cortex decreases the responsiveness of central amygdala output neurons. *Journal of Neuroscience, 23,* 8800–8807.

Radecki, D. T., Brown, L. M., Martinez, J., & Teyler, T. J. (2005). BDNF protects against stress-induced impairments in spatial learning and memory and LTP. *Hippocampus, 15*(2), 246–253.

Radley, J. J., Rocher, A. B., Miller, M., Janssen, W. G. M., Liston, C., Hof, P. R., et al. (2006). Repeated stress induces dendritic spine loss in the rat medial prefrontal cortex. *Cerebral Cortex, 16,* 313–320.

Raine, A., Buchsbaum, M. S., Stanley, J., Lottenberg, S., Abel, L., & Stoddard, J. (1994). Selective reductions in prefrontal glucose metabolism in murderers. *Biological Psychiatry, 36,* 365–373.

Rainnie, D. G., Bergeron, R., Sajdyk, T. J., Patil, M., Gehlert, D. R., & Shekhar, A. (2004). Corticotrophin releasing factor-induced synaptic plasticity in the amygdala translates stress into emotional disorders. *Journal of Neuroscience, 24,* 3471–3479.

Rakic, P. (1985). Limits of neurogenesis in primates. *Science, 227,* 154–156.

Ramachandran, V. S., Rogers-Ramachandran, D., & Stewart, M. (1992). Perceptual correlates of massive cortical reorganization. *Science, 258,* 1159–1160.

Rampon, C., Jiang, C. H., Dong, H., Tang Y. P., Lockhart, D. J., Schultz, P. G., et al. (2000). Effects of environmental enrichment on gene expression in the brain. *Proceedings of the National Academy of Sciences, USA, 97,* 12880–12884.

Ranote, S., Elliott, R., Abel, K. M., Mitchell, R., Deakin, J. F. W., & Appleby, L. (2004). The neural basis of maternal responsiveness to infants: An fMRI study. *Neuroreport, 15,* 1825–1829.

Rao, V. R., & Finkbeiner, S. (2007). NMDA and AMPA receptors: Old channels, new tricks. *Trends in Neurosciences, 30,* 284–291.

Rau, V., & Fanselow, M. S. (2007). Neurobiological and neuroethological perspectives on fear and anxiety. In L. J. Kirmayer, R. Lemelson, & M. Barad (Eds.), *Understanding trauma: Integrating biological, clinical, and cultural perspectives* (pp. 27–40). New York: Cambridge University Press.

Rauch, S. L., Jenike, M. A., Alpert, N. M., Baer, L., Breiter, H. C. R., Savage, C. R., et al. (1994). Regional cerebral blood flow measured during symptom provocation in obsessive-compulsive disorder using oxygen 15-labeled carbon dioxide and positron emission tomography. *Archives of General Psychiatry, 51,* 62–70.

Rauch, S. L., Shin, L. M., & Phelps, E. A. (2006). Neurocircuitry models of posttraumatic stress disorder and extinction: human neuroimaging research—past, present, and future. *Journal of Biological Psychiatry, 60,* 376–382.

Rauch, S. L., Shin, L. M., Segal, E., Pitman, R. K., Carson, M. A., McMullin, K., et al. (2003). Selectively reduced regional cortical volumes in post-traumatic stress disorder. *NeuroReport, 14,* 913–916.

Rauch, S. L., van der Kolk, B. A., Fisler, R. E., Alpert, N. M., Orr, S. P., Savage, C. R., et al. (1996). A symptom provocation study of posttraumatic stress disorder using positron emission tomography and script-driven imagery. *Archive of General Psychiatry, 53,* 380–387.

Rees, G., Kreiman, G., & Koch, C. (2002). Neural correlates of consciousness in humans. *Nature Reviews Neuroscience, 3,* 261–270.

Rees, S. L., Steiner, M., & Fleming, A. S. (2006). Early deprivation, but not maternal separation, attenuates rise in corticosterone levels after exposure to a novel environment in both juvenile and adult female rats. *Behavioral Brain Research, 175*(2), 383–391.

Regard, M., Oelz, O., Brugger, P., & Landis, T. (1989). Persistent cognitive impairment in climbers after repeated exposure to extreme altitude. *Neurology, 39,* 210–213.

Reich, W. (1945). *Character analysis.* New York: Simon & Schuster.

Reiman, E. M., Raichle, M. E., Robins, E., Mintun, M. A., Fusselman, M. J., Fox, P. T., et al. (1989). Neuroanatomical correlates of a lactate-induced anxiety attack. *Archives of General Psychiatry, 46,* 493–500.

Resnick, H. S., Yehuda, R., Pitman, R. K., & Foy, D. W. (1995). Effects of previous trauma on acute plasma cortisol level following rape. *American Journal of Psychiatry, 152*, 1675–1677.

Ressler, K. J., Rothbaum, B. O., Tannenbaum, L., Anderson, P., Graap, K., Zimand, E., et al. (2004). Cognitive enhancers as adjuncts to psychotherapy. *Archives of General Psychiatry, 61*, 1136–1144.

Rezai, K., Andreasen, N. C., Alliger, R., Cohen, G., Swayze, V., & O'Leary, D. S. (1993). The neuropsychology of the prefrontal cortex. *Archives of Neurology, 50*, 636–642.

Richards, M., & Deary, I. J. (2005). A life course approach to cognitive reserve: A model for cognitive aging and development? *Annals of Neurology, 58*, 617–622.

Rilling, J. K., Gutman, D. A., Zeh, T. R., Panoni, G., Berns, G. S., & Kilts, C. D. (2002). A neural basis for social cooperation. *Neuron, 35*, 395–405.

Rizzolatti, G., & Arbib, M. A. (1998). Language within our grasp. *Trends in Neurosciences, 21*, 188–194.

Rizzolatti, G., & Sinigaglia, C. (2008). *Mirrors in our brain: How our minds share actions and emotions.* New York: Oxford University Press.

Roberts, A. C., & Wallis, J. D. (2000). Inhibitory control and affective processing in the prefrontal cortex: Neuropsychological studies in the common marmoset. *Cerebral Cortex, 10*, 252–262.

Robinson, R. G., Kubos, K. L., Starr, L. B., Rao, K., & Price, T. R. (1984). Mood disorder in stroke patient: Importance of location of lesion. *Brain, 1*, 91–93.

Roffman, J. L., Marci, C. D., Glick, D. M., Dougherty, D. D., & Rauch, S. L. (2005). Neuroimaging and the functional neuroanatomy of psychotherapy. *Psychological Medicine, 35*, 1–14.

Rogan, M. T., & LeDoux, J. E. (1996). Emotion: Systems, cells, synaptic plasticity. *Cell, 85*, 469–475.

Rogan, M. T., Staubli, U. V., & LeDoux, J. E. (1997). Fear conditioning induces associative long-term potentiation in the amygdala. *Nature, 390*, 604–607.

Rogers, A. R. (1993). Why menopause? *Evolutionary Ecology, 7*, 406–420.

Rogers, C. R. (1942). *Counseling and psychotherapy.* Boston: Houghton Mifflin.

Rogers, R. D., Ramnani, N., Mackay, C., Wilson, J. L., Jezzard, P., Carter, C. S., et al. (2004). Distinct portions of anterior cingulate cortex and medial prefrontal cortex are activated by reward processing in separable phases of decision-making cognition. *Biological Psychiatry, 55*, 594–602.

Rokeach, M. (1964). *The three Christs of Ypsilanti.* New York: Columbia University Press.

Roozendaal, B. (1999). Glucocorticoids and the regulation of memory consolidation. *Psychoneuroendocrinology, 25*, 213–238.

Ropper, A. H., & Brown, R. H. (2005). *Adams and Victor's principles of neurology.* New York: McGraw-Hill.

Rorden, C., Mattingley, J., Karnath, H., & Driver, J. (1997). Visual extinction and prior entry: Impaired perception of temporal order with intact motion perception after unilateral parietal damage. *Neuropsychologia, 35,* 421–433.

Rosenkranz, J. A., Moore, H., & Grace, A. A. (2003). The prefrontal cortex regulates lateral amygdala neuronal plasticity and responses to previously conditioned stimuli. *Journal of Neuroscience, 23,* 11054–11064.

Rosenzweig, M. R. (2001). Learning and neural plasticity over the life span. In P. E. Gold & W. T. Greenough (Eds.), *Memory consolidation: Essays in honor of James L. McGauggh.* Washington, DC: American Psychological Association.

Ross, E. D., Homan, R. W., & Buck, R. (1994). Differential hemispheric lateralization of primary and social emotions: Implications for developing a comprehensive neurology for emotions, repression, and the subconscious. *Neuropsychiatry, Neuropsychology, and Behavioral Neurology, 7,* 1–19.

Rossi, E. L. (1993). *The psychobiology of mind-body healing.* New York: Norton.

Rothbart, M. K., Taylor, S. B., & Tucker, D. M. (1989). Right-sided facial asymmetry in infant emotional expression. *Neuropsychologia, 27,* 675–687.

Royer, S., Martina, M., & Paré, D. (1999). An inhibitory interface gates impulse traffic between the input and output stations of the amygdala. *Journal of Neuroscience, 19,* 10575–10583.

Rubens, A. B. (1985). Caloric stimulation and unilateral visual neglect. *Neurology, 35,* 1019–1024.

Rubia, K., Overmeyer, S., Taylor, E., Brammer, M., Williams, S., Simmons, A., et al. (1999). Hypofrontality in attention deficit hyperactivity disorder during higher-order motor control: A study with functional MRI. *American Journal of Psychiatry, 156,* 891–896.

Rubino, G. J., Farahani, K., McGill, D., Van de Wiele, B., Villablanca, J. P., & Wang-Maithieson, A. (2000). Magnetic resonance imaging-guided neurosurgery in the magnetic fringe fields: The next step in neuronavigation. *Neurosurgery, 46,* 643–654.

Ruby, P., & Decety, J. (2001). Effect of subjective perspective taking during simulation of action: A PET investigation of agency. *Nature Neuroscience, 4,* 546–550.

Rushworth, M. F. S., & Behrens, T. E. J. (2008). Choice, uncertainty and value in prefrontal and cingulate cortex. *Nature Neuroscience, 11,* 389–397.

Rushworth, M. F. S., Krams, M., & Passingham, R. E. (2001). The attentional role of the left parietal cortex: The distinct lateralization and localization of motor attention in the human brain. *Journal of Cognitive Neuroscience, 13,* 698–710.

Russo-Neustadt, A. A., Beard, R. C., Huang, Y. M., & Cotman, C. W. (2000). Physical activity and antidepressant treatment potentiate the expression of specific brain-derived neurotrophic factor transcripts in the rat hippocampus. *Neuroscience, 101*(2), 305–312.

Rutter, M., & Rutter, M. (1993). *Developing minds: Challenge and continuity across the life span*. New York: Basic Books.

Ryan, W. (1971). *Blaming the victim*. New York: Pantheon Books.

Saba, G., Rocamora, J. F., Kalalou, K., Benadhira, R., Plaze, M., & Lipski, H. (2004). Repetitive transcranical magnetic stimulation as an add-on therapy in the treatment of mania: A case series of eight patients. *Psychiatry Research, 128*, 199–202.

Sabbagh, M. A. (2004). Understanding orbitofrontal contributions to theory-of-mind reasoning: Implications for autism. *Brain and Cognition, 55*, 209–219.

Sackeim, H. A., Putz, E., Vingiano, W., Coleman, E., & McElhiney, M. (1988). Lateralization in the processing of emotionally laden information. I. Normal functioning. *Neuropsychiatry, Neuropsychology, and Behavioral Neurology, 1*(2), 97–110.

Sackheim, H. A., Greenberg, M. S., Weiman, A. L., Gur, R. C., Hungerbuhler, J. P., & Geschwind, N. (1982). Hemispheric asymmetry in the expression of positive and negative emotions: Neurologic evidence. *Archives of Neurology, 39*, 210–218.

Sakai, Y., Kumano, H., Nishikawa, M., Sakano, Y., Kaiya, H., Imavayashi, E., et al. (2006). Changes in cerebral glucose utilization in patients with panic disorder treated with cognitive-behavioral therapy. *NeuroImage, 33*, 218–226.

Sakamoto, H., Fukuda, R., Okuaki, T., Rogers, M., Kasai, K., Machida, T., et al. (2005). Parahippocampal activation evoked by masked traumatic images in posttraumatic stress disorder: A functional MRI study. *NeuroImage, 26*, 813–821.

Salm, A. K., Modney, B. K., & Hatton, G. I. (1988). Alterations in supraoptic nucleus ultrastructure of maternally behaving virgin rats. *Brain Research Bulletin, 21*, 685–691.

Santini, E., Ge, H., Ren, K., Peña de Ortiz, S., & Quirk, G. L. (2004). Consolidation of fear extinction requires protein synthesis in the medial prefrontal cortex. *Journal of Neuroscience, 24*, 5704–5710.

Sapolsky, R. M. (1985). A mechanism for glucocorticoid toxicity in the hippocampus: Increased neuronal vulnerability to metabolic insults. *Journal of Neuroscience, 5*, 1228–1232.

Sapolsky, R. M. (1987). Glucocorticoids and hippocampal damage. *Trends in Neurosciences, 10*, 346–349.

Sapolsky, R. M. (1990). Stress in the wild. *Scientific American, 262*(1), 116–123.

Sapolsky, R. M. (1996). Why stress is bad for your brain. *Science, 273*, 749–750.

Sapolsky, R. M. (2004). Mothering style and methylation. *Nature Neuroscience, 7*, 791–792.

Sapolsky, R. M., Krey, L. C., & McEwen, B. S. (1984). Glucocorticoid-sensitive hippocampal neurons are involved in terminating the adrenocortical stress response. *Proceedings of the National Academy of Sciences, USA, 81*, 6174–6177.

Sapolsky, R. M., Uno, H., Rebert, C. S., & Finch, C. E. (1990). Hippocampal damage associated with prolonged glucocorticoid exposure in primates. *Journal of Neuroscience, 10,* 2897–2902.

Sarrieau, A., Sharma, S., & Meaney, M. J. (1988). Postnatal development and environmental regulation of hippocampal glucocorticoid and mineralocorticoid receptors. *Developmental Brain Research, 43,* 158–162.

Sarter, M., & Markowitsch, H. J. (1985). The amygdala's role in human mnemonic processing. *Cortex, 21,* 7–24.

Satterfield, J. H., & Dawson, M. E. (1971). Electrodermal correlates of hyperactivity in children. *Psychophysiology, 8,* 191–197.

Sauseng, P., Klimesch, W., Schabus, M., & Doppelmayr, M. (2005). Fronto-parietal EEG coherence in theta and upper alpha reflect central executive functions of working memory. *International Journal of Psychophysiology, 57,* 97–103.

Saxe, G. N., Chinman, G., Berkowitz, R., Hall, K., Leiberg, G., Schwartz, J., et al. (1994). Somatization in patients with dissociative disorders. American *Journal of Psychiatry, 151,* 1329–1333.

Saxena, S., Brody, A. L., Ho, M. L., Zohrabi, N., Maidment, K. M., & Baxter, L. R. (2003). Differential brain metabolic predictors of response to paroxetine in obsessive-compulsive disorder, versus major depression. *American Journal Psychiatry, 160,* 522–532.

Scarmeas, N., Zarahn, E., Anderson, K. E., Honig, L. S., Park, A., Hilton, J., et al. (2004). Cognitive reserve-mediated modulation of positron emission tomographic activations during memory tasks in Alzheimer disease. *Archives of Neurology, 61,* 73–78.

Schaaf, M. J. M., de Kloet, E. R., & Vregeudenhil, E. (2000). Corticosterone effects on BDNF expression in the hippocampus. Implications for memory formation. *Stress, 3*(3), 201–208.

Schacter, D. L. (1976). The hypnagogic state: A critical review of the literature. *Psychological Bulletin, 83,* 452–481.

Schacter, D. L. (1986). Amnesia and crime. *American Psychologist, 41,* 286–295.

Schacter, D. L. (1996). *Searching for memory: The brain, the mind, and the past.* New York: Basic Books.

Schaefer, S. M., Jackson, D. C., Davidson, R. J., Aguirre, G. K., Kimberg, D. Y., & Thompson-Schill, S. L. (2002). Modulation of amygdalar activity by the conscious regulation of negative emotion. *Journal of Cognitive Neuroscience, 14,* 913–921.

Schaie, K. W., & Willis, S. L. (1986). Can decline in adult intellectual functioning be reversed? *Developmental Psychology, 22,* 223–232.

Schall, J. D. (2001). Neural basis of deciding, choosing and acting. *Nature Reviews Neuroscience, 2,* 33–42.

Schiffer, F., Teicher, M. H., & Papanicolaou, A. C. (1995). Evoked potential evidence for right brain activity during the recall of traumatic memories. *Journal of Neuropsychiatry and Clinical Neurosciences, 7,* 169–175.

Schmahmann, J. D. (1997). *The cerebellum and cognition.* New York: Academic Press.

Schmand, B., Smit, J. H., Geerlings, M. I., & Lindeboom, J. (1997). The effects of intelligence and education on the development of dementia: A test of the brain reserve hypothesis. *Psychological Medicine, 27,* 1337–1344.

Schneider, M. L. (1992). Prenatal stress exposure alters postnatal behavioral expression under conditions of novelty challenge in rhesus monkey infants. *Developmental Psychobiology, 25,* 529–540.

Schore, A. N. (1994). *Affect regulation and the origin of the self: The neurobiology of emotional development.* Hillsdale, NJ: Erlbaum.

Schore, A. N. (1997a). Early organization of the nonlinear right brain and development of a predisposition to psychiatric disorders. *Development and Psychopathology, 9,* 595–631.

Schore, A. N. (1997b). A century after Freud's project for a scientific psychology: Is a rapprochement between psychoanalysis and neurobiology at hand? *Journal of the American Psychoanalytic Association, 45,* 841–867.

Schore, A. N. (2000). Attachment and the regulation of the right brain. *Attachment and Human Development, 2,* 23–47.

Schore, J., & Schore, A. (2008). Modern attachment theory: The central role of affect regulation in development and treatment. *Clinical Social Work Journal, 36,* 9–20.

Schrott, L. M. (1997). Effect of training and environment on brain morphology and behavior. *Acta Paediatrica Scandanavia, 422* (Suppl.), 45–47.

Schrott, L. M., Denenberg, V. H., Sherman, G. F., Waters, N. S., Rosen, G. D., & Galaburda, A. M. (1992). Environmental enrichment, neocortical ectopias, and behavior in the autoimmune NZB mouse. *Developmental Brain Research, 67,* 85–93.

Schultz, R. T., Gauthier, I., Klin, A., Fulbright, R. K., Anderson, A. W., Volkmar, F., et al. (2000). Abnormal ventral temporal cortical activity during face discrimination among individuals with autism and Asperger syndrome. *Archives of General Psychiatry, 57,* 331–340.

Schultz, W. (1998). Predictive reward signal of dopamine neurons. *Journal of Neurophysiology, 80,* 1–27.

Schultz, W., Apicella, P., Scarnati, E., & Ljunberg, T. (1992). Neuronal activity in monkey ventral striatum related to the expectation of reward. *Journal of Neuroscience, 12,* 4595–4610.

Schultz, W., Dayan, P., & Montague, P. R. (1997). A neural substrate of prediction and reward. *Science, 275,* 1593–1599.

Schultz, W., Tremblay, L., & Hollerman, J. R. (2000). Reward processing in primate orbitofrontal cortex and basal ganglia. *Cerebral Cortex, 10,* 272–283.

Schulz, K. P., Fan, J., Tang, C. Y, Newcorn, J. H., Buchsbaum, M. S., Cheung, A. M., et. al. (2004). Response inhibition in adolescents diagnosed with attention deficit hyperactivity disorder during childhood: An event-related fMRI study. *American Journal of Psychiatry, 161,* 1650–1657.

Schutter, D. J. L. G. (2009). Antidepressant efficacy of high-frequency transcranial magnetic stimulation over the left dorsolateral prefrontal cortex in double-blind sham-controlled designs: A meta analysis. *Psychological Medicine, 39,* 65–75.

Schuz, A. (1978). Some facts and hypotheses concerning dendritic spines and learning. In M. A. B. Braizer & H. Petsche (Eds.), *Architectonics of the cerebral cortex* (pp. 129–135). New York: Raven.

Schwartz, D. A. (1979). The suicidal character. *Psychiatric Quarterly, 51,* 64–70.

Schwartz, J. M. (1996). *Brain lock: Free yourself from obsessive-compulsive behaviors.* New York: ReganBooks.

Schwartz, J. M., Stoessel, P. W., Baxter, L. R., Martin, K. M., & Phelps, M. E. (1996). Systematic changes in cerebral glucose metabolic rate after successful behavior modification treatment of obsessive-compulsive disorder. *Archives of General Psychiatry, 53,* 109–113.

Schwartz, S. (1964). Effects of neonatal cortical lesions and early environmental factors on adult rat behavior. *Journal of Comparative Physiological Psychology, 57,* 72–77.

Schwartz, S., Assal, F., Valenza, N., Seghier, M. L., & Vuilleumier, P. (2005). Illusory persistence of touch after right parietal damage: Neural correlates of tactile awareness. *Brain, 128,* 277–290.

Sear, R., Mace, R., & McGregor, I. A. (2000). Maternal grandmothers improve nutritional status and survival of children in rural Gambia. *Proceedings Biological Sciences, The Royal Society, 267,* 1641–1647.

Searleman, A. (1977). A review of right hemisphere linguistic capabilities. *Psychological Bulletin, 84,* 503–528.

Seidman, L. J., Faracone, S. V., Goldstein, J. M., Goodman, J. M., Kremen, W. S., Toomey, R., et al. (1999). Thalamic and amygdala-hippocampal volume reductions in first-degree relatives of patients with schizophrenia: An MRI-based morphometric analysis. *Biological Psychiatry, 46,* 941–954.

Seidman, L. J., Valera, E. M., & Makris, N. (2005). Structural brain imaging of attention-deficit/hyperactivity disorder. *Biological Psychiatry, 57,* 1263–1272.

Seitz, R. J., Nickel, J., & Azari, N. P. (2006). Functional modularity of the medial prefrontal cortex: Involvement in human empathy. *Neuropsychology, 20,* 743–751.

Selden, N. R. W., Everitt, B. J., Jarrard, L. E., & Robbins, T. W. (1991). Complimentary roles for the amygdala and hippocampus in aversive conditioning to explicit and contextual cues. *Neuroscience, 42,* 335–350.

Selye, H. (1979). *The stress of my life.* New York: Van Nostrand.

Semmes, J. (1968). Hemispheric specialization: A possible clue to mechanism. *Neuropsychologia, 6,* 11–26.

Sergent, J. (1986). Subcortical coordination of hemispheric activity in commissurotomized patients. *Brain, 109,* 357–369.

Sergent, J. (1990). Furtive incursions into bicameral minds. *Brain, 113,* 537–568.

Serieux, P., & Capgras, J. (1909). Misinterpretive delusional states. In *Les folies raisonnantes: Le delire d'interpretation* (pp. 5–43). Paris: Balliere.

Shapiro, D., Jamner, L. D., & Spence, S. (1997). Cerebral laterality, repressive coping, autonomic arousal, and human bonding. *Acta Scandinavica Physiologica, 640*(Suppl.), 60–64.

Shapiro, F. (1995). *Eye movement desensitization and reprocessing: Basic principles, protocols, and procedures.* New York: Guilford.

Shatz, C. J. (1990). Impulse activity and patterning of connections during CNS development. *Neuron, 5,* 745–756.

Sheline, Y. I., Gado, M. H., & Price, J. L. (1998). Amygdala core nuclei volumes are decreased in recurrent major depression. *NeuroReport, 9,* 2023–2028.

Sheline, Y. I., Wang, P. W., Gado, M. H., Csernansky, J. G., & Vannier, M. W. (1996). Hippocampal atrophy in recurrent major depression. *Proceedings of the National Academy of Sciences, USA, 93,* 3908–3913.

Shenton, M. E., Kikinis, R., Jolesz, F. A., Pollak, S. D., LeMay, M., Wible, C. G., et al. (1992). Abnormalities of the left temporal lobe and thought disorder in schizophrenia: A quantitative magnetic resonance imaging study. *New England Journal of Medicine, 327,* 604–612.

Sherry, D. F., Jacobs, L. F., & Gaulin, S. J. C. (1992). Spatial memory and adaptive specialization of the hippocampus. *Trends in Neurosciences, 15,* 298–303.

Sherry, D. F., & Schacter, D. L. (1987). The evolution of multiple memory systems. *Psychological Review, 94,* 439–454.

Shilony, E., & Grossman, F. K. (1993). Depersonalization as a defense mechanism in survivors of trauma. *Journal of Traumatic Stress, 6,* 119–128.

Shima, K., & Tanji, J. (1998). Role for cingulate motor area cells in voluntary movement selection based on reward. *Science, 282,* 1335–1338.

Shin, L. M., Rauch, S. L., & Pitman, R. K. (2006). Amygdala, medial prefrontal cortex, and hippocampal function in PTSD. *Annals of the New York Academy of Science, 1071,* 67–79.

Shmuelof, L., & Zohary, E. (2006). A mirror representation of others' actions in the human anterior parietal cortex. *Journal of Neuroscience, 26,* 9736–9742.

Siegel, D. J. (1995). Trauma and psychotherapy: A cognitive sciences view. *Journal of Psychotherapy Practice and Research, 4,* 93–122.

Siegel, D. J. (1996). Cognition, memory, and dissociation. *Child and Adolescent Clinics of North America, 5,* 509–536.

Siegel, D. J. (1999). *Developing mind: Toward a neurobiology of interpersonal experience.* New York: Guilford.

Silberman, E. K., & Weingartner, H. (1986). Hemispheric lateralization of functions related to emotion. *Brain and Cognition, 5,* 322–353.

Simon, O., Mangin, J., Cohen, L., Le Bihan, D., & Dehaene, S. (2002). Topographical layout of hand, eye, calculation, and language-related areas in the human parietal lobe. *Neuron, 33,* 475–487.

Simpson, J. R., Drevets, W. C., Snyder, A. Z., Gusnard, D. A., & Raichle, M. E. (2001). Emotion-induced changes in human medial prefrontal cortex: II. During anticipatory anxiety. *Proceedings of the National Academy of Sciences, USA, 98*, 688–693.

Simpson, J. R., Snyder, A. Z., Gusnard, D. A., & Raichle, M. E. (2001). Emotion-induced changes in human medial prefrontal cortex: I. During cognitive task performance. *Proceedings of the National Academy of Sciences, USA, 98*, 683–687.

Sirevaag, A. M., & Greenough, W. T. (1988). A multivariate statistical summary of synaptic plasticity measures in rats exposed to complex, social and individual environments. *Brain Research, 441*, 386–392.

Sirigu, A., Daprati, E., Ciancia, S., Giraux, P., Nighoghossian, N., & Posada, A., et al. (2003). Altered awareness of voluntary action after damage to the parietal cortex. *Nature Neuroscience, 7*, 80–84.

Sirigu, A., Duhamel, J., Coehn, L., Pillon, B., Dubois, B., & Agid, Y. (1996). The mental representation of hand movements after parietal cortex damage. *Science, 273*, 1564–1568.

Siviy, S. M., & Harrison, K. A. (2008). Effects of neonatal handling on play behavior and fear towards a predator odor in juvenile rats (rattus norvegicus). *Journal of Comparative Psychology, 122*(1), 1–8.

Smith, S. D., & Bulman-Fleming, M. B. (2004). A hemispheric asymmetry for the unconscious perception of emotion. *Brain and Cognition, 55*, 452–457.

Smythe, J. W., Rowe, W. B., & Meaney, M. J. (1994). Neonatal handling alters serotonin (5-HT) turnover and 5-HT2 receptor binding in selected brain regions: Relationship to the handling effect on glucocorticoid receptor expression. *Developmental Brain Research, 80*, 183–189.

Snyder, J., & Chatterjee, A. (2004). Spatial-temporal anisometries following right parietal damage. *Neuropsychologia, 42*, 1703–1708.

Snyder, L. H., Batista, A. P., & Andersen, R. A. (1997). Coding of intention in the posterior parietal cortex. *Nature, 386*, 167–170.

Solomon, Z. (1990). Back to the front: Recurrent exposure to combat stress and reactivation of posttraumatic stress disorder. In M. E. Wolf & A. D. Mosnaim (Eds.). *Posttraumatic stress disorder: Etiology, phenomenology, and treatment* (pp. 114–125). Washington, DC: American Psychiatric Press.

Sontheimer, H. (1995). Glial influences on neuronal signaling. *The Neuroscientist, 1*, 123–126.

Spangler, G., & Grossman, K. E. (1993). Biobehavioral organization in securely and insecurely attached infants. *Child Development, 64*, 1439–1450.

Spangler, G., & Schieche, M. (1998). Emotional and adrenocortical responses of infants to the strange situation: The differential function of emotional expression. *International Journal of Behavioral Development, 22*, 681–706.

Spear, L. P. (2000). The adolescent brain and age-related behavioral manifestations. *Neuroscience and Biobehavioral Reviews, 24*, 417–463.

Specter, M. (2001, July 23). Rethinking the brain. *The New Yorker*, 42–53.

Sperry, R. W. (1968). Hemispheric deconnection and unity in conscious awareness. *American Psychologist, 23*, 723–733.

Sperry, R. W., Gazzaniga, M. S., & Bogen, J. E. (1969). Interhemispheric relationships: The neocortical commissures; syndromes of hemisphere disconnection. In P. J. Vinken & G. W. Bruyn (Eds.), *Handbook of clinical neurology* (Vol. 4, pp. 273–290). Amsterdam: North Holland.

Spitz, R. (1946). Hospitalism: A follow-up report on investigation described in volume I, 1945. *Psychoanalytic Study of the Child, 2*, 113–117.

Squire, L. R. (1987). *Memory and brain.* New York: Oxford University Press.

Squire, L. R., & Zola-Morgan, S. (1991). The medial temporal lobe memory system. *Science, 253*, 2380–2386.

Staff, R. T., Murray, A. D., Deary, I. J., & Whalley, L. J. (2004). What provides cerebral reserve? *Brain, 127*, 1191–1199.

Stahl, S. M. (2008). *Stahl's essential psychopharmacology. Neuroscientific basis and practical applications.* New York: Cambridge University Press.

Stamatakis, A., Pondiki, S., Kitraki, E., Diamantopoulou, A., Panagiotaropoulos, T., Raftogianni, A., et al. (2008). Effect of neonatal handling on adult rat spatial learning and memory following acute stress. *Stress, 11*(2), 148–159.

St. Clair, M. (1986). *Object relations and self psychology.* Monterey, CA: Brooks/Cole.

Stein, M. B., Koverola, C., Hanna, C., Torchia, M. G., & McClarty, B. (1997). Hippocampal volume in women victimized by childhood sexual abuse. *Psychological Medicine, 27*, 951–959.

Stennett, R. G. (1957). The relationship of performance level to level of arousal. *Journal of Experimental Psychology, 54*(1), 54–61.

Stephan, H., & Andy, O. J. (1977). Quantitative comparison of the amygdala in insectivores and primates. *Acta Anatomica, 98*, 130–153.

Stern, D. N. (1985). *The interpersonal world of the infant.* New York: Basic Books.

Stern, D. N. (1995). *The motherhood constellation.* New York: Basic Books.

Stern, Y., Alexander, G. E., Prohovnik, I., & Mayeux, R. (1992). Inverse relationship between education and parietotemporal perfusion deficit in Alzheimer's disease. *Annals of Neurology, 32*, 371–375.

Stern, Y., Alexander, G. E., Prohovnik, I., Stricks, L., Link, B., Lennon, M. C., et al. (1995). Relationship between lifetime occupation and parietal flow: Implications for a reserve against Alzheimer's disease pathology. *Neurology, 45*, 55–60.

Stern, Y., Habeck, C., Moeller, J., Scarmeas, N., Anderson, K. E., Hilton, H. J., et al. (2005). Brain networks associated with cognitive reserve in healthy young and old adults. *Cerebral Cortex, 15*, 394–402.

Sterr, A., Muller, M. M., Elbert, T., Rockstroh, B., Pantev, C., & Taub, E. (1998a). Perceptual correlates of changes in cortical representation of fingers in blind multifinger Braille readers. *Journal of Neuroscience, 18*, 4417–4423.

Sterr, A., Muller, M. M., Elbert, T., Rockstroh, B., Pantev, C., & Taub, E. (1998b). Changed perceptions in Braille readers. *Nature, 391*, 134–135.

Stiles, J. (2000). Neural plasticity and cognitive development. *Developmental Neuropsychology, 18*, 237–272.

Stolorow, R. D., & Atwood, G. E. (1979). *Faces in a cloud: Subjectivity in psychoanalytic theory.* New York: Jason Aronson.

Stranahan, A. M., Khalil, D., & Gould, E. (2006). Social isolation delays the positive effects of running on adult neurogenesis. *Nature Neuroscience, 9*, 526–533.

Strange, B. A., & Dolan, R. J. (2004). b-Adrenergic modulation of emotional memory-evoked human amygdala and hippocampal responses. *Proceeding of the National Academy of Science, USA, 101*, 11454–11458.

Straube, T., Glauer, M., Dilger, S., Mentzel, H., & Miltner, W. H. R. (2006). Effects of cognitive-behavioral therapy on brain activation in specific phobia. *NeuroImage, 29*(1), 125–135.

Stuss, D. T., Gallup, G. G., & Alexander, M. P. (2001). The frontal lobes are necessary for "theory of mind." *Brain, 124*, 279–286.

Sullivan, R. M., Wilson, D. A., & Leon, M. (1989). Norepinephrine and learning-induced plasticity in infant rat olfactory system. *Journal of Neuroscience, 9*, 3998–4006.

Sulloway, F. J. (1979). *Freud: Biologist of the mind.* New York: Basic Books.

Sun, L., Jin, Z., Zang, Y. F., Zeng, Y. W., Liu, G., Li, Y., et al. (2005). Differences between attention-deficit disorder with and without hyperactivity: A 1H-magnetic spectroscopy study. *Brain Development, 27*, 340–344.

Svensson, T. H. (1987). Peripheral, autonomic regulation of locus coeruleus noradrenergic neurons in the brain: Putative implications for psychiatry and psychopharmacology. *Psychopharmacology, 92*, 1–7.

Swirsky-Sacchetti, T., Gorton, G., Samuel, S., Sobel, R., Genetta-Wadley, A., & Burleigh, B. (1993). Neuropsychological function in borderline personality disorder. *Journal of Clinical Psychology, 49*, 385–396.

Szyf, M., McGowan, P., & Meaney, M. J. (2008). The social environment and epigenome. *Environmental and Molecular Mutagenesis, 49*(1), 46–60.

Szyf, M., Weaver, I. C. G., Champagne, F. A., Dioro, J., & Meaney, M. J. (2005). Maternal programming of steroid receptor expression and phenotype through DNA methylation in the rat. *Frontiers in Neuroendocrinology, 26*, 139–162.

Szyf, M., Weaver, I., & Meaney, M. (2007). Maternal care, the epigenome and phenotypic differences in behavior. *Reproductive Toxicology, 24*(1), 9–19.

Taber, K. H., & Hurley, R. A. (2008). Astroglia: Not just glue. *Journal of Neuropsychiatry and Clinical Neurosciences, 20*(2), 124–129.

Takahashi, T., Ikeda, K., Ishikawa, M., Tsukasaki, T., Nakama, D., Tanida, S., et al. (2004). Social stress-induced cortisol elevation acutely impairs social memory in humans. *Neuroscience Letters, 363*, 125–130.

Tamietto, M., Geminiani, G., Genero, R., & De Gelder, B. (2007). Seeing fearful body language overcomes attentional deficits in patients with neglect. *Journal of Cognitive Neuroscience, 19*, 445–454.

Tamm, L., Menon, V., & Reiss, A. L. (2006). Parietal attentional system aberrations during target detection in adolescents with attention deficit hyperactivity disorder: Event-related fMRI evidence. *American Journal of Psychiatry, 163*, 1033–1043.

Tamm, L., Menon, V., Ringel, J., & Reiss, A. L. (2004). Event-related fMRI evidence of frontotemporal involvement in aberrant response inhibition and task switching in attention-deficit/hyperactivity disorder. *Journal of the American Academy of Child and Adolescent Psychiatry, 43*, 1430–1440.

Tang, Y. P., Shimizu, E., Dube, G. R., Rampon, C., Kerchner, G. A., Zhuo, M., et al. (1999). Genetic enhancement of learning and memory in mice. *Nature, 401*, 63–69.

Tanji, J., & Hoshi, E. (2001). Behavioral planning in the prefrontal cortex. *Current Opinion in Neurobiology, 11*, 164–170.

Taylor, G. J. (2000). Recent developments in alexithymia theory and research. *Canadian Journal of Psychiatry, 45*, 134–142.

Taylor, J. (2001). The central role of the parietal lobes in consciousness. *Consciousness and Cognition, 10*, 379–417.

Taylor, M. A. (1999). *The fundamentals of clinical neuropsychiatry.* Oxford: Oxford University Press.

Taylor, S. E., & Brown, J. D. (1988). Illusion and well-being: A social psychological perspective on mental health. *Psychological Bulletin, 103*, 193–210.

Teasdale, J. D., Howard, R. J., Cox, S. G., Ha, Y., Brammer, M. J., Williams, S. C. R., et al. (1999). Functional MRI study of the cognitive generation of affect. *American Journal of Psychiatry, 156*, 209–215.

Teicher, M. H., Dumont, N. L., Ito, Y., Vaituzis, C., Geidd, J. N., & Andersen, S. L. (2004). Childhood neglect is associated with reduced corpus callosum area. *Biological Psychiatry, 56*, 80–85.

Teicher, M. H., Ito, Y., Glod, C. A., Andersen, S. L., Dumont, N., & Ackerman, E. (1997). Preliminary evidence for abnormal cortical development in physically and sexually abused children using EEG coherence and MRI. *Annals of the New York Academy of Sciences, 821*, 160–175.

Tejedor-Real, P., Costela, C., & Gibert-Rahola, J. (1998). Neonatal handling reduces emotional reactivity and susceptibility to learned helplessness. Involvement of catecholaminergic systems. *Life Sciences, 62*(1), 37–50.

ten Cate, C. (1989). Behavioral development: Toward understanding processes. In P. P. G. Bateson & P. Klopfer (Eds.), *Perspectives in ethology* (Vol. 8, pp. 243–269). New York: Plenum Press.

Teneback, C. C., Nahas, Z., Speer, A. M., Molloy, M., Stallings, L. E., Spicer, K. M., et al. (1999). Changes in prefrontal cortex and paralimbic activity in depression following two weeks of daily left prefrontal TMS. *Journal of Neuropsychiatry and Clinical Neurosciences, 11*, 426–435.

Thatcher, R. W., Walker, R. A., & Giudice, S. (1987). Human cerebral hemispheres develop at different rates and ages. *Science, 236,* 1110–1113.

Thayer, J. F., & Cohen, B. H. (1985). Differential hemispheric lateralization for positive and negative emotion: An electromyographic study. *Biological Psychology, 21,* 265–266.

Thomas, K. S. (1987). General practice consultation: Is there any point in being positive? *British Medical Journal, 294,* 1200–1202.

Thompson, R. A., Lamb, M. E., & Estes, D. (1982). Stability of infant-mother attachment and its relationship to changing life circumstances in an unselected middle-class sample. *Child Development, 53,* 144–148.

Tillfors, M., Furmark, T., Marteinsdottir, I., Pissota, A., Langstrom, B., & Fredrikson, M. (2001). Cerebral blood flow in subjects with social phobia during stressful speaking tasks: A PET study. *American Journal of Psychiatry, 158,* 1220–1226.

Tillich, P. (1974). *The courage to be.* New Haven: Yale University Press.

Tomarken, A. J., & Davidson, R. J. (1994). Frontal brain activation in repressors and nonrepressors. *Journal of Abnormal Psychology, 103,* 339–349.

Tomarken, A. J., Davidson, R. J., Wheeler, R. E., & Doss, R. C. (1992). Individual differences in anterior brain asymmetry and fundamental dimentions of emotion. *Journal of Personality and Social Psychology, 62,* 676–687.

Torasdotter, M., Metsis, M., Henriksson, B. G., Winblad, B., & Mohammed, A. H. (1998). Environmental enrichment results in higher levels of nerve growth factor MRNA in the rat visual cortex and hippocampus. *Behavioral Brain Research, 93,* 83–90.

Trapolini, T., Ungerer, J. A., & McMahon, C. A. (2008). Maternal depression: Relations with maternal caregiving representations and emotional availability during the preschool years. *Attachment and Human Development, 10*(1), 73–90.

Travis, L. A., Bliwise, N. G., Binder, J. L., & Horne-Moyer, H. L. (2001). Changes in clients' attachment styles over the course of time-limited dynamic psychotherapy. *Psychotherapy: Theory, Research, Practice, Training, 38*(2), 149–159.

Tremblay, L., & Schultz, W. (1999). Relative reward preference in primate orbitofrontal cortex. *Nature, 398,* 704–708.

Trevarthen, C. (1993). The self born in intersubjectivity: The psychology of an infant communicating. In U. Neisser (Ed.), *The perceived self: Ecological and interpersonal sources of self-knowledge* (pp. 121–173). Cambridge: Cambridge University Press.

Triggs, W. J., McCoy, K. J., Greer, R., Rossi, F., Bowers, D., Kortenkamp, S., et al. (1999). Effects of left frontal transcranial magnetic stimulation on depressed mood, cognition, and corticomotor threshold. *Biological Psychiatry, 45,* 1440–1446.

Trojan, S., & Pokorny, J. (1999). Theoretical aspects of neuroplasticity. *Physiological Research, 48*(2), 87–97.

Tsoory, M. M., Vouimba, R. M., Akirav, I., Kavushansky, A., Avital, A., & Richer-Levin, G. (2008). Amygdala modulation of memory-related processes in the hippocampus: Potential relevance to PTSD. *Progress in Brain Research, 167,* 35–49.

Tucker, D. M. (1992). Developing emotions and cortical networks. In M. R. Gunnar & C. Nelson (Eds.), *Minnesota symposia on child psychology: Vol. 24. Developmental behavioral neuroscience* (pp. 75–128). Hillsdale, NJ: Erlbaum.

Tucker, D. M., Luu, P., & Pribram, K. H. (1995). Social and emotional self-regulation. In J. Grafman & K. J. Hoyoak (Eds.), *Structure and functions of the human prefrontal cortex* (pp. 213–239). New York: New York Academy of Sciences.

Tulving, E. (1985). How many memory systems are there? *American Psychologist, 40,* 385–398.

Turke, P. W. (1997). Hypothesis: Menopause discourages infanticide and encourages continued investment by agnates. *Evolution and Human Behavior, 18,* 3–13.

Tyrka, A. R., Wier, L., Price, L. H., Ross, N., Anderson, G. M., Wilkinson, C. W., et al. (2008). Childhood parental loss and adult hypothalamic-pituitary-adrenal function. *Biological Psychiatry, 63,* 1147–1154.

Uddin, L. Q., Kaplan, J. T., Molnar-Szakacs, I., Zaidel, E., & Iacoboni, M. (2005). Self-face recognition activates a frontoparietal "mirror" network in the right hemisphere: An event-related fMRI study. *Neuroimage, 25,* 926–935.

Ulfig, N., Setzer, M., & Bohl, J. (2003). Ontogeny of the human amygdala. *Annals of the New York Academy of Sciences, 985,* 22–33.

Ulrich, R. (1984). View through a window may influence recovery from surgery. *Science, 224,* 420–421.

Ungerleider, L. G. (1995). Functional brain imaging studies of cortical mechanisms for memory. *Science, 270,* 769–775.

Ungerleider, L. G., & Haxby, J. V. (1994). "What" and "where" in the human brain. *Current Opinion in Neurobiology, 4,* 157–165.

Urry, H. L., Nitschke, J. B., Dolski, I., Jackson, D. C., Dalton, K. M., Mueller, C. J., et al. (2004). Making a life worth living: Neural correlates of well-being. *Psychological Science, 15,* 367–372.

Urry, H. L., van Reekum, C. M., Johnstone, T., Kalin, N. H., Thurow, M. E., Schaefer, H. S., et al. (2006). Amygdala and ventromedial prefrontal cortex are inversely coupled during regulation of negative affect and predict the diurnal patten of cortisol secretion among older adults. *Journal of Neuroscience, 26,* 4415–4425.

Usdin, E., Kvetnansky, R., & Kopin, I. J. (1976). *Stress and catecholamines.* Oxford: Pergamon.

Vaidya, C. J., Austin, G., Kirkorian, G., Ridlehuber, H. W., Desmond, J. E., Glover, G. H., et al. (1998). Selective effects of methyphenidate in attention deficit hyperactivity disorder: A functional magnetic resonance study. *Proceedings of the National Academy of Sciences, USA, 95,* 14494–14499.

Vaina, L. M., Solomon, J., Chowdhury, S., Sinha, P., & Belliveau, J. W. (2001). Functional neuroanatomy of biological motion perception in humans. *Proceedings of the National Academy of Sciences, USA, 98,* 11656–11661.

Vallar, G., Sterzi, R., Bottini, G., Cappa, S., & Rusconi, M. L. (1990). Temporary remission of left hemianesthesia after vestibular stimulation: A sensory neglect phenomenon. *Cortex, 26,* 123–131.

Vallée, M., Maccari, S., Dellu, F., Simon, H., Le Moal, M., & Mayo, W. (1999). Long-term effects of prenatal stress and postnatal handling on age-related glucocorticoid secretion and cognitive performance: A longitudinal study in the rat. *European Journal of Neuroscience, 11,* 2906–2916.

Vallée, M., Mayo, W., Dellu, F., Le Moal, M., Simon, H., & Maccari, S. (1997). Prenatal stress induces high anxiety and postnatal handling induces low anxiety in adult offspring: Correlation with stress-induced corticosterone secretion. *Journal of Neuroscience, 17,* 2626–2636.

van der Kolk, B. A. (1988). The trauma spectrum: The interaction of biological and social events in the genesis of the trauma response. *Journal of Traumatic Stress, 1,* 273–290.

van der Kolk, B. A. (1994). The body keeps the score: Memory and the evolving psychobiology of post traumatic stress. *Harvard Review of Psychiatry, 1*(5), 253–265.

van der Kolk, B. A., Blitz, R., Burr, W., Sherry, S., & Hartmann, E. (1984). Nightmares and trauma: A comparison of nightmares after combat with lifelong nightmares in veterans. *American Journal of Psychiatry, 141,* 187–190.

van der Kolk, B. A., & Greenberg, M. S. (1987). The psychobiology of the traumatic response: Hyperarousal, constriction, and addiction to traumatic reexposure. In B. A. van der Kolk (Ed.), *Psychological trauma* (pp. 63–87). Washington, DC: American Psychiatric Press.

van der Kolk, B. A., Pelcovitz, D., Roth, S., Mandel, F. S., McFarlane, A., & Herman, J. L. (1996). Dissociation, somatization, and affect dysregulation: The complexity of adaptation to trauma. *American Journal of Psychiatry, 153,* 83–95.

Vanduffel, W., Fize, D., Peuskens, H., Denys, K., Sunaert, S., Todd, J. T., et al. (2002). Extracting 3D from motion: Differences in human and monkey intraparietal cortex. *Science, 298,* 413–415.

van Hoesen, G. W. (1981). The differential distribution, diversity and sprouting of cortical projections to the amygdala in the rhesus monkey. In Y. Ben-Ari (Ed.), *The amygdaloid complex* (pp. 77–90). Amsterdam: Elsevier/North Holland Biomedical Press.

Van Opstal, F., Verguts, G., & Fias, W. (2008). A hippocampal-parietal network for learning an ordered sequence. *NeuroImage, 40,* 333–341.

van Reekum, C., Urry, H., Johnson, T., Throw, M., Frye, F., Jackson, C., et al. (2007). Individual differences in amygdala and ventromedial prefrontal cortex activity are associated with evaluation speed and psychological well-being. *Journal of Cognitive Neuroscience, 19*(2), 237–248.

Vansteenwegen, D., Hermans, D., Vervliet, B., Francken, G., Beckers, T., Baeyens, F., et al. (2005). Return of fear in a human differential conditioning paradigm caused by a return to the original acquisition context. *Behavior Research and Therapy, 43* 323–326.

Vasterling, J. J., Brailey, K., Constans, J. I., & Sutker, P. B. (1998). Attention and memory dysfunction in posttraumatic stress disorder. *Neuropsychology, 12,* 125–133.

Vaughn, B., Egeland, B., Sroufe, L. A., & Waters, E. (1979). Individual differences in infant-mother attachment at twelve and eighteen months: Stability and change in families under stress. *Child Development, 50,* 971–975.

Vernadakis, A. (1996). Glia-neuron intercommunications and synaptic plasticity. *Progressive Neurobiology, 49,* 185–214.

Victor, M., & Ropper, A. H. (2001). *Adams and Victor's principles of neurology* (7th ed.). New York: McGraw-Hill.

Villarreal, G., Hamilton, D. A., Petropoulos, H., Driscoll, I., Rowland, L. M., Griego, J. A., et al. (2002). Reduced hippocampal volume and total white matter volume in posttraumatic stress disorder. *Biological Psychiatry, 52,* 119–125.

Vogeley, K., May, M., Ritzl, A., Falkai, P., Zilles, K., & Fink, G. R. (2004). Neural correlates of first-person perspective as one constituent of human self-consciousness. *Journal of Cognitive Neuroscience, 16,* 817–827.

Vogt, B. A. (2005). Pain and emotion interactions in subregions of the cingulate gyrus. *Nature Reviews Neuroscience, 6,* 533–544.

von Bonin, G. (1963). *The evolution of the human brain.* Chicago: University of Chicago Press.

Vondra, J. I., Shaw, D. S., Swearingen, L., Cohen, M., & Owens, E. B. (2001). Attachment stability and emotional and behavioral regulation from infancy to preschool age. *Development and Psychopathology, 13,* 13–33.

Vyas, A., Bernal, S., & Chattarji, S. (2003). Effects of chronic stress on dendritic arborization in the central and extended amygdala. *Brain Research, 965,* 290–294.

Vyas, A., & Chattarji, S. (2004). Modulation of different states of anxiety-like behavior by chronic stress. *Behavioral Neuroscience, 118,* 1450–1454.

Vythilingam, M., Heim, C., Newport, J., Miller, A. H., Anderson, E., Bronen, R., et al. (2002). Childhood trauma associated with smaller hippocampal volume in women with major depression. *American Journal of Psychiatry, 159,* 2072–2080.

Wada, J. (1961). Modification of cortically induced responses in brain stem by shift of attention in monkeys. *Science, 133,* 40–42.

Wager, T. D., Davidson, M. L., Hughes, B. L., Lindquist, M. A., & Ochsner, K. N. (2008). Prefrontal-subcortical pathways mediating successful emotion regulation. *Neuron, 59,* 1037–1050.

Wager, T. D., Rilling, J. K., Smith, E. E., Sokolik, A., Casey, K. L., Davidson, R. J., et al. (2004). Placebo-induced changes in fMRI in the anticipation and experience of pain. *Science, 303,* 1162–1167.

Wagner, A. D., Shannon, B. J., Kahn, I., & Buckner, L. (2005). Parietal lobe contributions to episodic memory retrieval. *Trends in Cognitive Sciences, 9*, 446–453.

Walach, H., & Jonas, W. B. (2004). Placebo research: The evidence base for harnessing self-healing capacities. *Journal of Alternative and Complementary Medicine, 10*(1), 103–112.

Walsh, R. N., Budtz-Olsen, O. E., Penny, J. E., & Cummins, R. A. (1969). The effects of environmental complexity of the histology of the rat hippocampus. *Journal of Comparative Neurology, 137*, 361–366.

Walsh, V., Ashbridge, E., & Cowey, A. (1998). Cortical plasticity in perceptual learning demonstrated by transcranial magnetic stimulation. *Neuropsychologia, 36*, 45–49.

Walton, M., Bannerman, D., Alterescu, K., & Rushworth, M. (2003). Functional specialization within medial frontal cortex of the anterior cingulate for evaluating effort-related decisions. *Journal of Neuroscience, 23*, 6475–6479.

Wanisch, K., Tang, J., Mederer, A., & Wotjak, C. T. (2005). Trace fear conditioning depends on NMDA receptor activation and protein synthesis within the dorsal hippocampus of mice. *Behavioral Brain Research, 157*(1), 63–69.

Warner-Schmidt, J. L., & Duman, R. S. (2006). Hippocampal neurogenesis: Opposing effects of stress and antidepressant treatment. *Hippocampus, 16*(3), 239–249.

Watanabe, M. (1996). Reward expectancy in primate prefrontal neurons. *Nature, 382*, 629–632.

Watanabe, Y., Gould, E., Daniels, D. C., Cameron, H., & McEwen, B. S. (1992). Tianeptine attenuates stress-induced morphological changes in the hippocampus. *European Journal of Pharmacology, 222*, 157–162.

Watanabe, Y. E., Gould, E., & McEwen, B. S. (1992). Stress induced atrophy of apical dendrites of hippocampal CA3 pyramidal neurons. *Brain Research, 588*, 341–345.

Waters, E., Merrick, S., Treboux, D., Crowell, J., & Albersheim, L. (2000). Attachment security in infancy and early adulthood: A twenty-year longitudinal study. *Child Development, 71*, 684–689.

Weaver, I. C. G., Cervoni, N., Champagne, F. A., D'Alessio, A. C., Sharma, S., Seckl, J. R., et al. (2004). Epigenetic programming by maternal behavior. *Nature Neuroscience, 7*, 847–854.

Weaver, I. C. G., Champagne, F. A., Brown, S. E., Dymov, S., Sharma, S., Meaney, M. J., et al. (2005). Reversal of maternal programming of stress response in adult offspring through methyl supplementation: Altering epigenetic marking later in life. *Journal of Neuroscience, 25*, 11045–11054.

Weaver, I. C. G., D'Alessio, A. C., Brown, S. E., Hellstrom, I. C., Dymov, S., Sharma, S., et al. (2007). The transcription factor nerve growth factor-inducible protein a mediates epigenetic programming: Altering epigenetic marks by immediate-early genes. *Journal of Neuroscience, 27*, 1756–1768.

Weaver, I. C. G., Grant, R. J., & Meaney, M. J. (2002). Maternal behavior regulates long-term hippocampal expression of BAX and apoptosis in the offspring. *Journal of Neurochemistry, 82,* 998–1002.

Weaver, I. C. G., Meaney, M. J., & Szyf, M. (2006). Maternal care effects on the hippocampal transcriptome and anxiety-mediated behaviors in the offspring that are reversible in adulthood. *Proceedings of the National Academy of Sciences, USA, 103,* 3480–3485.

Weaver, S. A., Aherne, F. X., Meaney, M. J., Schaefer, A. L., & Dixon W. T. (2000). Neonatal handling permanently alters hypothalamic-pituitary-adrenal axis function, behavior, and body weight in boars. *Journal of Endocrinology, 164,* 349–359.

Weiner, I. (1998). Principles of psychotherapy. New York: Wiley and Sons.

Weinfield, N. S., Sroufe, L. A., & Egeland, B. (2000). Attachment from infancy to young adulthood in a high-risk sample: Continuity, discontinuity, and their correlates. *Child Development, 71,* 695–702.

Weingarten, S. M., Cherlow, D. G., & Holmgren, E. (1977). The relationship of hallucinations to the depth structures of the temporal lobe. *Acta Neurochirurgica, 24*(Suppl.), 199–216.

Weinger, G., Lange, C., Sachsse, U., & Irle, E. (2008). Amygdala and hippocampal volumes and cognition in adult survivors of childhood abuse with dissociative disorders. *Acta Psychiatrica Scandinavica, 118,* 281–290.

Wellington, N., & Rieder, M. J. (1993). Attitudes and practices regarding analgesia for newborn circumcision. *Pediatrics, 92,* 541–543.

West, M. J. (1993). Regionally specific loss of neurons in the aging human hippocampus. *Neurobiology of Aging, 14,* 287–293.

Wexler, B. E., & Heninger, G. R. (1979). Alterations in cerebral laterality during acute psychotic illness. *Archives of General Psychiatry, 36,* 278–284.

Whalen, P. J., Johnstone, T., Somerville, L. H., Nitschke, J. B., Polis, S., Alexander, A. L., et al. (2008). A functional magnetic resonance imaging predictor of treatment response to venlafaxine in generalized anxiety disorder. *Biological Psychiatry, 63,* 858–863.

Whalley, L. J., Deary, I. J., Appleton, C. L., & Starr, J. M. (2004). Cognitive reserve and the neurobiology of cognitive aging. *Ageing Research Reviews, 3,* 369–382.

Wheeler, R. E., Davidson, R. J., & Tomarken, A. J. (1993). Frontal brain asymmetry and emotional reactivity: A biological substrate of affective style. *Psychophysiology, 30,* 82–89.

White, S. A. (2001). Learning to communicate. *Current Opinion in Neurobiology, 11,* 510–520.

Widom, C. S., DuMont, K., & Czaja, S. J. (2007). A prospective investigation of major depressive disorder and comorbidity in abused and neglected children grown up. *Archives of General Psychiatry, 64,* 49–56.

Wiens, S. (2006). Subliminal emotion perception in brain imaging: Findings, issues, and recommendations. *Progress in Brain Research, 156,* 105–121.

Willcutt, E. G., Dole, A. E., Nigg, J. T., Faraone, S. V., & Pennington, B. F. (2005). Validity of the executive function theory of attention deficit/hyperactivity disorder: A meta-analytic review. *Biological Psychiatry, 57*, 1336–1346.

Williams, L. M. (1994). Recall of childhood trauma: A prospective study of women's memories of child sexual abuse. *Journal of Consulting and Clinical Psychology, 62*, 1167–1176.

Williams, L. M., Kemp, A. H., Felmingham, K., Barton, M., Olivieri, G., Peduto, A., et al. (2006). Trauma modulates amygdala and medial prefrontal responses to consciously attended fear. *NeuroImage, 29*, 347–357.

Williams, L. M., Phillips, M. L., Brammer, M. J., Skerrett, D., Lagopoulos, J., Rennie, C., et al. (2001). Arousal dissociates amygdala and hippocampal fear responses: Evidence from simultaneous fMRI and skin conductance recording. *NeuroImage, 14*, 1070–1079.

Wilson, F. A. W., O'Scalaidhe, S. P., & Goldman-Rakic, P. S. (1993). Dissociation of object and spatial processing domains in primate prefrontal cortex. *Science, 260*, 1955–1958.

Wilson, F. R. (1998). *The hand*. New York: Vintage Books.

Winick, M., Katchadurian, K., & Harris, R. C. (1975). Malnutrition and environmental enrichment by early adoption. *Science, 190*, 1173–1175.

Winnicott, D. W. (1958). The capacity to be alone. In *Maturational processes and the facilitating environment: Studies in the theory of emotional development* (pp. 29–36). New York: International Universities Press.

Winnicott, D. W. (1962). Ego integration in child development. In *Maturational processes and the facilitating environment: Studies in the theory of emotional development* (pp. 56–63) New York: International Universities Press.

Winnicott, D. W. (1963). From dependence to independence in the development of the individual. In *Maturational processes and the facilitating environment: Studies in the theory of emotional development* (pp. 83–99). New York: International Universities Press.

Witelson, S. F., Kigar, D. L., & Harvey, T. (1999). The exceptional brain of Albert Einstein. *The Lancet, 353*, 2149–2153.

Wittling, W. (1997). The right hemisphere and the human stress response. *Acta Physiologica Scandinavica, 161*(640) (Suppl.), 55–59.

Wittling, W., & Pfluger, M. (1990). Neuroendocrine hemisphere asymmetries: Salivary cortisol secretion during lateralized viewing of emotion-related and neutral films. *Brain and Cognition, 14*, 243–265.

Wolf, N. S., Gales, M. E., Shane, E., & Shane, M. (2000). The developmental trajectory from amodal perception to empathy and communication: The role of mirror neurons in this process. *Psychoanalytic Inquiry, 21*, 94–112.

Wolpe, J. (1958). *Psychotherapy by reciprocal inhibition*. Stanford, CA: Stanford University Press.

Wolpert, D. M., Goodbody, S. J., & Husain, M. (1998). Maintaining internal representations: The role of the human superior parietal lobe. *Nature Neuroscience, 1*, 529–533.

Woolley, C. S., Gould, E., & McEwen, B. S. (1990). Exposure to excess glucocorticoids alters dendritic morphology of adult hippocampal pyramidal neurons. *Brain Research, 531,* 225–231.

Wu, J., Buchsbaum, M. S., Gillin, J. C., Tang, C., Cadwell, S., Wiegand, M., et al. (1999). Prediction of antidepressant effects of sleep deprivation by metabolic rates in the ventral anterior cingulate and medial prefrontal cortex. *American Journal of Psychiatry, 156,* 1149–1158.

Wykes, T., Brammer, M., Mellers, J., Bray, P., Reeder, C., Williams, C., et al. (2002). Effects of the brain of psychological treatment: Cognitive remediation therapy. *British Journal of Psychiatry, 191,* 144–152.

Yau, J. L. W., Olsson, T., Morris, R. G. M., Meaney, M. J., & Seckl, J. R. (1995). Glucocorticoids, hippocampal corticosteroid receptor gene expression and antidepressant treatment: Relationship with spatial learning in young and aged rats. *Neuroscience, 6*(3), 571–581.

Yehuda, R. (1999). Biological factors associated with susceptibility to posttraumatic stress disorder. *Canadian Journal of Psychiatry, 44,* 34–39.

Yehuda, R., Bierer, L. M., Schmeidler, J., Aferiat, D. H., Breslau, I., & Dolan, S. (2000). Low cortisol and risk for PTSD in adult offspring of holocaust survivors. *American Journal of Psychiatry, 157,* 1252–1259.

Yehuda, R., Kahana, B., Schmeidler, J., Southwick, S. M., Wilson, S., & Giller, E. I. (1995). Impact of cumulative lifetime trauma and recent stress on current posttraumatic stress disorder symptoms in holocaust survivors. *American Journal of Psychiatry, 152,* 1815–1818.

Yehuda, R., & Siever, L. J. (1997). Persistent effects of stress in trauma survivors and their descendants. *Biological Psychiatry, 41,* 1S–120S.

Yerkes, M., & Dodson, D. (1908). The relation of strength to rapidity of habit-formation. *Journal of Comparative Neurology and Psychology, 18,* 459–482.

Yovell, Y. (2000). From hysteria to posttraumatic stress disorder: Psychoanalysis and the neurobiology of traumatic memories. *Neuropsychoanalysis, 2,* 171–181.

Yu-Feng, Z., Yong, H., Chao-Zhe, Z., Qing-Jiu, C., Man-Qiu, S., Meng, L., et al. (2007). Altered baseline brain activity in children with ADHD revealed by resting-state functional MRI. *Brain and Development, 29,* 83–91.

Zahm, D. S. (2006). The evolving theory of basal forebrain functional-anatomical "macrosystems." *Neuroscience and Behavioral Reviews, 30,* 148–172.

Zald, D. H., & Kim, S. W. (2001). The orbitofrontal cortex. In S. P. Salloway, P. F. Malloy, & J. D. Duffy (Eds.), *The frontal lobes and neuropsychiatric illness* (pp. 33–69). Washington, DC: American Psychiatric Press.

Zang, Y., Jin, Z., Weng, X., Zhang, L., Zeng, Y., & Yang, L. (2005). Functional MRI in attention-deficit hyperactivity disorder: Evidence for hypofrontality. *Brain and Development, 27,* 544–550.

Zeitlin, S. B., Lane, R. D., O'Leary, D. S., & Schrift, M. J. (1989). Interhemispheric transfer deficit and alexithymia. *American Journal of Psychiatry, 146,* 1434–1439.

Zeitlin, S. B., & McNally, R. J. (1991). Implicit and explicit memory bias for threat in post traumatic stress disorder. *Behavior Research and Therapy, 29,* 451–457.

Zeltzer, L. K., Anderson, C. T. M., & Schecter, N. L. (1990). Pediatric pain: Current status and new directions. *Current Problems in Pediatrics, 20,* 415–486.

Zhang, L. X., Levine, S., Dent, G., Zhan, Y., Xing, G., Okimoto, D., et al. (2002). Maternal deprivation increases cell death in the infant rat brain. *Developmental Brain Research, 133,* 1–11.

Zhang, T. Y., Chretien, P., Meaney, M. J., & Gratton, A. (2005). Influence of naturally occurring variations in maternal care on prepulse inhibition of acoustic startle and the medial prefrontal cortical dopamine response to stress in adult rats. *Journal of Neuroscience, 25,* 1493–1502.

Zhang, T., Parent, C., Weaver, I., & Meaney, M. J. (2004). Maternal programming of individual differences in defensive responses in the rat. *Annals of New York Academy of Sciences, 1032,* 85–103.

Zhao, M., Toyoda, H., Lee, Y., Wu, L., Ko, S. W., Zhang, X., et al. (2005). Roles of NMDA NR2B subtype receptor in prefrontal long-term potentiation and contextual fear memory. *Neuron, 47,* 859–872.

Zhu, X. O., & Waite, P. M. E. (1998). Cholinergic depletion reduces plasticity of barrel field cortex. *Cerebral Cortex, 8,* 63–72.

Zola-Morgan, S. M., & Squire, L. R. (1990). The primate hippocampal formation: Evidence for a time-limited role in memory storage. *Science, 250,* 288–290.

Zubieta, J. K., Bueller, J. A., Jackson, L. R., Scott, D. J., Xu, Y., Koeppe, R. A., et al. (2005). Placebo effects mediated by endogenous opioid activity on μ-opioid receptors. *Journal of Neuroscience, 25,* 7754–7762.

Zuckerman, B., Bauchner, H., Parker, S., & Cabral, H. (1990). Maternal depressive symptoms during pregnancy, and newborn irritability. *Developmental and Behavioral Pediatrics, 11,* 190–194.

# Index

# THE NORTON SERIES ON INTERPERSONAL NEUROBIOLOGY

Allan N. Schore, PhD, Series Editor
Daniel J. Siegel, MD, Founding Editor

The field of mental health is in a tremendously exciting period of growth and conceptual reorganization. Independent findings from a variety of scientific endeavors are converging in an interdisciplinary view of the mind and mental well-being. An interpersonal neurobiology of human development enables us to understand that the structure and function of the mind and brain are shaped by experiences, especially those involving emotional relationships.

The Norton Series on Interpersonal Neurobiology will provide cutting-edge, multidisciplinary views that further our understanding of the complex neurobiology of the human mind. By drawing on a wide range of traditionally independent fields of research—such as neurobiology, genetics, memory, attachment, complex systems, anthropology, and evolutionary psychology—these texts will offer mental health professionals a review and synthesis of scientific findings often inaccessible to clinicians. These books aim to advance our understanding of human experience by finding the unity of knowledge, or consilience, that emerges with the translation of findings from numerous domains of study into a common language and conceptual framework. The series will integrate the best of modern science with the healing art of psychotherapy.